Motor Learning and Performance

From Principles to Application

SEVENTH EDITION

Timothy D. Lee, PhD
Richard A. Schmidt, PhD

HUMAN KINETICS

Library of Congress Cataloging-in-Publication Data

Names: Schmidt, Richard A. (Richard Allen), 1941-2015, author. | Lee, Timothy Donald, 1955- author.
Title: Motor learning and performance : from principles to application / Timothy D. Lee, PhD, Richard A. Schmidt, PhD.
Description: Seventh edition. | Champaign, IL : Human Kinetics, [2026] | Includes bibliographical references and index.
Identifiers: LCCN 2024045290 (print) | LCCN 2024045291 (ebook) | ISBN 9781718221093 (paperback) | ISBN 9781718221109 (loose-leaf) | ISBN 9781718221116 (epub) | ISBN 9781718221123 (pdf)
Subjects: LCSH: Motor learning.
Classification: LCC BF295 .S249 2026 (print) | LCC BF295 (ebook) | DDC 370.15/5--dc23/eng/20241121
LC record available at https://lccn.loc.gov/2024045290
LC ebook record available at https://lccn.loc.gov/2024045291

ISBN: 978-1-7182-2109-3 (paperback)
ISBN: 978-1-7182-2110-9 (loose-leaf)

Copyright © 2026, 2020 by Timothy D. Lee
Copyright © 2014 by Richard A. Schmidt and Timothy D. Lee
Copyright © 2008, 2004, 2000 by Richard A. Schmidt and Craig A. Wrisberg
Copyright © 1991 by Richard A. Schmidt

Human Kinetics supports copyright. Copyright fuels scientific and artistic endeavor, encourages authors to create new works, and promotes free speech. Thank you for buying an authorized edition of this work and for complying with copyright laws by not reproducing, scanning, or distributing any part of it in any form without written permission from the publisher. You are supporting authors and allowing Human Kinetics to continue to publish works that increase the knowledge, enhance the performance, and improve the lives of people all over the world.

The online audio content that accompanies this product is delivered on HK*Propel:* **HKPropel.HumanKinetics.com**. You agree that you will not use HK*Propel* if you do not accept the site's Privacy Policy and Terms and Conditions, which detail approved uses of the online content.

The online learning content that accompanies this product is delivered on HK*Propel*, **HKPropel.HumanKinetics.com**. You agree that you will not use HK*Propel* if you do not accept the site's Privacy Policy and Terms and Conditions, which detail approved uses of the online content.

To report suspected copyright infringement of content published by Human Kinetics, contact us at **permissions@hkusa.com**. To request permission to legally reuse content published by Human Kinetics, please refer to the information at **https://US.HumanKinetics.com/pages/permissions-translations-faqs**.

This publication is written and published to provide accurate and authoritative information relevant to the subject matter presented. It is published and sold with the understanding that the author and publisher are not engaged in rendering legal, medical, or other professional services by reason of their authorship or publication of this work. If medical or other expert assistance is required, the services of a competent professional person should be sought.

Permission notices for material reprinted in this book from other sources can be found on pp. xvii-xix.

The web addresses cited in this text were current as of July 2025, unless otherwise noted.

Acquisitions Editor: Diana Vincer; **Senior Managing Editor:** Anna Lan Seaman; **Copyeditor:** Joan Little, Pendulum Editing; **Proofreader:** A.E. Williams; **Indexer:** Rebecca L. McCorkle; **Permissions Manager:** Laurel Mitchell; **Graphic Designer:** Denise Lowry; **Cover Designer:** Keri Evans; **Cover Design Specialist:** Susan Rothermel Allen; **Photograph (cover):** Nick Wosika/Icon Sportswire via Getty Images; **Photographs (interior):** © Human Kinetics, unless otherwise noted; **Photo Asset Manager:** Laura Fitch; **Photo Production Manager:** Jason Allen; **Senior Art Manager:** Kelly Hendren; **Illustrations:** © Human Kinetics, unless otherwise noted; **Printer:** Walsworth

Printed in the United States of America 10 9 8 7 6 5 4 3 2 1

The paper in this book was manufactured using responsible forestry methods.

Human Kinetics
1607 N. Market Street
Champaign, IL 61820
USA

United States and International
Website: **US.HumanKinetics.com**
Email: info@hkusa.com
Phone: 1-800-747-4457

Canada
Website: **Canada.HumanKinetics.com**
Email: info@hkcanada.com

E9079 (paperback) / E9080 (loose-leaf)

In Memoriam

Laurie Wishart (1949-2019), my research partner and life partner, died in 2019. In preparing to write this memorial, I reread many cards, letters, and emails that I received following her death. Common themes in these tributes included her smile (it lit up the room); her charm, wit, and warmth; and an immense intellectual curiosity. But it was clear from the many tributes that Laurie's defining characteristic was not simply that she *cared* about people but rather the unique and deeply personal way in which she expressed that care as curiosity about, and attention to, the people in her life. One person wrote, "She was interesting, but moreover, interested." Another said, "She made you feel that you were the only person in the room that she wanted to pay attention to." Variations on those sentiments were repeated over and over by family, friends, colleagues, and former students.

Her essential caring nature defined Laurie's interaction with everyone, all the time. A cousin wrote that Laurie possessed that attribute even as a small child. Each undergrad and graduate student was mentored with respect and encouragement for their individuality and with fierce devotion. She made each grandchild feel uniquely special and loved. Her scientific inquisitiveness extended to the people behind the research. Our reflections on a day of conference attendance typically included my telling her about the exciting new research I'd learned and her telling me what she'd learned about the people who had done the research.

Although more than four years have passed since her death, Laurie's influence on this book and on scientific engagement and mentorship in the fields of motor learning and physical therapy remains as strong as ever. My name is listed on this book as a coauthor, but I could never have done it without her love, encouragement, and support, which I continue to cherish every day.

Tim Lee
Ancaster, Ontario
May 2024

Contents

PART II Principles of Skill Learning 177

Preface

Most of us feel excitement when we watch a close race, match, or performance, observing the complex, well-controlled skills displayed by the players or musicians. We marvel at those who succeed in executing their skill on the spot, at how people with high-level skills are able to excel, and how experts are able to adapt their skill to novel situations, sometimes under extreme circumstances.

Take another look at the front cover of this textbook. What do you see? A casual observer might notice a left-handed golfer using excellent form to hit a chip shot. A careful observer would notice that the golfer is actually right handed (see the golf glove on his left hand) and was hitting a right-handed golf club turned upside down. Look at how the toe of the club is pointed down; the toe of a left-handed club would have been pointing up. The golfer on the front cover is Davis Riley. At a 2022 PGA tournament event, Davis found his ball so close to a tree that he could not easily execute a right-handed shot. So, he stood on the other side of the ball, turned his club upside down, and executed a perfect left-handed shot.

This book was written for people who appreciate high-level skilled activity and for those who would like to learn more about how such expertise is attained. Readers in fields related directly to kinesiology (such as teaching and coaching) will benefit from the knowledge provided here. But the material extends far beyond these fields and should be relevant for those who study rehabilitation in physical and occupational therapy, as well as for instructors and facilitators of many other areas in which motor skills play an important role, such as medicine, music, ergonomics, law enforcement, and the military. The text is intended for beginners in the study of skill and requires little knowledge of physiology, psychology, or statistics.

The text's level of analysis focuses on motor *behavior*—the overt, observable performance of skilled movements. Of course, understanding skilled behavior involves many scientific areas or fields of study. Motor skill is the outcome of processes studied in many different fields, such as neurology, anatomy, biomechanics, biochemistry, and social and experimental psychology, and this text could have focused on any number of these fundamental fields. But the focus here is broader than the fundamental fields that support it. The focus is behavioral, with the major emphasis on humans' performing skills of various kinds. We will talk about these other levels of analysis from time to time throughout the book in an attempt to explain what processes or events occur to support these high-level skills. Therefore, this text should be appropriate for courses in elementary motor learning and motor performance in a relatively wide group of scientific areas.

An important component developed throughout the text is the construction of a conceptual model of human performance. The term *model* is used in a variety of ways in many branches of science. Models are found frequently and typically consist of a system of parts that, when assembled in a certain way, mimic aspects of the system we are trying to understand. One example is the pump-and-pipe model of our circulatory system, in which a pump represents the heart and pipes of various diameters and lengths represent the arteries and veins. One could actually construct a physical model to be used in classroom demonstrations or experiments on the effects of blood pressure on capillaries of the hand (although some models are purely conceptual).

Our first goal in writing this text was to build a strong, general, conceptual understanding (or overview) of skills. We believe that instructors, coaches, therapists, and trainers, as well as others dealing with learning or teaching skills, will profit greatly from such a conceptual understanding of skilled behavior. In striving toward this goal, we have adopted the idea that skills can be understood, for the most part, using concepts concerning information and its processing. We begin by considering the human as a very simple input–output system; then gradually, as we introduce new topics, we expand the model by adding processes that account for how these new concepts fit in the system. Gradually, by building on knowledge and concepts presented in earlier parts of the text, we add increasing complexity to the conceptual model. Simply presenting the finished conceptual model would make it very difficult for students to understand, and we hope that the systematic process of constructing the model, assembled with parts as they are presented in the text, forms a logical basis for increasing the model's complexity. This detailed construction process should make the final version of the model understandable.

Our second goal was to organize the book in the best way to aid student understanding based on many years of collective teaching experience. The text is divided into two parts. After the introduction to the study of motor skills in chapter 1, part I examines how the motor system works by investigating the major principles of human performance and progressively developing the conceptual model of human action. The focus is mainly on human performance from an information-processing perspective, although alternative theoretical approaches are also provided. Chapter 2 discusses the nature of information processing, decision-making, and movement planning. Chapter 3 explores the concepts of attention and memory. Chapter 4 concerns the information received from various sensory sources that is relevant to movement. Chapter 5 examines the processes underlying the production of movement, with a particular emphasis on the role of motor programs. Chapter 6 considers the basic principles of performance that form the building blocks of skilled performance—analogous to the fundamental laws of physics. Chapter 7 extends this analysis by examining different approaches to performing more complex skills—from the traditional approach of examining differences in movement abilities to the more contemporary examination of how movements are coordinated, both within and between individuals. On completion of part I, the reader should have a reasonably coherent view of the conceptual and functional properties of how the motor system works in performing already learned skills.

Part II of the text uses the conceptual model to impart an understanding of the processes involved in human motor *learning*. Much of this discussion uses the terms and concepts introduced in part I. This method works well in our own teaching, probably because motor learning is usually inferred from changes in motor behavior; therefore, it is logical to discuss these changes in terms of the behavioral principles presented in part I. In this second part, chapter 8 presents some methodological problems that are unique to the study of learning, such as how and when to measure performance to make inferences about learning. Chapter 9 considers broad issues of learning, retention, and transfer, such as the important role of practice. Chapter 10 concerns how and when to practice, dealing with the many factors that instructors can control directly to make practice more effective. Chapter 11 deals with the critical topic of augmented feedback, examining what kinds of movement information students need for effective learning, when it should be given, and so on. Chapter 12 is new to this edition, inviting readers to expand their thinking about the learning process by considering various theories and theoretical explanations for how learning occurs. By the end of the text, readers will have a progressive accumulation of knowledge that, in our experience, provides a consistent view of how skills are performed and learned while also providing alternative conceptualizations of these processes.

Many real-world examples of motor performance and learning principles are discussed in the main body of the text. In addition, we've included Focus on Application sections set off from the main textual materials. Strategically located directly after pertinent discussions of principles, these sections apply the material to real-world examples. We wanted to write a text that performers, teachers, coaches, physical therapists, and other instructors could use in various fields to enhance human performance in real-world settings. To meet this goal, we have worked to focus the text on the topics most relevant to practical application.

As a third goal, we wanted a presentation style that would be simple, straightforward, and highly readable for those without extensive backgrounds in the motor performance area. As a result, the main content does not expound on the research and data that contribute to our knowledge of motor skill acquisition and performance. Important points are illustrated by data from research, but the emphasis is on an integrated conceptual knowledge of how the motor system works and learns. However, for those who desire a tighter link to the basic data, we have included sections called Focus on Research, which are set off from the main text and describe the important experiments and concepts in detail.

Finally, we demanded that the principles discussed be faithful to the empirical data and thought in the study area. From decades of doing basic research in motor learning and motor performance, we have developed what we believe to be defensible, coherent, personal viewpoints (conceptual models, if you will) about how skills are performed and learned, and our aim was to present this model to the reader to facilitate understanding. Our viewpoints are based on a large literature of theoretical ideas and empirical data, together with much thought about competing ideas and apparently contradictory research findings. We have tried to write from this perspective, as we would tell a story. Every part of the story can be defended empirically, or it would not have been included. Our goal has been to write the truth, at least as we understand it and as it can be understood with the current level of knowledge.

Students will find a range of learning aids within each chapter, including chapter-opening outlines, objectives, and lists of key terms, as well as an end-chapter summary of the activities in the accompanying web study guide and Check Your Understanding and Apply Your Knowledge questions. Instructors using this text in their courses will find a wealth of updated ancillary materials on HK*Propel*, including a presentation package and image bank, instructor guide, and test package.

A short preview quiz is also presented at the beginning of each chapter, and pertinent questions are added throughout each chapter. One might wonder why the text presents questions before providing the answers later. The reason is simple: Research in education has repeatedly found that "testing" someone to retrieve or construct an answer or solution makes the information more memorable when it is later presented (the so-called "testing effect"). Those readers who have given an honest, valiant effort to answer these questions when they are presented will benefit later on with a better, longer-lasting understanding of the answer.

The book also provides an online resource that contains narratives from Tim Lee's book *Motor Control in Everyday Actions*. The narratives relate to real-life encounters with objects and tasks in day-to-day routines. The purpose of the narratives is not only to motivate interest in concepts important to this field of study but also to stimulate thinking regarding how to conduct new research on these topics and serve as a relevant and relatable companion to the present book. The narratives that correspond to topics in each chapter are indicated throughout the book.

This seventh edition of *Motor Learning and Performance* extends the approach used in the previous six editions—integrating the latest findings with research evidence that has remained relevant for longer periods. To this end, each chapter of the text has been extensively updated with references to the most relevant and exciting new research. Since motor learning and performance are probably the most widespread activities that humans from all walks of life experience daily, our goal was to touch on as many of these applications as possible. The generality and limitations of these principles represent a core of human existence, and we hope that our treatment of them in this book resonates well with each person who reads it.

Timothy D. Lee
Professor Emeritus, Department of Kinesiology, McMaster University, Hamilton, Ontario

Richard A. Schmidt
(deceased)

Student and Instructor Resources

Student Resources

Students, visit the online resource on HK*Propel*, which has been fully revised for the seventh edition to offer a more focused and interactive set of activities to aid learning. Student access codes are included with the purchase of a print book or ebook through Human Kinetics. Student access codes are also sold separately on the Human Kinetics website.

Each chapter presents a series of interactive activities that test your understanding of important concepts. These include matching, multiple-choice, and diagram-based activities. Each chapter also presents a principles-to-application exercise that prompts you to take your knowledge beyond the classroom by using principles of motor learning and performance to analyze an activity. There is no single right answer for the principles-to-application problems, but it is important to provide evidence and reasoning to support your ideas. Each principles-to-application exercise includes sample student answers and critiques of those answers to guide you as you develop your analysis. By completing the exercises on HK*Propel*, you will build your knowledge of important concepts from the textbook and learn to apply that knowledge to real-world situations.

The online resource also contains the narratives from Tim Lee's 2010 book, *Motor Control in Everyday Actions*. The narratives are referenced throughout this text and organized by chapter on HK*Propel*.

Finally, HK*Propel* includes the following multimedia content:

48 audio clips describing the processes shown in select figures.

Look for the icons and QR codes throughout the text to know when this additional content is available. As you work to understand a concept illustrated in a figure, refer to the audio for an explanation and to build your understanding.

Instructor Resources

The instructor guide, test package, chapter quizzes, presentation package, and image bank are free to course adopters and are accessed on HK*Propel*.

Instructor Guide

The instructor guide includes a sample syllabus, summary notes for each chapter for preparing lectures, ideas for presenting topics and engaging students in class discussions, as well as practical laboratory activities. The instructor guide also features answers to the questions posed in the captions of some photos in the book.

Test Package

The test package includes more than 350 true-false, matching, multiple-choice, fill-in-the-blank, and essay questions. The files may be downloaded for integration with a learning management system or printed for use as paper-based tests. Instructors may also create their own customized quizzes or tests from the test bank questions to assign to students directly on HK*Propel*. Multiple-choice and true-false questions are automatically graded, and instructors can review student scores on the platform.

Chapter Quizzes

Updated for the seventh edition, these ready-to-use short quizzes test students' understanding of the most important concepts in each chapter. Each quiz may be downloaded or assigned to students on HK*Propel*. The chapter quizzes are automatically graded, with scores available for review on the platform.

Presentation Package

The presentation package includes more than 250 PowerPoint text slides that highlight material from the text for use in lectures and class discussions. The slides can be used directly in PowerPoint or can be printed to make transparencies or handouts for students. Instructors can easily add, modify, and rearrange the order of slides, as well as search for images based on keywords. Access the presentation package by visiting HK*Propel*.

Image Bank

The image bank comprises most of the figures and tables from the text, sorted by chapter. These are provided as separate files for easy insertion into tests, quizzes, handouts, and other course materials, which can be used to develop a customized presentation.

Acknowledgments

Rainer Martens first conceptualized the idea of the book, and his encouragement led Dick Schmidt to write the first edition (Schmidt, 1991). Dick and Craig Wrisberg coauthored the next three editions (Schmidt & Wrisberg, 2000, 2004, 2008). I coauthored the fifth edition with Dick and prepared the sixth edition after Dick passed away in 2015 (Schmidt & Lee, 2020).

The current edition extends the team effort that I have enjoyed over the past 25 years working with the many wonderful and talented people at Human Kinetics (HK) publishing. Their encouragement, humor, and dedication made the sometimes tedious process much more enjoyable, for which I am very grateful. For this edition, I would especially like to thank Diana Vincer and Anna Lan Seaman for their efforts and support in seeing this project through to completion. I think of these people and their colleagues at HK as much more than just employees of a company. Rather, they are dedicated to producing the best possible learning experience for their readers, and I sincerely thank them for all their hard work. I also thank Liz Sanli (again) for preparing the book's ancillaries. Chapter 12 in this edition is new, pulling some parts from other chapters and adding new content to create an exciting new discussion. I thank Nikki Hodges and Diane Ste-Marie, two trusted and valued colleagues, for providing comprehensive reviews of early drafts. Last, I thank Catherine and our expansive family of children and grandchildren for helping me maintain a focus on the bigger picture.

Tim Lee
Ancaster, Ontario, Canada

Credits

Figures

Figure 1.2: Adapted from Chapanis (1951).

Figure 2.2: Adapted from Attneave (1959).

Figure 2.7: Reprinted by permission from R.A. Schmidt, T.D. Lee, C.J. Winstein, et al., *Motor Control and Learning: A Behavioral Emphasis,* 6th ed. (Champaign, IL: Human Kinetics, 2019). 65; Data from Merkel (1885).

Figure 2.8: Reprinted by permission from R.A. Schmidt, T.D. Lee, C.J. Winstein, et al., *Motor Control and Learning: A Behavioral Emphasis,* 6th ed. (Champaign, IL: Human Kinetics, 2019). 65; Data from Merkel (1885).

Figure 2.10: Data from table 1, Brosnan et al. (2017).

Figure 2.12*a*: RonBailey/E+/Getty Images

Figure 2.12*b*: David Arky/Tetra images/Getty Images

Figure 2.13: Adapted from Adams and Dijkstra (1966).

Figure 3.1: Based on Posner and Keele (1969).

Figure 3.3: Reprinted by permission from Simons and Chabris (1999).

Figure 3.4: vm/E+/Getty Images

Figure 3.5*a-b*: Data from Davis (1959).

Figure 3.5*c*: Reprinted by permission from R.A. Schmidt, T.D. Lee, C.J. Winstein, et al., *Motor Control and Learning: A Behavioral Emphasis,* 6th ed. (Champaign, IL: Human Kinetics, 2019), 108; Data from Davis (1959).

Figure 3.7: Reprinted by permission from M.I. Posner and S.W. Keele, "Attentional Demands of Movement," in *Proceedings of the 16th Congress of Applied Physiology* (Amsterdam, Amsterdam: Swets and Zeitlinger, 1969).

Figure 3.8: Adapted from Sherwood, Lohse, and Healy (2014).

Figure 3.9: Reprinted by permission from R.S. Weinberg and D. Gould, *Foundations of Sport and Exercise Psychology,* 8th ed. (Champaign, IL: Human Kinetics, 2024), 95.

Figure 4.8: Data from Keele and Posner (1968).

Figure 5.4: Reprinted by permission from R.A. Schmidt, T.D. Lee, C.J. Winstein, et al., *Motor Control and Learning: A Behavioral Emphasis,* 6th ed. (Champaign, IL: Human Kinetics, 2019), 185-86.

Figure 5.5: Reprinted by permission from W.J. Wadman, "Control of Fast Goal-Directed Arm Movements," *Journal of Human Movement Studies* 5 (1979): 10.

Figure 5.6: Adapted from T.R. Armstrong, *Training for the Production of Memorized Movement Patterns: Technical Report No. 26* (Ann Arbor, MI: University of Michigan, Human Performance Center, 1970), 35. By permission of the Department of Psychology, University of Michigan.

Figure 5.7: Reprinted by permission from R.A. Schmidt, T.D. Lee, C.J. Winstein, et al., *Motor Control and Learning: A Behavioral Emphasis,* 6th ed. (Champaign, IL: Human Kinetics, 2019), 203.

Figure 5.8: Adapted by permission from J.M. Hollerbach, *A Study of Human Motor Control Through Analysis and Synthesis of Handwriting,* Doctoral Dissertation, (Cambridge, MA: Massachusetts Institute of Technology, 1978).

Figure 5.9: Reprinted by permission from M.H. Raibert, *Motor Control and Learning by The State-Space Model: Technical Report No. A1-TR-439* (Cambridge, MA: Artificial Intelligence Laboratory, Massachusetts Institute of Technology, 1977), 50.

Figure 6.1: Adapted from Fitts (1954).

Figure 6.2: Adapted from Fitts (1954).

Figure 6.3: Reprinted by permission from R.A. Schmidt, T.D. Lee, C.J. Winstein, et al., *Motor Control and Learning: A Behavioral Emphasis,* 6th ed. (Champaign, IL: Human Kinetics, 2019), 217: Data from Fitts (1954).

Figure 6.4: Reprinted by permission from R.A. Schmidt et al., "Motor-Output Variability: A Theory for the Accuracy of Rapid Motor Acts," *Psychological Review* 86 (1979): 425. Copyright © 1979 by the American Psychological Association.

Figure 6.5: Reprinted by permission from R.A. Schmidt et al., "Motor-Output Variability: A Theory for the Accuracy of Rapid Motor Acts," *Psychological Review* 86 (1979): 425. Copyright © 1979 by the American Psychological Association.

Figure 6.7: Adapted by permission from R.A. Schmidt and D.E. Sherwood, "An Inverted-U Relation Between Spatial Error and Force Requirements in Rapid Limb Movements: Further Evidence for The Impulse-Variability Model," *Journal of*

Experimental Psychology: Human Perception and Performance 8 (1982): 165. Copyright © 1982 by the American Psychological Association.

Figure 6.9: Reprinted by permission from R.A. Schmidt, T.D. Lee, C.J. Winstein, et al., *Motor Control and Learning: A Behavioral Emphasis,* 6th ed. (Champaign, IL: Human Kinetics, 2019), 227.

Figure 7.2: Reprinted by permission from P.A. Bender, *Extended Practice and Patterns of Bimanual Interference.* Unpublished Doctoral Dissertation (Los Angeles, CA: University of Southern California, 1987).

Figure 7.3: Reprinted by permission from T.D. Lee et al., "Do Expert Golfers Really Keep Their Heads Still While Putting?" *Annual Review of Golf Coaching* 2 (2008): 135-143.

Figure 7.6: Based on Kelso, Scholz, and Schöner (1986).

Figure 8.3: Adapted by permission from R.B. Ammons and L. Willig, "Acquisition of Motor Skill: IV. Effects of Repeated Periods of Massed Practice," *Journal of Experimental Psychology* 51 (1956): 118-126. Copyright © 1956 by the American Psychological Association.

Figure 8.4: Adapted by permission from R.B. Ammons and L. Willig, "Acquisition of Motor Skill: IV. Effects of Repeated Periods of Massed Practice," *Journal of Experimental Psychology* 51 (1956): 118-126. Copyright © 1956 by the American Psychological Association.

Figure 8.5: Adapted by permission from H.P. Bahrick, P.M. Fitts, and G.E. Briggs, "Learning Curves: Facts or Artifacts?" *Psychological Bulletin* 54 (1957): 256- 268. Copyright © 1957 by the American Psychological Association.

Figure 9.1: Data from Leavitt (1979).

Figure 9.3: Adapted by permission from R.A. Schmidt, T.D. Lee, C.J. Winstein, et al., *Motor Control and Learning: A Behavioral Emphasis,* 6th ed. (Champaign, IL: Human Kinetics, 2019), 451; Adapted from MacKay (1976), personal communication.

Figure 9.4: Reprinted by permission from E. Neumann and R.B. Ammons, "Acquisition and Long Term Retention of a Simple Serial Perception Motor Skill," *Journal of Experimental Psychology* 53 (1959): 160. Copyright © 2011 by the American Psychological Association.

Figure 9.5: Reprinted from E.A. Fleishman and J.F. Parker, "Factors in the Retention and Relearning of Perceptual Motor Skill," *Journal of Experimental Psychology* 64 (1962): 218. Copyright © 1962 by the American Psychological Association.

Figure 9.6: Adapted from Lordahl and Archer (1958).

Figure 9.7: Monty Rakusen/DigitalVision/Getty Images

Figure 9.9: PHILIPPE LOPEZ/AFP via Getty Images

Figure 10.1: Reprinted by permission from R.A. Schmidt, T.D. Lee, C.J. Winstein, et al., *Motor Control and Learning: A Behavioral Emphasis,* 6th ed. (Champaign, IL: Human Kinetics, 2019), 323; Data from Baddeley and Longman (1978).

Figure 10.2: Reprinted by permission from L.E. Bourne and E.J. Archer, "Time Continuously on Target as a Function of Distribution of Practice," *Journal of Experimental Psychology* 51 (1956): 27. Copyright © 1956 by the American Psychological Association.

Figure 10.4: Data from Catalano and Kleiner (1984).

Figure 10.5: Reprinted by permission from K.M. Keetch, R.A. Schmidt, T.D. Lee, and D.E. Young, "Especial Skills: Their Emergence with Massive Amounts of Practice," *Journal of Experimental Psychology: Human Perception and Performance* 31 (2005): 970-978. Copyright © 2005 by the American Psychological Association.

Figure 10.6: Adapted by permission from J.B. Shea and R.L. Morgan, "Contextual Interference Effects on the Acquisition, Retention, and Transfer of a Motor Skill," *Journal of Experimental Psychology: Human Learning and Memory* 5 (1979): 179-187. Copyright © 1979 by the American Psychological Association.

Figure 10.7: Reprinted by permission from T.D. Lee et al., "Modeled Timing Information During Random Practice Eliminates the Contextual Interference Effect," *Research Quarterly for Exercise and Sport* 68 (1997): 100-105, permission conveyed through Copyright Clearance Center, Inc.

Figure 10.8: Adapted from Lee and Magill (1983).

Figure 10.9: Data from Simon and Bjork (2001).

Figure 10.10: Adapted by permission from B.A. Boyce, "Effects of Assigned Versus Participant-Set Goals on Skill Acquisition and Retention of a Selected Shooting Task," *Journal of Teaching in Physical Education* 11, no. 2 (1992): 227.

Figure 10.11: Based on Lewthwaite and Wulf (2010).

Figure 10.12: Data from Hird et al. (1991).

Figure 11.3: Adapted by permission. ©Bob Scavetta. Any adaptation or reproduction of "1.5 Seconds of Thought" is forbidden without the written permission of the copyright holder.

Figure 11.4: Reprinted by permission from R.A. Schmidt, T.D. Lee, C.J. Winstein, et al., *Motor Control and Learning: A Behavioral Emphasis,* 6th ed. (Champaign, IL: Human Kinetics, 2019), 338; Data from Kernodle and Carlton (1992).

Figure 11.5: Reprinted by permission from C.J. Winstein and R.A. Schmidt, "Reduced Frequency of Knowledge of Results Enhances Motor Skill Learning," *Journal of Experimental Psychology: Learning, Memory, and Cognition* 16 (1990): 910.

Copyright © 1990 by the American Psychological Association.

Figure 11.7: Data from Guadagnoli et al. (1996).

Figure 11.8: Based on Yao, Fischman, and Wang (1994).

Figure 11.10: Adapted by permission from R.A. Schmidt, T.L. Lee, C.J. Winstein, et al., *Motor Control and Learning: A Behavioral Emphasis,* 6th ed. (Champaign, IL: Human Kinetics, 2019), 338; Adapted from Armstrong (1970).

Figure 11.11: Reprinted by permission from S.P. Swinnen et al., "Information Feedback for Skill Acquisition: Instantaneous Knowledge of Results Degrades Learning," *Journal of Experimental Psychology: Learning, Memory, and Cognition* 16 (1990): 712. Copyright © 2011 by the American Psychological Association.

Figure 11.12: Based on Guadagnoli and Kohl (2001).

Figure 12.6: Reprinted by permission from K. Davids, C. Button, and S. Bennett, *Dynamics of Skill Acquisition: A Constraints-Led Approach* (Champaign, IL: Human Kinetics, 2008), 40.

Figure 12.7: Adapted by permission from R. Gray, "Comparing Cueing and Constraints Interventions for Increasing Launch Angle in Baseball Batting," *Sport, Exercise and Performance Psychology* 7 (2018): 318-332. Copyright © 2018 by the American Psychological Association.

Photos

Page iii: © Timothy D. Lee

Page xx: ti-ja/E+/Getty Images

Page 6 (top): LuisPortugal/E+/Getty Images

Page 10 (from top to bottom): Kohei Hara/Stone/Getty Images; Claude Beaubien/fotolia.com

Page 13 (top): Tim Mosenfelder/Getty Images

Page 22: Thomas Barwick/DigitalVision/Getty Images

Page 26 (from top to bottom): David Madison/Getty Images Sport/Getty Images; Renata Angerami/E+/Getty Images

Page 29: Christian Petersen/Getty Images

Page 35 (from top to bottom): FatCamera/E+/Getty Images; skynesher /iStockphoto/Getty Images

Page 36: Burazin/Getty Images/The Image Bank/Getty Images

Page 42: Mark Dadswell/Getty Images

Page 50: kajakiki/E+/Getty Images

Page 55: Michael H/DigitalVision/Getty Images

Page 56: Matthew Maxey/Icon Sportswire via Getty Images

Page 57: South_agency/E+/Getty Images

Page 69: Larry Marano/Getty Images

Page 78: Alexander Yakovlev/fotolia.com

Page 81 (from left to right): RichLegg/E+/Getty Images; ©DR P. MARAZZI/Science Source

Page 82: holgs/E+/Getty Images

Page 87: Nicki Pardo/Photodisc/Getty Images

Page 96: Photo courtesy of Philip de Vries.

Page 102: Clive Mason/Getty Images

Page 103: 945ontwerp/E+/Getty Images

Page 106: Black 100/Photodisc/Getty Images

Page 116: Marcus Chung/E+/Getty Images

Page 124: Michael Reaves/Getty Images

Page 129 (from top to bottom): ©Liv Friis-larsen - Fotolia.com; AscentXmedia/E+/Getty Images

Page 136: sturti/E+/Getty Images

Page 143 (clockwise from top to bottom): © Timothy D. Lee; ET-ARTWORKS/DigitalVision/Getty Images; JP Greenwood/Photodisc/Getty Images

Page 154: Stan Grossfeld/The Boston Globe via Getty Images

Page 157: vm/E+/Getty Images

Page 164 (from top to bottom): Plan Shooting 2/ImaZinS/Getty Images; © CORBIS / age fotostock

Page 170: Photo courtesy of University of Delaware.

Page 178: SCIENCE PHOTO LIBRARY/Science Photo Library/Getty Images

Page 180: Hill Street Studios/DigitalVision/Getty Images

Page 191: © Timothy D. Lee

Page 200: Ebet Roberts/Redferns

Page 204: RichLegg/E+/Getty Images

Page 206: Don Mason Photography LLC/The Image Bank RF/Getty Images

Page 207: imacoconut/Getty Images/Getty Images

Page 218: Dick Schmidt

Page 224: ViewStock/View Stock/Getty Image

Page 237: Hispanolistic/E+/Getty Images

Page 243: Zoom Agence/Stockbyte/Getty Images

Page 250: Tony Anderson/DigitalVision/Getty Images

Page 255: M_a_y_a/E+/Getty Images

Page 260: franckreporter/E+/Getty Images

Page 265: miniseries/E+/Getty Images

Page 273: Ethan Miller/Getty Images

Page 278: AleksandarGeorgiev/E+/Getty Images

Page 283: Photo courtesy of Sinah Lee.

Page 294: JMichl/E+/Getty Images

1

Introduction to Motor Learning and Performance

How Skills Are Studied

CHAPTER OUTLINE

Why Study Motor Skills?
The Science of Motor Learning and Performance
Defining Skills
Components of Skills
Classifying Skills
Measuring Skilled Performance
Understanding Performance and Learning
Summary

CHAPTER OBJECTIVES

Chapter 1 provides an overview of research in human motor skills with particular reference to their study in motor learning and performance. This chapter will help you understand

- the scientific method in skills research,
- different taxonomies used to classify skills,
- common variables used to measure motor performance, and
- the rationale for developing a conceptual model of motor performance.

CHAPTER PREVIEW QUIZ

1. What is the primary difference between a discrete skill and a continuous skill?
2. What is the primary difference in the environment in which open and closed skills are performed?
3. What is a correlation, and what does it mean when a set of scores for 50 people on two skill tests are correlated?

Parkour can be scary to watch, let alone perform. The traceur or traceuse displays acts of balance, agility, and dexterity, usually across great expanses of space and often at dizzying heights above ground. How people perform these skills with such grace and confidence, how such skills are acquired, and how you can help develop these skills in someone else represent a fascination that encourages an understanding of human learning and performance.

A description of the study of motor learning and performance starts here. This chapter introduces the concept of skill and discusses various features of its definition. The chapter then gives examples of skill classification schemes that are important for later applications. Finally, the logic behind the book's organization is described to help you understand skills effectively: First, it presents the principles and processes underlying skilled movement control (performance); then, it discusses how practice (learning) can improve such capabilities.

The remarkable capability to perform skills is a critical feature of our very existence and is almost uniquely human. Without the capacity for skilled performance, we could not type this text, and you could not read it. The study of motor learning and performance is critically important for students involved in physical education and kinesiology, coaching, physical (or speech or occupational) therapy, chiropractic, medicine, human factors (ergonomics), law enforcement, and many other disciplines in which motor skills play a critical role. Here is the opportunity to learn about the fundamentals of a wide variety of sports and athletic endeavors, music, and everyday actions that are fascinating and exciting.

Human skills take many forms—from those that emphasize the control and coordination of our largest muscle groups in relatively forceful activities (such as soccer, track and field, and firefighting) to those that require precise fine-tuning in the smallest muscle groups (as in typing, repairing a watch, or microsurgery). This book generally focuses on the full range of skilled behaviors because it is useful to understand that many common features underlie the performance of skills associated with industrial and military settings, sport, the reacquisition of movement capabilities lost through injuries or strokes, or simply the everyday activities of most people.

Most humans have the innate capability to develop many skills and require only maturation and experience to produce them in nearly complete form. Walking and running, chewing, balancing, and avoiding danger are some examples of these relatively innate behaviors. But imagine what simple and uninteresting creatures we would be if these innate actions were all that we could ever do. All biological organisms have the remarkable facility to profit from their experiences, to learn to detect important environmental features (and to ignore others), and to produce behaviors that were not part of their original capabilities. Humans have great flexibility to adapt, which allows gains in proficiency for occupations such as dentists or computer programmers, for competition in music or athletics, or simply for conducting their daily lives more efficiently. Thus, producing skilled behaviors and the learning that leads to their development are tightly intertwined in human experience.

What makes this field of study so interesting is that motor learning and performance involve much more than just movement. Skilled performers must observe what is going on around them by watching, touching, and listening to their environment so that actions that influence movement are relevant to the ever-changing world. A skilled police officer, for example, must be a careful observer of a suspect's behavior so that any actions taken maximize the safety of all individuals involved. As such, the study of perception, attention, and decision-making is very relevant to any discussion of human learning and performance.

Why Study Motor Skills?

Because skills make up such a large part of human life, scientists and educators are trying to understand the factors that affect their performance. The knowledge gained is applicable to numerous aspects of life, such as skill instruction, in which methods for efficient teaching and effective carryover to life situations are primary concerns. There is also considerable applicability for improving high-level performance in areas such as sport, music, surgery, and industry. Of course, much of what coaches and instructors do during their professional activities involves, in one way or another, skill instruction. Practitioners who understand these skill-related processes most effectively will undoubtedly have an advantage when their trainees perform their activities.

Other areas can be emphasized as well. There are many applications in training skills for industry, where effective job skills can mean success in the workplace and can be major determinants of satisfaction both with the job and with life in general. Teaching job skills most effectively and determining which of many individuals are best suited to particular occupations are common situations in which knowledge about skills can be useful in industry. Usually, these applications are considered within the field of human factors (ergonomics). The principles also apply to physical therapy and occupational therapy settings, where the concern is the (re)learning and production of movements disrupted by injury. Although all these areas may be different and the physical capabilities of the learners may vary widely, the principles that lead to successful application are generally the same (see chapter 12 for more discussion).

The Science of Motor Learning and Performance

It is not uncommon that as an area of interest grows, the systematic study of the principles involved also develops. Motor learning and performance are no different in that a science has emerged that allows the formalization of terms and concepts for others to use.

When we use the word *science*, what do we mean? The concept of a science implies several things:

1. The active use of theory and hypothesis testing to guide research and interpret results
2. A certain infrastructure that includes books, journals, podcasts, and other forms of media; scientific organizations that deal with both the fundamental aspects of the science and the application of knowledge to real-world situations; as well as granting agencies that fund research
3. The existence of courses of study in universities and colleges

Theories and Hypotheses

Certainly at the heart of every science are theories that are devised to explain how phenomena occur. The theorist devises hypothetical constructs—elements or pieces that interact in various ways in the theory. The theorist then describes how the hypothetical constructs interact with each other to explain some empirical phenomenon. Then, using logical deduction, scientists determine certain predictions that the theory makes in its current form. These predictions form the basis of hypotheses that can be tested, often in a controlled, experimental setting, but sometimes they can also be tested in real workplace or sport environments. These hypotheses take the form of statements such as "If learners practice under condition *x*, then learning should be better than for others who practice under condition *y*."

Theories are typically tested by doing experiments, which determine whether the hypothesis correctly predicted the results. In the motor learning and performance field, these experiments typically have at least two groups of research participants randomly assigned to experimental treatments, with one group performing a task under condition *x* (as in the example just mentioned) and the other group performing under condition *y*. In this example, if the group practicing under condition *x* outperforms the group in condition *y*, we can conclude that the hypothesis is supported. However, a given theory might predict an outcome that would make sense for several theories, so an experiment that supports the hypothesis does not prove that the theory is correct. If the results contradict the prediction of at least one theory, the logical inference is that the theory must be incorrect, allowing us to reject all or parts of it. A theory cannot survive for long if the results of controlled experiments do not support the prediction. Because of this difference in the power of how hypotheses are tested, scientists tend to search out predictions from a theory that might not hold if tested in the laboratory.

What Skills Have Been Studied, and Who Studies Them?

The science of motor learning and performance has been used to study many varieties of skills. Initially, skills research was primarily the domain of psychologists and physiologists who used various tasks as tools to examine theories of learning and coordination. For example, in the 1890s, Bryan and Harter studied the behaviors involved in sending and receiving Morse code. In the 1920s, the psychologist E.L. Thorndike used blindfolded line drawing to examine the role of augmented feedback to test predictions from the Law of Effect theory. Rotary-pursuit tracking was commonly used to examine Hull's theory of learning in the 1940s. And simple line-drawing tasks became popular again in the 1960s to study the forgetting of information over short retention periods.

In the late 19th century, physiologists such as Sir Charles Sherrington were interested in the role of various biological systems concerning the fundamental mechanisms of neural control of muscle and the study of the nervous system. Nikolai Bernstein and Erich von Holst contributed essential research to our understanding of movement coordination during the first half of the 20th century. And Edward Taub performed controversial experiments on monkeys that revealed evidence about lost and retained movement capabilities in the absence of sensory feedback.

Perhaps motivated by discoveries in these more traditional fields, researchers in other disciplines began to study motor skills as a means to answer domain-specific issues. Paul Fitts (see Focus on Research 1.1) contributed to the war effort in the 1940s by studying piloting errors—why errors occurred and how task demands limit movement's speed and accuracy. Fitts' work represented an emerging field called ergonomics (or human factors), which broadly studied the limits of human performance in the execution of industrial tasks.

FOCUS ON Research 1.1

Paul M. Fitts

Have you ever wondered why some keys on a calculator or your computer keyboard are larger than others, or why they are positioned in specific locations? If so, then you can probably credit Paul Fitts with the underlying rationale. His research was designed to answer fundamental questions about human performance in situations that required speed and accuracy, often in stressful situations. Some of his many contributions include research on stimulus–response compatibility effects (see chapter 2), the effects of target size and distance on movement time, now known as Fitts' Law (chapter 6), and the stages of learning (chapter 12).

FOCUS ON Research 1.2

Franklin M. Henry

Before World War II and during the 1950s and 1960s, when much effort was directed at military skills such as pilotry, most of the research in movement behavior and learning was done by experimental psychologists, studying relatively fine motor skills. Little effort was devoted to the gross motor skills applicable to many sports. Franklin M. Henry, trained in experimental psychology but working in the Department of Physical Education at the University of California, Berkeley, was filling this gap with a new tradition of laboratory experimentation that started an important new direction in research on movement skills. He studied gross motor skills, with performances intentionally representative of those seen on the playing fields and in gymnasiums. But he used laboratory tasks, which enabled the rigorous study of these skills employing methods analogous to those used in experimental psychology. Two of his major contributions to research were (1) evidence that reaction time increased as intended movements increased in complexity, providing evidence in support of the motor program concept (see chapter 5), and (2) evidence that skills are highly uncorrelated within individuals (see Correlation: The Association Strength Between Scores later in this chapter), which dispelled the general motor ability theory (see chapter 7). His research was so important that he is now generally regarded as the "father" of motor behavior research.

Physical education and kinesiology departments, led by researchers such as Franklin M. Henry (see Focus on Research 1.2), studied motor skills as a research topic of direct interest in and of itself. Later, researchers such as Jack Adams and Richard Schmidt added to this effort by establishing testable theories regarding the learning and control of motor skills (see chapter 12).

Since the 1980s, there has been an explosion of research conducted in various fields of application in which skills are used as components of daily living, such as medicine, dentistry, physical rehabilitation, fire prevention, law enforcement, and the interface of humans with various forms of computing devices (see Lee & Carnahan, 2021, for a retrospective). And, of course, the study of how highly skilled performance is acquired and executed remains an ongoing field of study in sport and music. All these influences, in the pursuit of both practical and theoretical advances to our knowledge, have served to drive the study of motor learning and performance.

Defining Skills

As widely represented and diverse as skills are, it is difficult to define them in a way that applies to all cases. Guthrie (1952) provided a definition that captures most of the critical features of skills that we emphasize here. He defined **skill** as "the ability to bring about some result with maximum certainty and minimum outlay of energy, or of time and energy" (p. 136). Next, we consider some of the important components (or features) of this definition.

First, performing skills implies some desired goal (or result), such as sinking a free throw in basketball, holding a handstand in gymnastics, expressing thoughts using a keyboard, or being able to walk again after a stroke. Skills are usually thought of as different from movements, which do not necessarily have any particular goal, such as idly wiggling one's little finger.

Second, to be skilled implies meeting this result with maximum certainty. For example, suppose that a darts player scores a bull's-eye. This, by itself, does not ensure that he is a skilled darts player, because there is no evidence that this result was achieved with much certainty. Such an outcome could have resulted from one lucky throw among hundreds of not-so-lucky ones. To be considered

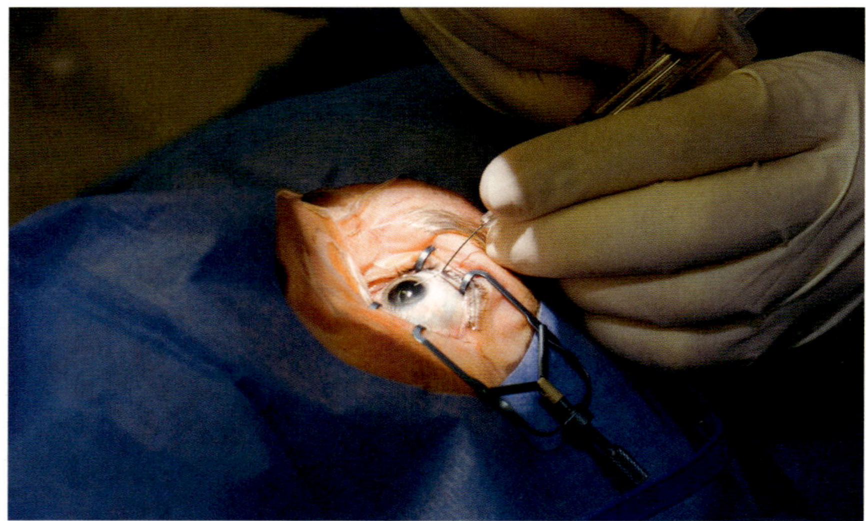

In each of these photos, identify the main emphases with respect to the definition of skill.

skilled, a person must possess the ability to produce the skill reliably, on demand, without luck playing a very large role.

Third, a major feature in many skills is the minimization, and thus conservation, of the energy required for performance. For some skills, this is clearly not the goal, as in the shot put, where the only goal is to achieve the maximum distance with the maximum outlay of energy. But for many other skills, the minimization of energy expenditure is critical, allowing the marathon runner to hold an efficient pace or the wrestler to save strength for the last few minutes of the match. Skilled musicians are renowned for their movement precision and lack of unwanted extra movements. This minimum-energy notion applies not only to the physiological energy costs but also to the psychological, or mental, energy required for performance. Performers have learned many skills so well that they hardly need to pay attention to them, freeing their cognitive processes for other features of the activity, such as strategic planning in team sports or artistic expressiveness in dance and music. A major contributor to the efficiency of skilled performance is, of course, practice, with learning and experience leading to the relatively effortless performances so admired in highly skilled people.

Finally, another feature of many skills is that highly proficient performers achieve their goals in a minimum amount of time. Many skills have this as the only goal, such as a swimming race. Minimizing time can interact with the other skill features mentioned, however. Surgeons who conduct invasive surgery need to work quickly to minimize the opportunity for infections to enter the body. Yet surgeons obviously need to work carefully too. Speeding up performance often results in imprecise movements that have less certainty in terms of achieving their goals. Also, increased speed generates movements for which the energy costs are sometimes higher. Thus, understanding skills involves optimizing and balancing several aspects of skill that are important to different extents in different settings. In sum, skills generally involve achieving some well-defined goal by

- maximizing the certainty of goal achievement,
- minimizing the physical- and mental-energy costs of performance, and
- minimizing the time used.

Components of Skills

The elegant performance of the skilled dancer and the artistic talents of an expert sculptor may appear simple, but the performance goals actually were realized through a complex combination of mental and motor processes. For example, many skills involve considerable emphasis on incoming information, such as detecting that a tennis opponent is going to hit a shot to your left or that you are rapidly approaching a car that has suddenly stopped on the road ahead of you. Often, this requires a split-second analysis of patterns of sensory input, such as discerning that the combined movements of an entire football team indicate that the play will be a pass to the left side. This information leads to decisions about what to do, how to do it, and when to do it. Such decisions are often a major determinant of success. Finally, of course, skills typically depend on the quality of movement generated because of these decisions. Even if the situation is correctly perceived and the response decisions are appropriate, the performer will not be effective in meeting the environmental goal if the actions are poorly executed.

These three elements are critical to almost any skill:

- Perceiving the relevant environmental features
- Deciding what to do, where to do it, and when to do it to achieve the goal
- Producing movements that achieve the goal

These various processes are present in almost all motor skills. Even so, all skills are not fundamentally the same. In fact, the principles of human performance and learning depend to some extent on the kind of movement skill to be performed. So next, we discuss how skills have been classified.

Classifying Skills

There are several skill classification systems that help organize the research findings and make their application somewhat more straightforward. These are presented in the following sections.

Open and Closed Skills

One way to classify movement skills concerns the extent to which the environment is stable and predictable throughout performance (see table 1.1). An **open skill** is one for which the environment is variable and unpredictable during the action. Examples include many team sports and police traffic stops, where it is difficult to predict the future actions of other people. A **closed skill**, on the other hand, is one for which the environment is stable and predictable. Examples include swimming in an empty lane in a pool and drilling a hole in a block of wood. These *open* and *closed* designations actually mark only the end points of a continuum, with the skills lying in between having varying degrees of environmental predictability or variability, such as driving a car in traffic where the actions of others are usually, but not always, predictable (see Gentile, 2000, for more discussion).

This classification points out a critical feature for skills, defining the performer's need to respond to moment-to-moment variations in the environment. These environmental variations require subprocesses associated with perception, pattern recognition, and decision-making (usually with the need to perform these processes quickly) so the action can be adapted to changes in the environment. These processes are minimized in closed skills, where the performer can evaluate the environmental demands without time pressure, organize the movement in advance, and carry it out without needing to make rapid modifications as the movement unfolds.

Discrete, Serial, and Continuous Skills

A second scheme for classifying skills concerns how the movement itself unfolds (see table 1.2). At one end of this dimension is a **discrete skill**, which usually has an easily

TABLE 1.1 Open and Closed Skills Continuum

Closed skills ⟵		⟶ Open skills
Predictable environment	**Semipredictable environment**	**Unpredictable environment**
Gymnastics	Walking a tightrope	Playing soccer
Darts	Driving a car	Wrestling
Typing	Invasive surgery	Police traffic stop

TABLE 1.2 Discrete–Serial–Continuous Skills Continuum

Discrete skills	Serial skills	Continuous skills
Distinct beginning and end	**Discrete actions linked together**	**No discrete beginning or end**
Throwing a dart	Hammering a nail	Steering a cart
Flipping a light switch	Working on an assembly-line	Swimming
Shooting a rifle	Performing parkour	Cycling

defined beginning and end, often with movement of a very brief duration, such as throwing a ball or turning on a light switch. Discrete skills are particularly important in both sport and daily actions, especially considering the large number of discrete hitting, kicking, and throwing skills that make up many sport activities, as well as everyday skills of fastening buttons, writing your signature, and pointing a computer mouse.

At the other end of this dimension is a **continuous skill**, which has no particular beginning or end, with the behavior flowing on for many seconds, minutes, or even hours, such as swimming or knitting. As discussed later, discrete and continuous skills can be quite different, requiring different processes for performance and demanding that they be taught somewhat differently as a result.

One frequently studied continuous skill is **tracking**, in which the performer uses limb movements to control a lever, a wheel, a handle, or some other device to follow a target. Steering a car involves tracking, with steering wheel movements made so the car follows the track defined by the roadway. Tracking movements are very common in real-world skill situations, and their performance and learning have been much researched.

Between the polar ends of the discrete–continuous skill continuum is the **serial skill**, which is a series of discrete skills strung together to make up a more complicated skilled action. Here, the word *serial* implies that the order of the elements is usually critical for successful performance. Cars that have a manual transmission to shift gears involve a serial skill that combines discrete arm movements with movements of both feet performed in a precisely timed sequence to create a larger action. Other examples include performing a gymnastics routine and most types of cooking—separate, discrete actions sequenced in a precise order.

Object Manipulation and Body Transport

Gentile (2000) identified two additional factors that help to more precisely define the nature of skills (see table 1.3). One concerns whether the body is stationary or in motion while performing the skill. For example, a dentist usually performs her work while standing still, in contrast to a table busser in a restaurant, who is constantly on the move. The other factor is whether the performer is manipulating an object during performance. Figure skaters express artistry in motion on ice skates without manipulating an object. In contrast, hockey players manipulate the stick to control the puck while skating.

The four factors described in this section—environment predictability, nature of the movement, body transport, and object manipulation—combine to define skills in a complex classification system. Ultimately, almost every skill that you can think of can be described as an interacting product of these four dimensions.

TABLE 1.3 Gentile's Taxonomy Involving Body Transport and Object Manipulation

		Object manipulation	
		Absent	**Present**
Body transport	Stationary	Communicating with sign language Directing traffic	Performing surgery Doing carpentry
	Moving	Performing a figure skating routine Executing a gymnastics floor routine	Playing in a marching band Skiing downhill

In each of these photos, differentiate the skills in terms of the open–closed continuum and Gentile's taxonomy.

Measuring Skilled Performance

Quite frequently, researchers compute scores for a participant who attempted to perform a series of trials on a test. As we shall see, there are various ways to calculate performance measures, depending on the nature of the task.

Error Scores in Discrete Tasks (One Dimension)

Suppose that you are testing individuals on a throwing task in which they are trying to toss a ball exactly 50 ft from where they are standing. Comparing the skill of two individuals based on just a single score is likely to be less reliable than comparing them based on the results of multiple throws, so researchers often carry out multiple trials when assessing skilled performance. So, in our example, two participants each make five trials. The results are illustrated in figure 1.1 and presented in table 1.4.

Which of these two individuals was more skilled at this task? From the figure, it appears that there is a difference in skill, but looking at a figure and making decisions based on one's impression is less precise than developing measures that are based on the actual numbers and inferential statistics. Therefore, researchers have devised ways of combining the scores on the five trials into a measure, represented by a single number, that reflects their skill in the task. Several candidate measures are possible, and each represents a unique assessment of skill.

The worksheet presented in table 1.4 presents a detailed description of how to calculate various methods that represent the skills of the two throwers in figure 1.1.

Visit HK*Propel* to read "Public Opinion Polls" and complete the self-directed learning activities.

Constant Error (CE)

The simplest way to determine which person was more skilled is to compute the error deviation of each throw relative to the target and then calculate the average of these error deviations (column four in table 1.4). For example, on trial 1, Chester's error score was –4 (his throw was 46 ft, and thus 4 ft short of the target of 50 ft). The error score on the second trial was +2 (his 52 ft throw was 2 ft too far), and so on. After the error scores for each trial are computed, the mean can then

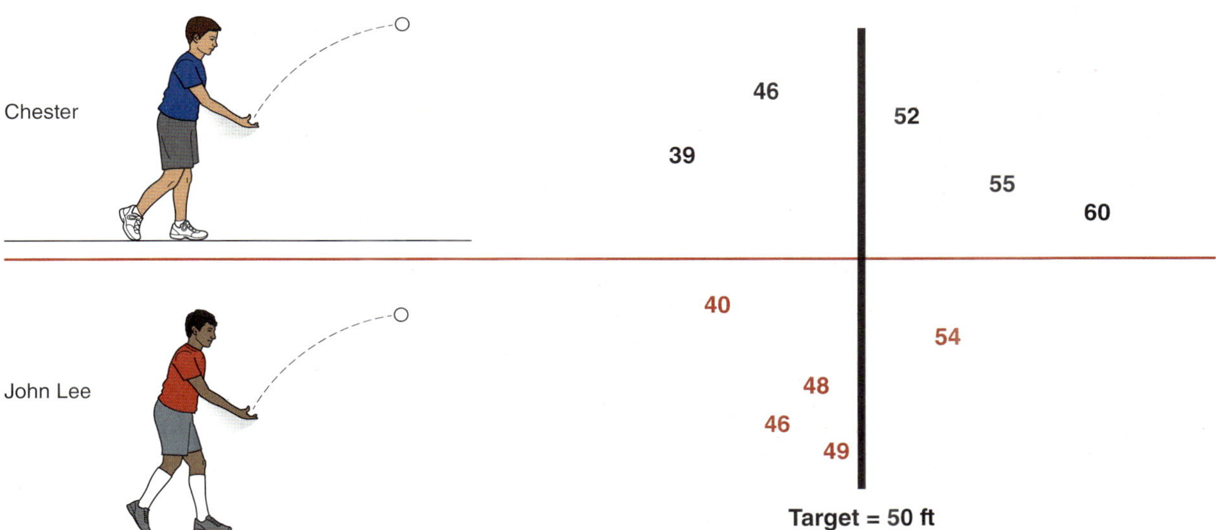

FIGURE 1.1 Two performers are attempting to toss a ball exactly 50 ft. The numbers represent the individual outcome results for each of the five trials. The results are used in table 1.4 to calculate error scores.

TABLE 1.4 Error Scores in Discrete Tasks

Chester					
			CE	AE	VE
Trial	X_i	T	$X_i - T$	$\|X_i - T\|$	$[(X_i - T) - CE]^2$
1	46	50	−4	4	19.36
2	52	50	+2	2	2.56
3	39	50	−11	11	129.96
4	55	50	+5	5	21.16
5	60	50	+10	10	92.16
			$\Sigma(X_i - T) = 2.0$	$\Sigma(\|X_i - T\|) = 32.0$	$\Sigma[(X_i - T) - CE]^2 = 265.2$
			$\Sigma(X_i - T)/N = +0.4$	$\Sigma(\|X_i - T\|)/N = 6.4$	$\Sigma[(X_i - T) - CE]^2 / N = 53.04$
					$\sqrt{[\Sigma[(X_i - T) - CE]^2 / N]} = 7.3$
John Lee					
			CE	AE	VE
Trial	X_i	T	$X_i - T$	$\|X_i - T\|$	$[(X_i - T) - CE]^2$
1	40	50	−10	10	54.76
2	54	50	+4	4	43.56
3	48	50	−2	2	0.36
4	46	50	−4	4	1.96
5	49	50	−1	1	2.56
			$\Sigma(X_i - T) = -13$	$\Sigma(\|X_i - T\|) = 21$	$\Sigma[(X_i - T) - CE]^2 = 103.2$
			$\Sigma(X_i - T)/N = -2.6$	$\Sigma(\|X_i - T\|)/N = 4.2$	$\Sigma[(X_i - T) - CE]^2 / N = 20.64$
					$\sqrt{[\Sigma[(X_i - T) - CE]^2 / N]} = 4.5$

be calculated to determine the average error deviation from the target. This is termed the participant's average **constant error (CE)**. The interpretation is that Chester tended to overthrow the 50 ft target by only 0.4 ft —that is, his average CE was +0.4. John Lee tended to underthrow the target by 2.6 ft —that is, his average CE was −2.6. Therefore, based on the average of outcomes of the five throws, Chester tended to be closer to the goal than John Lee.

The formula for constant error is

$$\text{CE} = \frac{\Sigma(X_i - T)}{N}$$

where Σ = the sum of, i = trial number, X_i = score for the ith trial, T = the target distance, and N = the number of trials.

Absolute Error (AE)

Another simple way to combine the scores into a single number is to disregard whether the throw was long or short of the target and consider the absolute value (i.e., with the sign ignored or removed) of the error on each trial. This measure calculates the average of those unsigned error scores for the various trials (column 5 in table 1.4). For example, Chester has an error of −4 ft on the first trial; when we take the absolute value, the first trial has an absolute error of 4 ft. The second trial has an error of +2 ft, whose absolute value is 2. If we do this procedure for the remainder of the trials for Chester and all the trials for John Lee, the computed average **absolute**

In each of these photos, classify the actions depicted along the four skill classification dimensions: discrete, continuous, or serial; open or closed; body in motion or stationary; object or no object.

error (AE) for Chester is 6.4; for John Lee, it is 4.2. Here, disregarding the direction of the errors, the interpretation is that John Lee was closer to the goal than Chester, a conclusion that is *opposite* to the conclusion based on the average CE.

The formula for average absolute error is

$$\mathrm{AE} = \frac{\Sigma(|X_i - T|)}{N}$$

where Σ, *i*, *X*, *T*, and *N* are defined as before for constant error, and the vertical bars (|) mean absolute value of.

Variable Error (VE)

The third measure of skill is not actually a measure of accuracy but an assessment of the participant's inconsistency—that is, how each individual score differed in comparison to the average CE score. To compute **variable error (VE)**, we square the difference between each trial's error score and the individual's own constant error $[(X_i - T) - CE]^2$, sum those squared values over all five trials, and divide by 5. Now, since these are squared values, we return them to their original state by computing the square root of this value (see column six in table 1.4).

In this example, for Chester's first trial, the difference between his throwing error $(X_1 - T)$ and Chester's average CE (which was +0.4) is [(−4 − (+0.4)] = −4.4 ft, which, when squared, is 19.36 ft. For the second trial, the difference is [(+2) − (+0.4)] = 1.6 ft, which, when squared, is 2.56 ft. Now do the same thing for trials 3, 4, and 5: add up all five squared differences; divide this number by $N = 5$; then take the square root of that number; and you finally have VE. The score reflects the inconsistency in responding—that is, how variable each performance is relative to the person's own average CE. Of course, when computing the value for John Lee, we would use his CE (which was −2.6) in the computations. The computed VE score for Chester was 7.3 ft, and for John Lee, the VE was 4.5 ft. The interpretation is that even though Chester's average CE was closer to the goal than John Lee's average CE, Chester was more inconsistent in those throws than was John Lee.

The formula for variable error is

$$VE = \sqrt{\frac{\Sigma[(X_i - T) - CE]^2}{N}}$$

where Σ, *X*, *i*, *CE*, and *N* are defined as before, and √ is the square root.

Researchers reported AE as a measure of error quite frequently until Schutz and Roy (1973) pointed out some statistical difficulties with it. Today, investigators tend to use CE (as a measure of average bias or directional error) and VE (as a measure of inconsistency). Sometimes investigators use the **absolute constant error (|CE|)** instead of CE for an individual's measure of bias. The |CE| is simply the average absolute value of the computed CE score as defined previously. The advantage is that |CE| retains the magnitude of average deviation from the target but prevents two scores from canceling out when data from more than one person are averaged together to present a group score. Chapter 2 of Schmidt and colleagues (2025) presents much more on these error scores for single-dimensional tasks.

Visit HK*Propel* to read "Cutting Wood and Missing Putts" and complete the self-directed learning activities.

Error Scores in Two-Dimensional Discrete Tasks

In some discrete aiming tasks, such as darts, archery, and pistol shooting, the goal is to hit a spot on a target. In figure 1.2, the results of two shooters who aimed five shots each at the bull's-eye are represented with different colored holes in the target. Can you identify which shooter is more highly skilled? A complication is that different measures of performance lead to different interpretations of skill.

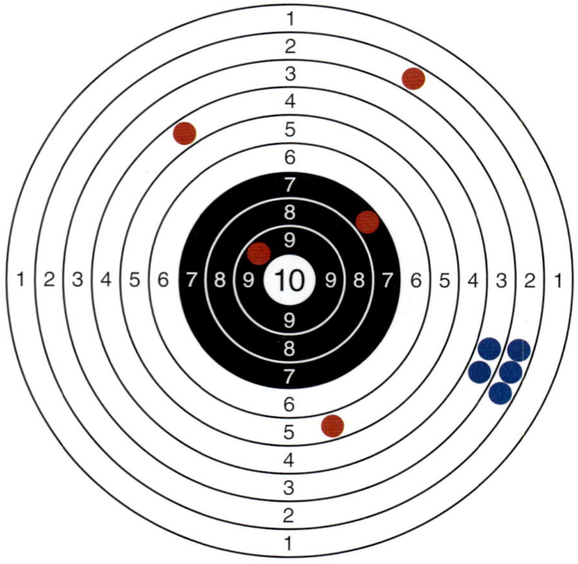

FIGURE 1.2 Two performers take five shots each at a target, trying to hit the bull's-eye. Which shooter is more skilled?

In figure 1.2, the concentric rings are scored outward from the bull's-eye in decreasing values, from 10 to 1. Using these values, the shooter denoted by the red dots in the target had scores of 9, 7, 5, 4, and 3, for a total of 28. The shooter denoted by the blue dots had scores of 3, 3, 2, 2, and 2, for a total of 12. If total points were the sole measure of skill in this task, then the conclusion would be that the shooter with the higher point total (red dots) was more highly skilled. Yet the figure illustrates that this clearly is not the case—the shooter with the higher point total scattered the shots all over the target, while the other shooter's scores were precise and tightly arranged. A simple adjustment for the shooter of the blue dots, perhaps in the gun sights or in response to environmental factors, could move this cluster closer to the bull's-eye. There is no simple change that the first shooter could make to bring the dispersion of red dots closer together—only improving skill could accomplish that.

Other measures can be used to score the performance of the shots represented in figure 1.2. The simplest is the average radial error: simply measure the distance from the center of the target to each of the shots, sum the distances, and divide by the number of shots. In this case, the average radial error would be similar to the average AE identified in the previous section for one-dimensional tasks. And for similar reasons, it, too, fails to capture the true nature of skilled performance in this task.

Better measures of performance would consider the two dimensions in which errors could occur in this task: up–down and left–right. In this method, a left–right value (relative to the vertical midline) and an up–down value (relative to the horizontal midline) could represent each shot. Measures of two-dimensional CE and VE could then be calculated from these two values. In the examples presented in figure 1.2, precise measures of two-dimensional CE would be smaller for the shots in red, but the two-dimensional VE would be much smaller for the shots in blue. Hancock and colleagues (1995) present details on how to calculate these two-dimensional error scores.

Error Scores in Continuous Tasks

Continuous tasks, such as tracking, can produce many error scores on a single trial. Consider figure 1.3 as an example of a portion of a single trial of a tracking task for one individual. The wide green path represents the goal, such as a highway lane along which a driver might navigate a car. The red line represents the exact (but usually unmarked) center of the track from edge to edge. The black dotted line represents a person's tracking behavior—in this case, how close the car stays to the center of the road. How might skill be measured in this single trial of a continuous performance?

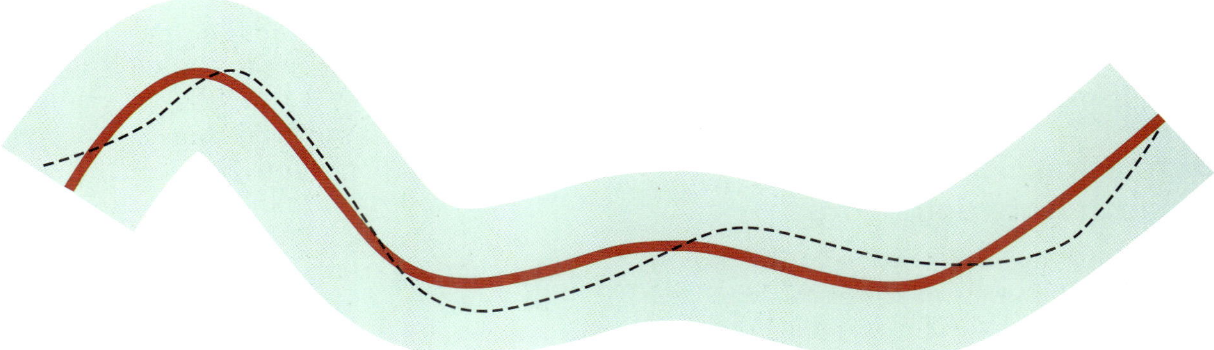

FIGURE 1.3 Measuring RMSE in a tracking task. The green area represents the track (e.g., a highway lane). The red (solid) line represents the (unmarked) center of the lane and can be considered the participant's goal track. The black dotted line represents the participant's performance in attempting to follow the red line.

A common method used by researchers who study tracking tasks is to compute a measure called **root-mean-square error (RMSE)**. One does this by computing the distance of the person's tracking behavior from the target line either at constant distance points along the track (e.g., every 10 ft of highway traveled) or at constant time intervals along the track (e.g., every 100 ms). This method effectively slices the continuous movement into equal, discrete intervals of tracking behavior from start to finish.

With each slice of the track, the researcher then computes how far the participant's tracking position is from the target. Because the red line in figure 1.3 represents the center of the track, it is convenient to define the red line as the zero position. Therefore, if the participant is to the right of the target, the measure receives a positive error value; if the tracking position is to the left of the target, the measure gets a negative value. Compute the RMSE score by first calculating the squared deviations for each measured position along the track, then taking the square root of the sum of those scores (see Schmidt et al., 2025, for more detail on how to calculate RMSE).

The RMSE is a more complex measure of performance than any of the error scores for discrete tasks because it represents two components of behavior. The RMSE reflects both the bias tendency (e.g., on average, to drive closer to the right edge of the lane than the left edge) and the inconsistency in the tracking behavior (how variable the performance tends to be). The RMSE is well recognized as a very good measure of how effectively the person tracked.

Correlation: The Association Strength Between Scores

Sometimes researchers are interested in discovering how sets of scores relate to each other. Franklin M. Henry (see Focus on Research 1.2) was an early pioneer of using correlations as a measure of determining one such relationship: the *general motor ability* hypothesis. Assume that a relatively large number of people are tested on each of two skills, A and B. Henry reasoned that if one person was an outstanding performer on skill A, then, according to the general motor ability hypothesis, that person should also score well on skill B. Conversely, if another person did not score well on skill A, at least part of the reason would be that this person had a weak general motor ability, and this person would be expected to score relatively poorly on skill B as well. In this way, skill A and skill B are related to each other in that good scores on A go with good scores on B, and poor scores on A go with poor scores on B. That is, performance scores on skills A and B should be highly correlated.

With this kind of relationship, if we were to plot performances of skill A against performances of skill B, as we have done in figure 1.4, where each dot represents a single individual measured on both tests A and B, these two tests should plot linearly with each other, which they tend to do in figure 1.4*a*. Note that these two skills might represent similar outcome measures, such as distance in a long jump versus height in a high jump. In this case, the two tests are *positively* correlated. But high correlations could also occur if good performances in the two measures went in opposite directions, such as if longer jumps correlated with lower times in a 100 m sprint. In such a case, the two tests should also plot linearly, as they do in figure 1.4*b* but in the opposite direction. In this case, the two tests are *negatively* correlated. However, if skill A and skill B are unrelated, then they should plot more or less as seen in figure 1.4*c*, which illustrates no correlation.

As we mentioned previously, however, determining conclusions based on the visual inspection of trends in data is imprecise. Fortunately, a statistic called the **correlation coefficient (*r*)** provides a way to determine the exact strength of a relationship, for example, between the scores illustrated in figure 1.4.

The correlation coefficient can range in size from −1.0 to +1.0. The size of the correlation indicates the strength of the relationship,

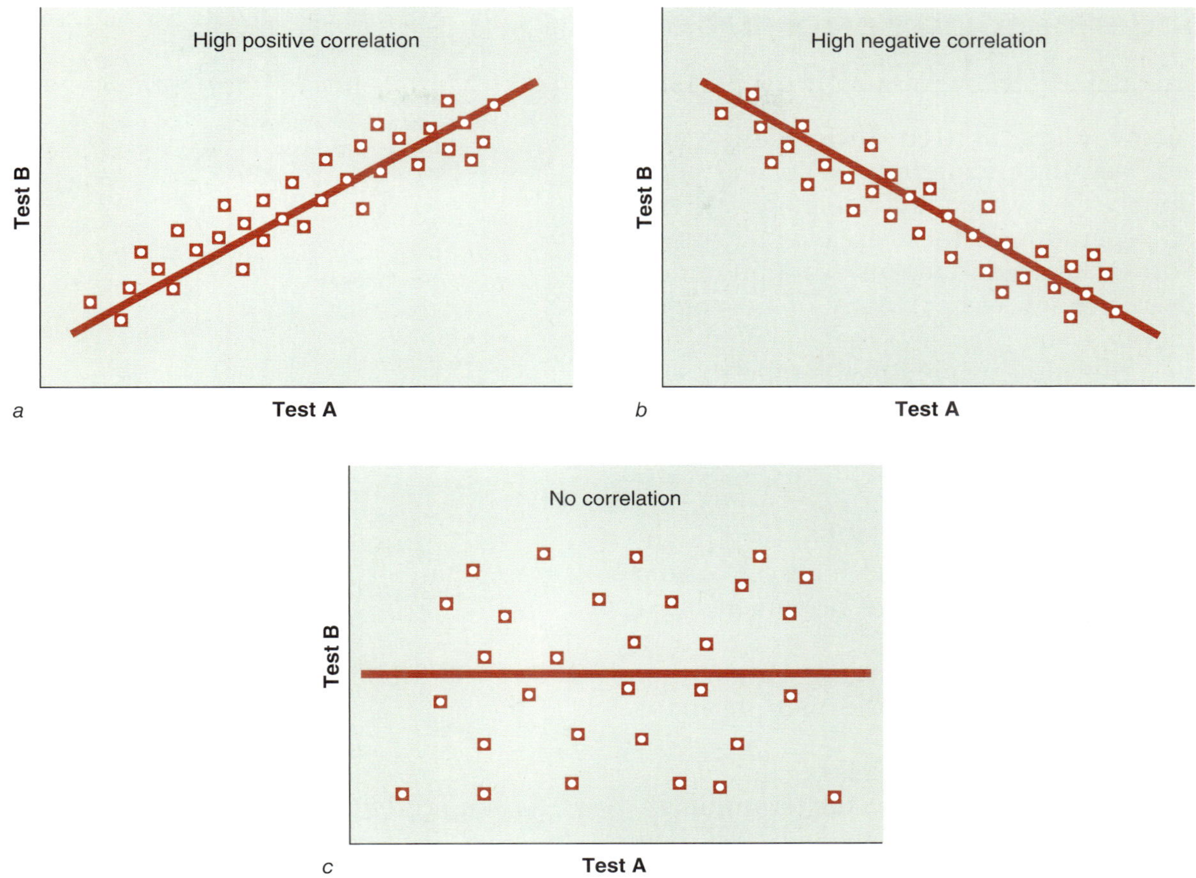

FIGURE 1.4 Scatter plot of two tests revealing *(a)* a high positive correlation, *(b)* a high negative correlation, and *(c)* no correlation. Each dot in the figure represents the performance of one individual, plotting performance along the axis representing one test against performance along the axis for the other test.

or how close the individual dots are to the best-fitting line passing through them. If the dots are close to the line, as in figure 1.4*a*, the positive correlation is close to +1.0, indicating a very strong tendency for skill in A to be associated with skill in B ($r = +.90$). Similarly, in figure 1.4*b*, the closeness of the dots to the line indicates a strong negative coefficient ($r = -.90$). If the dots lie relatively far from the line, as they do in figure 1.4*c*, the correlation is zero or very close to zero, indicating no tendency or a relatively weak tendency for scores in A to be associated with scores in B ($r \sim 0$). The strength of a relationship is estimated by the squared correlation coefficient multiplied by 100. Thus, a correlation of +.15, for example, means that the two tests have $.15^2 = (.15 \times .15) \times 100$, or about 2% in common with each other.

Note that the general motor ability hypothesis predicts that the correlation of scores for any two skills should be either highly positively or highly negatively correlated. A finding of zero or near-zero correlation would provide strong evidence against the hypothesis. We will have much more to say about the findings uncovered by Henry's research in chapter 7. In the meantime, do you predict that the evidence will support or reject the general motor ability hypothesis?

Visit HK*Propel* to read "The Hot Hand" and complete the self-directed learning activities.

Understanding Performance and Learning

In some ways, skilled performance and motor learning are interrelated concepts that cannot be easily separated for analysis. Even so, a separation of these areas is necessary for presentation and makes eventual understanding much easier. Many of the terms, principles, and processes that scientists use to describe improvements with practice and learning (motor learning) actually come from the literature on the underlying processes in the production of skilled motor performance (which includes both motor learning and human performance). Whereas it might seem more logical to teach motor learning before motor performance (a person must learn before performing), it is awkward to present information on learning without first providing background information about performance.

For this reason, this book is organized into two parts: Part I introduces the terminology, concepts, and principles related to skilled human performance with minimal reference to processes associated with learning. The principles discussed here probably apply most strongly to actions in which the performer is already skilled. Having examined the principles of how the motor system produces skills, part II then turns the discussion to how these processes can be altered, facilitated, and trained through practice, which involves motor learning.

Figure 1.5 illustrates a simplified relationship between motor learning and performance in the context of the issues discussed in this chapter. Measurable performance results from processes that culminate in movement. Just as the skill has different identifiable dimensions, so too does the individual. Part I of this book describes the processes that influence motor performance, while part II focuses on learning, which occurs by repeating and refining those processes, representing a relatively permanent improvement in the performance of a skill.

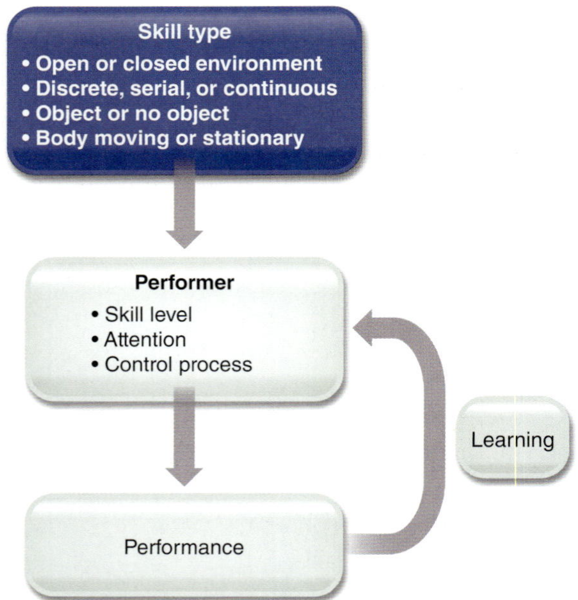

FIGURE 1.5 An overview of the processes involved in motor learning and performance. Part I is devoted to the processes that influence performance. Part II concerns issues that influence learning.

When studying motor performance and learning, it is helpful to understand where each concept fits into the complex process of performing a skill. For this reason and to help apply skills information to a variety of settings, this book develops a conceptual model. This model represents the big picture of motor performance. As new topics are introduced, they are added to the model, tying together most of the major processes and events that occur as performers produce skills. Models of this type are critical in teaching and in science because they embrace many seemingly unrelated facts and concepts, linking real-world knowledge with the concepts being discussed.

Models can be of many types, of course, such as the plumbing-and-pump model of the human circulatory system, the variety of balls that model the structure of atoms, the solar system, and molecules in chemistry. For skills, a useful conceptualization is an information-flow model, which considers how information of various kinds is used in producing a skilled action. The first part of the text builds this model, first considering how the sensory information that enters the system through the receptors is processed, transformed, and stored. To this is added how this sensory information leads to other processes associated with decision-making and planning action. Then features of the initiation of action and the activities involved during the action, such as controlling muscular contractions and detecting and correcting errors, are added to the emerging conceptual model. These features of action relate highly to the performer's analysis of the sensations produced resulting from performing the action—processes related to feedback. The second part of the text deals with learning, and the model provides an effective understanding of the processes that practice influences or does not.

Summary

People regard skills as an important and fascinating aspect of life. Knowledge about skills has come from a variety of scientific disciplines and can be applied to many settings, such as sport, teaching, coaching, industry, and physical therapy.

Skill is usually defined as the capability to bring about a desired result with maximum certainty and minimum time and energy. Many different components are involved; the major categories are perceptual or sensory processes, decision-making, and movement output. Skills may be classified along numerous dimensions, such as open and closed skills; discrete, serial, and continuous skills; body transport or stationary skills; and skills with or without object manipulation. These classifications are important because the principles of skills and their learning often differ for different skill categories.

The text's particular organization of materials should facilitate an understanding of skills. After this introduction, the remainder of part I addresses the principles of human skilled performance and the underlying processes, focusing on how the various parts of the motor system act to produce skilled actions. Part II examines how to modify these various processes through practice and motor learning. A conceptual model of human performance developed throughout the text facilitates an understanding of how all these components can operate together.

HK*PROPEL* ACTIVITIES

HK*Propel* offers these activities to help you build and apply your knowledge of the concepts in this chapter. Additionally, you'll find a key terms flashcard review activity and a key terms quiz, along with audio supplements for selected figures, as indicated by QR codes throughout the chapter.

Interactive Learning

Activity 1.1: Classify skills as discrete, serial, or continuous in nature by selecting the appropriate category for each of the five examples.

Activity 1.2: Review the types of errors measured in motor learning research by matching various error measures with their definitions.

Activity 1.3: Watch a short video clip highlighting technology use in measuring motor performance, then consider what technology is available to measure performance and error for a sport of your choice.

Activity 1.4: Match ways of measuring performance to specific skills and research questions.

Principles-to-Application Exercise

Activity 1.5: The principles-to-application exercise applies the concepts in this chapter to your own experience by asking you to analyze a motor skill that you have previously learned or are currently learning. You'll describe the skill as open or closed and as discrete, serial, or continuous and identify the goals of the skill and the factors that contribute to your success when performing it.

Motor Control in Everyday Actions Narratives

Public Opinion Polls

Cutting Wood and Missing Putts

The Hot Hand

Check Your Understanding

1. Define a skill and indicate why each of the following terms is important to that definition.
   - Environmental goal
   - Maximum certainty
   - Minimum-energy costs
   - Minimum time
2. Distinguish between open and closed skills and between discrete, serial, and continuous skills. Give one example of each.
3. List and describe three elements critical to almost any skill.
4. Define a theory and describe how scientists use theories to design experiments.

Apply Your Knowledge

1. List three motor skills that you have learned, either recently or when you were younger (e.g., swinging a baseball bat, tying your shoelaces, or playing a chord on the piano). Classify each of the skills you have listed, distinguishing between open and closed and between discrete, serial, and continuous skills. Are maximum certainty, minimum-energy costs, and minimum time equally important for each of the tasks you have listed? Why or why not?

PART I

Principles of Skilled Performance

Chapter 1 introduced a few types of motor performance that fascinate us—from the powerful movements of elite athletes to virtuoso musical performances. We now begin a two-part exploration of such skills. In part I, we emphasize the research-based principles that underlie motor performances. We build a conceptual model of human skilled performance as the various concepts concerning motor performance are introduced. This model contains and summarizes many of the major factors that underlie performance and is a useful guide for understanding how motor skills are performed. In part I, the focus is mainly on the factors that allow skilled motor performances to occur, without much reference to practice and learning. After we explain the terminology and fundamental concepts of human performance in part I, we turn in part II to some of the principles governing how motor skills are acquired with practice and augmented feedback.

2

Processing Information and Making Decisions

The Mental Side of Human Performance

CHAPTER OUTLINE

CHAPTER OBJECTIVES

Chapter 2 describes a conceptualization of how decisions are made in the performance of motor skills. This chapter will help you understand

- the information-processing approach to understanding motor performance,
- the stages that occur during information processing,
- various factors that influence information-processing speed,
- the role of anticipation in hastening response speed, and
- memory systems and their roles in motor performance.

CHAPTER PREVIEW QUIZ

1. Define reaction time—be very precise in the wording of your definition.
2. Describe examples of a compatible and an incompatible relationship between a stimulus and the response.
3. Define warm-up decrement and explain how it affects performance.

The batter felt ready this time. The pitcher had just thrown three curveballs in a row. Although the batter had two strikes against him, he was confident because he felt certain that the next pitch would be a fastball, and he was prepared for it. As the pitch was coming toward him, he strode forward and began to swing the bat to meet the ball, but he soon realized it was another curve. He could not modify his swing in time, and the bat crossed the plate long before the ball arrived. The pitcher had beaten him again.

How did the batter's faulty anticipation interfere with his performance? What processes were required to amend the action? To what extent did the stress of the game interfere with his batting? Certainly, a major concern for the skilled performer is the evaluation of information, leading to a decision about future action. But what information was the batter reflecting on while the pitch was coming toward the plate—the spin of the ball? its velocity? its location? the type, speed, and location of previous pitches? how fast to swing the bat? where to try to hit the ball? Processing all, or even some, of this information would surely have affected the batter's success in hitting the ball.

Visit HK*Propel* to read "Preventing Penalties and Batting Baseballs" and complete the self-directed learning activities.

One of the most important features of skilled performance is deciding what to do (and what not to do) quickly and accurately. After all, a perfectly executed baseball throw to first base is completely ineffective if the ball should have been thrown to a different base instead. This chapter considers factors contributing to these decision-making capabilities, including processing environmental information and some factors that contribute to the actual decision. We begin with a general approach for understanding how we use information, which will form the basis of the conceptual model of human performance.

The Information-Processing Approach

Researchers have found it useful to think of the human being as a processor of information, much like a computer. Information is presented to the human as input; various stages within the central nervous system generate a series of operations that process this information, and the eventual output is movement. Figure 2.1 shows the most basic representation to illustrate this approach to **information processing**.

What Is Input?

Appearing at the top of the diagram in figure 2.1 is the term *input*, which refers to the information to be processed by the human. Information comes in all sensory forms, with visual input being the most common in motor skills as well as the most complex. One important issue in information processing is the amount of input. Similar to a computer, the human processing system requires more time to process a larger amount of information than it does to process a smaller amount.

A useful way to understand the amount of information is to consider it equivalent to the amount of uncertainty in a situation. Figure 2.2 presents a good analogy (after Attneave, 1959). Suppose someone secretly placed an X in one of the 64 squares in figure 2.2, and your task was to guess the correct square by asking questions about its location. You could

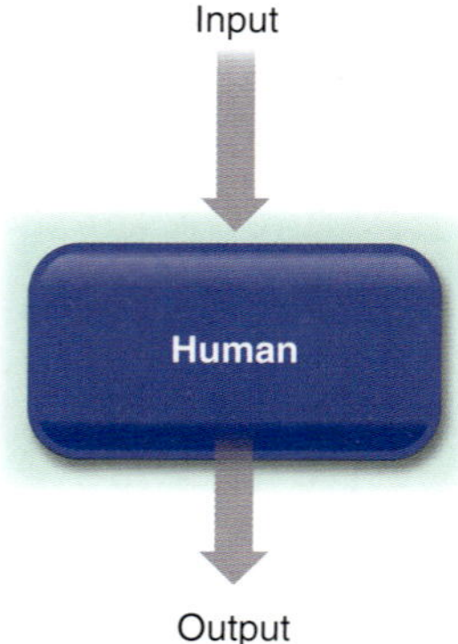

FIGURE 2.1 A simplified information-processing approach to thinking about human performance.

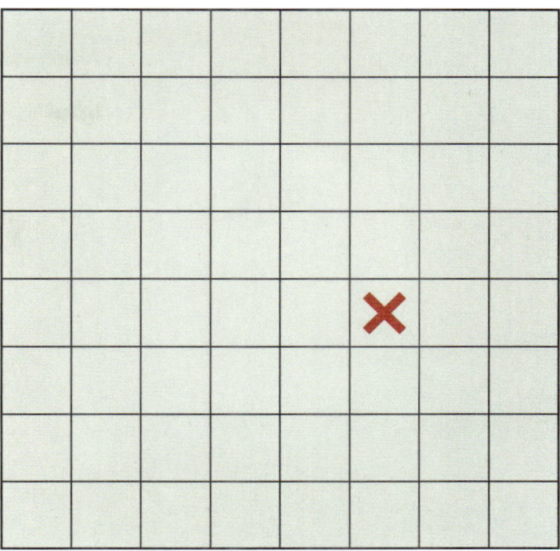

a

b

FIGURE 2.2 *(a)* There are 64 possible locations of the X, requiring 6 bits of information to process. *(b)* By asking two questions, one can eliminate 75% of the possible locations. The task now has been reduced to only 16 possible locations, or 4 bits of information.

discover the answer by asking only six questions, with each question eliminating one-half of the incorrect locations. For example, if your first question was "Is the X located in the top half of the squares?" the answer would be "no" because it is actually located in the bottom half. But even if your question had been "Is the X located in the bottom half of the squares?", it still would have eliminated the top half of the figure, effectively reducing the uncertainty by one-half, from 64 to 32 squares. By asking further questions in this manner, reducing uncertainty by one-half each time, you would solve the question by asking just six questions. Reducing the uncertainty by one-half each time allows the information gained to be quantifiable in terms of a base unit of 2. In the example in figure 2.2*a,* the potential amount of information to be gained is equal to 6 binary digits (bits) of information because 2 must be raised to the power of 6 (2^6) to reach 64.

Now suppose there was a situation in which three-quarters of the 64-square grid could be effectively eliminated as a possible location of the X, as in figure 2.2*b*. The uncertainty of its location is substantially reduced. In quantifiable terms, the amount of information to process has been reduced from 64 squares to 16 squares, or from 6 bits to 4 bits of information (because $2^4 = 16$). (Note that the idea is basically the same as the National Collegiate Athletic Association's March Madness in basketball. When starting with 64 teams, one team must win six games to become the champion, because each round eliminates half of the teams.)

The amount of information to be processed and the determination of ways to reduce that amount represent important components of our discussion in various parts of this book. Using anticipation is one method to reduce the amount of information to process. Performers who know what to expect in a certain situation or who can eliminate certain alternatives will reduce the amount of information to process. For example, most baseball batters know that a pitcher is likely to throw a fastball on a 3-and-0 count, because the pitcher needs a strike, and usually the pitcher's most accurate pitch is the fastball. Also, because the pitcher needs a strike, he is likely to throw the ball near the center of the strike zone. In this case, the batter can reduce the uncertainty about the upcoming pitch in terms of both its type (fastball) and its location (center of strike zone). Of course, there is no guarantee that the anticipation will be correct, but the reduction in the amount of information to process will make for an easier and faster decision about whether to swing at the pitch.

a

b

Identify situations in which *(a)* the defense or *(b)* the goalkeeper can reduce the amount of uncertainty (information) to process.

In many sports, part of an athlete's skill is the ability to effectively reduce the amount of information to process. Skilled athletes have the advantage of knowing what components of the environment are likely to reveal critical information and what components are unlikely to. Therefore, they can eliminate some of the uncertainty prior to the presentation of the input. Goalkeeping against a penalty kick in soccer is a good example. The completely inexperienced goalkeeper must wait to see the direction in which the ball has been kicked before she can begin to move in that direction to stop it. Usually, such an unanticipated response is ineffective in making the save. However, the skilled goalkeeper can pick up clues from the penalty taker before the kick, such as the angle of approach and gaze of the eyes, which improve the overall odds of being successful. The skilled keeper is essentially reducing the amount of uncertainty to process.

The Human

A major goal of researchers interested in the performance of motor skills is to understand the specific nature of the processes in the box labeled *human* in figure 2.1. There are many ways to approach this problem; a particularly useful one assumes that there are separable information-processing stages through which the information must pass on the way from input to output. For our present purposes, here are three of these stages:

1. Stimulus identification
2. Response selection
3. Movement programming

The stage analysis approach generally assumes that sensory information enters the system and is processed in the first stage. Only after this stage has completed its operations is the result passed on to the second stage, which carries on the information processing, then the stage two result is passed to the third stage, and so on. A critical assumption is that the stages do not overlap. All the processing in a given stage is completed before the product is passed to the next stage; processing in two different stages cannot occur at the same time (referred to as *parallel processing*). This process finally results in an output—the action. Let's consider some of what goes on in these stages of processing.

Stimulus Identification Stage

During this first stage, the processing system's role is to decide whether information is present and, if so, what it is. Thus, **stimulus identification** is primarily a sensory stage, analyzing environmental information from a variety of sources, such as vision, audition, touch, proprioception, and smell. The components, or separate dimensions of these stimuli, are thought to be assembled in this stage, such as the combination of edges and colors that form a representation of a car in traffic. Patterns of movement are also detected, such as whether other objects are moving, in what direction and how quickly they are moving, and so on, as would be necessary for driving a car in heavy traffic. The result of this stage is thought to be some internalized representation of the input, with this information being passed on to the next stage: response selection.

Visit HK*Propel* to read "Friendly Fire" and complete the self-directed learning activities.

Response Selection Stage

The activities of the **response selection** stage begin after the stimulus identification stage provides information about the input. This stage has the task of deciding what response to make (if any), given the nature of the situation and current intentions. In the driving example, the choice from available responses might be to go around another vehicle, to slow the car, to make an avoidance maneuver, or to do nothing different. Thus, this stage requires the key process of determining what to do and how to do it.

Movement Programming Stage

Upon receiving the decision determined by the response selection stage about what movement to make, the final stage begins its processing. The **movement programming** stage has the task of preparing the motor system to make the desired movement. Before producing a movement, the system must ready the lower-level mechanisms in the brainstem and spinal cord for action, and it must retrieve and organize a motor program that will eventually control the movement. In the driving example, if the response selection stage determined that a braking response was required, then the organization of the motor program responsible for executing a braking action would occur in the movement programming stage.

Output

Once the movement programming stage has completed its information processing, the result is passed along to further stages that are responsible for producing a motor output. The stages involved in producing movement will occupy the middle chapters of this book and represent a major focus of researchers whose interests lie in motor control.

Expanding the Conceptual Model

Figure 2.3 adds some detail to the simple notion of information processing described in figure 2.1 by including the stages of processing just described. This elaboration is the first expansion of our conceptual model, which will continue throughout the text as we introduce more fundamental ideas about human performance.

Clearly, these stages are all included within the human information system and are not directly observable under usual circumstances. As described in Focus on Application 2.1, however, it is clear that these stages take time to complete. But how much time do they take? Several laboratory methods allow scientists to learn many details about these stages. **Reaction time (RT)** is one of the most important tools that researchers have used for many decades to learn about these stages. We will examine RT in much more detail to understand how information processing operates.

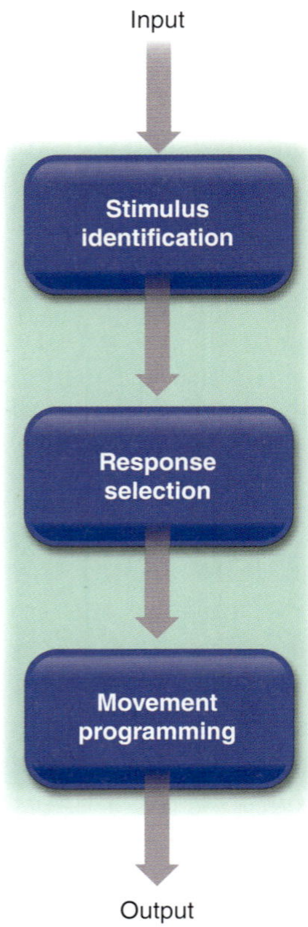

FIGURE 2.3 An expanded information-processing model highlighting three critical processing stages in thinking about human performance.

Reaction Time and Decision-Making

An important performance measure indicating the speed and effectiveness of decision-making is the RT interval—the interval of time that elapses until the response begins following a sudden, often unanticipated stimulus. The concept and assessment of RT are important because they represent a part of some everyday events, such as braking rapidly in response to an unanticipated traffic event, responding to catch an accidentally tipped-over glass, and, in such sports events as sprint races, beginning a race with stimulus from an auditory tone.

There is an old saying that a picture is worth a thousand words. The redrawn photo of a long-ago sprint race certainly bears this out (figure 2.4), reprinted from Scripture

FOCUS ON Application 2.1

Intent to Blow Whistle Rule in the NHL

Few sports build the stages of information processing into the official rule book. The National Hockey League (NHL) is a rare exception. A game in early 2017 provides an example of when a rule specifically applied an information-processing concept. A play in the first period of a game between the Nashville Predators and Vancouver Canucks saw a scramble for the puck in front of the Canucks' goalie Ryan Miller. The referee, Ghislain Hebert, no longer able to see the puck loose in the goal crease, justifiably determined that the goalie had covered the puck with his body and blew his whistle to stop play. As it turned out, the puck crossed the goal line just milliseconds before the sound of Hebert's whistle. After a meeting with the other officials, Hebert confirmed that the apparent goal would not count.

The Predators' players and coaches were enraged—it was clear that the sound of the whistle occurred after the puck crossed the goal line, so why would the goal not count? In response, the officials cited rule 78.5, section xii, which states, "Apparent goals shall be disallowed . . . when the Referee deems the play has been stopped, even if he had not physically had the opportunity to stop play by blowing his whistle" (*National Hockey League Official Rules [2021–2022]*, p. 119-120). This ruling is further clarified by rule 31.2, which states, "As there is a human factor involved in blowing the whistle to stop play, the Referee may deem the play to be stopped slightly prior to the whistle actually being blown. The fact that the puck may come loose or cross the goal line prior to the sound of the whistle has no bearing if the Referee has ruled that the play had been stopped prior to this happening" (p. 51).

The key phrase in the cited rule is the "human factor involved in blowing the whistle." The human factor that the rule refers to involves the stages of processing described in this chapter, all of which add up to a time lag that applies in the intent to blow rule: The time lag starts when the referee detects the stimulus (in this case, the puck no longer being visible), decides on the appropriate response (the intention to stop play by blowing the whistle), begins the movement programming process (the action involved in blowing the whistle), and executes the action (resulting in the sound of the whistle). As we shall see in this chapter and those to follow, these stages of processing can take up to several hundred milliseconds, leaving plenty of time for a puck to cross the goal line after the decision has been made to blow the whistle.

The intent to blow whistle rule allows referees to make a final decision based on the timing of the intention, not when the whistle was actually blown. Identify another situation in a different sport where an official's decision or a player's intent did not match what was actually seen or heard.

> *continued*

Application 2.1: Intent to Blow Whistle Rule in the NHL > *continued*

The rationale underlying these rules may not be well understood and represents a source of frustration for fans and players. The rule is designed to let the referee's decision at the time the decision was made be the key determining factor. In our view, by acknowledging this human factor, the NHL has achieved a remarkably insightful way to protect the integrity of their referees.

(1905). The starter on the left side of the photo has already fired his gun, perhaps a couple of hundred milliseconds earlier, as you can see by the position of the pistol smoke rising above the starter. Yet the runners are all still in their ready positions and are only now beginning to move. The photo illustrates nicely the substantial delay involved in RT. Being able to minimize RT in such a situation is critical to getting the movement under way as rapidly as possible. Because RT is a fundamental component of many skills, it is not surprising that researchers have directed much attention toward it.

Visit HK*Propel* to read "Jumping the Gun" and complete the self-directed learning activities.

But RT has important theoretical meaning as well, which is the major reason it has attracted so much research attention. Sometimes there is confusion about what RT is and how it is measured. To review, researchers define the RT interval very precisely; it is the period of time beginning when the stimulus is first presented and ending when the movement response starts. Note that the RT interval does not include the time that is taken to complete the movement, as illustrated in figure 2.5. That period of time, from the beginning of the response until the completion of the movement, is specifically called the **movement time (MT)**. For example, as it is frequently used, the term *brake RT* is technically incorrect because it describes the time it takes a person to react to an unexpected event (RT) and press the brake pedal in a car (MT). The time taken to press the brake includes the foot's movement from its initial position (usually on the accelerator) to depress the brake. This movement occurs

FIGURE 2.4 Illustration of the RT delay in a sprint start: the starting gun has been fired (as the smoke rising from the starter's pistol implies), yet the athletes are still on their marks because of the delay in processing the signal from the starting gun (the delay is contained in the reaction-time interval).

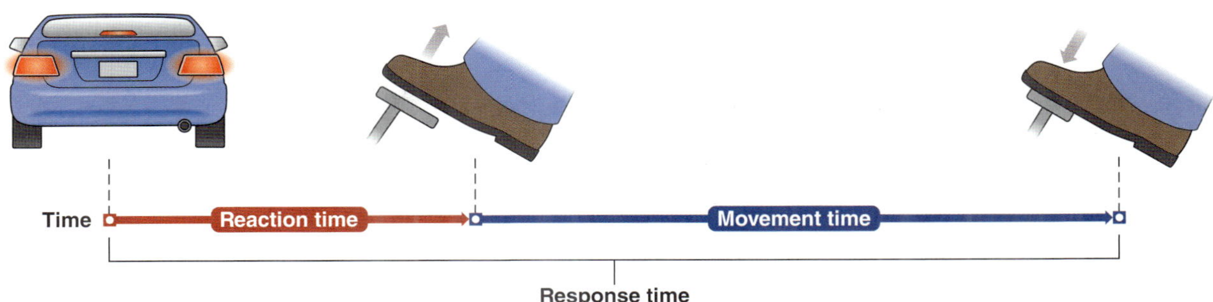

FIGURE 2.5 Illustration of the relationship between reaction time, movement time, and response time in sudden braking. The timeline depicts the brake lights in the car ahead appearing, the foot lifting off the accelerator, and the same foot pressing the brake pedal.

after the measurement of the RT interval is completed. What many refer to as brake RT is actually the total of RT plus MT, which would more appropriately be termed the brake **response time**. The brake RT would, in fact, end as the foot began to leave the accelerator pedal.

Visit HK*Propel* to read "Red Light, Green Light" and complete the self-directed learning activities.

Factors Influencing Decision-Making

The RT interval is a measure of the accumulated durations of the three stages of processing seen in figure 2.3. Any factor that increases the duration of one or more of these stages will lengthen RT. For this reason, scientists interested in information processing have used RT to measure the duration of these stages. Some of the many important factors related to human performance are considered in the next sections.

Number of Stimulus–Response Alternatives

Consider the following example of driving a car: In light traffic, the number of situations that require an emergency evasive response is less than in heavy traffic. One of the most important factors influencing the time to start an action is the number of stimuli (each having its own response) that can possibly occur at any given time. For example, your response to someone who swerves into your lane might be a rapid evasive turn into an empty lane, whereas the appearance of brake lights on the car you are following might require you to apply your brakes. In such situations, unexpected events from multiple vehicles around you amplify the number of possible situations that could occur, compared to situations with extremely light or no traffic. Controlled laboratory experiments conducted to examine the effects of the number of choices generally involve very simple situations such as multiple stimuli (e.g., lights) and multiple responses from which the research participant must choose (e.g., pressing different keys depending on which stimulus light has been illuminated).

Figure 2.6 illustrates a typical experimental setup in which the stimulus array contains eight lights and a response panel with eight corresponding keys. In each of the four panels in figure 2.6, focus only on the yellow light bulbs and corresponding fingers. Although all eight stimulus lights and response keys are seen in each version of the experiment, the participant is instructed to expect one light from a limited set of stimulus–response (S-R) alternatives to illuminate. For example, in figure 2.6*c*, the participant would know that only one of the middle four lights would be lit, which would require pressing the assigned corresponding key with the appropriate finger. It is important to note that, across conditions, RTs for only one response key are compared (e.g., the right index finger RT under one vs. two vs. four vs. eight choice conditions).

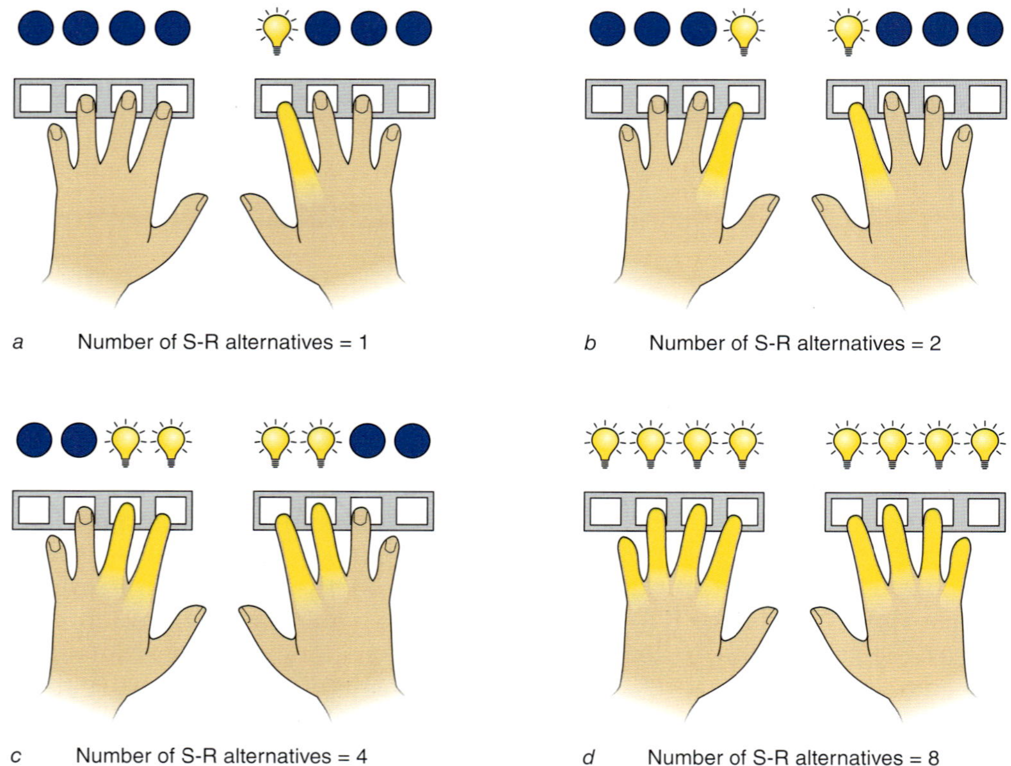

FIGURE 2.6 Different combinations of the number of stimulus–response alternatives. The yellow light bulbs and corresponding finger-button responses represent potential stimulus–response alternatives in various experiment conditions: *(a)* a block of trials uses only one stimulus–response alternative; *(b)* the stimulus could be one of the two yellow lights, responding with the associated finger-button response, and so on. *(a-d)* In all situations, the critical comparison is the time taken to respond with the right index finger.

This experimental situation is termed a **choice reaction time** task, in which the participant must choose one response from a subset of possible predetermined responses. Typically, the participant receives a warning signal, followed by a **foreperiod** of unpredictable length (e.g., 2, 3, or 4 s, the order being randomly determined). The participant knows exactly which button to press only when the stimulus is suddenly presented. As always, RT is the measured duration that starts at the presentation of the stimulus and ends when the response is initiated. In this particular example, RT is the time required to detect and recognize the stimulus and select and initiate the proper response.

Generally, as the number of possible S-R alternatives increases, the time required to respond to any one of them increases. The fastest situation involves only one stimulus and one response, termed **simple RT**. The increase in RT is very large when the number of alternatives increases from one to two. As seen in figure 2.7, RT might increase from about 190 ms with simple RT (figure 2.6*a*) to more than 300 ms for a two-choice case (figure 2.6*b*)—a 58% increase in the time required to process the stimulus information, then choose and initiate the response! Adding extra choices still increases RT, but the increases become smaller and smaller (e.g., the increase from 9 to 10 choices might be only 20 ms, or about 2% or 3%). But even this small amount of delay can be critical in determining success in many situations. Increased RT due to a greater number of S-R alternatives is of critical importance in understanding skilled performance, forming the basis of **Hick's Law** (see Focus on Research 2.1).

FOCUS ON Research 2.1

Hick's Law

In a very early RT experiment by Merkel (1885, cited in Woodworth, 1938), participants pressed a reaction key when presented with one of up to 10 possible stimuli. Figure 2.7 shows Merkel's results, where RT is plotted as a function of the number of S-R alternatives. There was a sharp rise in RT (roughly 120 ms; see figure 2.7) when the number of alternatives increased from $N = 1$ to $N = 2$; this rise becomes smaller as the number of alternatives increases toward 10 (e.g., RT increases only 3 ms from $N = 9$ to $N = 10$; see figure 2.7).

The relationship between RT and the number of S-R alternatives in figure 2.7 can be described as curvilinear. Much later, Hick (1952) and Hyman (1953) showed that when the RT was plotted against the logarithm to the base 2 of the number (N) of S-R alternatives, abbreviated $\log_2(N)$, the relationship was linear (see figure 2.8). This relationship has become known as Hick's Law, and it holds for a wide variety of situations using different movements and stimulus materials. It is one of the most important laws of human performance. (See the earlier discussion and figure 2.2, in which $\log_2(N)$ is the power to which the base 2 must be raised to equal N.)

Hick's Law in equation form is $RT = a + b \log_2(N)$, where a is the RT-intercept and b is the slope. The relationship implies that RT increases a constant amount every time the number of stimulus–response alternatives (N) doubles (e.g., from $N = 2$ to $N = 4$, where the $\log_2(N) = 1$ and 2, respectively; or from $N = 8$ to $N = 16$, where the $\log_2(N) = 3$ and 4, respectively). This led to an important interpretation of Hick's Law: RT is linearly related to the amount of information that must be processed to resolve the uncertainty about the various possible stimulus–response alternatives. Doubling the amount of information to be processed by doubling N therefore increases RT by a constant amount, equal to the slope (b) in the Hick's Law equation.

Exploring Further

1. How does the concept of uncertainty relate to the amount of information in Hick's Law?
2. Name two factors that would be expected to influence the magnitude of the slope (b) of Hick's Law and describe how variations in these factors would be predicted to increase or decrease the slope.

Stimulus–Response Compatibility

An important determinant of RT is **stimulus–response (S-R) compatibility**, usually defined as the extent to which the stimulus and the response connect in a natural way. Turning the handlebars of a bicycle to the right to move toward the right is an example of S-R compatibility because the movement of the handlebars and the change in direction are the same—that is, they are directionally compatible. Imagine how difficult it would be to have to move the handlebars to the left in order to turn right (in fact, someone has done just that—search *backwards bicycle* online for a video). Perhaps that explains why steering a sailboat is trickier than steering a bicycle—the sailor needs to move the tiller to the left in order to change the boat's heading to the right.

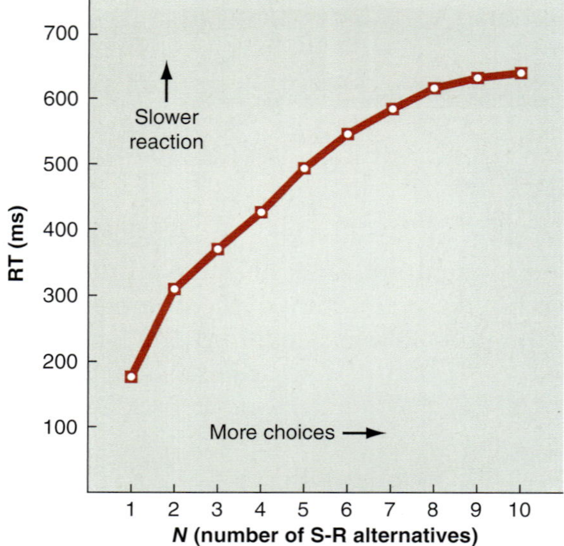

FIGURE 2.7 The relationship between the number of possible stimulus–response (S-R) alternatives and reaction time (cited in Woodworth, 1938).

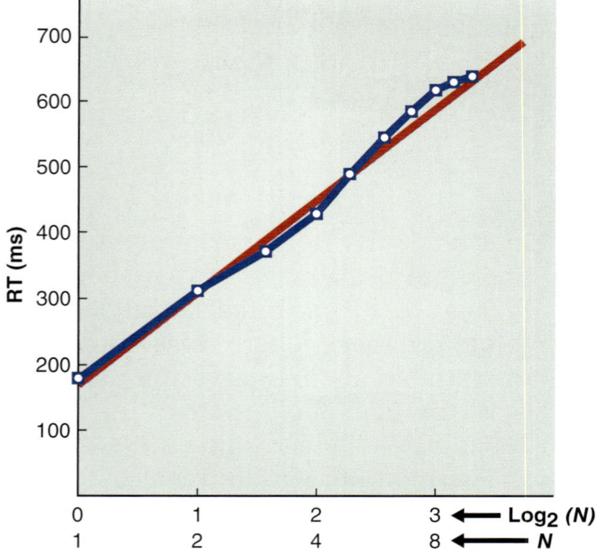

FIGURE 2.8 Hick's Law: The relation between RT and the number of S-R alternatives (N) is replotted using Merkel's data from figure 2.7, with RT as a function of $\log_2(N)$. The red straight line represents the fitted linear equation.

Figure 2.9 illustrates a simple example of how S-R spatial compatibility mappings are studied in research. The S-R ensemble illustrated in figure 2.9*a* is more compatible than the ensemble in figure 2.9*b* because, in figure 2.9*a*, either stimulus light calls for the participant to respond in the same direction and on the same side of the body as the light. In figure 2.9*b*, however, the right light calls for the use of the left hand, while the left light calls for the right hand. The spatial mapping of the stimuli and required response is not

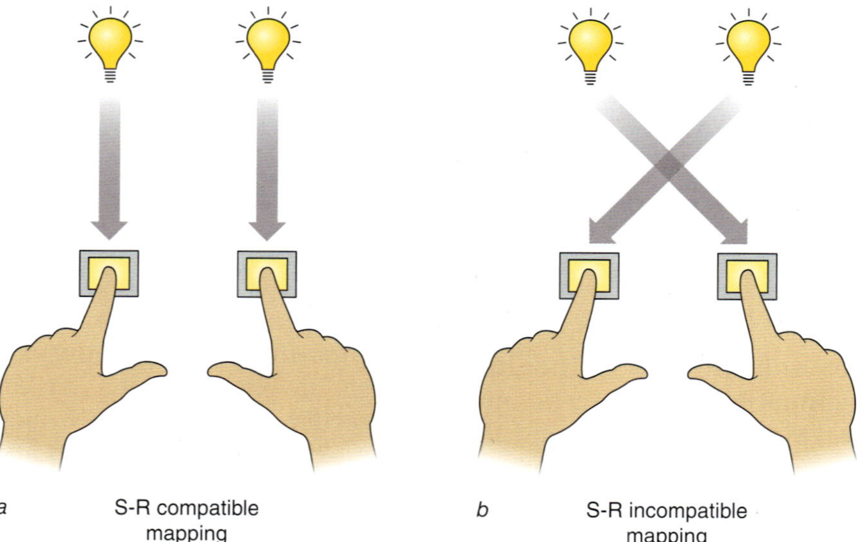

FIGURE 2.9 The relationship between the two stimuli and the two responses is more spatially S-R compatible in *(a)* the array on the left than in *(b)* the array on the right.

a

b

In each of these photos, how can *(a)* the team or *(b)* the player who controls the ball increase the amount of information that the opponent must process by creating more uncertainty?

Practice is required to overcome low stimulus–response compatibility. For example, a boater needs to move the tiller in the opposite direction the boat needs to turn.

nearly so spatially direct and unambiguous; the situation in 2.9*b* is S-R incompatible (or, more accurately, less spatially compatible than that in figure 2.9*a*).

It is well established that, for a given number of S-R alternatives, increasing S-R compatibility decreases RT. This is thought to be the effect of the relative difficulty of information processing in the response selection stage, where the more natural linkages between compatible stimuli and responses lead to faster resolution of uncertainty and thus shorter RTs. Note, however, that the general rules regarding the number of possible stimuli and RT still apply to incompatible S-R arrangements (i.e., Hick's Law).

So, what exactly makes a linkage "natural" and how does it improve S-R compatibility (or conversely, what makes a linkage unnatural)? As we have discussed, the spatial relationship between a movable object and what it controls is an obvious candidate. A rightward movement of the mouse on my desktop sends the cursor on the computer screen to the right. Any other result would be less natural from a spatial compatibility view. The movement of the mouse has a direct influence on the movement of the cursor and, when compatible, results in faster and more efficient performance.

Visit HK*Propel* to read "Push or Pull?" and complete the self-directed learning activities.

Spatial S-R relationships can also have an indirect effect on performance. For example, suppose you were wearing stereo headphones and were told to respond rapidly to a message presented to one ear (such as "press the key under the right hand"). Such a task is performed faster and more accurately if the message is presented to the right ear rather than the left ear. The effect is indirect because the interpretation of the stimulus and nature of the response are the same regardless of the ear to which the command is presented. Response selection is faster when the effector is more spatially compatible with the source of the message, even though it has no direct influence on the choice of response.

Compatibility has also been studied regarding the intention of the movement. Suppose a friend asked you to move an upside-down glass from one spot on the table to another. Your response would likely be to simply pick up the glass and move it using a normal upright hand posture. However, if she asked you to place the glass upside down after you had moved it, then you would likely have inverted your hand posture before picking up the glass so that it was in the normal upright position when you placed it on the table. Note that in both cases, the stimulus (the glass) was the same—the hand posture selected to perform the task differed as a function of what David Rosenbaum termed **end-state comfort**. The initially selected hand posture was compatible with the anticipated comfort of the final hand posture (see Rosenbaum, 2010).

Many S-R compatibility effects are logically considered to occur naturally. Others, however, have no known natural precedent and have emerged instead as a function of societal norms. For example, we tend to turn dials clockwise to increase the loudness of an auditory source or the speed of a fan, even though there is no natural reason to do so. In North America, we move a light switch upward to turn the light on; in many other countries, the light is turned on by moving the switch down. In these cases, it is more difficult to argue that the mapping of the stimulus and response represents a naturally existing relationship and not a purely arbitrary one. Instead, the likely association is a learned societal one—we sometimes act habitually due to learned, specific cultural (or industrial) tendencies, referred to by ergonomists as **population stereotypes** (see Focus on Application 2.2).

FOCUS ON Application 2.2

Population Stereotypes

Stimulus–response (S-R) compatibility and population stereotypes are a large part of our daily existence. We usually only take notice of them when unexpected issues arise. One common example occurs when you walk into a room and flip a switch to turn on a light or a bank of lights. In North American culture (but not in some other parts of the world), we turn lights on by flipping the light switch up; moving it down turns the lights off. We act accordingly when we enter a room and tend not to give the action a moment's thought. However, a light switch that has been installed opposite to our expectations will bring the issue to our conscious attention.

A similar issue occurs regarding the spatial organization of switches in relation to the spatial locations of the lights in the room that they control. Suppose you enter a room that has three lights controlled by three separate switches. One light is near you, one is in the middle of the room, and one is in the far corner of the room, and they are controlled by the switches located on the wall near the room entrance. Which switch would you flip to turn the middle light on? A panel that has been compatibly mapped will have the nearest switch control the nearest light, the middle switch control the

> *continued*

Application 2.2: Population Stereotypes *> continued*

light in the middle of the room, and so on. But how often have you been tricked into turning on the wrong light because of incompatible light-to-switch mapping? Once again, the issue mainly comes to our attention when the unexpected occurs.

Colors are associated with population stereotypes too. Red often represents stop or danger and green means go or safe. Traffic lights exploit this relationship, as do many other lights in our environment. The small LEDs (light-emitting diodes) on my coffee machine are red while the coffee is being brewed, and they turn green when the coffee is ready to drink. Importantly, we really only pay attention to these stereotypes in our day-to-day activities when the expected relationship is violated.

Visit HK*Propel* to read "The Grocery Store" and complete the self-directed learning activities.

Anticipation: Minimizing Processing Delays

As mentioned earlier in this chapter, one fundamental way to reduce RT is to anticipate. In many open-skill environments, a highly skilled performer predicts what is going to happen in the environment and when it will occur, then performs various information-processing activities before the stimulus actually occurs. A soccer goalkeeper anticipates that a player taking a penalty will aim her kick at the upper-left corner of the goal, so the goalkeeper starts moving in that direction prior to the kick. An experienced long-haul truck driver knows that many car drivers do not understand the stopping distance of an 18-wheeled vehicle, so he takes evasive actions to avoid a potential accident. These predictions are not just good guesses; instead, they rely on picking up subtle cues from the environment (e.g., an opponent) that tip off what is likely to happen so that the response can begin sooner than would otherwise be possible. Focus on Research 2.2 describes some strategies that researchers have used to uncover how skilled performers pick up these cues.

Highly skilled people know what stimuli are likely to be presented, where they are likely to appear, and when they will occur, so they can predict the required actions to take with a high level of probability. Armed with this information, a performer can complete some or all the information-processing activities usually conducted during the response selection or movement programming stage before the actual stimulus presentation. This allows the performer to initiate the movement much earlier or in coordination with the timing of movements in the environment, such as a boxer predicting where and when a left hook will arrive to block and counteract it. Because of these capabilities to anticipate, skilled performers seem to behave almost as if they had all the time they needed without rushing to respond to stimuli by using the reaction-time processes previously discussed.

Types of Anticipation

Anticipation can occur in different ways. One type is called **spatial anticipation**. For example, two important shots in badminton are the clear and drop shots. The clear shot is high and long and sends the opponent to the back of the court. The drop shot should land just slightly over the net, which brings the opponent to the front of the court. Spatial anticipation in badminton involves predicting the type of shot your opponent will hit and being in the correct position to return the shot.

In other situations, it might be obvious what is going to occur and where, but there might be uncertainty about *when* it will occur, as in anticipating the snap of the ball in American football. This is usually called **temporal anticipation**. Although there is a

FOCUS ON Research 2.2

Studying the Expert Advantage

What skills distinguish an expert from a novice? Most would agree that an expert possesses motor skills that are more accurate, less variable, and generally more efficient than those of a novice. For some skills, however—and most importantly, for open skills—researchers have shown that experts also have a large perceptual advantage (anticipating the movements of objects in the outside world). How do the researchers know this?

Video occlusion is one experimental technique frequently used to assess athletes' speed and accuracy in making perceptual judgments. The method asks viewers of varying skill levels to make predictions while watching edited videos of athletes in action. For example, a video of a baseball pitcher might be shown in which a certain body part (e.g., the pitching arm) has been edited out of the video. Presumably, occluding a body part (e.g., the grip on a fastball or a curveball) from the video would interfere with an anticipation only if the viewer was skilled at using that critical perceptual information. In contrast, editing out a noncritical body part should not interfere with anticipation. Another editing method is to suddenly stop the video at certain points in the action. Presumably, a skilled viewer who has picked up important information early in the video would be better than the novice at predicting what would happen next. The purpose that underlies both occlusion methods is to discover how and when expert performers use information. Understanding what critical cues tip off predictive information should then be useful in training the less-skilled performers.

Another method that researchers use to study expertise is gaze, which examines how athletes use vision to pick up information about an opponent or the environment. Gaze analyses provide data about visual fixations (locking in on a location) and saccades (rapid shifts in fixation from one location to another). Fixations provide visual information for processing; saccades do not. The common finding in many open sports is that experts use fewer but longer fixations than novices. This would support the view that the expert's visual search strategies are more efficient in picking up information from the environment than the novice's.

Exploring Further

1. What is the quiet-eye effect?
2. What are point-light displays? How are they used in research to assess biological motion?

strong advantage in knowing what will occur, not being able to predict when it will occur prevents the performer from organizing the movement completely in advance.

Benefits of Anticipation

Several factors affect the capability to predict effectively. One is the regularity of the events. For example, if our racquetball opponent always serves the ball to our (weak) backhand side, we can predict this event and try to counter it in various ways. Our capability to anticipate would be minimized if our opponent instead randomly used three or four different serves. Similarly, if the football quarterback always has the ball snapped on the second of two rhythmical verbal signals, the defensive team can anticipate the critical event and be highly prepared for it. Varying the timing of the snap signals keeps the defensive team from anticipating temporally, yet it still allows the quarterback's offensive teammates to anticipate both temporally and spatially (because they have learned what is to be done and when in the huddle). The goals here are for the offensive team to respond as a unit to the snap count and to allow the defensive team no capability to anticipate the ball snap.

Costs of Anticipation

There are several strong advantages to anticipation, but, as with most strategies for trying to gain an advantage, it comes with risks (see Focus on Application 2.3). The primary disadvantage occurs when the anticipated action

FOCUS ON Application 2.3

Cost–Benefit of Anticipating in Sprint Starting

The story "Jumping the Gun" on HK*Propel* describes how and why a false start is determined in a sprint race. Recall earlier that we defined RT as the period of time from the start of an unanticipated signal until the initiation of the response. Of course, in a sprint race, all the runners know what the signal will be (the sound of the electronic "pistol"). What is unanticipated is exactly when it will occur. In fairness to all, race officials will disqualify any sprinter who has anticipated the signal. They penalize a sprinter who has a measured RT of less than 100 ms. Can you guess why, then, RTs became longer for both males and females in the period 2004 to 2009 and longer again in the period 2010 to 2014 (see figure 2.10)? The answer lies in a cost–benefit analysis of anticipating.

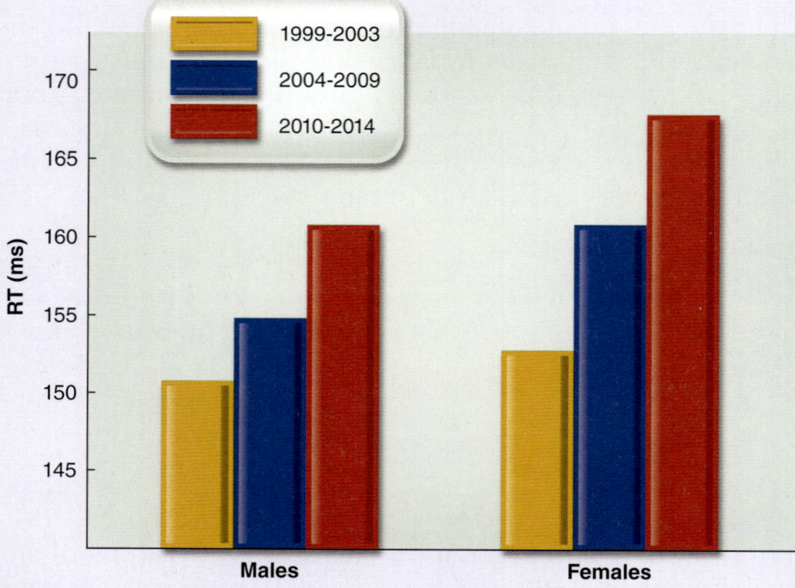

FIGURE 2.10 International sprint race median RTs during three separate eras under which different rules for false starting had been implemented.

Prior to 2004, the rules of sprint racing permitted each runner to make one false start. The runner was disqualified only if he or she made a second false start in that race. Thus, there was a slight strategic benefit to anticipating the sound of the gun. If the sprinter started his response just before hearing the sound of the gun but not too much before, then a legal RT (of 100+ ms) would be a huge advantage over the other racers. The cost of such a strategy was that if RT was less than 100 ms, then the sprinter would be charged with a false start and would need to be more cautious not to jump the gun in the do-over.

A rule change in 2004 changed the cost–benefit trade-off because each runner could no longer make a second false start. Instead, only one runner in the field could make a false start. After that, the entire field of runners for that race was essentially put on notice—any subsequent false start would result in an immediate disqualification, regardless of who had made the false start. Such a rule change made the false start much more penalizing, and as a result, sprinters tended to be more cautious about jumping the gun, especially after the field was put on notice. Hence, RTs, on average, increased.

The cost of anticipating became even more devastating following a further rule change in 2010. The new rule change removed the "on notice" clause—now, any sprinter who had a false start was disqualified immediately. The rule change made the cost of jumping the gun catastrophic, and sprinters responded by lengthening their average RTs even more (see figure 2.10).

is not what actually happens. In American football, if the defensive lineman anticipates that the snap will occur on the second sound but the quarterback takes the snap on the third sound, the lineman could move too early, incurring an offside penalty. In a similar way, when anticipating that an opponent will hit the ball to the left side of the court, a tennis player may move in that direction before the shot but is at risk of losing the point if the opponent actually hits the shot to the right.

Anticipating correctly can result in many benefits, but the costs of anticipating incorrectly can be worse than not anticipating at all. Earlier, we discussed the idea that anticipating allows various information-processing activities to take place in advance, before the stimulus is presented. Suppose that a performer has gone through these preparatory processes but now the events in the environment change. The information-processing costs in this case are actually magnified. First, the performer must stop the already prepared (falsely anticipated) action, and this process will require time to complete. Then the new, correct action must be prepared and initiated, which extends the processing delay even further. Thus, while a correct anticipation might reduce the lag period to essentially 0 ms, an incorrect anticipation will require more processing activities and longer delay compared to a response to a neutral or unanticipated event.

Visit HK*Propel* to read "Method to His Bratness" and complete the self-directed learning activities.

Errors in Decision-Making

Reaction time is the most commonly used method to study decision-making. Experimenters make fine adjustments to the stimuli and required responses and assess changes in RT to better understand specific information-processing stages. A different approach to understanding decision-making involves the study of human error—why intentions fail to unfold as planned. Many studies of human error do not use **experimental methods** but instead analyze naturally occurring events in daily life. The study of human error lacks the precision of experimental methods but has the ecological advantage of studying real people in natural settings.

The effects of S-R compatibility, discussed previously regarding the impact on RT, can be inferred readily from the scene in figure 2.11. Most stovetop burners are manufactured with a set of spatially incompatible controls: four burners arranged with two on the left side (front and rear) and two on the right side, controlled by four dials ordered linearly on a panel. The spatial incompatibility of the dials with the burners they control can produce a harmless error, such as failing to turn on the correct burner, or a more serious result, such as a severe burn. A more spatially compatible arrangement would match the control panel configuration to

Penalties for a false start in sprinting have become stricter, resulting in longer average RTs.

the burner configuration and virtually eliminate the errors seen in turning on the wrong burner (see "Push or Pull?" on HK*Propel*).

FIGURE 2.11 A watched pot never boils, and neither will this one. Turning on the wrong stovetop element because of spatially incompatible controls is an all-too-frequent problem when cooking. Identify two other spatially incompatible situations that cause problems where you live.

Errors in decision-making can occur for many of the same reasons that we saw in the previous sections, leading to slower RTs and MTs. In fact, the error may be the very cause of the delays in responding (e.g., the indecision in what to do) or in the movement when responding (such as reversing movement of the light switch after realizing the mistake). Errors can occur at any stage of information processing.

Misinterpreting a curve ball as a fastball in baseball can lead the batter to initiate a swing at a ball that may eventually be unhittable. In some cases, the error may be corrected before it is too late; in other cases, the error detection has passed a point of no return, and no correction is possible. Sometimes, the error persists well beyond the point of no return. The driver in the Santa Monica Farmer's Market case (see "The Farmers' Market" on HK*Propel*) was so convinced that his foot was on the brake pedal that he gave no thought to correcting his mistake.

Other high-profile cases may have similar links. Several instances of weapon confusion error have occurred in recent years in which a police officer who had intended to fire a Taser instead fired a handgun. Figure 2.12 illustrates two weapons used commonly by police. There are many differences between them (color, grip, size, weight), which, like the brake pedal and accelerator in a car, should make them easily distinguishable.

a

b

FIGURE 2.12 Two weapons used in law enforcement: *(a)* a Glock handgun and *(b)* a Taser 7. The differences in physical properties (size, weight, grip, and color) are expected to make them easily distinguishable, yet weapon confusion errors still occur, likely because the same action is required to discharge both.

However, in a moment of heightened anxiety (hypervigilance), an error occurred in which the officer unintentionally drew and fired the gun instead of the Taser. Like pedal misapplication errors, in which both the brake and accelerator require pushing movements, both the gun and Taser are fired by squeezing a trigger. The virtually identical action in both cases of unintentional errors likely contributed significantly either to the wrong device being used or to the failure to notice the mistake before it was too late.

Decision errors signify that the wrong action was chosen, even though that (incorrect) action was carried out faithfully. Many reasons for these types of errors relate to attention, which is the topic of the next chapter. Movement execution errors, on the other hand, suggest that the correct decision was made but the movement itself was flawed, leading to the failure to achieve the intended goal. Chapters 4, 5, 6, and 7 discuss movement control, including errors of execution.

Visit HK*Propel* to read "Is the Bean Dizzy?" and complete the self-directed learning activities.

Memory

Not yet discussed in this chapter is a concept that is critical to processing information and making decisions: memory. The environment constantly bombards us with stimuli, of which we only process a minor portion. How is this done, and what becomes of that information? Based on the model first proposed by Atkinson and Shiffrin (1968), memory is conceptualized to involve three different systems: short-term sensory store, short-term memory, and long-term memory. The various types of memory and their characteristics will be useful later during the discussion of several aspects of human performance.

Short-Term Sensory Store

The briefest of all memories, the **short-term sensory store (STSS)**, retains sensory information for a very short period of time. We rely on the STSS to briefly hold information taken in by the visual, auditory, and haptic systems. How long does the sensory information last? Research suggests that visual information is retained for less than 1 s in STSS. Auditory and haptic information can be retained slightly longer, perhaps as much as 3 or 4 s. The sensory information deemed relevant is attended to for future processing. Nonrelevant (or unattended) information is lost quickly, either due to rapid decay over time or due to displacement caused by new sensory information entering STSS.

Short-Term Memory

Short-term memory (STM), which researchers sometimes call *working memory*, is a temporary holding place for information that has been briefly stored in STSS. As an example, suppose that someone had verbally given you their phone number, and you were trying to remember it long enough to enter it into your phone's contact list. You know that the auditory sensory information will not last long enough, so you repeat the number to yourself long enough to enter the contact. The process of repeating (by subvocalizing) is one rehearsal strategy to retain information in STM. Rehearsal is a process in which you pay attention to the information that you wish to retain long enough to complete a task. Early research on STM provides some ideas about how rehearsal can be effective and what happens if rehearsal is prevented.

For example, participants in a study by Peterson and Peterson (1959) were asked to remember verbal information (a three-letter trigram, e.g., XMK) but were prevented from rehearsing it by having them subtract backward by threes from a two-digit number (e.g., 87, 84, 81, 78, and so on). Within about 10 s, the probability of successfully recalling the trigram was less than 20%, and after about 20 s, it was below 10%. The conclusion from this and other research was that verbal information in STM is retained longer than in STSS but is still lost quite rapidly when not given sustained attention.

Adams and Dijkstra (1966) conducted a study similar to Peterson and Peterson's, although they used motor skills to study the STM of movement information. In one condition (labeled 1 in figure 2.13), blindfolded participants moved a slide on a track from a start position to a mechanical stop, then tried to reposition the slide in the same final location (with the stop removed) after various periods of time (retention intervals). In two other conditions, the movement of the slide to the mechanical stop was repeated either 6 or 15 times, amounting to additional rehearsals of the movement. In this experiment, memory loss is represented by an increase in absolute error over time. Figure 2.13 shows two important results from the Adams and Dijkstra data. First, as in the Peterson and Peterson study, rapid **forgetting** occurred during the first 20 s of the retention period, with further decreases occurring over the next 60 s, especially if there were no additional rehearsals provided (i.e., the condition labeled 1 in figure 2.13). Second, the addition of rehearsals (6 or 15) reduced the amount of forgetting over the retention intervals. This evidence suggests that information can be retained for a period of time that is much longer than STSS but is subject to forgetting if not given sustained attention. As well, the strength of the representation in memory also affects forgetting, because information retention that was strengthened by rehearsals slowed the speed of memory loss.

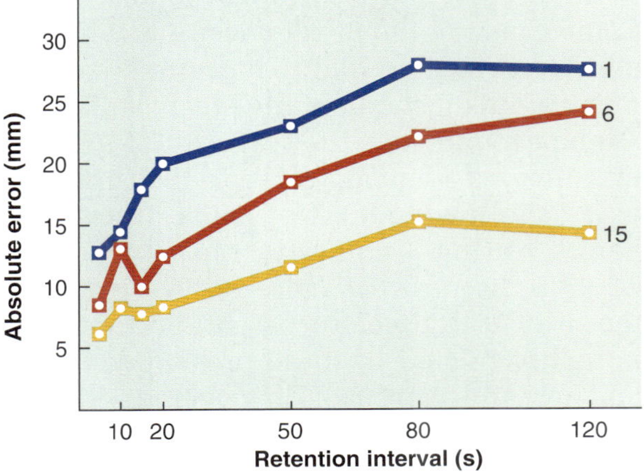

FIGURE 2.13 Absolute error in blind positioning recall increases rapidly over different retention intervals (5 to 120 s) depending on the number of rehearsals (1, 6, or 15 rehearsals).

Long-Term Memory

Long-term memory (LTM) contains information that has accumulated over a lifetime. Experiments show that LTM must be essentially limitless in capacity, as indicated by the vast amount of information that can be stored for very long periods of time. Some researchers suggest that LTM can be further parsed into different types of representations. One dichotomy, for example, suggests a difference between declarative (or explicit) memory for facts (what you *know*) and procedural (or implicit) memory for skills (what you can *do*). This helps our understanding of why some individuals with specific lesions to the brain can learn perceptual-motor skills but cannot remember new facts (see "H.M." on HK*Propel*). The dichotomy also helps to explain differences in retention characteristics for memories. For many motor skills, particularly continuous ones such as riding a bicycle or swimming, evidence and common experience suggest almost perfect retention after years, even decades, without intervening practice. In contrast, well-learned verbal and cognitive skills (e.g., foreign language vocabulary) are seemingly forgotten over time. Chapter 9 presents more on retention.

Visit HK*Propel* to read "H.M." and complete the self-directed learning activities. 

Information Transfer Between STM and LTM

In general, transferring information from STM (which is prone to rapid forgetting) into LTM (which is much more permanent) requires effort. Preparing for an exam, for example, takes time and repetition for the material to be stored and retrievable from LTM. There are exceptions, of course—burning one's hand on a hot stove is an experience that does not require much repetition to learn. Be careful to note that not all methods are equally successful in getting information into LTM. Rereading lecture notes and passages from a textbook, using highlighting pens, and so on are frequent techniques used to store information in preparation for an exam. Some may be surprised to learn, for example, that these methods are relatively ineffective compared to taking practice tests (Agarwal et al., 2021).

Motor learning and performance presume the transfer of information between STM and LTM. Learning requires that skills be stored in LTM; performance requires that memory for skills be retrieved from LTM. Practice is generally considered the most effective means of learning. However, the methods used to conduct practice are vastly different in their effectiveness in creating representations that last in LTM. In fact, we devote the last four chapters of this book to the methods that best promote the learning of motor skills.

Performing a skilled motor activity requires retrieval from LTM, which is prone to error if the system is not optimally prepared to execute it. For example, performing a skill for the first time after a layoff, sometimes even a very brief layoff, often results in an execution decrement. Many examples exist. The basketball player who steps to the free-throw line must perform an action that she has not performed in some time. Evidence suggests that the first of two or three consecutive free throws is performed less accurately than the second or third (Morgulev et al., 2020; see also "Shooting Two From the Line" on HK*Propel*). Professional darts players, who rotate taking turns with other players, are less accurate with the first dart throw than with the next two (Wunderlich et al., 2020), even though the delay since the last set of throws may have been less than a minute. Why has such a performance decrease happened, and are there ways to boost performance after a short layoff?

Visit HK*Propel* to read "Shooting Two From the Line" and complete the self-directed learning activities.

The observance of an initial decrement to performance after a layoff has, in fact, been studied for many years. That these decrements to performance are relatively large and that they appear reliably in so many different tasks and under so many different circumstances has earned this research area its very own term: **warm-up decrement** (Adams, 1961). Note that the term *warm-up* is not used here in the same sense as warming up physiologically to run a race, for example. Rather, warm-up decrement is considered a psychological impediment that is brought on by the passage of time away from a task and is eliminated quickly when performance begins, but not before some diminished performance occurs.

The cause of warm-up decrement has been a subject of considerable debate. One view is that it represents a type of forgetting of the skill itself (Adams, 1961). An alternate view is that warm-up decrement results from a loss of the set rather than forgetting the skill itself (Nacson & Schmidt, 1971). The **set** is a collection of psychological states or processes (e.g., the target of attentional focus, mental effort, postural adjustments) that had facilitated performance before the break. Resuming performance initiates a recalibration process of the movement system that overcomes the loss of set, but not before incurring a brief warm-up decrement (Ajemian et al., 2010). Common to both views of warm-up decrement is the notion of a loss from STM of processes that had supported performance prior to the break.

Is there a way of overcoming warm-up decrement prior to resuming performance without actually performing the task itself? Some consider the preshot routine, when an athlete performs a highly individualized set of behaviors just before the "real" action, an attempt to reinstate the set into STM. These may involve bouncing the basketball a certain way or following a set of ritual procedures before hitting a golf ball. Most high-level athletes do these activities in a very consistent way each time. Successful performance is highly related to these preshot routines, and research suggests that overcoming the negative effects of warm-up decrement is part of the reason for their success (Boutcher & Crews, 1987).

Warm-up decrement can obviously have more serious life-altering consequences when they occur in other aspects of life. The initial start-up of a driving cycle has been linked to automotive accidents, such as pedal misapplication errors (Schmidt, 1989). The occurrence of warm-up decrement at the start of a surgery is an example that could have negative consequences for a patient. Interestingly, research has found that certain activities can benefit a surgeon prior to the first cut. For example, a recent review of the literature found that performing various types of specific simulation (e.g., using virtual reality) resulted in enhanced initial surgical performance (Feeley et al., 2022). The simulation "primed" the surgeons to ready themselves for actual surgery due, at least in part, to overcoming the negative effects of warm-up decrement.

Visit HK*Propel* to read "The Preshot Routine" and complete the self-directed learning activities.

Summary

The human motor system can be thought of as an information processor—for motor skills, information is received from the environment, processed through various stages, and output as movements. Processing involves three main stages: a stimulus identification stage, which detects the nature of environmental information; a response selection stage, which resolves uncertainty about what action should be made; and a movement programming stage, which organizes the motor system for action. Reaction time is an important measure of information-processing speed. Its duration is strongly affected by stimulus–response alternatives (described by Hick's Law), by the naturalness of the relationship between stimuli and their associated movements (stimulus–response compatibility), and by anticipation of the upcoming events. The nature of errors and why they occur also hold many clues about the stages of processing. Three memory systems are described: Short-term sensory store (STSS) holds sensory information for a few seconds at most. Short-term memory (STM) can hold about eight items of information for longer periods of time, but these items last only as long as attention can be maintained. Long-term memory (LTM) can hold information permanently.

HK*PROPEL* ACTIVITIES

HK*Propel* offers these activities to help you build and apply your knowledge of the concepts in this chapter. Additionally, you'll find a key terms flashcard review activity and a key terms quiz, along with audio supplements for selected figures, as indicated by QR codes throughout the chapter.

Interactive Learning

Activity 2.1: Identify the stage of information processing in which each of a list of actions occurs.

Activity 2.2: Arrange the stages of information processing in the correct order.

Activity 2.3: Review the memory systems by matching each to its definition.

Activity 2.4: View several images of examples of poor design, then practice explaining why one example demonstrates poor stimulus–response compatibility.

Principles-to-Application Exercise

Activity 2.5: The principles-to-application exercise for this chapter prompts you to choose a skill you can perform or are learning how to perform. You will describe the skill, including the goal of the movement and the basic actions involved. You will also select someone else to perform this skill and describe one processing activity for each stage of information processing and one factor that might influence decision-making about the skill.

Motor Control in Everyday Actions Narratives

Preventing Penalties and Batting Baseballs

Friendly Fire

Jumping the Gun

Red Light, Green Light

Push or Pull?

The Grocery Store

Method to His Bratness

Is the Bean Dizzy?

H.M.

Shooting Two From the Line

The Preshot Routine

Check Your Understanding

1. Describe the information-processing activities that might occur in the stimulus identification, response selection, and movement programming stages for a hockey goalie in a game and for a kayaker navigating a set of rapids.
2. Describe and provide an example where spatial anticipation is important to a sport outcome, and describe and provide an example where temporal anticipation is important to a sport outcome.
3. Provide an example of stimulus–response compatibility and an example of stimulus–response incompatibility that you have encountered today.

Apply Your Knowledge

1. Three memory systems are involved in the learning process. The short-term sensory store (STSS) stores large amounts of sensory information before processing by short-term memory (STM), which is a temporary holding place for information. Information can remain in STM through rehearsal, and it can be processed for storage in long-term memory (LTM). This processing from STM to LTM can be described as learning. Explain how each of the three memory systems (STSS, STM, and LTM) is involved in learning a new dance routine. Provide examples of specific information that would be processed.

2. Anticipation can play a role in many contexts. One activity where the success or failure of anticipation can be particularly clear is racket sports, where players must anticipate the next shot of their opponent. Discuss how anticipation in a game of squash can be both beneficial and harmful, depending on the situation. What factors can affect the outcome of anticipation?

3

Attention and Performance

Information-Processing Limitations

CHAPTER OUTLINE

CHAPTER OBJECTIVES

Chapter 3 describes the role of attention as a factor that limits human performance. This chapter will help you understand

- attention and its various properties and definitions,
- attention as a limitation in the capacity to process information,
- attention as a limitation in the capability to perform actions, and
- performance under conditions of increased stress.

CHAPTER PREVIEW QUIZ

1. How are you limited in doing two things at the same time?
2. What is the difference between an internal and an external attentional focus?
3. Why does choking occur in sports?

The task of driving to the store illustrates why the concept of attention is complicated. Consider the following:

- On the drive to the supermarket, you suddenly remember that you left the shopping list on the refrigerator and try to reconstruct what might have been on it—eggs, milk, peanut butter, hmm, no, not milk; I bought some yesterday. . . . You receive a phone call. It's your roommate, and she asks you to pick up some pasta, as well as some green peppers, for dinner.
- There's an intersection ahead; the light has been green for quite a while and may turn yellow at any moment, so I'd better be ready . . .
- It's pretty warm today; maybe I should turn on the air conditioning. How do I work the climate control again?
- What was it that my roommate asked me to get? Think hard, remember . . . oh yeah, pasta and . . . green onions—that's it.
- Oops, the lane departure feature on my car just made my steering wheel vibrate and nudged the car back toward the center of the lane.
- There's the yellow light; do I have time to make a safe stop, or should I accelerate through the intersection?

And on it goes. Although the scenario illustrates many common ways that we experience attention, it also highlights some important differences. Consider the following facets of attention and factors that influence it (see Focus on Application 3.1).

- Attention appears to be *limited* in that only a certain amount of information-processing capacity seems to exist. If attention is overloaded, much information can be missed.
- Attention appears to be *selective* in that it can be focused on one thing, then on another, and only with great difficulty (if at all) can we focus attention on two things at once.
- Attention can be *directed* in various ways, such as to external sensory events (e.g., where the climate control is located), to internal mental operations (e.g., trying to remember the shopping list), or to internal sensory information (sensations from the muscles and the joints, such as feeling the steering wheel vibrate).

What Is Attention?

All the preceding examples represent different uses of attention. But what is attention? In our view, attention is a resource (or pool of resources) that is available and can be used for various purposes. The ways in which these attentional resources are allocated define how we use attention.

One way to think of attention relates to doing two things at the same time. The limitations in information processing determine how well (or poorly) two things can be done simultaneously. If performing each task requires attention, the total amount required compared to the limited amount available determines the quality of the simultaneous performance. When the amount of attention required is greater than the amount available, performance suffers.

The pie graphs in figure 3.1 illustrate how the fixed amount of attention (capacity resource) must be divided between two tasks (a main task and a secondary task). The entire circle (or pie) represents the total capacity of resources available for allocation. When the main task is relatively simple and does not require very much attention, as depicted in figure 3.1*a*, more attentional capacity remains available to allocate to the secondary tasks. When the main task is complex, however, more attention must be allocated to performing it, thereby reducing the amount available to allocate to the secondary task (figure 3.1*b*).

FOCUS ON Application 3.1

William James on Attention

Consider the following statement, made over a century ago by the famous psychologist William James (1890):

> Everyone knows what **attention** is. It is the taking possession by the mind, in clear and vivid form, of one out of what seem several simultaneously possible objects or trains of thought. Focalization, concentration of consciousness, is of its essence. It implies withdrawal from some things in order to deal effectively with others.

In just a few words, William James quickly captures the complexity of the concept of attention. In his statement, James suggests that attention takes on at least three different roles. First, he says that attention involves "taking possession by the mind . . . of one out of . . . several . . . trains of thought." In this statement, James suggests that attention involves a selective process in which the individual juggles several ongoing lines of thinking, each competing for current resources (or consciousness). Second, he states that attention involves "focalization . . . of consciousness." This is a subtle, but important, departure from the first idea because it implies an active, directive process of current thinking, presumably one that is dynamic—that changes with the evolving needs of the performer or the environment. Last, James suggests that attention requires "withdrawal from some things in order to deal effectively with others." Here, James is again implying something subtly different—that we have a limited amount of attention to allocate, which may not be sufficient to allocate to two or more tasks simultaneously. Therefore, the performer must be able to shift the amount of attention allocated as changes occur in the demands of the task.

As we will discuss in this chapter, James' intuitions and descriptions about attention in 1890 have been supported by research and remain quite accurate today.

By analogy, attention is like a bank account, which contains financial resources that fund our daily living. The full pies in figure 3.1 would represent all the money available. Suppose the money allocated to paying your rent is like a primary task. When that rent amount is relatively small, as in figure 3.1*a*, more money is available to spend elsewhere. However, when the rent is relatively large, as in figure 3.1*b*, much less is available for other things.

Visit HK*Propel* to read "Gumbo" and complete the self-directed learning activities.

Attention, as a limited capacity, has strong implications for understanding skilled performance. For example, when driving an overwhelming amount of information could be processed, some of it relevant to performance (e.g., what other drivers are doing) and some of it irrelevant to performance (e.g., the color of other cars on the road). The problem is how to cope with this potential overload of information. The performer must learn what information is important to attend to, when to attend to it, and how to shift attention skillfully between events in the environment: monitoring and correcting actions, planning future actions, and doing many other processes that compete for the limited attentional capacity.

One way to understand attention is to consider its role in the stages of information processing described in chapter 2—stimulus iden-

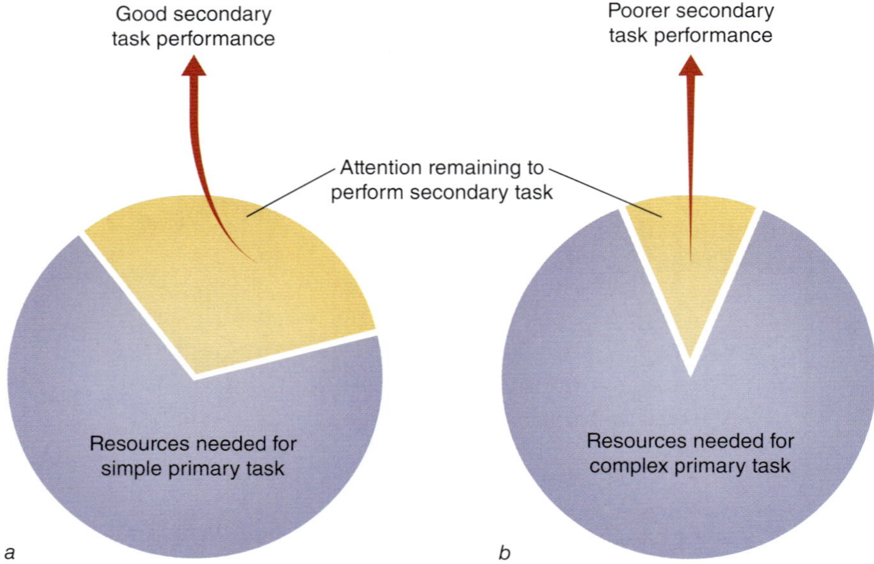

FIGURE 3.1 Attention remaining for a secondary task *(a)* when the primary task is simple compared to *(b)* when the primary task is more complex.

tification, response selection, and movement programming (see figure 2.3). What processes compete for available attention within each stage? As a preview, there is evidence that some processing can occur in parallel (i.e., without attention) in the stimulus identification stage but that much less parallel processing occurs in the response selection stage. Finally, considerable competition often exists among tasks in the movement programming stage.

Attentional Limitations in Stimulus Identification

Some evidence suggests that processing activities in the initial stages of the information-processing model can be done in parallel. With parallel processing, two or more streams of information can enter the system and be processed together without interfering with each other (i.e., both tasks can be performed as well together as they can be performed alone). For other tasks, however, two or more streams of information exceed the capacity limits of attention, requiring that we switch attention back and forth between competing sources. Still other research reveals that **sustained attention** tends to wane after extended periods of information processing. These influences on sensory information processing are discussed in the next sections.

Stroop Effect

Information from different aspects of the visual display, such as the color and shape of objects, can be processed together without interference. One line of evidence for parallel processing in stimulus identification comes from an analysis of the **Stroop effect** (Stroop, 1935; MacLeod, 1991, 2015). Imagine that you were asked to read out loud, as fast as possible, a list of words by naming the color of the font in which each word is printed. In some cases, the words have no semantic relationship to the colors in which they are printed, as in figure 3.2*a*. In other cases, as in figure 3.2*b*, a strong semantic relationship exists—the names of the font colors compete with the names of the words. The Stroop effect refers to the finding that finishing the list in figure 3.2*b* requires more time and incurs more errors than the list in figure 3.2*a*. Even though you try to ignore the name of the word and focus solely on the font color, that word name gets at least some automatic processing in parallel with processing the font color. Performance is affected because the

Multitasking is an example of an attentional capacity problem in which the demands of the individual tasks exceed the capability to devote full attention to each of them. Explain how the performer in this photo might try to achieve multitasking.

parallel processing of the two stimuli (word name and font color) competes for different responses in a later stage of processing.

FIGURE 3.2 The Stroop effect. Time yourself while naming the font colors of the words printed in each list. Font colors with *(a)* no semantic relationship are faster to name than *(b)* those with a strong semantic relationship.

Although the Stroop effect was discovered initially using the word and font color paradigm, similar "Stroop-like" effects have been found using various other types of stimuli. One example is the no-look pass in basketball, hockey, and other team sports (see Focus on Research 3.1).

Cocktail Party Effect

Imagine yourself in a large room at a party where many groups of people are engaged in conversations. There is considerable noise surrounding your conversation—loud music, other conversations, and so on—yet you can still engage in your conversation successfully, effectively shutting out the background noise.

Not all information is blocked, however. If your name is spoken in a conversation in a different part of the room, you have the amazing capacity to hear it, even though you were not involved in that conversation

FOCUS ON Research 3.1

A Stroop-Like Effect in Basketball

Recall from the Stroop effect that response times are slower and errors increase when the font color name of a printed word competes with the name of the word itself (e.g., responding with *red* when the word *green* is printed in a red font). The effect occurs because generating the name of a word is an overlearned, automatic process that must be inhibited before generating the font color name. Research suggests that something similar to the Stroop effect occurs when responding to head fakes in sports—such as a basketball player who passes the ball in the direction opposite to where he is looking or a soccer player who kicks the penalty to the left of the goalkeeper while looking to her right.

Kunde and colleagues (2011) conducted a set of elegantly simple studies in which participants responded to static pictures of a basketball player who was passing a ball to his left or to his right. The player in the photo was either looking in the same direction or in the opposite direction of the pass. The findings were clear: responses to incongruent photos (looking and passing in opposite directions) were 7% slower and three times more erroneous than responses to congruent photos. However, Kunde and colleagues also found that when the player's face was blocked, there were no differences between responses to the congruent and incongruent photos. These findings indicate that humans automatically process the implied direction of someone's gaze and have difficulty ignoring it when the direction of action is incongruent with the gaze direction (for more on deceptive processes in sports, see Jackson & Cañal-Bruland, 2019 and Güldenpenning et al., 2023).

These results are not surprising. As Kunde and colleagues point out, humans are very attuned to the faces of other people. Even very young infants try to imitate the actions of others, such as attempting to stick out their tongues in response to observing an adult. But, like the Stroop effect (and its many variations), this is a learned behavior that can largely be eliminated with practice. For example, expert basketball players are less prone to head fakes because they have learned to focus less on opponents' heads and eyes and fixate more on what the hands and the ball are doing when playing defense.

In this photo, the offensive player is trying to create a Stroop-like delay in the defense by using a no-look pass. Describe another sports situation in which an offensive player's gaze direction is intended to fool the behavior of the defender.

at all. Although you had effectively shut out that background noise to attend to your own conversation, at least some of that information must have been processed in parallel in the stimulus identification stage in order that you could hear your own name. Cherry (1953) called this the **cocktail party effect**. Like the Stroop effect, the cocktail party effect illustrates that even some unattended sensory features are processed in parallel with other attended information in the very early stages of information processing.

Cherry developed the dichotic listening task to empirically test the cocktail party effect. Participants wore stereo headphones with separate streams of auditory information directed to each ear and were instructed to pay attention by shadowing (repeating) the information presented in one channel and disregarding the other. Unexpectedly, they were sometimes asked to repeat the information presented to the unattended ear. Participants were largely unable to remember the content of the information from the unattended ear, although they could identify some surface features of the message, such as the speaker's gender and loudness of the voice, thus showing that some information sent to the unattended ear was processed in parallel.

In this photo, what stage of information processing is illustrated by the cocktail party effect?

Inattentional Blindness

The Stroop and cocktail party effects illustrate how stimuli and information are processed in parallel, even despite efforts to prevent it. Yet sometimes a very simple, goal-directed visual search, such as looking for something specific, such as a person or street sign, seems to make us "blind" to other things by limiting parallel processing. Some remarkable findings have shown that we can miss seemingly obvious features in our environment when we are engaged in a directed visual search. For example, research participants in the now-famous Simons and Chabris (1999) study watched a video of six people who passed basketballs among themselves while all players were in motion. Three players on one team wore black shirts, and the other three players wore white shirts. Each team passed the ball among players on their own team. The research participants who watched a video of this activity were told to count the number of passes made by the team dressed in white shirts. (The original Simon and Chabris video and many imitations of it are easy to find on the Internet.)

After the 30 s video ended, the experimenter asked the participants how many passes were made and followed this by asking if they had seen anything unusual in the video. About half of all participants responded "no" to the second question. The other half responded by saying that they had seen someone dressed in a gorilla suit walk through the group of players, pound his chest, and walk away (see figure 3.3). When the video was replayed to the participants who had not seen the gorilla, they were shocked at having missed it, some even claiming that the researcher must have shown them a different video (Chabris & Simons, 2010).

Visit HK*Propel* to read "Turn Right at the Next Gorilla" and complete the self-directed activities.

Neisser and Becklen (1975) originally discovered this phenomenon, termed **inattentional blindness**. These findings reveal that missing the rather obvious gorilla is likely to

FIGURE 3.3 The inattentional blindness effect. Observers of the video counted the number of basketball passes made among the players in white shirts. About half of these observers did not recall seeing the gorilla walk through the middle of the group.

occur only when the viewer is engaged in a specific search task (i.e., counting the number of passes). Other findings reveal that the inattentional blindness effect is not restricted to watching videos but can be demonstrated in live-action events. For example, people who are engaged in attention-demanding tasks are likely to miss obvious things such as a change in a person to whom they are giving directions (Simons & Levin, 1998) or a person dressed in a clown suit riding a unicycle (Hyman et al., 2010).

The cause of **looked-but-failed-to-see automotive accidents** is closely related to the inattentional blindness effect (Wolfe et al., 2022). Typically, in these accidents, a car is driven into the path of a clearly visible pedestrian, bicycle, or other vehicle (Brown, 2005; Langham et al., 2002). The failure of the driver to notice the other object, even though he looked at it, often occurred because he was searching for something else in the environment, such as a specific sign or building. A similar type of looked-but-failed-to-see error has been reported in medical image diagnoses, when a specific search item (e.g., tumor) leaves the radiologist blind to a different problem. For example, in a humorous callout to the Simon and Chabris experiment, Drew and colleagues (2013) found that 83% of radiologists missed seeing the image of a small gorilla in a CT chest scan.

Inattentional blindness also helps us understand why we momentarily fail to recognize a friend that we walk past while looking for someone else in a crowd. Our search has been directed toward a person with specific visual characteristics, and we become temporarily oblivious to people who don't match those search criteria, even though we would have instantly recognized them had we not been specifically searching for someone else. Magicians and pickpockets exploit essentially the same concept. When directed by the magician or thief to focus attention on one thing, the victim becomes essentially blind to another person's actions (Stephen et al., 2008).

Sustained Attention

World War II generated research on sustained attention to better understand why the performance of radar operators, who were on enemy lookout, deteriorated over time. One task used to study sustained attention was devised by Mackworth (1948), who asked participants to watch the pointer of a clocklike apparatus jump second by second. Occasionally, after long, irregular (unpredictable) intervals, the pointer would jump by 2 s. Detection of these 2 s jumps was found to decline dramatically after the first 30 min of work and gradually thereafter. These were termed *vigilance decrements* and have been reported in many other tasks in which sustained attention is required (see Hancock, 2017, for a historical overview).

A number of factors are known to affect sustained attention (or vigilance); these include the operator's motivation, arousal, secondary tasks, and, of course, fatigue (related to the accumulated amount of time spent performing the task). Environmental factors, such as temperature and noise, are also important contributions (see Davies & Parasuraman, 1982). Sustained attention becomes progressively more difficult over time for various reasons, such as a decreased sensitivity for stimulus identification.

These effects can be readily observed daily because they influence many occupations in which sustained attention is a necessity (see figure 3.4). For example, consider the task of

FIGURE 3.4 Vigilance decrements would be expected after prolonged periods of work, such as when screening carry-on luggage.

working as a security agent at a busy airport. Before people can board their aircraft, they must go through a series of security checks, which includes an X-ray scan of their carry-on luggage. Each X-rayed piece of luggage must undergo a visual search by a human operator, who looks for objects that are not permitted on the aircraft. The obvious ones (guns, knives) should be relatively easy to spot. But the problems faced by the security agent include trying to decide whether something is a banned object and deciding when to terminate the search and move on to the next object. Experiments on visual search tasks reveal that the number and similarity of distracting objects play an important role in the search's success. The occurrence of banned objects is rare, which makes the agent's task even more difficult, so sustained attention to the task is of primary concern (Wolfe et al., 2005).

Long periods of driving without rest are hazardous to sustained attention. However, the very actions involved in driving provide some benefits to maintaining vigilance. How will automated driving vehicles taking over the roads affect sustained attention (Greenlee et al., 2018)? Will drivers be prepared to assume rapid control of the vehicle in an emergency? These are important questions for future research.

Attentional Limitations in Response Selection

Competition for attention is never more obvious than when two actions are performed simultaneously, with each task requiring mental operations, such as drinking a cup of coffee while navigating a computer screen with a touchpad. The competition is thought to occur during response selection because choices must be made among several possible alternatives—which hand to use for picking up the cup and navigating the touchpad, tracking both the cup to your mouth and the cursor on the screen, and so on. These activities are governed by **controlled processing**, which is thought to be

1. slow,
2. attention demanding, with interference caused by competing processes, and
3. serially organized, with attention switching between tasks if necessary.

Relatively effortful, controlled processing is a very large part of conscious information-processing activities, involving mental operations among relatively poorly learned, or even completely novel, activities. Performing two tasks together that require information processing can disrupt one or both tasks.

A separate, very different kind of information processing seems to occur for other tasks, especially highly learned ones. For example, basketball players have very little difficulty bouncing a basketball while walking or running, and guitarists can rapidly play a series of chords by applying pressure to various strings with one hand while strumming strings using a guitar pick with the other hand. It is as if much of the information processing necessary to perform these tasks was fundamentally different from controlled processing, requiring little attention. This way of dealing with information, **automatic processing**, is

1. fast,
2. not attention demanding in that such processes do not compete (very much) with other tasks, and
3. organized in parallel, occurring together with other processing tasks.

Automatic information processing is thought to result from an enormous amount of practice. Your capability to quickly recognize collections of letters as the words you are reading now has resulted from years of practice. Many years ago, Bryan and Harter (1897, 1899) conducted studies of telegraph operators, whose job it was to identify (receive) and send Morse code, which is composed of serial bursts of brief noise (called dots and dashes) that combine to define letters and numbers. Bryan and Harter found that telegraph operators focused on individual letters at the earliest stage of learning but that as they gained proficiency, they processed Morse code as combinations of letters, then as whole words, and even as phrases. For skilled operators, identifying and sending the combinations of dots and dashes that comprised individual letters was an automatic process.

Automaticity allows highly skilled athletes to process information about their opponents' movements and respond quickly.

Costs and Benefits of Automaticity

Automatic performances are related to processing information in parallel, quickly, and without interference from other processing tasks. Automaticity can have drawbacks as well as benefits. Although very fast processing is effective when the environment is stable and predictable, it can lead to terrible errors when the environment (or an opponent) changes suddenly. Thus, automaticity seems most effective in closed skills, where the environment is relatively predictable, and less so in open environments.

For example, after much practice, high-level volleyball players can interpret their opponents' movement patterns automatically to mean that the ball will be spiked from, for example, their left side (e.g., see Allard & Burnett, 1985). But what if, after consistently producing a pattern leading to a play to the left, the opposing team uses the same pattern leading to a play to the right? The defenders' automatic processing of the pattern, leading to a quick decision and a movement to counter the expected play, would result in a hopeless defense for the actual play. In this case, the automatic processing would put the defense at a disadvantage.

Developing Automaticity

How do people develop the capability to process information automatically? Experiments by Schneider and Shiffrin (1977) address one approach to this question. They found that practice, and lots of it, was a very important ingredient. Automaticity developed gradually and most effectively under a consistent mapping condition, where the response generated related consistently to a particular stimulus pattern. For example, the response to a red light while driving is always to bring the vehicle to a stop. This contrasts with a varied-mapping condition, where the same environmental event sometimes leads to one response and sometimes to another. An example is the variety of button layouts on different brands of remote control units, where a given function (changing the volume) requires pressing different buttons depending on the brand and the type of device being controlled. The diversity of such varied-mapping conditions makes automatic processing almost impossible to achieve, and such tasks require considerable controlled processing to avoid making errors.

Response Selection and Distracted Driving

The NHTSA (National Highway Traffic and Safety Administration) in the United States defines distracted driving as "any activity that diverts attention from driving, including talking or texting on your phone, eating and drinking, talking to people in your vehicle, fiddling with the stereo, entertainment or navigation system—anything that takes your attention away from the task of safe driving" (NHTSA, n.d., para. 1). Distracted driving is an excellent example of attention's limited capacity and, more specifically, the limitations due to response selection and movement programming.

Manual texting is an obvious distraction problem because it reduces stimulus identification due to sensory disengagement with driving activities (e.g., looking away from the road), response selection (e.g., deciding what buttons to touch), and movement programming (e.g., sequencing a series of presses). The NHSTA states that, at a speed of 55 mph (89 km/h), spending just 5 s reading or sending a text is like driving the entire length of a football field with eyes closed.

Many countries, as well as states in the United States, have banned the use of handheld cell phones while driving but allow the use of hands-free units. The underlying assumption is that the manual handling of a cell phone interferes with the operation of a motor vehicle. This argument lays the blame for the cell phone–driving dual-task deficit as a movement programming limitation. But the research suggests otherwise and is quite conclusive that hands-free and handheld phones are almost equally distracting. The source of the problem lies in the attention demanded by the communication itself and not whether the driver is holding on to, looking at, or manipulating the phone (e.g., Strayer & Johnston, 2001). The physical actions involved in manipulating the cell phone do not add significantly to the attention demands required in carrying on a conversation while driving (see Ishigami & Klein, 2009; Caird et al., 2018, for important reviews of this research). The discussion in Focus on Research 3.2 provides more information about the methods used to understand the attention demands of distracted driving.

Combining cell phone use with other types of activities can also be dangerous. For example, Thompson and colleagues (2013) found that people who texted or talked on a cell phone while they crossed a busy intersection walked about 20% slower than nondistracted pedestrians and were much less likely to look for oncoming traffic.

Attentional Limitations in Movement Programming

As discussed in chapter 2, the movement programming stage is the third in the sequence of information-processing stages. Here, after the performer has perceived information from the environment and has chosen an appropriate action, the performer must still organize the motor system to actually execute the movement. In this stage, the performer must make critical adjustments that occur at various levels (e.g., in the limbs, muscles, and spinal cord). These adjustments take time, of course. A good example is the action of a fencer, who must preprogram a movement despite having to execute the movement in the face of a potentially changing environment.

A fencer moves the foil toward the opponent's shoulder but then quickly alters the direction and contacts the waist instead. Responding to the first move (the fake) will

FOCUS ON Research 3.2

Distracted-Driving Research

Researchers have used a variety of approaches to understand the effects of distractions on driving. The obvious problem with doing the most logical type of research—using drivers in real traffic situations—is that it brings other drivers, the research participants, and sometimes the experimenters themselves into potentially dangerous situations, which is an unethical research practice. So, researchers have devised different methods to assess the attentional cost of performing various tasks while driving.

A statistical approach to the issue of distracted driving uses call records of individuals who were involved in an accident. The findings of one study using this method revealed that the likelihood of being involved in a car accident increased by 400% when a driver was talking on a cell phone (Redelmeier & Tibshirani, 1997). These authors claimed that the increase in accident rate when talking on a cell phone while driving is about the same as when driving with a .08% blood alcohol concentration—which exceeds the legal definition of driving under the influence of alcohol concentration in some states and countries.

The most common type of experimental procedure involves using driving simulators in laboratory environments. Some simulators provide extremely realistic driving environments, enabling researchers to have control over the traffic conditions and varying distractions without creating a dangerous experimental setup.

A few experimenters have created outdoor environments using an actual car and a simulated driving environment in an otherwise safe area, such as a large, empty parking lot. In fact, one of the very first studies of this kind was performed over a half-century ago, and the authors suggested back then that mobile phones and automobile drivers were a dangerous mix (Brown et al., 1969).

Each research method has advantages and disadvantages. Phone records involve actual data about calls that have occurred. But the co-occurrence of an accident and call records tells us very little about the individual's state of mind during the call. Simulators provide the researcher with excellent control of mental workloads, ongoing distractions, the timing of critical events, the measurement of behaviors, and so on. But these simulations of a driving environment are not the real thing. Outdoor environments, in actual cars but with simulated driving conditions, have the advantage of good experimental control of events but, again, without the reality of an actual driving experience in real traffic. In the end, the cumulative information provided by all types of research methodologies provides researchers with the best answers to critical questions about distracted driving (see Simmons et al., 2016, for more).

Exploring Further

1. How might the nature of a particular cell phone conversation affect a person's capacity to attend to the task of driving?
2. Do you think that a driver having a discussion with an in-car passenger would be as distracting as talking on a cell phone? Why or why not?

often delay the opponent's response to the second move. The delay in responding occurs because of competition in the movement programming stage, which has the task of organizing the motor system to make the desired movement. Specifically, the programming of one response (to block the fake to the shoulder) interferes with the programming of a second response (to block the lunge to the waist).

Visit HK*Propel* to read "Fakes" and complete the self-directed learning activities.

Support for this reasoning comes from considerable research evidence using the **double-stimulation paradigm**, in which the participant must respond with separate responses to each of two stimuli presented very closely together in time (see Focus on Research 3.3). In many ways, this paradigm mimics the problem facing the fencer who first responds to one move (the fake) and then to another in rapid succession. The delay in responding to the second move occurs because of the competition that arises in programming the first and second movements as rapidly as possible.

Psychological Refractory Period

An important question in human performance concerns how soon a person can switch from making a response to one stimulus to making a different response to another stimulus. If a

FOCUS ON Research 3.3

The Double-Stimulation Paradigm

Research on the **psychological refractory period (PRP)** uses what is called the *double-stimulation paradigm*, where the participant reacts to each of two stimuli with two separate responses. For example, the participant might be asked to respond to a tone (S_1, the first stimulus) by lifting the right hand from a reaction key as quickly as possible. A light (S_2, the second stimulus) might then appear after a very short time delay (called the **SOA,** or **stimulus-onset asynchrony**). The participant's task is to respond to the light by lifting the left hand from another key as quickly as possible. The SOA might range from zero to a few hundred milliseconds. The timelines shown in figure 3.5*a* (long SOA) and 3.5*b* (short SOA) might help to make this paradigm easier to understand.

Note that the important comparison is not the difference in reaction time (RT) between the two different stimuli (i.e., RT_2 vs. RT_1). Rather, of critical interest are the differences in the RT_2 under different SOAs. Figure 3.5*c*, which plots RT_2 versus lengthening SOAs, presents the findings from one study using this paradigm. The horizontal dashed line (control RT_2) is the value of RT_2 when the first stimulus is not presented at all; it represents the normal RT to this stimulus using this response when there is no competition from S_1. Responding to S_2 following a presentation of S_1 often results in an RT_2 that is much longer than the control RT_2, depending on the length of the SOA. When the SOA is about 50 ms, the response delay is very large and can more than double the value of RT_2 compared to its control value. As the SOA lengthens, the delay in RT_2 decreases, but there is still some delay in producing RT_2 until the SOA is more than 250 ms (see figure 3.5*c*). This delay is called the *psychological refractory period (PRP)*.

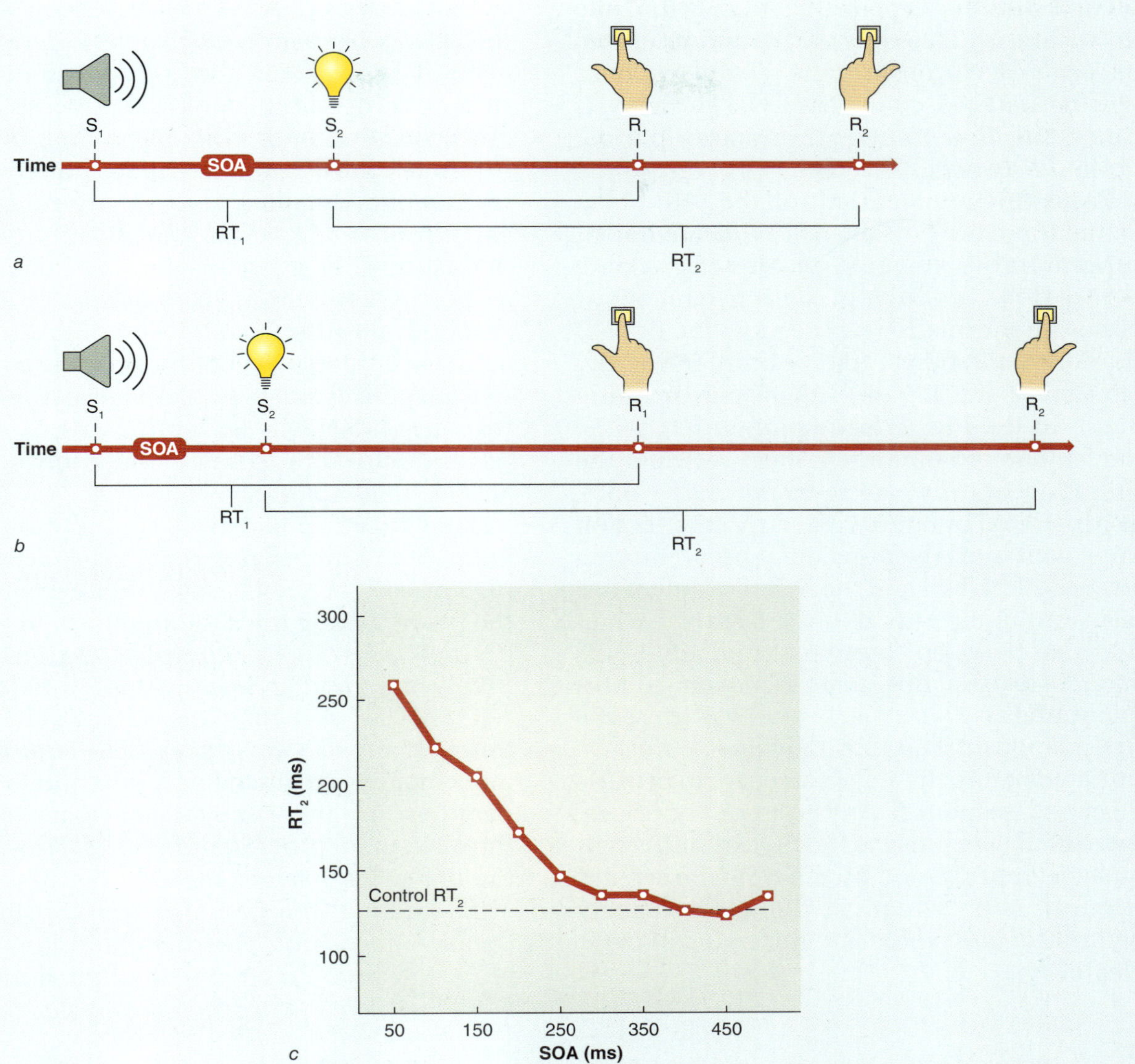

FIGURE 3.5 Illustration of critical events in the double-stimulation paradigm with a relatively *(a)* long SOA and *(b)* short SOA, with *(c)* results from an experiment by Davis (1959, cited in Schmidt et al., 2025), showing that RT_2 is lengthened greatly at the shortest SOAs.

The original single-channel hypothesis (Welford, 1952) argues that the processing of the first stimulus and response delays the processing of the second stimulus and response until the processing of the first stimulus and response has been completed. More recent thinking about data such as these holds that the major delay in RT_2 arises from interference between the movement programming stages of these actions, a bottleneck that is much later in the information-processing sequence than the original single channel hypothesized (Klapp et al., 2019).

Exploring Further

1. Why is the RT to the second of two closely spaced stimuli (RT_2) the most important result in this paradigm rather than the RT to the first stimulus (RT_1)?
2. How would the magnitude of the PRP effect be expected to change depending on the number of choices involved in responding to the first stimulus?

second stimulus is presented during the time the system is processing the first stimulus and its response, the onset of the second response will be delayed considerably. The delay is called the *psychological refractory period*, or the *PRP effect*.

A leading explanation for the PRP effect is that there is a bottleneck in the movement programming stage. A bottleneck occurs when flow is slowed, which can occur either intentionally (e.g., to slow the flow of liquid from a soda bottle) or unintentionally (as with a traffic jam, illustrated in figure 3.6*a*). In the PRP effect, competition at the movement programming stage restricts the initiation of only one movement at a time, as illustrated in figure 3.6*b*. Any other action must wait until the movement programming stage has finished and the first movement has been initiated. This delay is greatest when the time between the two stimuli (SOA) is short, because at this time the movement programming stage has just begun to process the first response. The first movement must be initiated before the stage can begin to process a second response. As the SOA increases, more of the response to the first stimulus will have been processed by the time the second stimulus is presented, so there is less delay before the movement programming stage is cleared.

One more finding is of interest here. When the SOA is very short—for example, less than 40 ms—the second stimulus is processed in a very different way. The two stimuli are processed as if they were one, which produces both responses simultaneously. In this phenomenon, termed *grouping*, the early processing stages presumably detect both stimuli as a single event and organize a coordinated action in which both limbs respond simultaneously. The coordinated action eliminates the bottleneck because the two responses are selected together as one response (Maslovat & Klapp, 2024). We will have much more to say about coordinated actions in chapter 7.

The PRP effect just discussed accounts for many of the underlying delays that occur in response to fakes. In basketball, for example, the player taking the shot might preprogram a single, relatively complex action that involves a move to begin a shot, a delay to withhold it, and then the actual shot—all done in rapid succession. The shooter's movement is organized as a unit and is prepared as any other movement would be in the movement programming stage. However, the defensive player sees only the first part of this action (the first stimulus [S_1] in the double-stimulation paradigm) and jumps to block the shot. Processing the first stimulus

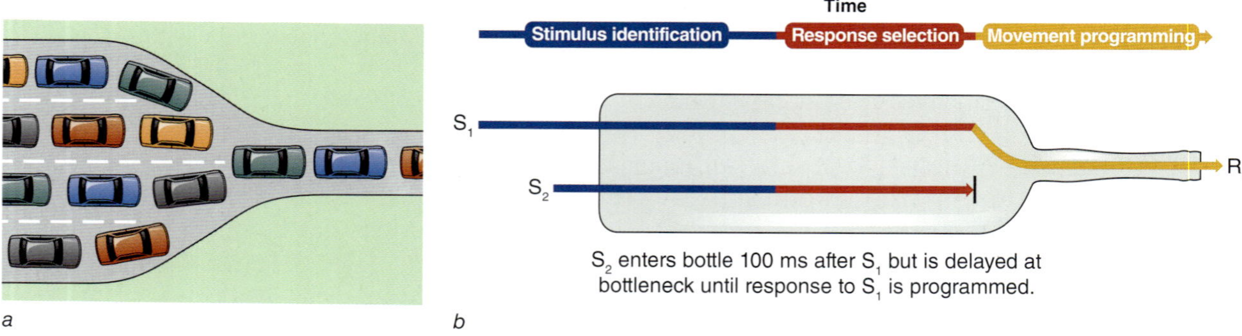

FIGURE 3.6 *(a)* The bottleneck analogy conveys the idea that the rate of flow from the bottle is restricted—in this case, specifically at the movement programming stage—similar to what happens when the flow of multiple lanes of traffic merges into a single lane. *(b)* An information-processing bottleneck in the movement programming stage occurs when two stimuli (S_1 and S_2) are presented closely together in time. The first stimulus enters the information-processing system initially, followed closely by the second stimulus. Processing of S_2 is delayed at the bottleneck until a response to S_1 has been programmed.

leads to large delays in responding to the new information that the shot was a fake (as indicated by the fact that the second stimulus, S_2, the actual shot, pass, or dribble, is now being made). The result is that the first response (movement to block) cannot be withheld, and it occurs essentially as originally planned. This creates a very large delay in initiating a second, corrective response to block the actual play, which is made at about the same time that the defensive player is dropping back to the floor after "taking the fake." However, the grouping effect also suggests that the offensive player needs to "sell" the fake by giving the defensive player enough time to begin to program a response, or the deception will be unsuccessful.

The Secondary-Task Methods

The secondary-task methods refer to different approaches to studying the attention demanded during the movement programming stage. Two versions commonly used in research have a similar goal: to understand the attentional demands of one task (the primary task) performed simultaneously with another task (the secondary task; Abernethy, 2001).

In one version (the **dual-task method**), the secondary task is executed for the duration of the primary task's performance. This method often uses a continuous primary task, such as performing a pursuit tracking task. The experimenter will pair performance of this task with different types of secondary tasks that vary in attentional demand. For example, adding 2s to a two-digit number is less demanding than subtracting 7s from a three-digit number. Performance of the primary task is likely to suffer more as the difficulty of (and hence, attention demanded by) the secondary task increases. Experiments of this type explain why a cell phone conversation while driving is more dangerous than performing other secondary tasks, for example.

A second version of the secondary-task method (the **probe-task method**) is typically designed to specifically assess attention at different times of the movement programming stage of a discrete task. In this method, the performer executes a primary task, and at some unexpected point, the researcher probes (or tests) the attention it demanded by suddenly presenting a tone or light (the probe stimulus). The participant's secondary task is to respond to the probe stimulus as rapidly as possible with either a manual response (e.g., a key press) or a vocal response (e.g., saying "stop"), and RT measures the delay in responding to the probe. With this strategy, the delay in RT to the probe provides a measure of the attention the primary task demanded; a more attention-demanding primary task would have slower RTs to the probe stimulus than a primary task that demanded less attention.

A study by Posner and Keele (1969) is a good example of how the probe technique is used in research. In their study, participants were asked to make a rapid, curvilinear movement with a lever toward a target (the primary task). Participants made these movements to either large or small targets—the idea being that smaller targets require more attentional capacity due to the increased precision requirements of aiming. The probe technique was used to assess attention demands at various points during the movement, including the start and end positions. Control trials were also conducted that assessed RT, in which no aiming movement was made.

Figure 3.7 presents the results of the Posner and Keele study. There are several things of interest here. First, the control-RT value (represented as the dashed line across the figure at a value of 260 ms) was considerably less than the probe RTs for any other data points in the graph. This was interpreted as indicating that aiming at both small and large targets required some attention throughout the movement, because RT in all conditions with a primary-task movement was elevated relative to the no-movement (control) condition. Second, the bowed nature of both the small-target and large-target curves in figure 3.7 suggests that attention demands were not evenly distributed throughout the movement. The elevated probe RTs at positions representing the beginning (0° position) and end (135° position) of the movement suggest that these were more attention-demanding parts than were the middle positions of the movement (i.e., the 15°, 45°, 75°, and 105° positions). Last, the probe RT for the small target was generally larger than for the large target, indicating that movements with greater precision requirements are more attention demanding than movements with less precise requirements.

Probe techniques are not without their limitations and problems, however. As we will see in chapter 7, producing two movements simultaneously (i.e., combining primary-task movement with secondary-task movement responses) introduces special coordination challenges to the processing system. If the movements are compatible (e.g., keeping a rhythmic beat with two hands, as in drumming), then two limbs can be coordinated in such a way that there is no detriment to performance (e.g., Helmuth & Ivry, 1996). A concern arises when two or more separate actions have distinct and incompatible spatial or temporal requirements. The problem with the probe technique is that responding manually to a probe can produce specific interference effects (over and above those associated with attention) with a manual primary task. McLeod (1980) found that much less competition occurred between a primary limb task and a vocal probe response, for example, and provided a less contaminated assessment of attention demand.

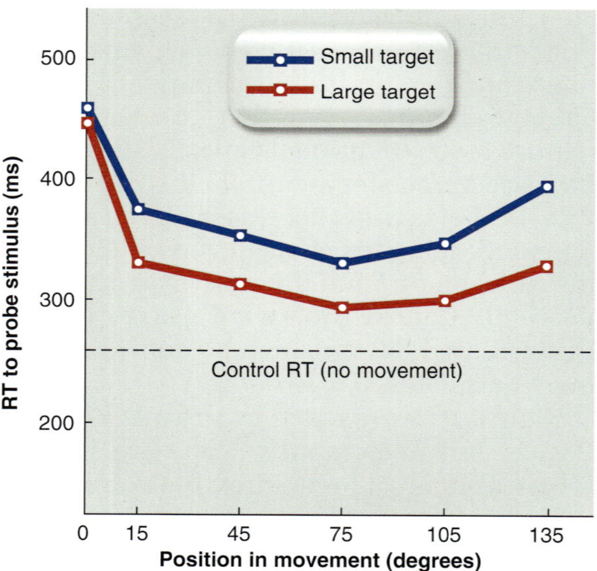

FIGURE 3.7 Assessing the attention demands at various points during the visually guided pointing movement to either a small or large target. Probe stimuli during movements to small targets revealed longer RTs than during movements to large targets. The straight dashed line denotes RTs for control trials to the probe stimulus when no pointing movement was made.

Attentional Focus During Action

A different approach to investigating the role of attention during movement concerns the object, or focus, to which attention is directed. Although the bulk of empirical research on the topic has been relatively recent, theorists speculated about it many years ago. Cattell (1893) wrote, "In piano playing, the beginner may attend to his fingers but the practiced player attends only to the notes or to the melody. In speaking, writing and reading aloud, and in games and manual work, attention is always directed to the goal, never to the movement. In fact, as soon as attention is directed to the movement, this becomes less automatic and less dependable." Later, Bernstein (published in Russian in the 1940s and translated into English in 1996) offered this advice: "The attention of a person who has learned to ride a bicycle should be fixed not on his legs or arms but on the road in front of the bicycle; the attention of a tennis player should be directed at the ball, the top edge of the net, the movements of the opponent,

Producing two or more movements simultaneously introduces a greater challenge if the tempos are incompatible, such as when a drummer plays a different beat with one hand than with the other hand or foot. Experienced drummers, such as the late Neil Peart of Rush, can do this skillfully.

but certainly not at his own legs or on the racket."

Cattell and Bernstein distinguish between the beneficial effect of focusing attention on something external to the body and the detrimental effect of focusing internally on the movement itself. Interestingly, these ideas about attentional focus have only been studied experimentally in the past few decades, beginning with the work of Gabriele Wulf and her colleagues. Moreover, the results of those studies mostly agreed with the introspections of Cattell and Bernstein. In almost all situations, an **external attentional focus** results in better performance than an **internal attentional focus**. These studies have revealed very impressive benefits to performance in a wide variety of laboratory and sport tasks for people of all ages (see Wulf, 2007, 2013; Chua et al., 2021 for reviews).

External Versus Internal Attentional Focus

Investigations typically address the issue of attentional focus by giving participants explicit instructions concerning how to direct their attention during movement execution. For example, instructions to focus internally could involve cues to think about the shape of the fingers when releasing a football, the tension in the arms when putting in golf, or the force exerted in the legs when performing an ice-skating jump. These instructions encourage an internal focus because the participant attends to how the body parts are moving, either by focusing on the commands used to produce the movement or the sensations arising from movement. In contrast, instructions to focus externally might direct the participant to think about the intended target of the football, where on the putter face the golf ball is being struck, or the projected elegance of an ice-skating jump. With an external focus, the instructions serve to direct the performer's attention to some intended end-product of the action or the influence of the action on the environment.

A running sprint-start experiment by Ille and colleagues (2013) is a good example of the effects of internal versus external attentional focus instructions. On separate days of study, the participants were instructed to think about the motions of the arms and legs during the sprint start (internal instructions) or were told simply to get across the finish line as quickly as possible (external instructions). Even this seemingly minor difference in instructions had a large impact on performance. The external-focus instructions resulted in RTs that were about 9% faster and MTs that were about 3% faster than under internal-focus instructions—percentages that seem small but are potentially quite impactful in a sprint race.

Sherwood and colleagues (2014) used a different method to influence attentional focus in a dart-throwing task. Rather than varying instructions, Sherwood and colleagues asked their participants to make a performance assessment after each throw, with the specific nature of the assessment designed to induce either an internal or external attentional focus on subsequent throws. Reflective, postthrow judgments about elbow position were considered to encourage the performer to think internally on subsequent throws; judgments about the final position of the dart relative to the target encouraged an external focus. Two experiments were conducted: one that used inexperienced dart throwers and another that gave the throwers three days of dart practice before the experiment was conducted. The results for radial error (see chapter 1) in both experiments were comparable to the Ille and colleagues (2013) study—external-focus throws were more accurate than internal-focus throws (see figure 3.8).

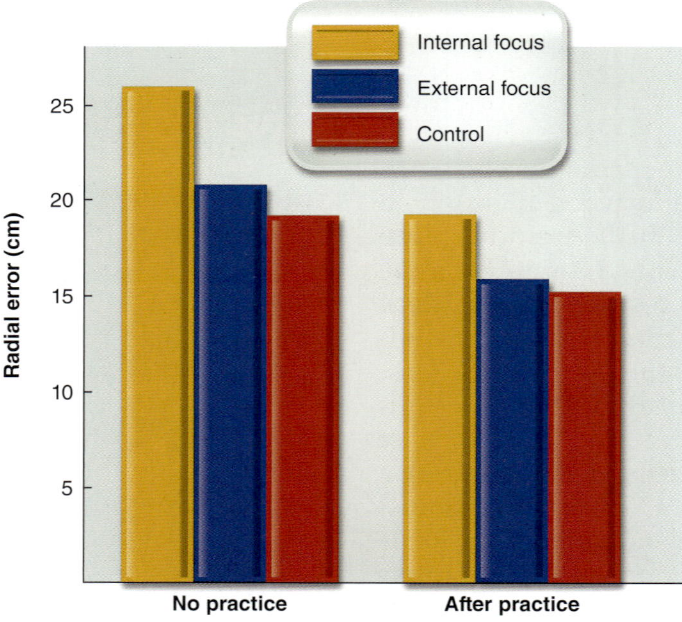

FIGURE 3.8 Regardless of whether dart throwers were inexperienced (left side) or after they had three days of practice (right side), an internal attentional focus was detrimental to throwing accuracy compared to external focus and control conditions.

The Sherwood and colleagues (2014) study also contained a very important third (control) condition, in which there were no postmovement assessments. Dart throws in this control condition were as accurate as the throws in the external condition. This finding is important because it suggests that the critical impact of attentional focus was not necessarily the positive benefit induced by the external focus but the negative effect of an internal focus.

A leading explanation of attentional focus effects on performance was termed the **constrained action hypothesis** by Wulf and colleagues (2001). They theorized that an internal attentional focus produces conscious, moment-to-moment movement control, which is typical of movement control used by inexperienced or less skilled performers. An external attentional focus, on the other hand, results in more free-flowing, automated movement control, which is more characteristic of skilled performers. Hence, the performance differences observed under internal and external-focus conditions are consistent with the differences expected when performed by less skilled versus more skilled performers.

Herrebrøden (2023) proposed an alternative explanation for the attentional focus effect that centers on the information cues promoted by internal and external instructions. According to this view, external instructions focus the performer's attention on information that is more relevant and predictive for successful skill performance than the information cued by internal-focus instructions. For many tasks (especially aiming tasks), the most relevant, or reliable, information for successful performance is usually contained in the environment, not within the body. But that is not true for all tasks. For example, a study on ergonomic rowing performance in novices by Neumann and colleagues (2020) found that instructions to focus on internal feedback (e.g., exerting force through the arms and legs) produced better power and distance performance than focusing externally on features of the ergometer (e.g., moving the handle or the seat). In ergometer rowing, the more relevant cues for successful performers might be found internally rather than externally. Exceptions to the research that have revealed an internal-focus advantage suggest that not all tasks benefit from cues that support externally available information.

At a more conceptual level, the existence of more nuanced research findings and explanations in the attentional focus literature is evidence of an exciting field of study that will generate further research that is both theory-driven and relevant for instructors and coaches. Like all research fields, new findings will tip the balance of evidence in favor of one view or another, or perhaps a completely new explanation (see chapter 12 for more on the value of theory-driven research).

Visit HK*Propel* to read "The Toad and the Centipede" and complete the self-directed learning activities. 

Choking

One of the most dramatic occasions in high-profile sporting events occurs when an individual, seemingly on the way to certain victory, does the unimaginable and loses. Famous examples of **choking** under pressure in sports include Boston Red Sox first-baseman Bill Buckner's error on a routine ground ball at a critical point in the World Series and collapses by Rory McIlroy (in 2011) and Jordan Spieth (in 2016) on the final nine holes of the Masters golf tournament. Everyone can probably recall events like this, and there appear to be no shortage of examples in every sport.

What is a choke, why does it occur, and how can it be avoided? By most accounts, choking is more than simply a failed performance in an important situation. Researchers such as Beilock (2010) suggest that choking often occurs when there is a change in one's attentional focus. Consistent with both explanations of attentional focus discussed previously, as the pressure builds to perform well in a critical situation, athletes who choke often shift their perspective. Consistent with a constrained action view, they may shift from performing in an overlearned, automatic type of movement control to thinking about how to perform the movement or how the movement will feel when it is performed. Consistent with an information view, the shift might be from using an optimal to a suboptimal environmental cue. Viewed in this way, choking is considered to result from a change in attentional focus to one that is less desirable for the task at hand. Moreover, the heightened anxiety that accompanies poor performance can lead to further internalized focus and a dismal, downward spiral toward failure.

Visit HK*Propel* to read "Choking Under Pressure" and complete the self-directed learning activities.

Ironic Effects

An anecdotal belief among many athletes is that trying *not* to do something will often result in doing that very thing, revealing a specific type of choking. For example, golfers who see a large lake to the right of the fairway might say to themselves, "Don't hit it to the right," and more often than not, do just that. Pitchers who try to not walk a batter seem more likely to do so compared to simply trying to throw strikes. And football linemen who tell themselves "don't jump offside" seem to be prone to doing just that (Janelle, 1999).

Wegner (1994), based on a number of findings about counterintentional errors, termed this tendency to do something you are trying not to do the **ironic effect**. Wegner found, for example, that holding a pendulum in an outstretched arm and trying not to let it sway in the *y*-dimension resulted in more *y*-dimensional sway than under various other instructions. Although other nonmotor ironic effects are known to exist (e.g., "try not thinking about a fuzzy, white puppy"), the influence of negative thoughts on motor control is largely considered the result of an inappropriate attentional focus.

Decision-Making Under Stress

Arousal, the level of excitement produced under stress, is common in skill performance situations. This is certainly true of many athletic events, where the pressure to win and the threat of losing, as well as crowd influences, are important sources of emotional arousal for players. The level of arousal is an important determinant of performance, particularly if the performance depends on the speed and accuracy of decision-making.

Inverted-U Principle

One can think of arousal as the level of excitement, or activation, generated in the central nervous system. For example, low levels of arousal are associated with sleeplike states, and high levels are associated with agitated and extremely alert states, such as those found in life-threatening situations. The influences of arousal level on performance have been studied for many years. The **inverted-U principle**, sometimes called the Yerkes-Dodson Law (1908), represents an early view of the relationship between arousal and performance. The basic idea is that increasing the arousal level generally enhances performance but only to a point. Performance quality peaks at some intermediate value of arousal and begins to deteriorate as the arousal level rises further—hence the inverted-U function (see figure 3.9). A disastrous result often occurs when one reaches the highest levels of arousal, such as described in Focus on Application 3.2.

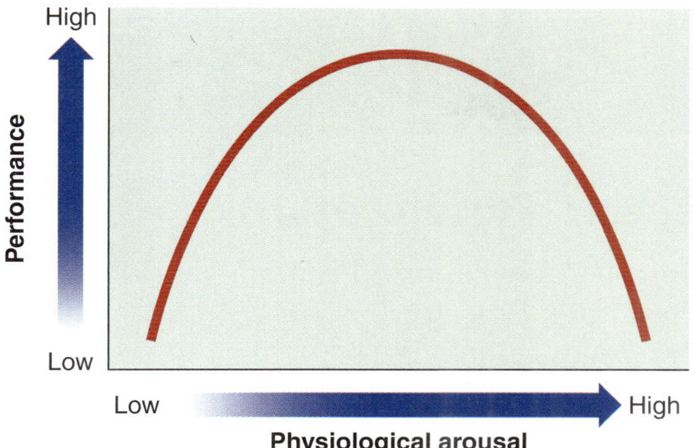

FIGURE 3.9 Illustration of the inverted-U principle. Increases in arousal are expected to improve performance, but only to a point, after which further increases decrease performance.

Variations of the Inverted-U Principle

Over the years, the general shape of the inverted U has been an acceptable heuristic for thinking about the relationship between arousal and performance. However, it is probably best not to put too much faith in the symmetrical shape of this U function. As shown in figure 3.10, task differences, as well as individual differences in the participant's natural excitability, can result in changes to the shapes of the curve, with optimal performance occurring at either the lower or higher ends of the arousal continuum.

Consider the three hypothetical curves illustrated in figure 3.10. The red curve labeled A shows a steep rise in performance at relatively low levels of arousal, with performance peaking and then beginning to decline even before a moderate level of arousal. Such a curve might represent the shape of the arousal–performance function for a particularly complex task, perhaps requiring fine motor control (threading a needle) or cognition (playing chess), or for an individual who functions best under calm conditions. In contrast, the yellow curve labeled C could represent the arousal–performance function for a very simple task, perhaps requiring great amounts of force with very little cognition (e.g., powerlifting) or for a person who thrives under pressure. The point here is that a symmetrical inverted U (the blue curve labeled B in figure 3.10) might best represent tasks that have medium levels of complexity, cognitive involvement, and so on. These principles have been recognized and studied in the fields of sports and exercise psychology, where the general

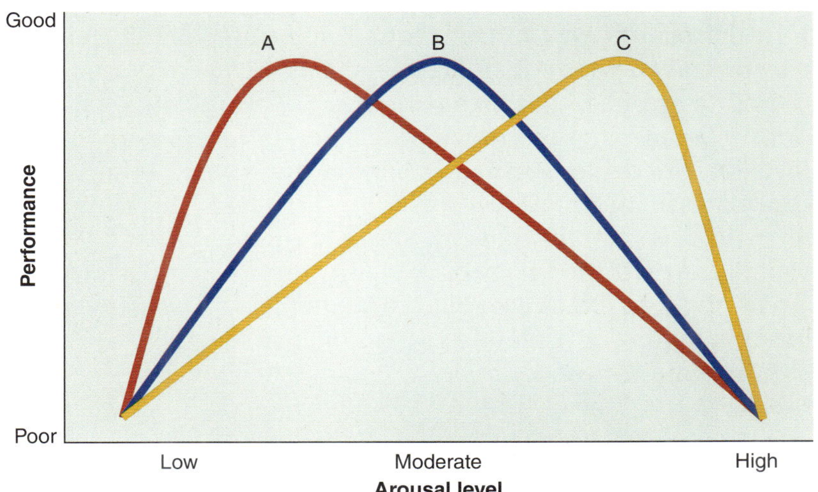

FIGURE 3.10 Variations to the inverted-U principle.

FOCUS ON Application 3.2

Driver Panic and Unintended Acceleration

It was a fairly normal morning—the 35-year-old teacher reported that she had just dropped her son at day care before heading to school. She stopped for coffee at the local drive-through and moved the transmission lever from Drive to Neutral in order to reach for her purse. After putting her coffee in the cup holder, she intended to put her foot on the brake while she changed the transmission from Neutral back to Drive. Suddenly, the car lurched forward and gathered speed. Pressing harder on the brake pedal seemed only to make the car go faster. Thinking that the brakes had failed, the teacher pressed harder still, and this time, the pedal went all the way to the floor. The car sailed across the parking lot, wildly out of control, with the driver in a complete panic state, before crashing into a parked vehicle on the other side of the street. The airbags engaged, and fortunately, nobody was seriously hurt. It was only then, as the motor continued to race with the wheels still squealing, that the woman realized her mistake—she had pressed the accelerator instead of the brake.

This story illustrates a number of important issues about motor control that we will return to later in the book: how we guide movements in the absence of visual feedback; how movement selection errors can occur without our detection; how and when we make error corrections; and last, and most important for our present discussion, the fact that normal modes of information processing can cease to operate when we are in a heightened state of panic, sometimes called **hypervigilance**.

As you reflect on this story, there are a number of easy solutions to the situation that come to mind. Turning off the ignition, moving the transmission into Neutral, and removing the foot from the pedal would have all solved the problem. But in these cases of **unintended acceleration** (also called *pedal misapplication errors*), a phenomenon that occurs far too commonly, none of these corrective actions are typically taken (Schmidt, 1989). Instead, it is usually some external agent, such as a tree, wall, or another vehicle, that brings the car to a halt.

Hypervigilance occurs at the very highest levels of arousal. In cases of unintended acceleration, the driver seems to freeze at the wheel, in terms of both normal movement control and information-processing activities. In a hypervigilant state, decision-making is severely limited, resulting in an inability to produce creative actions (e.g., switching off the ignition key) and ineffective performance generally. Fortunately, hypervigilant states are relatively rare. But when they do occur, the fate of the individual is almost completely turned over to the fight-or-flight functioning of a panicked information-processing system.

problem has been to understand the effects of stress and arousal on performance and to examine how mood-regulating procedures can manage arousal levels before performance (e.g., Weinberg & Gould, 2024).

Visit HK*Propel* to read "The Farmers' Market" and complete the self-directed learning activities.

Summary

A good way to think about attention is to imagine a pool of resources such that, if the information-processing activities from a given task exceed the resources available, performance of this task and perhaps a second task attempted at that same time will suffer. Under a limited set of circumstances, processing can be done in parallel—that is, performance on two tasks can be done together without the negative effects of competition for attention. In common party circumstances, we can ignore the conversations around us, focusing on a conversation with a given person until, for example, your name is spoken in a nearby conversation. Other findings tend to agree; information about the font color of a word and the meaning of the word appear to be processed in parallel, but there is considerable competition when selecting an action (the Stroop test). People can become blind to certain stimuli if attention is directed strongly elsewhere, for example, by failing to perceive the gorilla in plain sight when attention is directed to another target. This type of blindness appears to be related to a class of motor vehicle crashes in which the driver looked but failed to see an oncoming vehicle. On the other hand, many highly practiced tasks tend to be performed without very much attention; this is difficult to achieve without extensive practice under the proper conditions. While we might appear to be able to drive a car without any attention, studies of drivers attempting to drive and text or talk on a cell phone show that this is a dangerous combination. The biggest attentional limitation of all appears to be in the movement programming stage. The psychological refractory period (PRP) provides good evidence. The overall viewpoint appears to be that, while we may be able, under certain circumstances, to respond without attention in the stimulus identification and response selection stages, only one action can be programmed at a time during the movement programming stage.

Attentional focus on an external event results in generally better performance than internally focused attention. And changing attentional focus sometimes results in dramatic performance changes, such as choking. Shifts in attention are also associated with changes in an individual's levels of arousal, resulting in dramatic effects on performance.

HK*PROPEL* ACTIVITIES

HK*Propel* offers these activities to help you build and apply your knowledge of the concepts in this chapter. Additionally, you'll find a key terms flashcard review activity and a key terms quiz, along with audio supplements for selected figures, as indicated by QR codes throughout the chapter.

Interactive Learning

Activity 3.1: Review the concepts associated with limitations in attention by matching related terms to their definitions.

Activity 3.2: Indicate whether each in a list of characteristics applies to controlled processing or automatic processing.

Activity 3.3: Using a figure from the text, explore how the inverted-U relationship between arousal and performance varies by situation and person.

Activity 3.4: Indicate whether each instruction applies to external focus of attention or internal focus of attention.

Activity 3.5: Listen to a discussion about focus of attention and the sport of golf, then consider instructions that would encourage an external focus of attention for a different sport of your choice.

Principles-to-Application Exercise

Activity 3.6: The principles-to-application exercise for this chapter prompts you to choose an activity and analyze the attentional demands of three performance situations within that activity. You will also indicate whether the demand for attention relates primarily to stimulus identification, response programming, or movement programming, and examine how stress might affect decision-making during this activity.

Motor Control in Everyday Actions Narratives

Gumbo

Turn Right at the Next Gorilla

Fakes

The Toad and the Centipede

Choking Under Pressure

The Farmers' Market

Check Your Understanding

1. Both parallel and serial processing can occur during the stimulus identification stage of information processing. Provide examples of the types of information that a rock climber might process in parallel and in serial when deciding which move to make next.
2. Explain how a fake in wheelchair basketball illustrates a strong competition between activities in the movement programming stage of information processing.
3. Regarding attention, explain why a lifeguard at a crowded pool may find it more difficult to perform his job as he nears the end of his shift. What factors influence his ability to sustain attention? Suggest two policies that a pool could put in place to make sustained attention easier for lifeguards.

Apply Your Knowledge

1. The way novices and experts process information during the response selection stage of information processing can be very different. Describe the differing types of processing, highlighting the key features of each. How is task interference related to

each type of processing? How might a person performing a waltz perform differently as a novice and as an expert?

2. When mountain biking, some cyclists who have no trouble riding along a straight trail have difficulty performing the identical task (riding in a straight line) on a bridge that is the same width (or wider) than the trail, resulting in a less smooth performance or even a fall. What role might attentional focus play in this phenomenon? How could the inverted-U principle be used to help explain why a bridge over a ravine may make the task of riding in a straight line more difficult?

4

Sensory Contributions to Skilled Performance

Feedback Processing in Motor Control

CHAPTER OUTLINE

CHAPTER OBJECTIVES

Chapter 4 describes the roles of sensory feedback in human motor control. This chapter will help you understand

- the types of sensory information important for movement,
- motor control as a closed-loop processing system,
- the role of feedback and feedforward information in the conceptual model, and
- the roles of vision and audition in motor control.

CHAPTER PREVIEW QUIZ

1. What is a closed-loop system in motor performance?
2. How much time is needed to process visual feedback to aid performance?
3. What is sonification and how is it used as feedback?

Success in skilled performance often depends on how effectively the performer detects, perceives, and uses relevant information derived from the senses. A surgeon uses skilled touch (haptic) perception to detect an abnormal growth during a physical exam of a patient. A figure skater will decide whether to try a double- or a triple-salchow depending on the evaluation of body position in the early stages of the jump. Processing sensory information to detect and correct errors during performance is a skill that, if refined, can lead to large improvements.

Sources of Sensory Information

Information that is used for skilled performance can be categorized into two major types: **Exteroception** refers to information about the state of the environment in which one's body moves, and **proprioception** is information about the state of the body itself. In general, the term **feedback** refers to information that is "fed back" to the performer. In this chapter, we will focus on information that occurs when the body moves through the environment. For example, when we move from one place to another, information is available from the contracting muscles, the balance receptors, and what we see and hear while moving.

Inherent (or intrinsic) feedback sources provide both exteroception and proprioception. Inherent feedback refers to information that is naturally available in the environment and fed back by the senses. A major distinction is made later in the book when we discuss augmented feedback—information that is provided by an external source, not normally available to the performer from the inherent sources. An example is an instructor who provides a critical assessment of a learner's performance after executing a skill, or perhaps simply a video of that performance. The augmented feedback (verbal, visual, etc.) is not what the performer would "naturally" have available and represents information that has been added (or augmented) to the learner's inherent feedback for further processing.

Exteroception

The most prominent exteroceptive information source, of course, is vision. Seeing serves the important function of providing information about the physical structure of the environment, such as the edge of a stairway or an object blocking one's path. Vision also provides information about the movement of objects in the environment in relation to your own movements—such as the flight path of a ball—which can be used to make predictive judgments while you are running to catch it. Another function of vision is to detect and predict your own movement within the environment, such as your path toward an external object and how much time will elapse before you arrive.

The second major kind of exteroceptive information comes from hearing, or audition. Although audition is not generally as important in motor skills as vision, there are many activities that depend heavily on well-developed auditory skills; obvious examples are the sounds of a musical instrument as it is played and the role of hearing in speech production. Audition is important for many other skills too, such as using the sounds of a sailboat's hull moving through the water as cues to boat speed, the sound of a power tool as a skilled carpenter cuts through different materials, or the sounds of an engine as an auto mechanic makes adjustments.

Proprioception

The second major type of information arises from body movements, usually termed *proprioception*. This term refers to sensing information about the state of the body parts in relation to each other and to the environment. Several important receptors provide this information.

The **vestibular apparatus** in the inner ear provides information about head movements and body orientation in the environment (e.g., when you are upside down). The vestibular

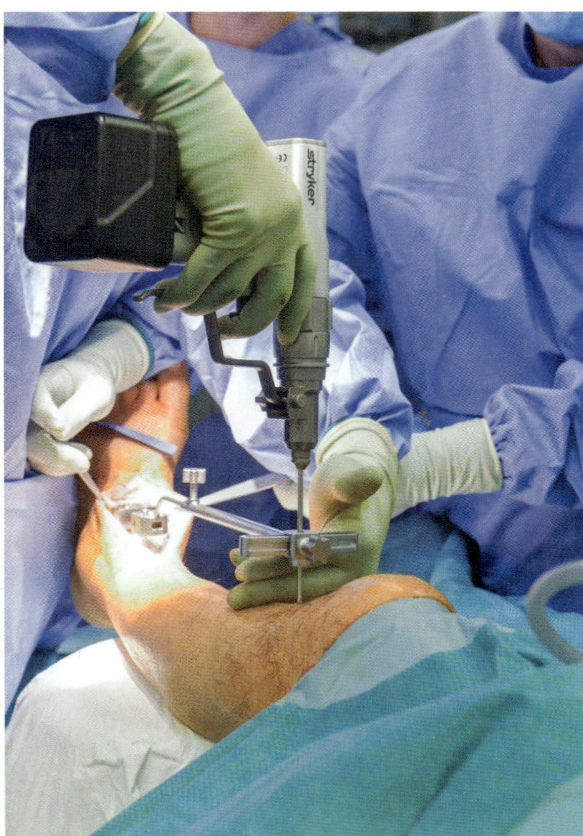

In each of these photos, identify the types of sensory information likely used by the performers.

apparatus consists of three structures (the saccule, utricle, and semicircular canals), which are positioned to detect the head's orientation with respect to gravity. Not surprisingly, these structures are critical in posture and balance control.

Several other structures provide information about what the limbs are doing. Receptors in the capsule surrounding each of the joints, called the **joint receptors**, give information about extreme positions of the joints. Embedded within the belly of the skeletal muscle are **muscle spindles**, oriented in parallel with the muscle fibers. Muscle spindle lengths change when muscle lengths change, providing information about joint position and the state of the muscle (e.g., stretch information). Near the junction between the skeletal muscle and its tendon lie the **Golgi tendon organs**, which are sensitive to muscle tension in the attached muscle. Finally, most skin areas have **cutaneous receptors**, including several kinds of specialized detectors of pressure, temperature, and pain. The cutaneous receptors are critical for the haptic sense, the sense of touch.

None of these proprioceptors respond to just one physical characteristic, however. The signal from a particular source, such as the muscle spindles, provides ambiguous information about joint position because several other physical stimuli (movement velocity, muscle tension, and the orientation with respect to gravity) can simultaneously affect the receptor. For this and other reasons, the central nervous system is thought to use a complex combination of the inputs from these various receptors as a basis for body awareness.

Alterations in proprioception can be used positively, as when human factors engineers exploit these alterations in designing equipment. Experienced typists prefer keyboards that have some haptic and auditory feedback, providing the satisfying auditory click and slight movement of the key, indicating that the key has been fully pressed (Asundi & Odell, 2011). Supplying aircraft instrument knobs of different shapes and locations for specific functions reduces confusion by associating distinct proprioceptive sensations with each knob. A similar strategy can be seen in the brew pub photo in this section.

Multisensory information produces redundancies that provide assistance during performance. For example, automobiles are equipped with sensors that provide visual and auditory feedback about the location of objects in a driver's blind spot, as well as auditory and haptic feedback for lane departures and other safety measures. Multisensory redundancies increase the likelihood that at least one of these inputs will trigger a rapid and accurate response.

However, more information is not always better information because multiple inputs can also lead to performance failures. Gray (2008) describes situations in which visual, proprioceptive, and vestibular information conflict to confuse airplane pilots about the spatial orientation of the plane's heading. Conflicts such as the size–weight illusion and the McGurk effect are just two examples of illusions that can lead to perception errors (see Focus on Application 4.1).

Visit HK*Propel* to read "The Magnetic Hill" and complete the self-directed learning activities.

There are many different sources of sensory information for motor control, varying not only in terms of where the information is detected but also in terms of how it is processed and used. We reduce the complexity of this discussion in the next sections by considering this variety of sensations as a single group, focusing on the common ways the central nervous system processes sensory information for skilled performance.

A brew pub uses draft tap handles that differ in shape, size, color, and proprietary design. These different designs encourage rapid decision-making while reducing errors.

FOCUS ON Application 4.1

When Vision Distorts Performance

In chapter 3, we discussed the various properties of attention. Directing one's attention toward a specific external source is considered an important mechanism, and vision can provide information critical for effective performance. However, performers often find that visual control dominates the other senses and that visual information leads to an unavoidable capture of attention. In fact, many believe that vision tends to dominate all other sources for our attention, and this dominance does not always produce positive outcomes. In many activities, performers have a choice of the modes of control they use, such as the race car driver or pilot who can monitor the sounds of the engine or kinesthetic information as opposed to the visual information provided by numerous cockpit gauges. And sometimes this nonvisual information is more reliable than the information provided by vision.

Visual information is obviously very important in many situations, but in others, an overreliance on vision can result in ineffective performance. A good example comes from sailboat racing, which is rich in visual information about the aerodynamic shapes of the sails and the way the wind flows over them. This visual information can yield relatively good performance. However, focusing on vision means ignoring other forms of information, such as the sounds the boat makes as it goes through the water, the action and position of the hull felt by the "seat of the pants," and forces on the tiller, which provide additional useful information about speed—but only if the person at the helm is attending to them. Some racing sailors have used blindfolded training methods to learn to decrease their reliance on vision and share attentional resources among other internal targets (senses) to optimize performance. The idea is that by preventing vision for a long time, the sailors will develop sensitivity to the less dominant sources of information.

Visual illusions provide a powerful demonstration of visual dominance effects. In the size–weight illusion, for example, two opaque containers, one much larger than the other, are filled with equal amounts of sand so that they are of identical weight. The participant is asked to lift both and judge which one is heavier. Vision (and experience) tells us that a larger container is usually heavier than a smaller one, and when proprioception fails to confirm that, we naturally come to the opposite conclusion—that the smaller container must have more weight in it than the larger container. Here, visual information is overriding proprioceptive judgments.

The McGurk effect reveals a vision–audition interaction. For example, a participant is asked to watch and listen to a video of someone speaking a word (e.g., *blow*). If you close your eyes and listen to the audio portion of the video, it is obvious that the person is saying *blow*. But the video actually shows someone mouthing the word *flow*, despite *blow* being heard on the audio. Most people who simultaneously watch the video and listen to the audio track report that the person is saying *flow*, even though what is actually heard is *blow*. Sometimes people even report something completely different from either *flow* or *blow*. Here, vision is distorting the (true) information provided by audition.

Auditory information can also conflict with vision, creating a distorted perception in sports. For example, a softball outfielder might be fooled into predicting that a line drive seen leaving a batter's bat will go over her head. In fact, the sound of the bat–ball contact correctly indicated that it was a softly hit ball, requiring the outfielder to run forward rather than back. Here, the visual information distorted the correct information provided by sound (see Gray, 2009, for more).

Processing Sensory Information

One important way to think about how sensory information is processed during movement is by analogy to closed-loop control systems, a class of mechanisms used in many applications in everyday life. Figure 4.1 provides an example of a simple closed-loop system.

Closed-Loop Control Systems

The simple **closed-loop control system** illustrated in figure 4.1 can be started in several ways. One common way occurs when you input a desired state or system goal, such as the desired indoor room temperature in the winter. Sensory information about the system's actual state (the room's actual temperature) is measured by a thermometer and is compared to the expected state (the desired temperature). Any difference between the expected and actual temperature represents an error (e.g., the temperature is too low); this error signal is transmitted to an executive that decides what action to take to eliminate or reduce the error. The executive then sends a command to an effector to carry out the action (in this case, turning on the furnace). This action raises the room temperature until the actual state equals the expected state (where the error in temperature is now zero). This updated information is sent to the executive, and the executive sends a new instruction to switch off the furnace. This process continues indefinitely, maintaining the temperature near the desired value throughout the day. This kind of system is termed *closed-loop* because the loop from the executive to the effector and back to the executive again is completely closed by sensory information, or feedback.

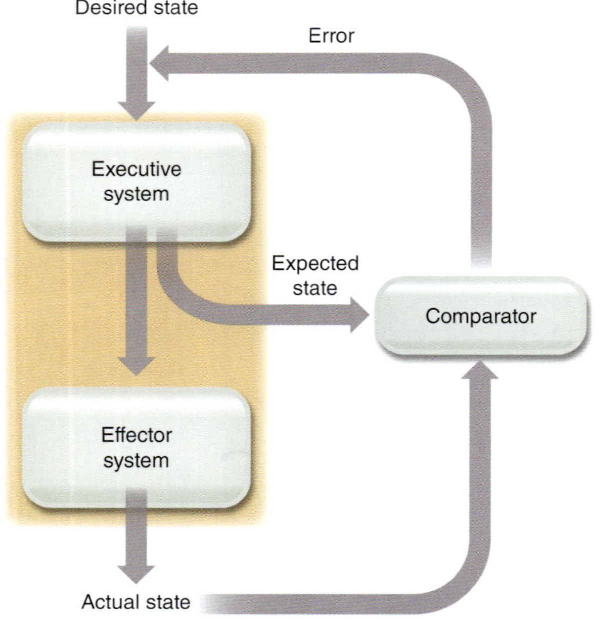

FIGURE 4.1 A basic closed-loop control system.

Analogous closed-loop processes operate in some motor skills, such as reaching to pick up a cup (the desired state). Visual information about the hand's position relative to the cup represents the movement error, which serves as feedback. An executive determines a correction that modifies the effector system to bring the hand into the proper location, reducing or eliminating the error. Of course, in most skills, feedback consists of a collection of different kinds of sensory information arising from a variety of receptors both within and outside the body (proprioceptors and exteroceptors).

All closed-loop control systems have four distinct parts:

1. An executive system for making decisions about errors
2. An effector system for carrying out the decisions
3. A referent that compares the actual state to the expected state to detect errors
4. An error signal, which is the information fed back to the executive

Visit HK*Propel* to read "The Curling Draw" and complete the self-directed learning activities.

Closed-Loop Control in the Conceptual Model

These closed-loop processes fit within the expanded conceptual model for movement control, as shown in figure 4.2. This is an expansion of the conceptual model of human performance presented in chapter 2, which introduced the stages of information processing (see figure 2.3). However, the features of closed-loop control seen in figure 4.1 have now been added to achieve a more complete model of human motor performance.

This conceptual model is useful for understanding the processes involved in both slow

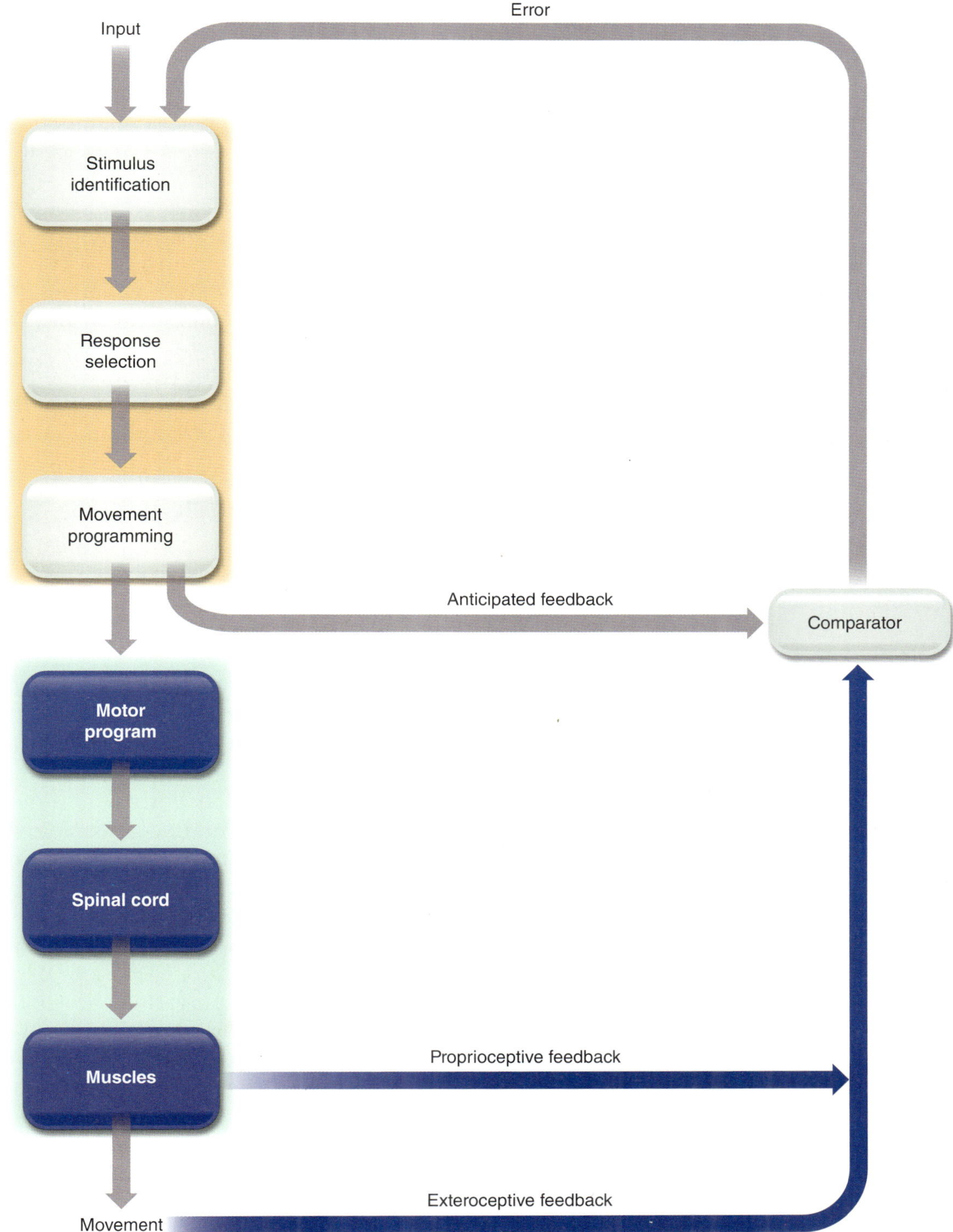

FIGURE 4.2 Expanded conceptual model with the addition of closed-loop components.

and very fast movements. In relatively slow movements (e.g., painting), error corrections can be made during the action. However, in very fast movements (e.g., swinging an axe), sometimes an error cannot be corrected because the movement is completed in less time than it takes to use the feedback to make the correction.

The executive system consists of the decision-making processes discussed in chapter 2—the stimulus identification, response selection, and movement programming stages. The output from the executive is a set of commands sent to an effector system consisting of several parts. One is the motor program, which produces commands for lower centers in the spinal cord that finally result in the contraction of muscles and the movement of joints.

Feedforward Information

At the same time as output commands are sent to the effector system, information is sent to the **comparator** that defines the sensory qualities of a correct movement, such as the feel of an effective golf swing. This information represents the expected sensory feedback—that is, the sensations that would be generated if the movement were performed correctly.

In the heating analogy, when the thermostat is set to 70°, incoming feedback from the room's air temperature (the actual feedback) is compared to the anticipated feedback (70°), and an error is computed, which is then delivered to the executive. The information specifying that the thermostat should be anticipating a temperature of 70° is often termed **feedforward** information. The term *feedforward* is used to distinguish it from *feedback*, which refers to the sensory information resulting from the action itself. Feedforward information represents the expected sensory consequences of the movement that should be received if the movement is correct.

Feedforward information serves important roles in skilled human performance. One of the most important is to help us understand sensory information that might otherwise be confusing. For example, gently but rapidly nudge your eyeball in different directions for a few seconds. The visual world will seem to jump around, as in a blurred video. However, if you intentionally make very rapid jumps of eye fixations from one scene to another (called *saccades*), the result will be an unblurred exploration of your visual space. The difference in blurring is due to the feedforward information: The signals that result in voluntary eye movements also send expected consequences that serve to dampen or cancel the actual feedback that would otherwise result in blurred vision.

The dampening (or canceling) of feedback by feedforward information also explains why we can't tickle ourselves or why a minor dispute between two siblings often gets out of hand (see Focus on Application 4.2). It also helps us understand why a noise seems louder if it is unexpected (Reznik et al., 2015). For example, a slammed door seems less noisy if we do it than if someone else does it unexpectedly.

Feedback Information

The output of the system (movement) results in proprioceptive and exteroceptive feedback information, collectively termed *movement-produced feedback*. When muscles contract, the processing system receives feedback about the forces produced as well as the pressures exerted on objects in contact with the skin. Contracting muscles cause movement and, therefore, feedback from moving joints and changes in body position with respect to gravity. Finally, movements usually produce alterations in the environment, which are sensed by the receptors for vision and audition, generating yet more feedback. These movement-produced stimuli, whose nature depends on the production of a particular action by the performer, are analyzed against their anticipated states in the comparator. The computed difference represents error, which is the information returned to the executive. This process refines and maintains the performer's behavior with the purpose of holding errors at acceptably low levels.

Notice that the stages of processing are critically important in the closed-loop model in figure 4.2. Every time an action's feedback

FOCUS ON Application 4.2

Force Escalation Between Siblings

How often have you seen (or done) this? One sibling pokes the other. The other pokes back. The first pokes again, and then the other pokes back. Soon the light poke becomes a jab, then a shove, and usually a parent steps in before things escalate too far. The first words are almost always the same: "she started it." But for the student of motor control, the more interesting questions are why and how the escalation occurred, perhaps even though neither sibling really intended it to escalate.

The most reasonable explanation appears to be related to the part of the conceptual model that goes from movement programming to the comparator, labeled *anticipated feedback* (figure 4.2). The anticipated feedback refers to the sensory consequences expected to arise from movement—the feedforward information. One important feature of feedforward information is that it has a dampening effect on the actual feedback signals received, reducing the intensity of the actual feedback experienced. In fact, sometimes the anticipated feedback can actually cancel out the impact of the actual sensory signals altogether, such as when you try to tickle yourself.

A clever study by Shergill and colleagues (2003) showed this force-escalation effect quite clearly. They used a force-reproduction task between pairs of participants, in which each member of the pair simply tried to replicate the force that they had received from the other participant by pressing on a force transducer. The results were dramatic—the force produced by each participant escalated by about 38% on each turn. The explanation for the escalation was that because the actual feedback from each self-generated press was dampened (or attenuated) by the anticipated signal, a higher force would need to be generated in order for it to feel like the one just received from the other person. The back-and-forth increase in force production was not an attempt to injure or "one up" the other. It was simply a means to overcome the attenuation of the actual proprioceptive feedback caused by the anticipated feedback to produce a force that matched the one received.

Attenuation of actual feedback sensations often leads to an escalation of force production.

goes to the executive for correction, it must go through the stages of processing. The various stages of processing are all subject to the mechanisms of attention, as discussed in chapter 3. There are exceptions, however, and we discuss various lower-level, reflex-like loops later in the chapter.

The closed-loop model in figure 4.2 is useful for understanding the maintenance of a particular state because it is necessary to perform many long-duration activities. For example, simply maintaining posture, where the goal is a natural, upright position, requires feedback. Various learned postures might be controlled in the same way, such as positioning the body in a handstand on the still rings in gymnastics. Many skills involving actions of the upper limbs require an accurate, stable posture as a platform. Without this stable base, such as in throwing darts or shooting a pistol, the movement would be inconsistent. The comparator is thought to define and maintain the desired relative positions of the various limbs as well as the general orientation in space.

Other tasks, in which continuous closed-loop control is critical, are far more dynamic. For instance, in a continuous tracking skill, a performer must follow a constantly varying track by manipulating a control. Steering a car is a classic example, where movements of the steering wheel result from visually detected errors in the car's position on the road. There are countless other examples because this class of activity is one of the most frequently represented in real-world functioning.

Without a doubt, closed-loop control models such as those shown in figure 4.2 are the most effective for understanding these kinds of behaviors. Thus, understanding how such a model operates provides considerable insight into human performance and allows for many important applications. Understanding the model's limitations for movement control is also important, as discussed next.

Visit HK*Propel* to read "The Tickle" and complete the self-directed learning activities.

Limitations of Closed-Loop Control

The inclusion of the information-processing stages in the system, as depicted in figure 4.2, illustrates the flexibility in movement control, allowing various strategies and options and altering the nature of the movement produced, depending on the circumstances. However, these stages of processing are slow and represent a big disadvantage when there is high demand for processing time, resources, or both, as in many complex actions (discussed in chapter 3). The following sections describe tasks in which the closed-loop model is relatively ineffective for guiding movement.

Unpredictable Tracking Tasks

One important generalization from chapters 2 and 3 is that the stages of information processing require considerable time. Hence, movement control in a closed-loop system with these processes embedded will be slow as well. The stages of processing are critical components in reaction-time (RT) situations, where presenting a stimulus requires various processes leading to a movement. The closed-loop model can be regarded in the same way, with the stimulus as the error information sent to the executive and the movement as the correction selected by the executive. Numerous studies of tracking suggest that the system can produce corrections at a maximum rate of about three corrections per second. This is approximately the rate that would be expected if the system were using RT processes as a critical component, reacting to errors by making corrections.

In the conceptual model presented in figure 4.2, each correction is based on information about the errors that have occurred over the past few hundred milliseconds. This error is processed in the stimulus identification stage; a movement correction is chosen in the response selection stage; and the correction is organized and initiated in the movement programming stage. Therefore, tracking tasks that involve more than three changes in direction per second are often performed very poorly. What makes a fumbled football difficult to retrieve is the frequently unpredictable nature of the bounces it takes. For this reason, closed-loop control processes are most relevant to tasks that are relatively slow, predictable, and have a long duration.

Rapid, Discrete Tasks

A closed-loop view of movement control fails to account adequately for movement production in skills that are very quick, such as the ballistic actions in sports skills (e.g., throwing and kicking) and keypressing while texting. In general, a performer initiates a fully planned movement in most rapid, discrete tasks. If later sensory information indicates that the movement will be incorrect and thus should be stopped or radically altered, this information is processed relatively slowly and sluggishly. Thus, the first few hundred milliseconds of the original movement occur more or less without modification. As you will see later in this chapter, sensory information plays an increasingly important and effective role for tasks in which the movement is performed slowly.

This sluggishness of feedback processing has implications for controlling the moment-to-moment adjustments in very rapid movements (e.g., movements less than 250 ms), such as typing a text message or plucking the strings of a banjo in a bluegrass song. According to the conceptual model, feedback arising from the rapid movement would not have enough time to be processed before the movement was completed. Thus, the feedback could not influence the fine, moment-to-moment control. More than any other observation, this sluggishness of feedback control has led scientists to believe that most rapid movements must be organized (programmed) in advance. In this view, the moment-to-moment control of rapid movement is included in the preorganized program and is not dependent on the relatively slow processes associated with feedback (this idea is discussed more fully in chapter 5).

However, there are exceptions in which feedback is used in a closed-loop manner to quickly modify movement control. Feedback can act reflexively (bypassing the information-processing stages) to modify movements far more quickly than indicated by the basic closed-loop model presented in figure 4.2. This aspect of feedback control is discussed next.

Reflexive Closed-Loop Control

To this point, only one kind of closed-loop process has been considered: conscious, voluntary control of actions using sensory information. But there are other ways in which sensory information is involved in movement control. These involve the many kinds of corrections, modifications, and subtle changes in skills that occur automatically (without conscious awareness).

Monosynaptic Reflexive Control

There are a number of reflexive mechanisms that operate below our level of consciousness. One of the most well known of these is the so-called knee-jerk (or patellar) reflex. If one sits on a table with knee bent and lower leg freely hanging and a small tap is applied to the patellar tendon (usually with a small rubber hammer), the response to the tap is a brief contraction of the quadriceps muscle, resulting in a small extension (straightening) of the lower leg. The time from the tap until the quadriceps is activated is less than 50 ms. This reflexive response occurs without any active, voluntary control and occurs far too quickly to have come via the stages of information processing.

Here is what happens: In this seated position, a tap to the patellar tendon, which attaches the patella to the tibia of the lower leg, applies a brief downward movement of the kneecap. Then, because the patella is attached to the quadriceps muscle, which (together with the muscle spindles in the quadriceps) is stretched a small amount too, the muscle spindles respond by sending a signal to the spinal cord via afferent (sensory) neurons. These neurons synapse with efferent (motor) neurons that lead back to the same muscle that was stretched (here, the quadriceps), causing a brief contraction.

This occurs very quickly and involuntarily, in part because the afferent and efferent neurons travel a relatively short distance and are connected by a single synapse. This reflex is called a *monosynaptic* stretch reflex, or **M1 response**.

Look at figure 4.3, which is a further expansion of our conceptual model. Within

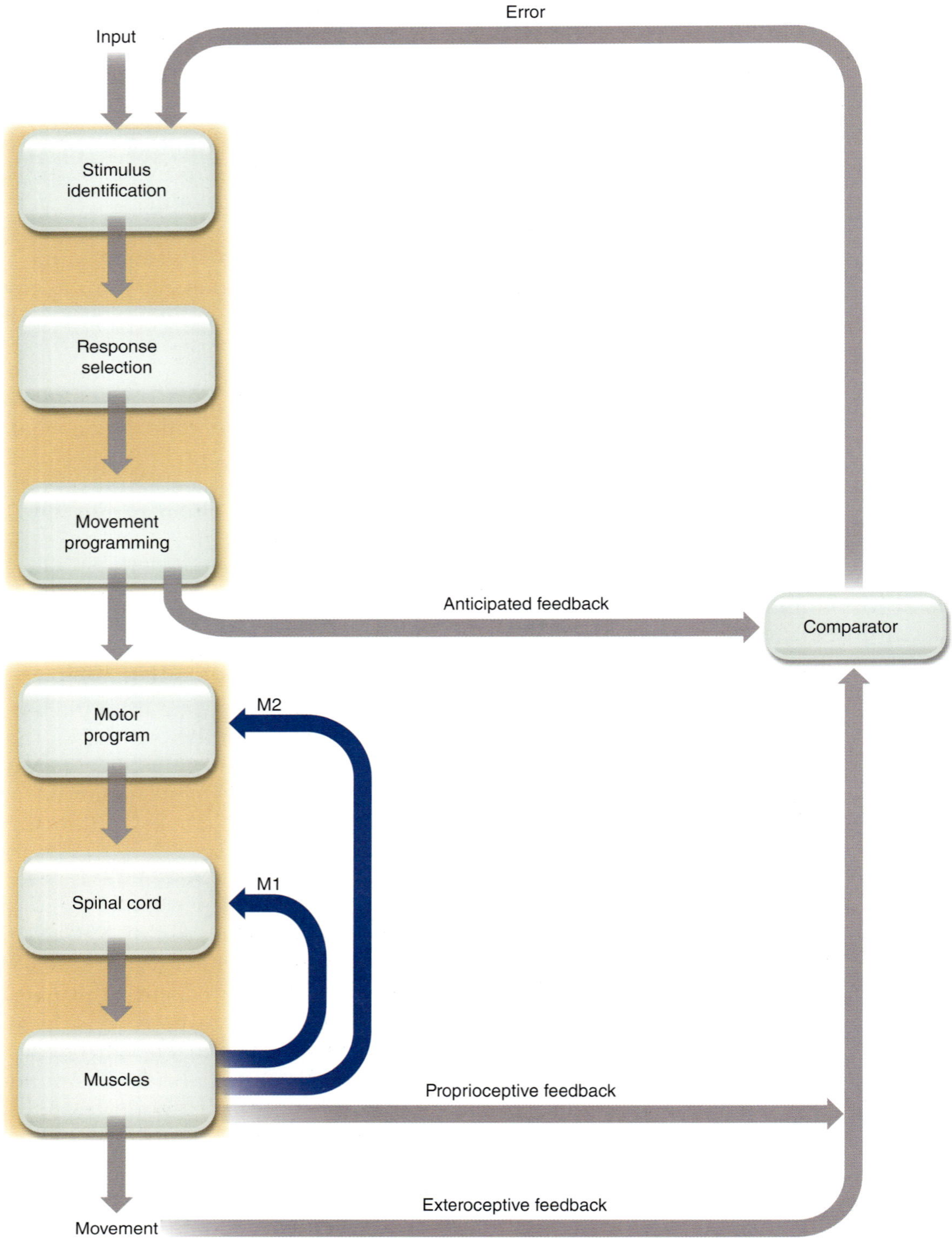

FIGURE 4.3 Conceptual model with the addition of M1 and M2 loops.

the effector box (motor program–spinal cord muscles), we have added a feedback loop (the M1 loop) from the muscle to the spinal cord and back to the same muscle. This loop is an important component of the monosynaptic stretch reflex. This feedback loop is at a relatively low level in the spinal cord, so the responses do not involve conscious, voluntary control and reflect stereotyped, involuntary, usually very rapid responses to stimuli.

Polysynaptic Reflexive Control

Imagine that you are a participant in the following experiment. You are standing, and your task is to hold one of your elbows at a right angle to support a moderate load (such as a book) on your outstretched, palm-up hand. You are instructed to hold the book at the same height and to maintain that position. Suddenly, without anticipating it, the experimenter adds another book to the load. Your hand begins to drop, but after a delay, you compensate for the added load and bring your hand back to its original position. In all likelihood, your response was nearly immediate and involuntary, but this time, more than one reflex was involved. The monosynaptic reflex just described was responsible for an initial, very brief, response to the added load. However, bringing the hand back to the target position likely involved one or more additional reflexes.

The slightly slower response occurs because the stretched biceps muscle delivers a signal (via afferent neurons from the muscle spindles) to the spinal cord. However, in this reflex, the signal is also sent up the spinal cord, and these neurons synapse with higher-level neurons. A signal is then sent back down the pathway in the spinal cord, where it synapses with the motor neurons leading to the biceps muscle, causing a second burst of biceps activity. This second burst of activity (labeled M2 in figure 4.3) is stronger and more sustained than the first one (the monosynaptic or M1 response), but it arrives after a slightly longer delay (50-80 ms) because the signal had to travel farther and because more synapses were involved. The M2 loop in figure 4.3 goes from the muscle to higher levels in the central nervous system. Together, these monosynaptic (M1) and polysynaptic (**M2 response**) reflexes are just two of the many types of reflexive mechanisms by which actions can be modified quickly (and automatically), leading toward goal achievement in a closed-loop manner.

Vision and Motor Control

Using vision for movement control is quite different from the reflexive closed-loop system just discussed. Vision, of course, has a very important role in everyday activities and deserves a place of its own in this chapter.

Two Visual Systems

Over the past 40 years or so, evidence has accumulated that two essentially separate visual systems underlie human functioning, rather than just one. Visual information is delivered from the retina of the eye along two separate processing streams to different places in the brain, and these two pathways of information are used differently in the control of behavior.

These two systems, illustrated in figure 4.4, are called the **dorsal stream** and the **ventral stream** because of their anatomical distinctions (Ungerleider & Mishkin, 1982). Visual information in both streams travels first from the retina of the eye to the primary visual cortex. However, at that point, it is thought that visual information processing becomes specialized. Information useful for the identification of an object is sent to the inferotemporal cortex via the ventral stream. Information that is used for the control of movement is sent to the posterior parietal cortex via the dorsal stream.

The ventral stream is specialized for conscious identification of objects that lie primarily in the center of the visual field. Its major function is to provide answers to the general question: What is it? Hence, we use this system to look at and identify something, such as the words being read on this page. This system contributes to conscious

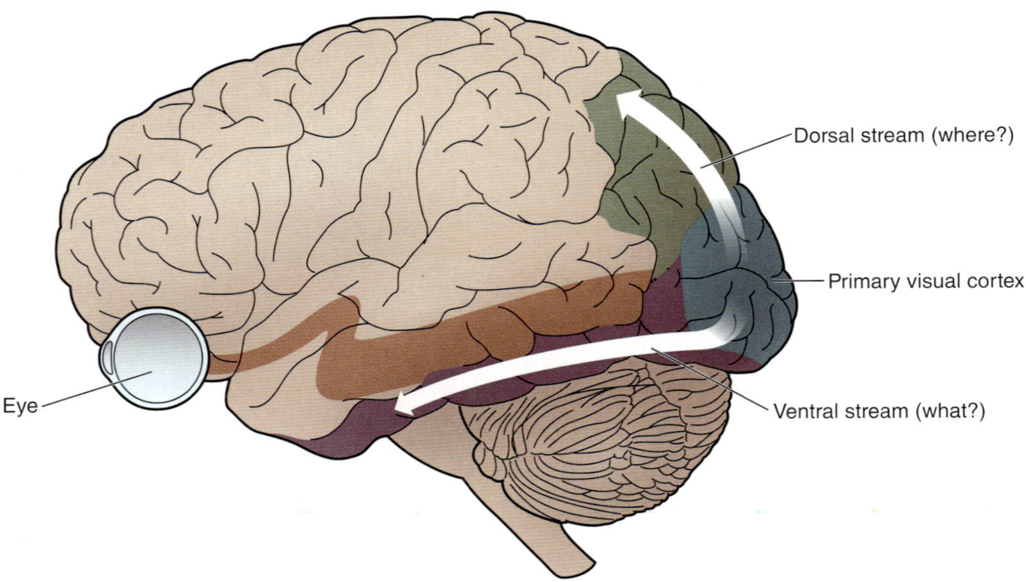

FIGURE 4.4 Illustration of dorsal and ventral stream pathways in the brain.

perception of objects and is severely degraded by poor lighting conditions, such as trying to read a physical book without adequate light or a document on a computer with the background lighting dimmed.

The dorsal stream is believed to be specialized for movement control. Distinct from the ventral stream, which is sensitive only to events in central vision, dorsal vision involves the entire visual field, both central and peripheral. Dorsal vision operates nonconsciously, contributing to the fine control of movements without our awareness (see Focus on Research 4.1). Its function is to provide an answer to the question, Where is it? Or perhaps, where am I relative to it?

Visual Control of Movement

How is visual information used for movement control, and what factors determine its effectiveness? It is useful to divide this discussion into separate parts, particularly because it deals with the separate roles of the dorsal and ventral systems.

Despite the characterization of ventral vision as a system for object identification, it would be wrong to conclude that it has no role in movement control. Ventral vision has access to consciousness, so it is processed through the information-processing stages discussed in chapter 2, leading to action in much the same way as any other information source. In the conceptual model in figure 4.3, vision can be seen as just another source of information arising from action, so its only access to the loop would be through the stages of information processing. In one sense, this is obvious. You can look at and consciously identify an oncoming car, which would then lead to the decision to try to avoid it. Ventral vision is critical here, and failures to identify objects properly can lead to serious errors. This is particularly important in night driving, when the ventral system's accuracy (visual acuity) is degraded considerably.

Before realizing there could be a dorsal system for movement control, scientists believed that a conscious ventral system was the only way visual information could influence action. In this outdated view, a baseball batter watching a pitch come toward the plate relied only on the relatively slow processes in the information-processing stages to detect the ball's flight pattern and to initiate changes in movement control. This idea was supported by numerous experiments that seemed to show that visual control of action was particularly slow and cumbersome. However, recent information

FOCUS ON Research 4.1

Blindsight Reveals Dorsal and Ventral Stream Processing

The term **blindsight** might seem like an oxymoron, but this curious phenomenon led to the discovery of the dorsal visual system. Blindsight is usually defined as a medical condition in which the person can respond to a visual object without consciously perceiving it. According to Weiskrantz (2007), the idea originally stemmed from work on the visual cortex of monkeys, where it was demonstrated that the animal, although technically blind, could still respond to various kinds of visual stimuli. Later studies demonstrated the phenomenon in humans (e.g., Humphrey, 1974; Weiskrantz et al., 1974).

Perhaps the most startling and convincing evidence came from the study of two human neurological patients, TN and DB (the patients' initials). Following two successive strokes, TN had major neurological damage in his visual cortex, which rendered him blind in both eyes by all traditional measures of vision. Researchers took TN to a hallway and asked him to walk down the hallway without his usual cane. Unbeknownst to TN, researchers had placed several objects in the hall around which he would have to negotiate. To the researchers' amazement, TN avoided them all, even pressing himself against the wall to avoid a trash can. Patient DB, whose occipital cortex had been removed surgically because of a tumor, was also blind according to traditional measures of vision. Researchers used forced-choice tests, in which DB was asked to guess where, between two locations in front of him, an object had been placed. His guesses were considerably more accurate than chance, even though he could not see the objects. He was also sensitive to long or short object presentation intervals, color, contrast, and motion, and the onset and offset of the target's presence. Very clearly, both of these patients were "seeing" objects about which they were not consciously aware (de Gelder et al., 2008; Weiskrantz et al., 1974).

These findings eventually were interpreted to mean that we possess two visual systems: a ventral system with access to consciousness (which DB and TN had lost completely) and a dorsal system that does not have access to consciousness (which was intact in DB and TN). (Figure 4.4 illustrates the anatomical pathways for these systems.) These observations involving patients, together with experimental evidence involving sighted individuals performing actions under visual illusion conditions (e.g., Bridgeman et al., 1981), demonstrate that we can respond to objects in our environment unconsciously, guided by visual information of which we are completely unaware.

Exploring Further

1. Neurophysiologists have studied patients with optic ataxia and visual agnosia. What information have these patients provided to researchers regarding the distinction between ventral and dorsal visual streams?
2. What types of visual illusions have been used in research to separate dorsal and ventral stream processing?

about the dorsal visual system, together with ideas about optical-flow processes in vision, has markedly changed our understanding of visual information processing for action.

Ventral Stream in Movement Control

The ventral stream provides information about the "what" in motor control. An expert baseball batter knows that different types of pitches have different spins—seeing the rotation of a pitched ball will help the batter predict its trajectory. A dental assistant must not only know the difference between the shape of a sickle probe and a periodontal probe but also be able to identify each with an associated verbal label. Thus, the ventral stream usually needs information presented in well-lit visual conditions in order to identify objects, which then can be used for conscious decision-making processes for action.

Object identification, via the ventral stream, plays a crucial role in movement planning before the initiation of an action. For example, look at the objects in figure 4.5 and predict the grip you would use to pick up each object. For the juice glass, a full-hand grip is needed. A three- or four-finger grip is needed for the beer mug, but a thumb-and-finger grip is appropriate for the teacup. The pen is usually picked up with a precision grip if the performer intends to use it to write something. However, if the performer intends to use the pen as a tool—say, to stab a hole in a cardboard box—then a power grip would be used. Thus, information provided by the ventral stream, combined with the intended use of the object in the action goal, becomes further processed in the movement planning stages (see Rosenbaum et al., 2013, for a more detailed discussion).

Dorsal Stream in Movement Control

James J. Gibson changed the way scientists theorized about the visual control of movement (e.g., Gibson, 1966). Patterns of optical flow were a particularly important concept promoted by Gibson. These patterns represent information used to control body movement (such as balance) and to provide information about the timing of events, such as the time required to close a gap between the performer and an object.

For example, riding a bicycle along a busy path or street requires rapidly processing many sources of visual information. The cyclist needs to be aware of traffic signs and signals, pedestrians crossing the street, cars turning away and into the oncoming path, and, of course, the dreaded opening of a car door. As the cyclist looks into this textured environment, each visible feature reflects rays of light, which enter the eyes at specific angles. Collectively, this is called the **optical array**. Because the cyclist is moving, each object in the environment shifts its position relative to the cyclist continuously, causing a change in the information provided by the optical array. This change in information is termed **optical flow** and can be thought of as a flow of light across the retina. The important point is that optical flow provides numerous significant kinds of information about the cyclist's movement through the environment, such as

- time before a collision between the cyclist and an object,
- direction of movement relative to objects in the environment,
- movement of environmental objects relative to the cyclist,
- stability and balance of the cyclist, and
- velocity of movement through the environment.

Time-to-Contact Information Figure 4.6 presents an example of how the optical array picks up information about an object first seen in the distance (e.g., 50 m away—position A), then at a closer distance (15 m away—position B), then at a very close distance (5 m—position C). The angle of light given from the edges of the object at distance A is very small (α_1); the angles increase slightly as the object gets 35 m closer (α_2), and then it expands at a much more rapid rate over the next 10 m (α_3).

The change in the optical-flow pattern from an oncoming object, such as a parked

FIGURE 4.5 The ventral stream identifies the visual properties of an object for the purpose of action. In this figure, the object's physical properties provide information about how to grip it. However, the visual properties of objects do not tell the whole story—intentions about how the object will be used also determine which grip to use. For example, think about how you would grip the pen if you were planning to write with it, and compare that to how you would grip the pen if you planned to use it to stab a hole in a cardboard box (see Rosenbaum et al., 2013).

car, indicates the time remaining until the object reaches the plane of the eye (Lee & Young, 1985). The retinal image of an approaching object expands as the object approaches, and it expands more quickly as the object approaches more quickly. The dorsal system picks up these changes in optical flow, providing information about object distance as well as the time until the object will contact the plane of the eye. This time-to-contact information, or **tau** (τ), is defined as the retinal image size divided by the image's rate of change in size, which is proportional to the time remaining until contact. Thus, τ is derived from optical-flow information and used by the dorsal stream to specify time-to-contact with the object. This information is critical for interceptive actions involving coincident timing, such as striking or catching a ball, driving, or preparing the body for entry into the water during a dive.

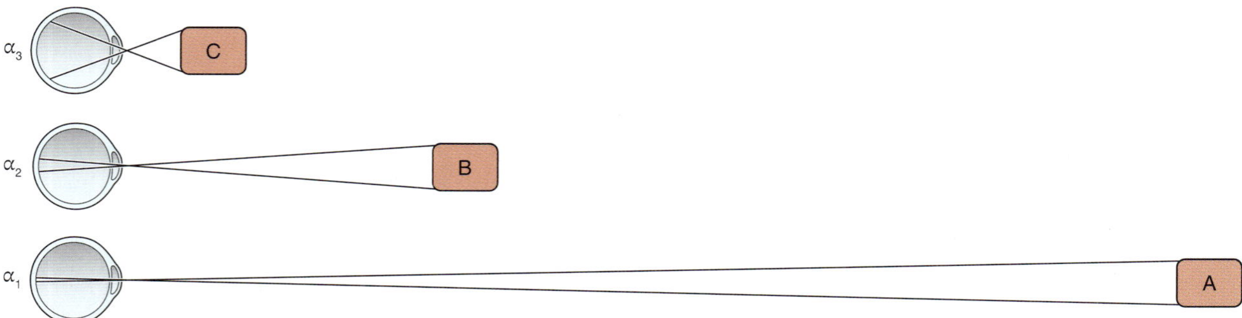

FIGURE 4.6 An object is traveling at the same velocity in the right-to-left direction toward the eye. The sizes of the object's optical image on the rear of the eye (the retina) at different distances are α_1, α_2, and α_3. Notice that when the object travels from positions A to B, the size of the retinal image changes at a slower rate than it does for the smaller distance covered from B to C. The dorsal system picks up these changes in optical flow, providing information about object distance and time until the object will contact the plane of the eye.

As a mountain biker navigates the trail, she processes a continuously changing stream of visual information about the environment. Describe one example of information processed by the mountain biker's ventral system and one example of information processed by the dorsal system.

Direction of Movement of Objects One can run through a forest, avoiding trees successfully, by using optical-flow information about the relative rates of change in the visual angles of the trees. For example, assume that the objects shown in figure 4.7 are trees. For tree A, the angles of light from the left and right edges expand at the same rate from both sides, indicating that the eye is traveling directly toward tree A and will collide with it. For tree B, on the other hand, the angles of light from the right side are expanding more slowly than those from the left side. This indicates that the eye will pass to the right of tree B.

Balance Maintaining balance has traditionally been the domain of proprioceptive information in detecting sway and loss of stability. For example, when the body sways forward, the ankle joint moves and the associated musculature stretches, producing movement signals from the muscle spindles and other proprioceptors. Also, receptors in the inner ear are sensitive to head movements, providing information about body sway and balance.

However, vision also plays a key role in balance control. Look straight ahead at an object on the wall. Without shifting your gaze direction, move your head slightly forward and backward and pay attention to the changes in visual information. You will probably notice that the objects in peripheral vision seem to sweep rapidly back and forth and that these changes depend on your head movement. Could this peripheral information serve for balance control?

Lee and Aronson (1974) demonstrated that balance is strongly affected by varying the visual information, suggesting that the optical-flow variables in peripheral vision are critical to balance. In their experiment, the participant stood in a special small room surrounded by walls suspended from a very high ceiling; the walls did not quite touch the floor. The walls could be moved with the floor kept still to influence only the optical-flow information. Moving the walls slightly away caused the participant to sway slightly forward, and moving the walls closer caused the participant to sway backward. With a young child, an away movement of the walls could cause the participant to stumble forward, and a toward movement of the walls could cause a rather ungraceful plop into a sitting position.

Moving the wall toward the person generates optical-flow information that ordinarily means the head is moving forward—that is, that the person is out of balance and falling forward. The automatic postural compensation is to sway backward. Such visually based compensations are far faster than can be explained by conscious processing in the ventral system, with latencies of about 100 ms (Nashner & Berthoz, 1978). These experiments suggest that optical-flow information and the dorsal system are important in controlling normal balancing activities.

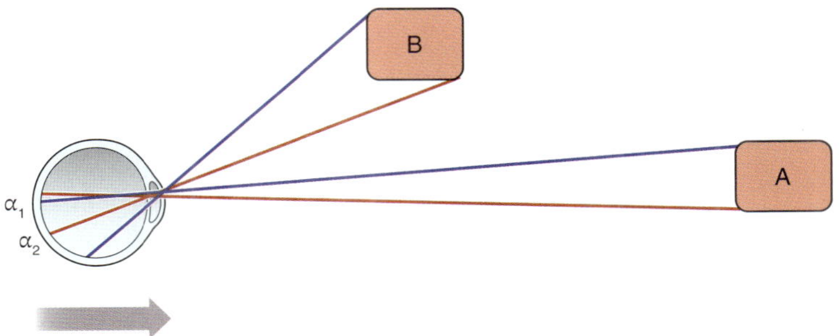

FIGURE 4.7 The observer, represented here by an eye, is heading directly toward object A but will pass to the right of object B. The dorsal system detects that the rays of light from both sides of object A are expanding at about the same rate, whereas the light rays from the left side of object B are expanding more quickly than those from the right side. This indicates that if the observer doesn't change course, she will collide with object A but will pass to the right of object B.

Processing Visual Feedback In some situations, visual information can be used very rapidly (with latencies less than 100 ms) to make adjustments in the control of movement. In other situations, however, visually based corrections involve the relatively slow stages of information processing. One line of research has been to identify exactly how much time is needed to conduct this processing activity.

Following the initial work by Woodworth (1899), Keele and Posner (1968) devised a unique strategy to measure the time required to process visual feedback. The participant's goal was to complete an aimed hand movement to a target within specific MT (movement time) goals. The target distance was 15 cm, and there were four MT goals (150, 250, 350, and 450 ms). Thus, the movements were completed in times that ranged from very rapid (150 ms goal, although actually completed in 185-190 ms) to fairly slow (450 ms). Participants were given verbal feedback about their actual MTs after each trial to help them move toward the instructed goal MT. A critically important feature of the research design was that participants completed some of the trials in the dark—the ambient lights were suddenly and randomly extinguished on one-half of the trials just as the movement was initiated. The prediction was simple: If visual feedback was used to guide the movement onto the target, then having the ambient lights on should produce more accurate aims than when the ambient lights were off. But if the movement was too fast to use visual feedback, then no differences in accuracy would be expected.

Figure 4.8 presents Keele and Posner's results. As the MTs became longer, the accuracy of hitting the target improved, mainly for the movements made with the lights on. Of importance, the accuracies in the lights on condition, compared to the lights off condition, were identical for the shortest MT (190 ms). It was only when the MTs became longer (> 250 ms) that having the lights on resulted in better accuracy. Therefore, these data suggest that the minimum time to use visual feedback in these aiming movements was between 190 and 250 ms.

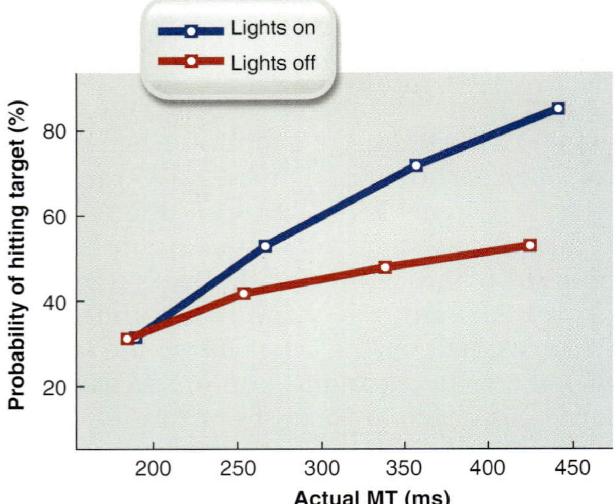

FIGURE 4.8 Movements completed in less than about 200 ms showed no benefit in accuracy with the ambient lights on (compared to lights off). Movements completed in 250 ms or more benefited from the availability of visual feedback.

Estimates of the minimum time for visual information processing have provided more clarity since the research of Keele and Posner. If the vision offset is unexpected, as in Keele and Posner's task, the time needed to process the visual feedback is roughly similar to that for an RT task. However, if the availability of visual feedback can be predicted, the processing time is reduced considerably (Elliott et al., 2010).

Visit HK*Propel* to read "Cool Papa Bell" and complete the self-directed learning activities.

Digby Elliott and colleagues have studied visual feedback processing using a different approach. In this method, ambient light is provided intermittently—participants wear special goggles that cycle periods of light and darkness, and the experimenter varies the duration of these cycle times. In a series of studies using stationary and moving targets, the researchers found that accurate performance was maintained as long as no more than 80 ms elapsed between periods of visual feedback. This work reveals that a

FOCUS ON Research 4.2

Gaze Control and the Quiet Eye

Eye-movement recording devices provide researchers with precise measures of gaze—where a person is looking during an action or perceptual event. These studies have revealed that we voluntarily control gaze using two different types of eye movements: smooth-pursuit eye movements and discrete, saccadic movements.

The goal of smooth-pursuit movements is to keep the target of our gaze fixed on the fovea of the retina. The eyes fixate on an object that is either motionless or moving slowly, allowing the viewer to pick up precise detail. Faster object movements, on the other hand, are characterized by brief fixations and rapid shifts (called *saccades*, mentioned earlier) to a different location in the visual environment. Information is picked up during the fixations but not picked up during the saccades between fixations. These rapid eye movements and fixations provide us with the capability to pick up information rapidly from a wide range of sources in our visual environment, such as when driving (looking out the front and side windows, checking the various mirrors, etc.).

Researchers have discovered something very interesting about the way highly skilled and less-skilled athletes use vision just before the onset of action. Expert performers keep their eyes fixated on a target for a longer period of time just before movement onset than do nonexperts. Moreover, individuals can improve their performance if they are trained to fixate their gaze for a longer period of time just before action. These findings have been replicated in many different types of activities (e.g., basketball free-throw shooting, target shooting, golf, juggling) and have been termed the **quiet-eye effect** (see Wilson et al., 2015, for a review).

What are the underlying mechanisms responsible for the quiet-eye effect? Several hypotheses exist (Gonzalez et al., 2017). One is that a prolonged gaze period might stabilize the perceptual system, facilitating movement processes dependent on them. Another view is that this period of eye inactivity provides an opportunity to shift attentional resources to an optimal focus (see discussion in chapter 3). Another idea is that more extensive movement programming processes are undertaken during these prolonged quiet-eye periods. Although other possible reasons cannot be excluded, there seems to be considerable generality to the benefits of the quiet-eye effect.

Exploring Further

1. What are the rods and cones of the eye, and what specific information do they contribute to vision?
2. What is the difference between looking and seeing? How does the activity known as parkour reveal that what traceurs and traceuses see is different from what the rest of us see?

visual snapshot goes a relatively long way in supporting performance when continuous vision is unavailable. Vision need not always be available in order to make feedback-based corrections (see Elliott & Bennett, 2021, for a review).

Vision in the Conceptual Model

The distinction between dorsal and ventral stream visual processing has obvious implications for our conceptual model, as presented in figure 4.3. Although ventral stream processing would still occur as suggested in the model (through the slow processing stages in the outer loop), dorsal stream processing would be expected to be unconscious. Because dorsal stream processing is nonconscious and relatively fast, it is fed back to relatively low levels in the central nervous system, considerably downstream from the processes that select and initiate movement but upstream from the muscles and the spinal cord. Thus, dorsal vision can be thought of as operating at intermediate levels of the system to make minor adjustments in already programmed actions, such as compensation for head movement in the golf swing and alterations in posture to maintain balance on the still rings. For this reason, we have added a dorsal vision feedback loop from the resulting movement to the level of the motor program in figure 4.9.

Auditition and Motor Control

The role of auditory feedback in movement control is not well understood, perhaps because of the dominant role of vision and all the attention researchers give to it. Yet we know that audition can have profound effects on motor control. For example, a speaker who talks into a microphone at a large concert hall with the voice projected from the sound system at the very back of the hall will experience a delay in hearing the auditory feedback. Such delays are well known to increase speech errors and slow speaking rates. Auditory delays can disrupt other forms of movement control, such as playing a musical instrument (Pfordresher & Dalla Bella, 2011) or typing buttons on a phone with briefly delayed sounds.

A good example of the important role of audition in sports is the sound made when a tennis ball is contacted by the racket. Research has found that predictive judgments of ball landing position corresponded to the loudness of the ball contact—the louder the contact, the further (deeper) into the court was the predicted landing position of the ball (Cañal-Bruland et al., 2018). Ironically, this important role of audition has led to a controversy involving players such as Maria Sharapova and Rafael Nadal. These (and other players) were well known for making loud grunts as they contacted the ball with the racket. A study by Sinnett and Kingstone (2010) found that watching video clips of tennis ground shots accompanied by a burst of white noise at the point of contact with ball disrupted the speed and accuracy of respondents much more than when the same videos shown without the white noise. Thus, attempts to mask or interfere with the ball contact sound could be a disadvantage for the player receiving the volley because they disrupt the predictive information that is provided by the auditory feedback. Together, these findings highlight the critical, if sometimes overlooked, importance of auditory information.

Visit HK*Propel* to read "Craps and Weighted Bats" and complete the self-directed learning activities.

Echolocation

Using feedback to orient oneself in space is primarily the role of vision and the vestibular apparatus. However, in some visually impaired animals, the role can be accurately performed using audition. Discovered initially with bats and dolphins, **echolocation** involves the emission of sound waves that bounce off objects, which are then used as auditory feedback to orient flying or swimming patterns to find food or avoid objects.

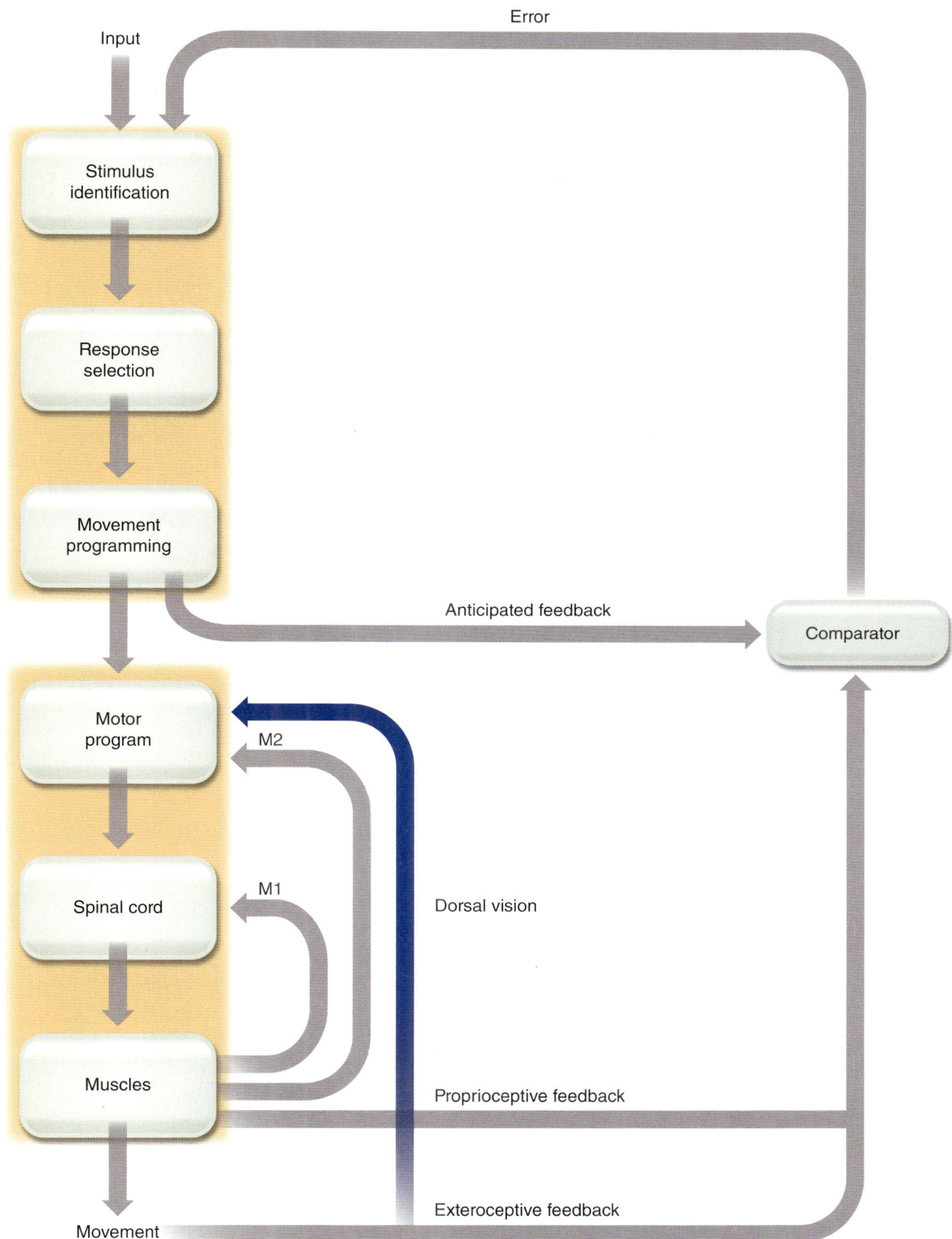

FIGURE 4.9 Conceptual model with the addition of dorsal vision feedback loop.

The great Rafael Nadal, who retired at the end of the 2024 season at the Davis Cup in Málaga, Spain, put his opponents at a disadvantage by interfering with the sound of the ball leaving his racket with his auditory grunts.

Some humans, particularly those who are blind, have acquired the capability to echolocate too. By tapping a cane or making very brief (3-15 ms) mouth clicks, humans send out sound waves that, when fed back after bouncing off objects, can be used to perceive rather precise information about the distance, size, and location of objects (Kolarik et al., 2014; Thaler & Goodale, 2016).

Sonification

As mentioned earlier, inherent auditory feedback plays an obviously important role when talking, typing, playing a musical instrument, tap dancing, and other forms of continuous behavior and disrupts performance when masked, distorted, or delayed. Recently, some researchers have been using augmented auditory feedback to improve performance in sports and rehabilitation. The method is called **sonification**. In general, sonification refers to the process of converting movement-related data into a form of auditory feedback. In sports and rehabilitation, these data refer to the output resulting from movement or the movement of an object.

As a simple example, imagine that a tone is sounded when you touch a tabletop with your fingertip. As you move your finger to the right, the tone increases in loudness; moving it to the left decreases the loudness. In the absence of vision, the auditory feedback would help you know approximately where your finger was located on the table. This is a simple example of sonification: transforming data (finger movement) into auditory feedback (loudness).

Now suppose that you wanted to provide auditory feedback about something more

In this photo, what is echolocation, and how is it used by bats to avoid objects and locate food sources?

complicated, such as the speed of a golf swing. One could map the swing's velocity with a change in auditory pitch. The backswing might have an initial increase in pitch (corresponding to the increase in velocity of the backswing), followed by a decrease in pitch (as the backswing transitions to a forward swing), then a massive increase in pitch as the club accelerates toward the ball. Considering all the various body segments, measurable outcomes (e.g., position, kinematics, kinetics), varieties of objects that could be moved, and the sundry auditory features available, there exists an incredibly large array of sonification possibilities.

Sonification research, which is quite dependent on technology, is still in a period of rapid growth (Schaffert & Schlüter, 2022). Providing auditory feedback about factors such as boat speeds in rowing and pedal forces exerted by cyclists has led to impressive gains in performance. Sonification techniques have also been used in the treatment of Parkinson's disease and stroke, with promising results (Schaffert et al., 2019). Chapter 11 provides more discussion of augmented feedback and its role in learning. However, initial indications about the immediate and long-term impacts of sonification in both sports and rehabilitation make this an exciting and vibrant area for applied research in the future.

Summary

The effectiveness with which a performer processes various forms of sensory information often determines the overall performance level. Sensory signals from the environment are usually termed *exteroceptive* information, whereas those from the body are termed *proprioceptive* information. For human performance, it is useful to think of these signals as operating in a closed-loop control system, which contains an executive for decision-making, an effector for carrying out the actions, feedback about the state of the environment, and a comparator to contrast the environmental state with the system's goal.

In the conceptual model of human performance, we added closed-loop control to the information-processing stages discussed in previous chapters. This model is particularly effective for understanding how slower actions as well as continuous tasks (such as tracking) are performed. We then added to the conceptual model several reflex-like processes that account for corrections without involving the information-processing stages. A special case of closed-loop control is vision. We introduced two visual streams: a dorsal stream for motor control and a ventral stream for object identification, and we considered the role of the dorsal stream in balance and in producing and correcting actions. Last, the understudied role of audition is beginning to emerge as an important contributor to human motor performance. These sensory systems were integrated into the conceptual model, which helps to show how these various sensory events can support or modify skilled actions and under what conditions they operate.

HK*PROPEL* ACTIVITIES

HK*Propel* offers these activities to help you build and apply your knowledge of the concepts in this chapter. Additionally, you'll find a key terms flashcard review activity and a key terms quiz, along with audio supplements for selected figures, as indicated by QR codes throughout the chapter.

Interactive Learning

Activity 4.1: Identify the roles of the sensory organs involved in proprioception by matching each receptor with its location and function.

Activity 4.2: Identify which component of a closed-loop control system relates to each of a series of actions.

Activity 4.3: Indicate whether each in a list of characteristics applies to the dorsal or ventral visual processing stream.

Activity 4.4: Choose the labels for the conceptual motor control model to review its stages, including closed-loop control pathways and visual stream information.

Activity 4.5: Listen to a discussion about the quiet-eye effect, perception–action coupling, and eye tracking in sport research; link the discussion to information-processing concepts.

Principles-to-Application Exercise

Activity 4.6: The principles-to-application exercise for this chapter prompts you to choose an activity, identify sources of proprioceptive and exteroceptive information during the activity, and evaluate which sources of information are useful to the performer. You will also apply the concept of closed-loop control to the activity.

Motor Control in Everyday Actions Narratives

The Magnetic Hill

The Curling Draw

The Tickle

Cool Papa Bell

Craps and Weighted Bats

Check Your Understanding

1. Name the four distinct parts of a closed-loop control system. Describe how each of these parts might function for a child stacking toy blocks.
2. Explain how the pattern of optical flow can inform an outfielder attempting to catch a fly ball about when and where the ball will reach the height of the fielder's glove.
3. How does ventral stream movement control play a role in movement planning when opening various doors throughout your day?

Apply Your Knowledge

1. Several sources of sensory information are available to a skier as she makes her way down an alpine ski run. Describe and provide examples of exteroceptive and proprioceptive information that she might receive during her run, and indicate why this information is important for movement.
2. How closed-loop control processes are used (if at all) is dependent on the task that is performed. Contrast the role played by closed-loop control processes for casting a fishing line and tracing a clothing pattern onto fabric. Would this role change if either of the tasks were sped up?

5

Motor Programs

Motor Control of Brief Actions

CHAPTER OUTLINE

CHAPTER OBJECTIVES

Chapter 5 describes how motor programs are used in movement control. This chapter will help you understand

- motor control as an open-loop system and the role of motor programs,
- experimental evidence for motor programs,
- limitations and problems in the simple motor program concept, and
- generalized motor programs and evidence for this expanded concept.

CHAPTER PREVIEW QUIZ

1. In your own words, define *motor program*.
2. What happens when you are startled?
3. What components of your signature are easy to forge, and what parts are difficult to forge?

Watching a diver complete a rapid, complex, acrobatic maneuver while free-falling through space toward the water raises several questions. How does a skilled diver produce so many movements so quickly? What controls them? How are they combined to form a whole fluid motion? The skilled diver gives us the impression that these quick movements might be organized in advance and performed without much modification, or at least not using the relatively slow kinds of feedback processing that we discussed in chapter 4.

This chapter investigates the idea of open-loop control, introducing the concept of the motor program as responsible for this kind of movement control. Then we discuss how the various feedback pathways interact with motor programs, giving a more complete picture of the interplay of central and peripheral contributions to movements. The chapter describes and raises problems about specific motor programs—underlying neural structures responsible for specific actions. Later, we focus on the concept of a **generalized motor program (GMP)**, a theory that can account for the common observation that movements can be varied along certain dimensions—for example, playing the guitar or a piano sequence slower or faster (or louder or softer) without sacrificing its underlying structure (i.e., the rhythm).

In many actions, particularly quick ones produced in stable and predictable environments (e.g., springboard diving, hammering), most people would assume that a performer somehow plans the movement in advance and then triggers it, allowing the action to run its course without much modification of the individual elements. Also, the performer does not seem to have much awareness or conscious control over the movement once it's triggered into action; the movement just seems to "take care of itself." Perhaps this is obvious. Certainly, you cannot have direct, conscious control of the thousands of individual muscle contractions and joint movements—all the **degrees of freedom** that must be coordinated as the skilled action is unfolding. There is simply too much going on for the limited-capacity attentional mechanisms (which we discussed in chapters 3 and 4) to control all of them consciously.

If processes you are aware of do not directly control these individual contractions, how are they controlled and regulated? In many ways, this question is one of the most fundamental to the field of motor behavior because it goes to the heart of how biological systems of all kinds control their actions. This chapter focuses on the ways the central nervous system functions before and during an action and how it contributes to the control of the unfolding movement. As such, this chapter is a close companion to chapter 4, which considered the ways sensory information contributes to movement production. This chapter adds the idea of centrally organized commands that sensory information may modify somewhat. A key feature of this idea involves the important concept of a **motor program**, which is a predetermined set of movement commands that defines the essential details of a movement.

Motor Program Theory

The concept of the motor program, which is central to this entire chapter, is based on a kind of control mechanism that is in some ways the opposite of the closed-loop system discussed throughout chapter 4. This type of functional organization is called **open-loop control**.

Open-Loop Control

Figure 5.1 illustrates the basic open-loop system and consists essentially of two parts: an executive and an effector. This open-loop structure has two of the main features used in closed-loop control (figure 4.1), but missing are the feedback and comparator mechanisms for determining system errors. Open-loop control begins with input about the desired state being given to the executive (or decision-making) level, whose task it is to define what action needs to be taken. The executive

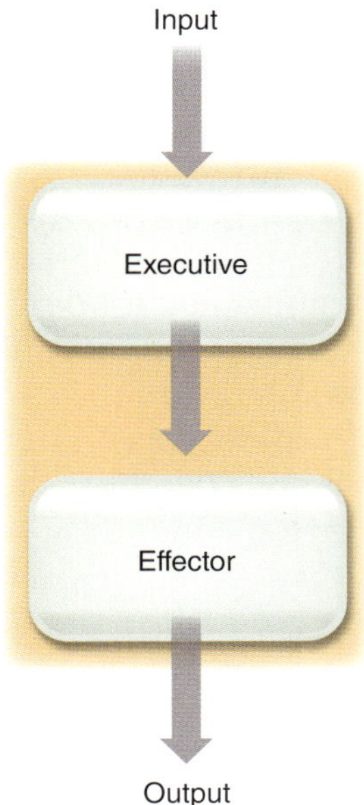

FIGURE 5.1 A basic open-loop system.

then passes instructions to the effector level, which is responsible for carrying out these instructions. Once the actions are completed, the system's job is over until the executive is activated again. Of course, without feedback, the open-loop system is not sensitive to whether the actions generated were effective in meeting the goal. And since feedback is not present, modifications to the action cannot be made while the action is in progress.

This kind of control system can be observed in many different real-world mechanisms. For example, most traffic signals use an open-loop system, where it sequences the timing of the red, yellow, and green lights that control the traffic flow. If an accident should happen at that intersection, the open-loop system continues to sequence the lights as if nothing were wrong, even though the standard pattern would be ineffective in handling this unexpected traffic flow problem. Thus, an open-loop system is effective as long as things go as expected, but it is inflexible in the face of unpredicted changes.

A basic microwave oven is another example of an open-loop system. The user might place a frozen entree in the oven and program it to defrost for 5 min and then to cook on high power for another 2 min. Here, the program tells the machine what operations to do at each step and when to do them. Some microwave ovens are sensitive to the temperature of the item being cooked because a feedback mechanism (temperature sensor) has been added. But many are not, and without a feedback mechanism, these machines follow the predetermined set of instructions without regard for whether they will result in the desired state.

Generally, the characteristics of a purely open-loop control system can be summarized as follows:

- Predetermined instructions specify the operations to be done, their sequencing, and their timing.
- Once the program has been initiated, the system executes the instructions essentially without modification.
- There is no capability to detect or to correct errors because feedback is not involved.
- Open-loop systems are most effective in stable, predictable environments in which the need for modification of commands is low.

Motor Programs as Open-Loop Systems

Many movements—especially those that are rapid, brief, and forceful, such as kicking and key pressing—seem to be controlled in an open-loop fashion, without much conscious control once the movement is under way. The performer in these tasks does not have time to process information about movement errors and must plan the movement in its entirety before movement initiation. This is quite different from the style of control discussed in the previous chapter, where the movements were slower (or longer in duration) and were largely based on feedback processes of various kinds.

Open-loop control seems especially important when the environmental situation is predictable and stable. Under these circumstances, human movements appear to be carried out without much possibility of, or need for, modification. This general idea was popularized more than a century ago by the psychologist William James (1891) and has remained one of the most important ways to understand movement control.

Consider a goal such as hitting a pitched baseball. The executive level, which consists of the decision-making stages of the system defined in chapter 2, evaluates the environment in the stimulus identification stage, processing such information as the speed and direction of the ball and the anticipated location of the ball when it enters the hitting area. The decision about whether to swing is made in the response selection stage. If the decision is to swing, the movement's speed, trajectory, and timing are determined in the movement programming stage.

Control is then passed to the effector level for movement execution. The selected motor program now carries out the swing by delivering commands to the spinal cord, which eventually directs the operations of the skeletal system involved in the swing. This movement then influences the outcome, resulting in the desired movement (hitting the ball squarely) or not (e.g., missing the ball, popping the ball up).

Although the decision-making stages determine what program to initiate and have some role in the eventual form of the movement (e.g., its speed and trajectory), the conscious decision-making stages do not actually control movement execution. Therefore, a system not directly under conscious control carries out the movement. By this view, the motor program is the agent determining which muscles are to contract, in what order, when, and for how long.

Visit HK*Propel* to read "Moving Sidewalks and Beer Glasses" and complete the self-directed learning activities.

Open-Loop Control in the Conceptual Model

How does this concept of open-loop control and the motor program fit with the conceptual model of human performance? Figure 5.2 shows the last evolution of the conceptual model in chapter 4 (figure 4.9), now with the portions that comprise the open-loop components highlighted (light-green shading). The conceptual model here reflects motor performance as an open-loop control system with feedback added (the parts not shaded) to enable corrections through the other loops discussed previously. This more complete conceptual model has two basic ways of operating, depending on the task. If the movement is very slow or of long duration (e.g., threading a needle), the feedback processes dominate control. If the movement is very fast or brief (e.g., a punch or kick), then the open-loop portions tend to dominate. In most tasks, motor behavior is neither entirely open- nor closed-loop alone but a complex blend of the two.

For very brief actions, the theory of motor programs is useful because it provides a set of ideas to talk about a functional organization of the motor system. If a given movement is said to be a *programmed action*, it appears to be organized in advance, triggered more or less as a whole, and carried out without much modification from sensory feedback. Programmed action is a style of motor control with a central movement organization—details are determined by the central nervous system and sent to the muscles, rather than controlled by peripheral processes involving feedback. Of course, both styles of control are possible, depending on the nature of the task, the time available, and other factors.

Evidence for Motor Programs

A number of separate lines of evidence support the existence of motor program control. This evidence comes from some rather diverse areas of research: (1) studies of RT (reaction time) in humans, (2) experiments and case studies involving animals and humans in which feedback has been removed, (3) studies of central pattern generators, (4) the analysis of behaviors when humans attempt to stop or change an action, and (5) the impact on

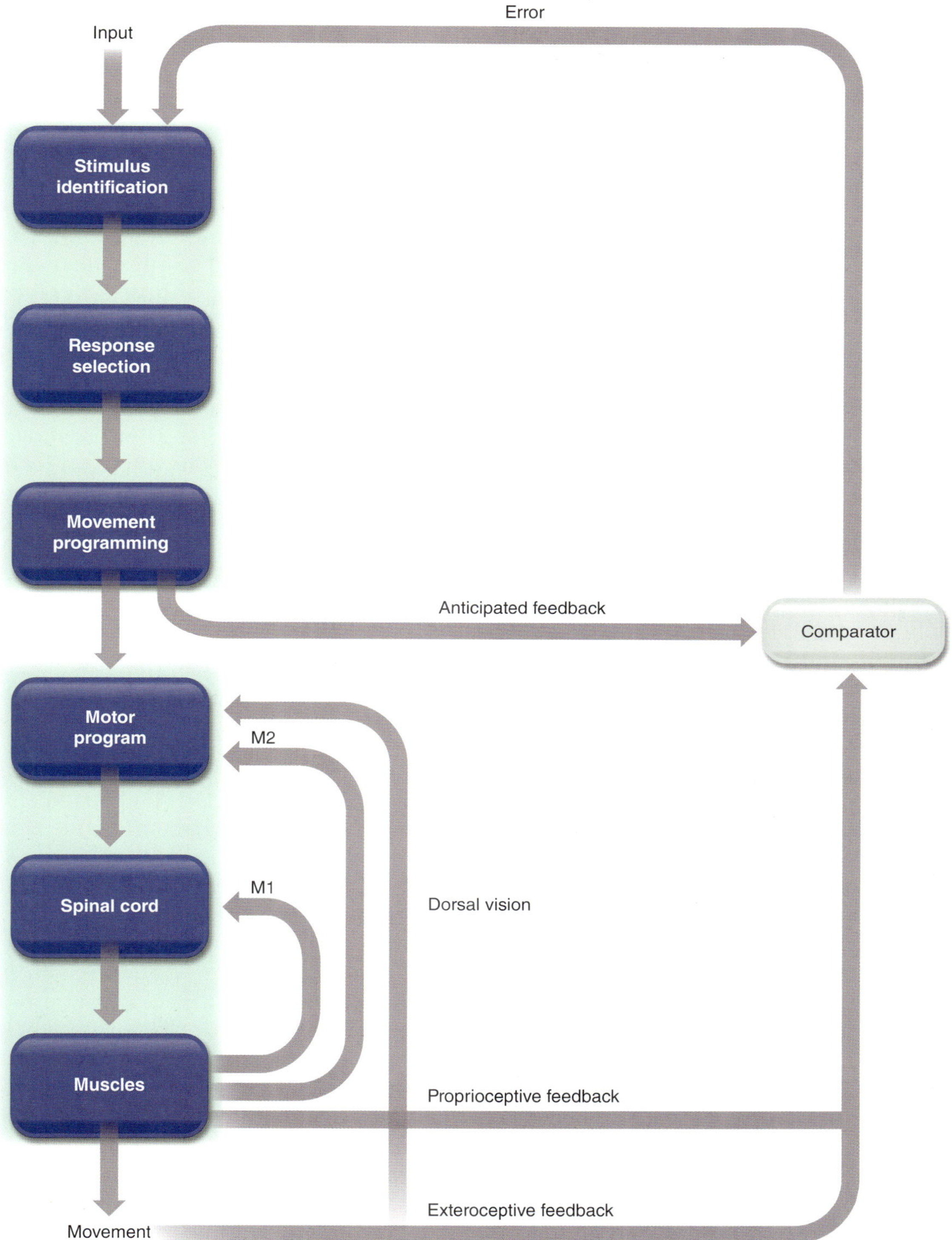

FIGURE 5.2 Conceptual model with the open-loop processes highlighted in light green.

muscle activation patterns when movement is unexpectedly blocked. We will summarize these lines of evidence in support of motor program theory before presenting two critical logistic problems with the idea that specific, entirely predetermined motor programs underlie skilled actions.

Reaction-Time Evidence

In chapter 2, we discussed evidence that RT was longer when factors slowed the stimulus selection (e.g., Hick's Law) and response selection (e.g., S-R incompatibility) stages. In this section, we review evidence that the factors affecting the movement programming stage also influence RT.

Response Complexity Effects

Participants in RT experiments are typically asked to respond to a stimulus by initiating and carrying out a predetermined movement as quickly as possible (as discussed in chapter 2). Duration of the RT is measured as the interval from the presentation of the stimulus until the movement begins, so any added time for movement completion itself does not contribute directly to RT. However, beginning with the work of Henry and Rogers (1960; see Focus on Research 5.1), research has shown that RT is affected by several features of the movement to be performed in the future, presumably by influencing the complexity (and duration) of the programming stage that occurs prior to movement.

Henry and Rogers (1960) found that increases in the complexity of the upcoming movement to be performed increased RT—that is, the time delay in initiating the response. This finding, plus much more research since the publication of Henry and Rogers' work, has produced the following set of findings (Klapp, 1996):

- RT is slower when additional elements in a series are added to the action (e.g., typing one letter would be initiated faster than typing a sequence of letters).
- RT is slower when more limbs must be coordinated (e.g., a one-handed piano chord would be initiated with a faster RT than a two-handed chord).
- RT is slower when the duration of the movement becomes longer (e.g., a 100 ms bat swing would be initiated with a faster RT than a 300 ms bat swing).

The interpretation of the research findings is that when the to-be-produced movement is more complex in any of these ways (number of elements, number of limbs involved, the overall duration of the action), RT is slower because more time is required to organize the motor system before the initiation of the action. This prior organization occurs, as discussed in chapter 2, in the movement programming stage. The effect on RT of the complexity of the to-be-performed movement provides evidence that at least some of the action is organized in advance, as predicted by motor program theory.

Visit HK*Propel* to read "Antilock Brakes" and complete the self-directed learning activities.

Startled Reactions

In the previous section, we discussed the idea that RT *lengthens* as the movement to be performed increases in complexity. Here, we focus on research showing that RT can be dramatically *shortened* under certain conditions.

We have all been in situations where a completely unexpected, extremely loud noise caused a severe startled reaction. The typical startle reaction includes contractions in the muscles of the face and neck and protective movements of the upper limbs. Because all these reactions are initiated much faster than a voluntary response to a stimulus, the **startle RT** has been used as a technique to reveal insights about movement programming. In these studies (reviewed in DeLuca et al., 2022; Maslovat et al., 2021), the participant is typically asked to prepare to make a rapid, forceful, sometimes complex response to an auditory or visual stimulus. Occasionally, the stimulus is accompanied by an unexpected, extremely loud acoustic signal (e.g., 130 decibels [dB]; by compari-

FOCUS ON Research 5.1

The Henry–Rogers Experiment

One of Franklin Henry's many important contributions was research that he and Donald Rogers published in 1960. The experiment was simple, which is typical of many important experiments. Participants responded as quickly as possible to a stimulus by making one of three movements that had been prepared in advance. Note that only one of these movements would be required for a long string of trials, so this was essentially a simple-RT paradigm (see chapter 2). The three different types of movements, designed to be different in complexity, were (1) a simple finger lift, (2) a simple finger lift plus a reach to slap a suspended ball, and (3) a simple finger lift followed by slapping a distant ball with the back of the hand, then moving to the push button, and then grasping a near ball (see Fischman et al., 2008, for details). Each of these actions was to be completed as quickly as possible.

Henry and Rogers measured the RT to initiate each of these actions—the interval from the presentation of the stimulus until the beginning of the required movement, which always began with a simple finger lift. (Remember that RT does not include the time to complete the movement itself.) They found that the time to initiate the movement increased with added movement complexity.

1. The simple finger-lift movement had an RT of 150 ms.
2. The intermediate-complexity movement had an RT of 195 ms.
3. The movement with two reversals in direction had an RT of 208 ms.

Notice that in each case, the stimulus to signal the movement (processed during the stimulus identification stage) and the number of movement choices (processed during the response selection stage) remained the same for all three movement complexities. Thus, because the only factor that varied was the complexity of the movement, the interpretation was that the elevated RTs were somehow caused by increased time for movement programming to occur before the action began. This notion has had profound effects on the understanding of movement organization processes and has led to many further research efforts to study these processes more systematically (see Christina, 1992; Klapp, 2010). Most importantly, these data support the idea that rapid movement is organized in advance, which is consistent with the motor program concept.

Exploring Further

1. Analyze the differences in actions required for the three movements in the Henry and Rogers study. Describe at least three differences in the movements' requirements that might have led to increases in the complexity of the motor program.
2. What additional changes could be made to the action requirements of the most complex movement that might be expected to increase movement programming time?

son, the sounds of a chainsaw and music at a rock concert typically only reach 120 dB). This loud acoustic signal usually produces the typical startle indicators (clenched neck and jaw muscles, etc.). However, what also happens is that the prepared movement is carried out as planned but initiated with an RT up to 100 ms faster than on the control trials.

These findings fit quite well with the motor program concept. The idea here is that the executive has prepared a motor program in advance of the stimulus to respond, which is normally released by a voluntary, internal go-signal from the executive to the effectors. The startle RT hastens the release of this signal by either speeding up the executive's processing time or perhaps even bypassing the executive altogether. Evidence for this interpretation was supported by an experiment by Maslovat and colleagues (2014), which combined the movement complexity and startle methodologies. They found that simple, voluntary RT increased as the movement to be made became more complex, replicating the effect discussed in the last section (Henry & Rogers, 1960). Importantly, they also found that RTs elicited by a startle also increased with more complex movements—suggesting that as the movement increased in complexity, even its involuntary release (via the startle) was influenced by the complexity of the movement to be made.

The Gunslinger Effect

Have you ever noticed that in a Western action movie in which two combatants duel in a gunfight, the person who draws first almost always dies (figure 5.3)? According to Kelso (1995), this curiosity was first noted by the famous physicist Niels Bohr, who occasionally took his research team to see old Western movies to lighten up the mood in the lab. Could this really happen? Would starting to move before the other person be a bad idea?

Studies that addressed this question asked pairs of research participants to play a competitive game in which the simple goal was to complete an upper-arm movement faster than their opponent (Welchman et al., 2010). As Bohr had observed, when a participant moved first, they did so more slowly than when they were reacting (Welchman et al., 2010), especially when kinematics such as peak velocity and the time to reach peak velocity were measured (LaDelfa et al., 2013). Nicknamed the "gunslinger effect" by LaDelfa and colleagues, this somewhat surprising finding has been replicated in experiments using more complex actions, such as a karate punch (Martinez De Quel & Bennett, 2014) or a whole-body sidestep (Wakatsuki & Yamada, 2020).

The gunslinger effect is consistent with the evidence provided in this section. Voluntary movements (such as drawing a pistol) require

FIGURE 5.3 The gunslinger effect: In the lore of Western movies, the person who draws first usually dies.

the planning and initiation of a motor program. The initiation process can be hastened with a signal to respond, especially if it is startling. Seeing another person draw first is both a visual signal to respond and mildly startling, having the effect of releasing the motor program earlier than in a voluntary initiation (Weller et al., 2018).

Deafferentation Experiments

In chapter 4, we mentioned that information from the muscles, joints, and skin is collected in sensory nerves, which enter the spinal cord at various levels. A surgical technique termed **deafferentation** involves severing (via surgery) an animal's afferent nerve bundles where they enter the cord, so the central nervous system can no longer receive information from some portion of the periphery. This procedure does not affect the motor pathways because information about motor activity passes through the (uncut) ventral (front) side of the cord. Sensory information from an entire limb or even from several limbs can be eliminated by this procedure.

What are experimental animals capable of doing when deprived of feedback from their limbs? Monkeys with deafferented upper limbs can still climb, playfully chase each other, groom, and feed themselves essentially normally. It is indeed difficult to recognize that these animals have a total loss of sensory information from the upper limbs (Taub, 1976; Taub & Berman, 1968). The monkeys are impaired in some ways, however; they have difficulty with fine finger control, such as picking up a pea or manipulating small objects. On balance, it is remarkable how little impaired these animals are in most activities.

Human case studies also show that some types of movement control are preserved in the absence of sensory feedback. Lashley (1917) reported that a patient with a gunshot wound to the back, leaving him without sensory feedback from the legs, could still position his lower leg quite accurately while blindfolded. And individuals who have lost much of their sensory feedback (called **sensory neuropathy** patients) can perform quite well in their environments as long as visual information is available (Blouin et al., 1996).

These studies suggest that sensory information from the moving limb is not absolutely critical for movement production because many movements can occur nearly normally without it. This evidence suggests that theories of movement control must be generally incorrect if they require sensory information from the responding limb. Because feedback-based theories cannot account for these actions, many theorists have argued that the movements must be organized centrally via motor programs and carried out in an open-loop way, not critically dependent on feedback (e.g., Keele, 1968). In this sense, the deafferentation evidence supports the idea that movements can be organized centrally in motor programs.

Central Pattern Generators

The idea of motor programs has some similarity to that of the **central pattern generator (CPG)**, which was developed to explain certain features of locomotion in animals, such as swimming in fish, chewing in hamsters, and slithering in snakes (Forssberg et al., 1975). A genetically defined central organization is established in the brainstem or the spinal cord. When this organization is initiated by a brief triggering stimulus from the brain, sometimes called a *command neuron*, it produces rhythmic, oscillating commands to the musculature as if it were defining a sequence of right–left–right activities, such as might serve as the basis of locomotion. These commands occur even if the sensory nerves are cut (deafferented), suggesting that the organization is truly central in origin.

The notion of the CPG is almost identical to that of the motor program. The main difference is that the motor program involves learned activities that are centrally controlled (such as kicking and throwing), whereas the CPG involves more genetically defined activities, such as locomotion, chewing, and breathing (Zehr, 2005).

The concept of a central pattern generator is used to describe simple, genetically defined activities such as walking, whereas motor program theory applies to learned skills such as riding a bicycle. List two other activities performed by animals in this photo that are likely controlled by CPGs.

Inhibiting Actions

Another line of evidence to support motor program control can be found in experiments in which participants are required to inhibit or stop a movement after having initiated the process of making the action. This is the kind of activity that one sees quite frequently in baseball batting (see Focus on Application 5.1). A question frequently asked by researchers concerns what is called *the point of no return*—at what point after starting the processing stages that lead to a movement is one committed to making, or at least starting, the action? In other words, at what point is the signal released to send the motor program to the muscles?

The *stop-signal paradigm* is the method most frequently used to study action inhibition. Slater-Hammel (1960) provided an early contribution to this research, which Focus on Research 5.2 and figure 5.4 describe in detail. The findings of this study, which involved a very simple finger lift off a key (presumably with little biomechanical delay), suggest that the point of no return occurred about 150 to 170 ms before the time when the movement was initiated. Other evidence suggests that a motor program is released that is responsible for initiating and carrying out the entire action unless a second motor program is initiated in time to stop or change its completion (see Verbruggen & Logan, 2008).

Visit HK*Propel* to read "The Point of No Return" and complete the self-directed learning activities.

Muscle Activity in Blocked Movements

The final line of evidence supporting the existence of motor programs comes from

FOCUS ON **Application 5.1**

Checked Swings in Baseball

The bat swing in baseball is a good example of an attempt to halt a motor program after it has been initiated. The typical swing consists of a coordinated action involving a step with the lead foot toward the oncoming ball, followed by a rapid rotation of the trunk and shoulders, propelling the bat with a large angular velocity and minimum overall movement time. There is good reason to believe that the step and swing are part of a single motor program initiated by elite batters on almost every pitch but that latter parts of the swing are *inhibited* before a full execution on many of those pitches. How do batters do this, and how successful are they?

The physics of baseball tell us that there is very little time available for a major league batter to hit a baseball. For pitches over 85 mph (137km/h), the ball takes less than a half second to reach the hitting zone after being released from the pitcher's hand. The batter typically prepares for the pitch and may initiate the step before the pitcher has actually released the ball. At some point along the way, usually before the ball reaches the midpoint in its flight toward the plate, the batter must decide whether to proceed with the swing (including where to aim the bat for its intended collision with the ball) or inhibit its execution. The result is four different types of batter responses (see Gray, 2009, for more on these ideas):

1. The batter successfully completely inhibits the motor program, and the swing is never initiated.
2. The batter starts the swing but inhibits the completion of the motor program, resulting in the bat stopping before it crosses the plate (defined as a *nonswing* in baseball rules).
3. The batter starts the swing but fails to inhibit the motor program in time, resulting in a slowed velocity of the bat as it crosses the plate (resulting in a completed swing).
4. The batter starts and completes the motor program with no attempt to inhibit the swing—a classic example of a completed swing.

experiments that examine patterns of muscle activity during a brief limb action. Figure 5.5 illustrates integrated electromyogram (EMG) tracings from a quick elbow extension movement (Wadman et al., 1979). In the normal movement (red lines), first there is a burst of the agonist muscle (here, the triceps). Then the triceps turns off, and the antagonist muscle (the biceps) is activated to decelerate the limb. Finally, the agonist comes on again near the end to stabilize the limb at the target area. This triple-burst pattern (agonist–antagonist–agonist) is typical of quick movements of this kind.

On some trials, occasionally and quite unexpectedly, the experimenter mechanically blocked the lever so that no movement was possible. Figure 5.5 also shows what happens to the EMG patterning on these blocked trials (blue lines). Even though the limb does not move at all, there is a similar pattern of muscular organization, with the onset of the agonist and the antagonist occurring at about the same times as when the movement was not blocked. Later, after about 120 ms or so, there is a slight modification of the patterning, probably caused by the reflex activities

FOCUS ON Research 5.2

Initiating a Motor Program

Before sprint officiating was automated, races like the 100 m were timed by hand with a stopwatch. The timing judge, positioned at the finish line, started her stopwatch when she saw the smoke of the starter's pistol and stopped it when she *anticipated* the runners crossing the finish line. If she stopped it when she *actually* saw the runner cross the line, then the clock would be stopped a short time later, because completing her action would be delayed by two factors: (1) the time required to send the motor instructions to the hand holding the watch and (2) the biomechanical delay in pushing the button. Therefore, the problem for the judge in accurately timing the point when the sprinter actually crossed the finish line is that she must initiate her command signal by a duration that equals the sum of the two factors just defined prior to the runner's arrival at the finish line. In other words, she had to anticipate how long this sum would be and initiate the motor program to stop her watch at exactly that amount of time prior to the runner crossing the line.

Our interest, of course, concerns how long it takes to send the motor instructions. Arthur Slater-Hammel (1960) provided one answer to this question. Participants held a finger on a key while watching an analog timer rotate at one revolution per second; lifting the finger off the key brought the sweep hand to an instantaneous stop. Participants were instructed to lift their finger from the key such that the clock hand would stop at exactly the point marked "800," or roughly at the 10 o'clock position on the clock (see figure 5.4*a*, the "800" label refers to a lapse of 800 ms after the start from the 12:00 position). Note that in order to do this task accurately, similar to the sprint timing judge, participants in the study would need to initiate the motor instructions to lift the finger at some point before the clock hand actually reached the 800 position. But how long before?

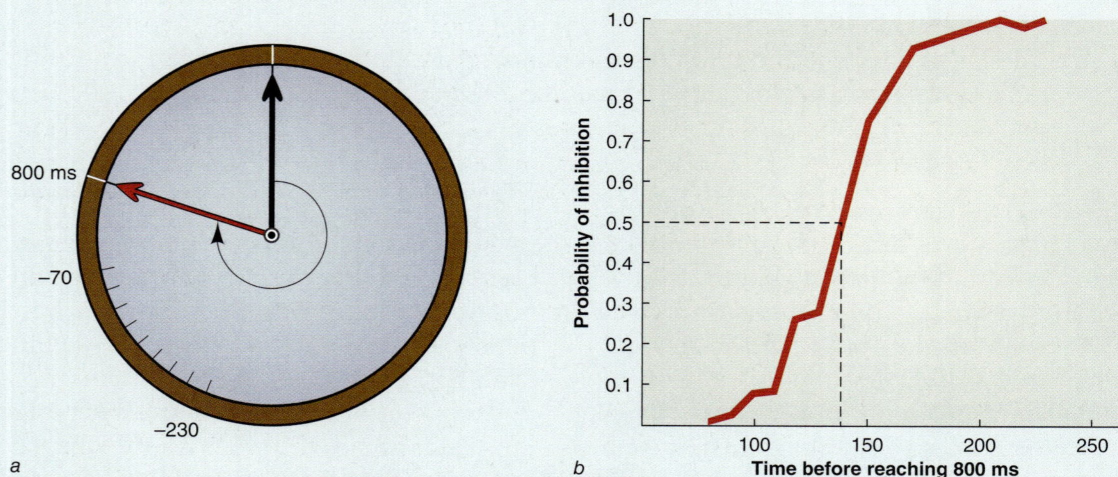

FIGURE 5.4 Slater-Hammel's (1960) *(a)* task and *(b)* results.

A critically important aspect of the Slater-Hammel study was the insertion of special probe trials that occurred rarely and unpredictably. On these probe trials, the experimenter would stop the clock hand at various locations before it reached 800 (locations denoted by the tick marks on the clock face in figure 5.4*a*, occurring between −70 and −230 ms before the 800 mark). If the sweep hand stopped at one of these tick mark locations, the participant's job was simply to keep his or her finger on the key. Thus, the probe trials required an inhibition of the normal task of lifting the finger to stop the sweep hand. The rationale was elegantly simple—if the motor instructions had not yet been sent to the muscles when they saw the sweep hand stop, then the participant should be able to successfully inhibit the finger lift. Conversely, there would be little chance of inhibiting such a short, ballistic action if the command to lift the finger had already been sent. Therefore, plotting inhibition success as a function of the tick mark location where the sweep hand stopped should provide an estimate of how long it takes to send the motor command to lift the finger.

The probability of successfully inhibiting the finger lift by Slater-Hammel's participants is shown in figure 5.4*b*. When the time before the 800 mark was relatively large (e.g., at the −230 tick mark on the clock in figure 5.4*a*), seeing the clock hand stop resulted in successfully inhibiting the movement almost all the time (probability of inhibition near 1.0 in figure 5.4*b*). However, as this interval decreased (i.e., became closer to 800), the participants became less successful at inhibiting their finger lift, to the point that when the clock hand stopped at the −70 mark in figure 5.4*a* (70 ms before the 800 mark), the participants almost never inhibited the movement (probability of inhibition near 0 in figure 5.4*b*). Generally, when the sweep hand was stopped about 130 to 150 ms before the intended finger lift, the participant could inhibit the movement successfully about half the time (corresponding to an average probability of inhibition equaling .5 in figure 5.4*b*). This finding means that the motor command to lift the finger was issued about 130 to 150 ms before the intended action, on average. This go-signal is a trigger for action, after which the movement occurs even though new information indicates that the movement should be inhibited.

Exploring Further

1. Slater-Hammel's estimate of the time required to anticipate the sweep hand's arrival at the 800 position is complicated by the fact that participants had a +26 ms constant error (CE) on the normal trials (the non-probe trials). What implications does this positively biased CE have for the estimated time when the internal go-signal is issued?
2. How could this stop-signal paradigm be adapted to examine the time required to make anticipatory actions in sport tasks such as batting a baseball?

(e.g., stretch reflexes) discussed in chapter 4. But the most important findings are that the antagonist (biceps) and second agonist (triceps) muscles even contracted at all when the movement was blocked, and that they contracted in approximately the same pattern as in the normal (unblocked) movements.

How is it possible for this essentially normal EMG activity to be produced for a movement that is never made or, indeed, even started? The feedback from the blocked limb must have been massively disrupted, yet the EMG patterning was essentially normal for 100 ms or so. These data contradict theories arguing that feedback from the moving limb (during the action) acts as a signal (a trigger) to activate the antagonist muscle contraction at the proper time. Rather, these findings are

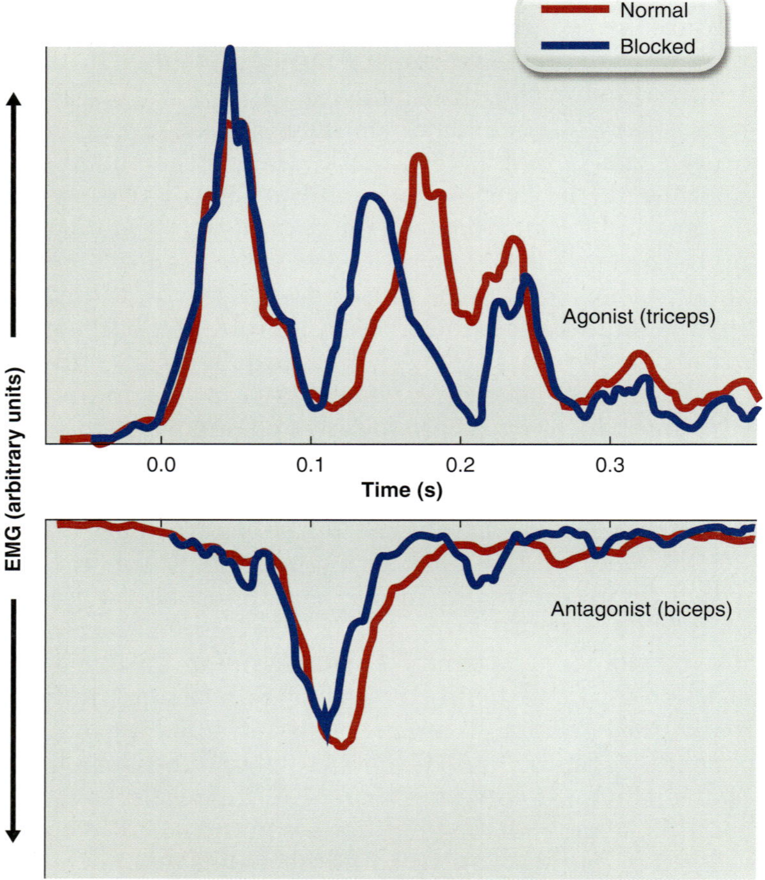

FIGURE 5.5 Electromyographic results from agonist (upper traces) and antagonist (lower traces) muscles when the participant actually produced the movement (normal trials—red lines) and when the movement was mechanically blocked (blocked trials—blue lines).

some of the strongest data in support of the motor program idea that movement activities are organized in advance and briefly run off unmodified by sensory information until the first reflexive activities can become involved.

Motor Programs and the Conceptual Model

Motor programs are a critical part of the conceptual model in figure 5.2; they operate within the system, sometimes in conjunction with feedback, to produce flexibly skilled actions. The open-loop part of these actions provides the organization, or pattern, that the feedback processes can later modify if necessary. Some of the major roles of these open-loop organizations are

- to define and issue the commands to musculature that determine when, how forcefully, and for how long muscles are to contract and which ones are to contract;
- to organize the many degrees of freedom of the muscles and joints into a unit;
- to specify and initiate preliminary postural adjustments necessary to support the upcoming action; and
- to modulate the many reflex pathways to ensure that the movement goal is achieved.

In the following sections, we discuss research examples of how motor programs use anticipatory and feedback information to regulate movement control.

Anticipatory Movement

Imagine that you are standing with your arms at your sides and an experimenter gives you a command to raise an arm quickly to point straight ahead. What will be the first detectable EMG (muscular) activity associated with this movement? Most people would guess that the first contraction would be in the shoulder muscles that raise the arm. But, in fact, the EMG activity in these muscles occurs relatively late in the action. Instead, the first muscles to contract are in the lower back and legs, some 80 ms before the first shoulder muscle contracts (Belen'kii et al., 1967).

This ordering of muscle contractions may sound strange, but it is really quite a smart way for the motor system to operate. Because the shoulder muscles are mechanically linked to the rest of the body, their contractions influence the positions of the segments connected to the arm—the shoulder and the back. That is, the movement of the arm affects posture. If no compensations in posture were made first, then raising the arm would cause the trunk to flex as well as shift the center of gravity forward, causing a loss of balance. Therefore, rather than adjusting for these effects *after* the arm movement, the motor system compensates for the anticipated destabilization *before* the arm movement.

There is good evidence that these preparatory postural adjustments are part of the movement program for making the arm movement (Lee, 1980). When the arm movement is organized, the motor program contains instructions to adjust the posture in advance as well as instructions to move the arm so that the action is a coordinated whole. Thus, we should not think of the arm movement and the posture control as separate events; rather, these are simply different parts of an integrated action of raising the arm and maintaining posture and balance. Interestingly, these preparatory adjustments vanish when the performer leans against a support, because a postural imbalance is not anticipated.

Integration of Central and Feedback Control

Although central organization of movements is a major source of motor control, it is also very clear (see chapter 4) that sensory information can modify these commands in several important ways, as illustrated in the conceptual model in figure 5.2. Thus, the question becomes how and under what conditions these commands from motor programs interact with sensory information to define the overall movement pattern. This is one of the most important research issues for understanding motor control.

Reflex-Reversal Phenomenon

In addition to the various classes of reflex mechanisms discussed in chapter 4 that can modify the originally programmed output (figure 4.10), another class of reflexive modulations exists that has very different effects on the movement behavior. Several experiments show how reflex responses are integrated with open-loop programmed control.

In one study, for example, the experimenter applied a light tactile stimulus to the top of a cat's foot while it was walking on a treadmill. When this stimulus was applied as the cat was just *placing* its foot on the surface of the treadmill (in preparation for load bearing), the response was to extend the leg slightly, as if to carry more load on that foot. This response has a latency of about 30 to 50 ms and is clearly nonconscious and automatic. When the same stimulus was applied when the cat was just *lifting* the foot from the surface (in preparation for the swing phase), the response was very different. The leg flexed upward at the hip and the knee, so the foot traveled above the usual trajectory in the swing phase. Thus, the same stimulus has different (reversed) effects when it is presented at different locations in the step cycle.

These alterations in the reflex—reversing its effect from extension to flexion (or vice versa) depending on where in the step cycle the stimulus is applied—have been called the **reflex-reversal phenomenon** (Forssberg et al., 1975). It challenges our usual conceptualizations of a reflex, which is typically defined as an automatic, stereotyped, unavoidable response to a given stimulus. Here, the same stimulus has generated two different reflexive responses.

Movement Flexibility

Complex reflex responses play an important role in the flexibility and control of skills. The cat's reflexes are probably organized to have an important survival role. Receiving a tactile stimulus on the top of the foot while it is swinging forward probably means that the foot has struck some object and that the cat will trip if the foot is not lifted quickly over the object. However, if the stimulus is received during the beginning of stance, flexing the leg would cause the animal to fall because it is swinging the opposite leg at this time.

Analogous findings have been shown in speech research, where slight, unexpected tugs on the lower lip during the production of a sound cause rapid, reflexive modulation, with the actual responses critically dependent on the particular sound being attempted (Abbs et al., 1984; Kelso et al., 1984). The concern for the motor system in such situations is to ensure that the intended action is generated and that the goal is achieved (in this case, making the desired speech sound).

This adaptable feature of a movement program provides considerable flexibility in its operation. The movement can be carried out as programmed if nothing goes wrong. If something does go wrong, then appropriate reflexes are allowed to participate in the movement to ensure that the goal is met.

Problems in Motor Program Theory: Novelty and Storage

Open-loop control allows the motor system to organize an entire, usually rapid, action in advance without having to rely on the relatively slow information-processing stages involved in a closed-loop control mode. Several processes must be handled by this prior organization. At a minimum, the following must be specified in the programming process in order to generate skilled movements:

- The *muscles* that are to participate in the action
- The *order* in which these muscles are to be activated
- The **relative timing** and sequencing of these contractions
- The *duration* of each contraction
- The *forces* of the muscle contraction

Most motor program theories assume that a movement is organized in advance by the establishment of a neural mechanism, or network, that contains time and event information. Some type of movement "script" specifies certain essential details of the action as it runs off in time. Therefore, scientists speak of *running* a motor program, which is analogous to the processes involved in running computer programs.

However, motor program theory, at least as developed so far in this chapter, does not account for several important aspects of movement behavior. Perhaps the two most severe limitations of motor program theory are (1) the lack of efficiency that would be required to store in memory the massive number of motor programs that would be required and (2) the failure to account for how novel movements are produced.

This capability for producing novel actions raises problems for the simple, detailed motor program theory as we have developed it so far. To this point in the chapter, we have provided evidence for the view that details for producing a rapid, discrete movement are stored as a program in long-term memory. For example, each variation in a tennis stroke used to produce shots that differ in the height and speed of the ball, the intended location of the ball placement, the distance to the net, and so on, would need a unique and separate program stored in memory because the instructions for the musculature would be different for each variation. Extending this view further suggests that we would need, quite literally, a countless number of motor programs stored in memory just to play tennis. Add to this the number of movements possible in all other activities of daily living, and the result would be an impossibly large number of programs stored in long-term memory. This represents the **storage problem** (Schmidt, 1975), which concerns the capacity required for storing all these separate programs in memory and making them instantly accessible when needed.

Many years ago, the British psychologist Sir Fredrick Bartlett (1932), in writing about tennis, said this: "When I make the stroke, I do not . . . produce something absolutely new, and I never repeat something old" (p. 202). What did he mean? The first part of his statement means that, even though a movement is in some sense novel, it is never totally brand new. Each of his ground strokes resembles his other ground strokes, possessing his own style of hitting a tennis ball. The second part of Bartlett's statement conveys the idea that every movement is novel in that it has never been performed exactly that way before. This raises the crux of the **novelty problem**—if motor programs stored in memory are responsible for all such rapid movements, how could something essentially new be based on something previously stored in memory? The simple, detailed motor program theory, as presented here to this point, fails to explain the performance of such novel actions.

The novelty and storage problems of motor program theory motivated a search for alternative ways to understand motor control. There was a desire to keep the appealing parts of motor program theory but to modify them to solve the storage and novelty problems. The idea that emerged was that motor programs must be generalized (Schmidt, 1975). This generalized motor program (GMP) consists of a representation that is stored in memory and retrieved and adjusted at the time of movement execution, allowing the action to meet the current needs.

Generalized Motor Program Theory

The quote from Bartlett captures the essence of GMP theory: Some features of the tennis stroke remain the same from shot to shot, and some features of the stroke are changed each time. According to GMP theory, what remains the same are the **invariant features** of a motor program—those features of the movement pattern that remain essentially the same, time after time. Invariant features are the reason our unique writing style appears the same regardless of whether we are using a pen to write in a notebook, using a marker to write large enough on a whiteboard for everyone in a large class to read, or using our toe to write something in the sand on a beach.

In GMP theory, the relatively superficial or **surface features** of a movement represent those aspects that change from stroke to stroke (in Bartlett's quote). If the general pattern represents the invariant features of your writing style, then modifying what are called **parameters** determines how it is executed at any one time, representing its surface features. Writing something slow or fast, large or small, on paper or in the sand, with a pen or a toe, and so on, represents how the GMP is executed at that particular time.

The word *parameter* is borrowed from mathematics and represents values that can be applied to an equation but do not change the form of the equation itself. For example, in a linear equation whose general form is $Y = a + bX$, the values a and b are parameters—Y and X are related to each other in the same way by the equation regardless of the values used for a and b. In making a movement, the unique performance that occurs when certain parameters are applied does not alter the invariant characteristics of the GMP—the parameters change only how the GMP is expressed as a movement at any given time.

In GMP theory, movements are thought to be produced as follows: A GMP for throwing (as opposed to kicking), for example, is determined as appropriate in the stimulus identification stage and then retrieved from long-term memory during the response selection stage. One of the necessary processes after the GMP has been retrieved is to define how to execute this program. Decisions regarding which limb to use, how fast to throw, which direction to throw, and how far to throw must be based on the available environmental information. These decisions result in the assignment of movement parameters—characteristics that define the nature of the program's execution without influencing the invariant characteristics of the GMP. Parameters include the speed of movement, its amplitude (overall size), and the limb used. Once the parameters have been determined, the movement can be executed using this particular set of surface features.

According to GMP theory, the key variables to consider are what constitute the invariant features of the GMP and what constitute the parameters, or surface features. These important issues will be discussed in the next sections.

Invariant Features of a GMP

To understand the nature of GMPs, we need to know what features of the movement patterns remain invariant, or constant, as the surface features (such as movement speed, movement amplitude, and forces) are altered. When movement time is altered, for example, almost every other aspect of the movement changes too. The forces and durations of contractions, the speed of the limbs, and the distances the limbs travel all can change markedly as the movement speeds up.

However, what if some aspects of these movements could be shown to remain constant even though just about everything else was changing? If such a constant could be found, scientists argued, it might indicate something fundamental about the basis for all these movements, thus providing evidence for how motor programs are represented in long-term memory. Such a constant value is termed an *invariance*, and the most important

Generalized motor program theory suggests that the motor program for signing your name retains its invariant features, no matter what you are writing on.

invariance concerns the temporal structuring of the pattern (the rhythm or relative timing).

Relative Timing

Rhythm, or relative timing, is a fundamental feature of many of our daily activities. Of course, rhythm is critically important in such activities as music and dance. But timing is also a key feature of many sporting activities (such as baseball batting) and work activities (e.g., typing, hammering). There is strong evidence to suggest that relative time is an invariant feature of the GMP. An example is the evidence provided in the Armstrong (1970) study, discussed in Focus on Research 5.3. Compare the peaks of the red line with the peaks of the blue line in figure 5.6—you will notice that the whole movement appeared to speed up as a unit. That is, each of the peaks (movement reversals) occurred sooner and sooner in real (or absolute) time but occurred at about the same point relative to the overall timing structure of the pattern; hence the term *relative time* (see Gentner, 1987, or Schmidt et al., 2025, for more on these issues).

Relative timing is the fundamental temporal structure of a movement pattern that is independent of its overall speed or amplitude. Relative timing represents the movement's fundamental "deep structure," as opposed to the surface features seen in the easily modified alterations in movement time. This deep temporal organization in movements seems to be invariant, even when the actions are produced at different speeds or amplitudes.

More specifically, as illustrated in figure 5.7, *relative timing* refers to the ratios of the durations of several intervals within the movement. Consider two hypothetical arm throwing movements, with movement 1 being performed with a shorter movement time than movement 2. Imagine that you measure and record the EMGs from three of the important muscles involved in each action (in principle, nearly any feature of the movement could be measured, not just EMG). If you measure several of these contraction durations, you can define relative timing by a set of ratios, each defined as part of the action's duration divided by the total duration. For example, in

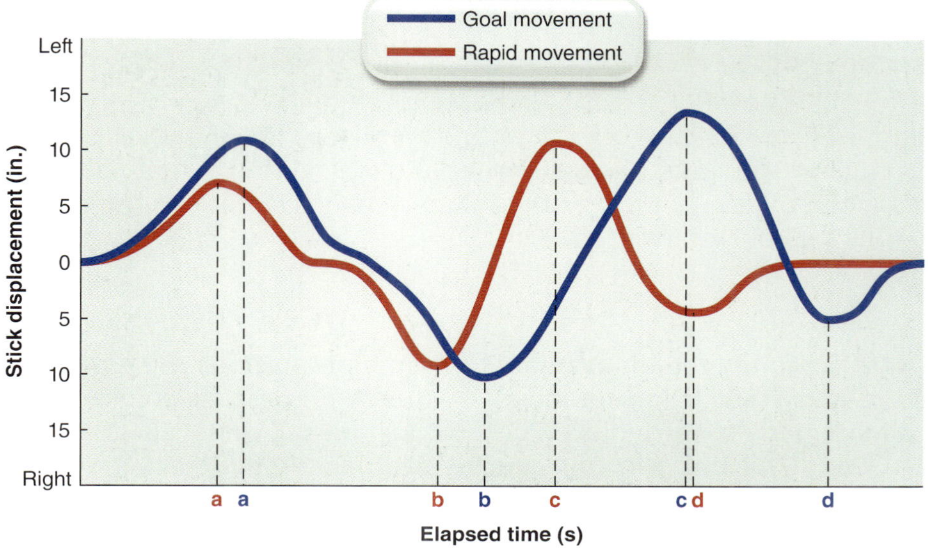

FIGURE 5.6 Participants learned to make timed left and right reversal movements of a lever. The blue line depicts the goal movement pattern. The red line represents a trial in which the movement is made too rapidly. The error in the timing of the reversals increases as the movement unfolds, which is what would happen if the movement depicted by the red line were simply a speeded-up version of the movement depicted by the blue line.

FOCUS ON Research 5.3

Invariances and Parameters

Armstrong (1970) made an important contribution to the development of the GMP theory by analyzing the patterns of movements that participants had learned to make. In Armstrong's experiment, learners attempted to move a lever to the left and right with a timing pattern that resulted in the blue line in figure 5.6. This goal movement (blue line) had four major reversals in direction, each of which was to be produced at a particular time in the action, with the total movement lasting about 4 s. Many practice trials were conducted, resulting in a well-learned movement pattern.

Of particular interest here, Armstrong noticed that when the learner happened to make the first reversal movement too quickly, the whole movement was also done too quickly. This is shown as the red line in figure 5.6. Notice that the red line's first peak (at reversal) was just a little bit early (compare the blue and red *a* positions). The discrepancy between the actual and goal reversal times increased roughly proportionally as the movement progressed (compare the reversal positions on the red vs. blue lines at positions *b*, *c*, and *d*). This gives the impression that every aspect of the movement pattern was produced essentially correctly but that the entire pattern was simply performed too quickly on this trial.

Armstrong's findings provided early evidence for the idea that the motor program can be generalized (Schmidt, 1975). The program controlled the relative timing of the movement reversals. When an early reversal appeared sooner or later than the goal time, all the subsequent reversals sped up or slowed proportionally.

Exploring Further

1. In Armstrong's figure (figure 5.6), sketch a line on the graph of how you predict an action with a 4.5 s overall movement time would look if the participant had preserved the same relative-timing structure.
2. Suppose Armstrong's participants had performed the pattern again, one month after the original practice sessions. Which do you think would be remembered better, the overall timing or the relative-time structure of the pattern? Give reasons for your answer.

movement 1, *a* refers to the total movement duration, and *b*, *c*, and *d* refer to the durations of three measurable parts of the action. The ratios $b/a = .40$, $c/a = .30$, and $d/a = .60$ can then be calculated. This pattern of ratios is characteristic of this throwing movement, describing its temporal structure relatively accurately.

In movement 2, despite a longer overall duration, this set of ratios stays the same because the values of b/a, c/a, and d/a are the same proportions as in movement 1. When this set of ratios is constant in two different movements, we say that the relative timing is invariant. Notice that movement 2 seems to be simply an elongated (horizontally stretched) version of movement 1, with all the temporal events occurring more slowly in a systematic manner. This will always be found when relative timing is invariant. According to the theory, the same GMP was used to produce both movements 1 and 2, but movement 2

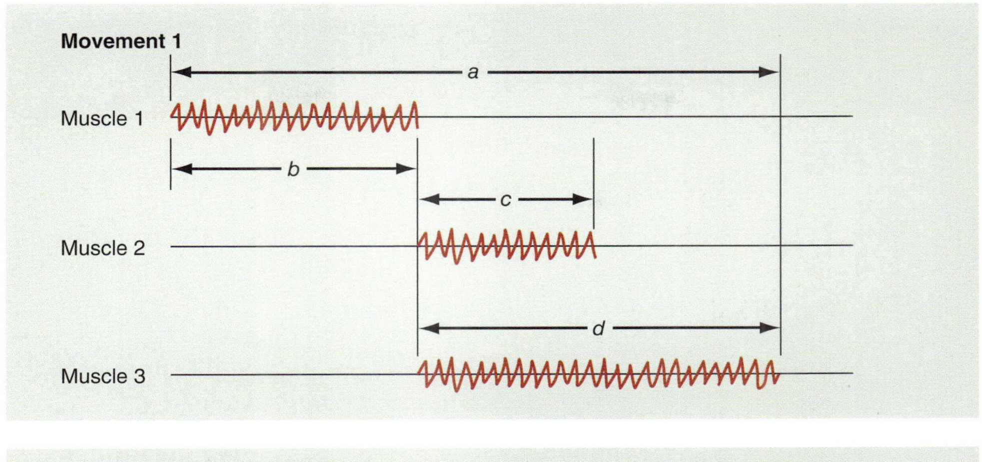

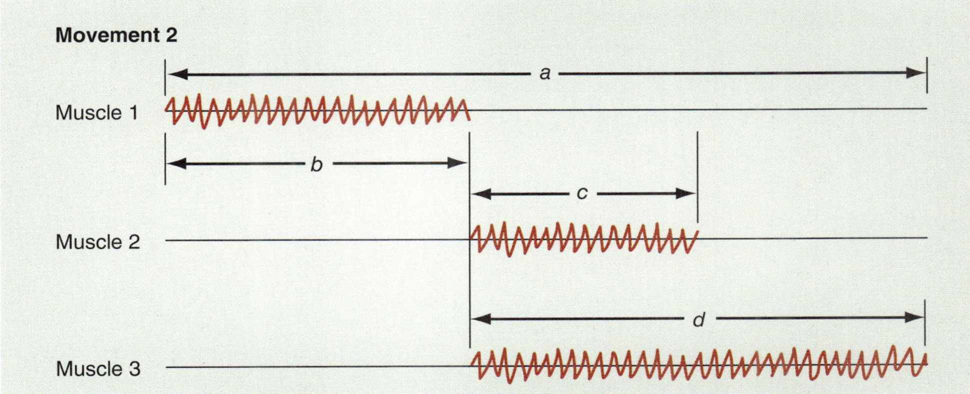

FIGURE 5.7 Hypothetical relative timing of EMG traces from three muscles for two hypothetical throwing movements. The relative-time ratios are computed by dividing the muscle EMG durations (i.e., *b*, *c*, and *d*) for each muscle by the overall movement time (i.e., *a*). Notice that these ratios remain roughly constant when the movement time of the action changes (movement 1 performed with less overall MT than movement 2).

was produced with a slower timing parameter than movement 1. The whole movement was slowed down as a unit, but its relative timing was preserved.

One of the important principles of movement control is that when a well-learned, brief, rapid movement is altered, it is done so with invariant relative timing. This occurs, for example, when changing the speed of the movement (a fast vs. a slow throw), the size of the movement (making your signature large or small), or the trajectory of the movement (throwing overarm vs. sidearm). Relative timing is invariant across different kinds of modifications, so the form of the movement is preserved even though the superficial features may change. There is some controversy about whether relative timing is perfectly invariant (Gentner, 1987; Heuer, 1988), but there can be no doubt that relative timing is at least approximately invariant.

Note that the relative timing actually produced by a performer can be thought of as a kind of "fingerprint" that is unique to a particular movement class. This pattern can be used to identify which of several motor programs has been executed (Schneider & Schmidt, 1995; Young & Schmidt, 1990). Focus on Application 5.2 provides more examples of how our GMPs reflect other kinds of biological fingerprints.

Classes of Movements

An activity like overarm throwing represents a class of movements consisting of a nearly infinite number of specific activities (e.g.,

FOCUS ON Application 5.2

Relative-Timing Biometrics

There are three types of identity verification methods: 1) something physical that you *possess*, such as a key; 2) something that you *know*, such as a password; or 3) something that you *are*, such as your fingerprint. Included in this last category of biometrics is your signature, traditionally used to verify you as the rightful owner of a check or credit card. A person's signature is usually considered unique and different from anyone else's signature. Forging the spatial characteristics of a signature is not a difficult task, however. All the forger needs to do is obtain the target signature, compare the illegal and legal signatures, and continue to practice by making improvements on the imperfections until a realistic forgery is difficult to distinguish from the real signature. A password that is typed into an account on a computer is even easier to forge if the fraudster knows the correct characters to enter. However, relative timing is the missing ingredient in both of these cases of fraud.

Suppose, for example, that when you signed your name, the spatial and temporal recordings of each of the various loops and cursives in producing the letters, as well as the timing of crossing your t's and dotting your i's and so on, were compared to a large data bank in which many examples of your previous signature time stamps had been stored. According to GMP theory, the invariant characteristics of your signature would be repeated regardless of the tool you used to sign your name (e.g., familiar or unfamiliar pen), the surface on which you wrote it (e.g., paper or digital tablet), or the size of your signature. Most importantly, the fraudster who had access only to the spatial characteristics of your signature would be at a loss to replicate its relative timing.

Typing your password also has a relative-timing characteristic that is uniquely yours, especially for those such as the authors of this book who are not trained typists. We each have our own unique style of typing—which letters are typically contacted with which fingers, how long each key is held down (dwell time), and the transition times between specific letters. Once again, a data bank of previous executions of our passwords would give rise to a range of overall timings of these dwell and transition times, from which a relative-timing profile could be derived and to which the fraudster (hopefully) would not have access.

Fortunately for us, these methods of using digital knowledge of our GMPs are now a reality. A field of research that examines keystroke dynamics reveals an emerging technology and industry that is designed to improve identity verification (Thomas & Mathew, 2023). In many ways, your signature and typed passwords are relative-timing fingerprints that are unique to you.

throwing various objects with different velocities and trajectories). The theory holds that the entire class is represented by a single GMP with a specific relative-timing structure. This program can have parameters in several dimensions (e.g., movement time, amplitude), making possible an essentially limitless number of combinations of specific throwing movements, each of which contains the same relative timing.

Locomotion represents another class of movements that a GMP could control. Research by Shapiro and colleagues (1981) suggests that, in fact, there are at least two separate GMPs for gait, each with unique relative timings—one for walking and another for running. Similar to the throwing example, however, we can speed up and slow down either the walking or running gait selectively without necessarily having to abandon the GMP.

Shapiro and colleagues (1981) studied the shifts in relative timing in locomotion. They recorded people on a treadmill at speeds ranging from 3 to 12 km/h and measured the durations of various phases of the step cycle as the movement speed increased. When the treadmill speed ranged from 3 to 6 km/h, all participants walked. Regardless of the speed, the relative time used for each phase of the step cycle remained about the same. When the treadmill speed was increased to 8 km/h, however, where now all participants were running, the relative-timing pattern was completely different compared to walking. But as the running speed increased from 8 to 12 km/h, there again was a tendency for these (new) proportions to remain nearly invariant.

The interpretation is that there are two GMPs operating here—one for walking and a different one for running. Each gait has its own relative-timing pattern that is quite different from the other. When the treadmill speed increases for walking, the parameter values change, but the relative timing remains the same, which speeds up the movement with the same program. At about 7 km/h, a critical speed is reached, and the participant abruptly shifts to a running program. Now there is a different relative timing (compared to walking) that is maintained nearly perfectly as running speed is increased further. (Note that alternative interpretations of the walk–run transition are discussed in chapter 7.)

Visit HK*Propel* to read "Forensic Motor Control" and complete the self-directed learning activities.

Adding Parameters to the GMP

In the previous section, we discussed some features of movement that remain the same

a

b

In each of these photos, identify one invariant characteristic of the movement and one parameter.

from one time to the next—the invariant features of the GMP. According to the theory, surface features need to be specified each time a movement is performed. That is, the GMP needs to be parameterized before it can be executed. What are some of these parameters?

Movement Time

Both the Armstrong study (1970) and the gait study by Shapiro and colleagues (1981) provided strong evidence that overall movement time could be varied without affecting the relative timing of the GMP. In Armstrong's study, the participant who accidentally sped up the movement pattern still retained the same relative timing of reversals in the movement. And the participants in the study by Shapiro and colleagues could vary speeds of walking and running without disrupting the relative timing of the step cycle. This also agrees with the common experience that we can speed up or slow down a given movement, such as throwing a ball at various speeds, without disrupting the rhythm of the component parts. These findings indicate that when duration parameters are added, the movement preserves the essential temporal-pattern features of the GMP. Therefore, overall movement time is a parameter of the GMP.

Movement Amplitude

The amplitude of movements can also be modulated easily in a way that is much like varying the time. For example, you can write your signature on a page as you would normally or five times larger on a whiteboard, and in each case, the signature is clearly "yours" (Lashley, 1942; Merton, 1972). Making this size change seems almost trivially easy.

The handwriting phenomenon was studied more formally by Hollerbach (1978), who had participants write the word *hell* in different sizes. He measured the acceleration patterns of the pen (revealing the forces delivered to the pen) during the production of the words. Figure 5.8 illustrates these accelerations. Traces that move upward indicate acceleration (force) away from the body; downward traces indicate acceleration toward the body. Of course, when the word is written larger, the overall magnitude of the accelerations produced must be larger, seen as the uniformly larger amplitudes for the larger word. But what is of most interest is that the temporal patterns of acceleration over time are almost identical for the two words, with the accelerations having similar modulations in upward and downward fluctuations.

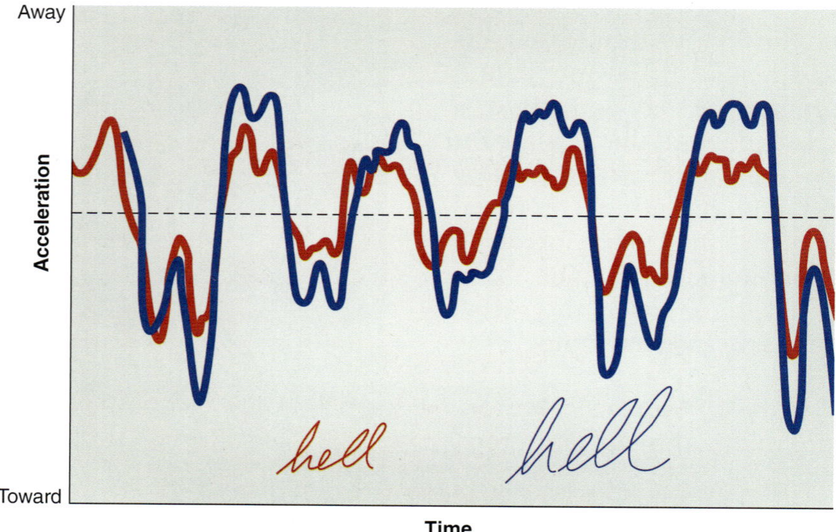

FIGURE 5.8 Acceleration-time tracings of two instances of writing the word *hell*, once in small script (red) and again in larger script (blue). Although the amplitudes (which are proportional to the forces exerted on the pen) for the two traces are markedly different, the temporal organization of the patterning remains nearly the same in the two instances.

This leads to an observation similar to the one just made about movement time. Increasing the amplitude of the movements is easy by uniformly increasing the accelerations (forces) that are applied while preserving their temporal patterning. Therefore, the same word written twice with different amplitudes can be based on a common underlying structure that can be executed with scaled forces that govern the entire movement to produce different actions of overall different sizes. Therefore, the overall amplitude of force is a parameter of the GMP.

Effectors

A performer can also modulate a movement by using a different limb—and, hence, different muscles—to produce the action. In the signature example, writing on a whiteboard involves very different muscles and joints than writing on a piece of paper. In whiteboard writing, the fingers are mainly fixed, and the writing is done with the muscles controlling the elbow and the shoulder. In writing on a piece of paper, the elbow and the shoulder are mainly fixed, and the writing is done with the muscles controlling the fingers. Yet the writing patterns produced are essentially the same. This indicates that a given pattern can be produced even when the effectors—and the muscles that drive them—are different.

These phenomena were studied by Raibert (1977), who wrote the sentence "Able was I ere I saw Elba" (a palindrome, spelled the same way backward as forward) with different effectors (i.e., limbs). In figure 5.9, line *a* shows his writing with the right (dominant) hand, line *b* with the right arm with the wrist immobilized, and line *c* with the left hand. These patterns are very similar. Even more remarkable is that line *d* was written with the pen gripped in the teeth, and line *e* used the pen taped to the foot! There are obvious similarities among the writing styles, and it seems clear that the same person wrote each of them, yet the effector system was completely different for each.

This evidence indicates that the essential features of the movement pattern are preserved despite radical changes in the effector system. Therefore, the selection of effectors can be thought of as a kind of parameter that is added to the GMP at the time of movement execution. There is an underlying structure common to these actions, which can be executed with different effector systems using the same GMP.

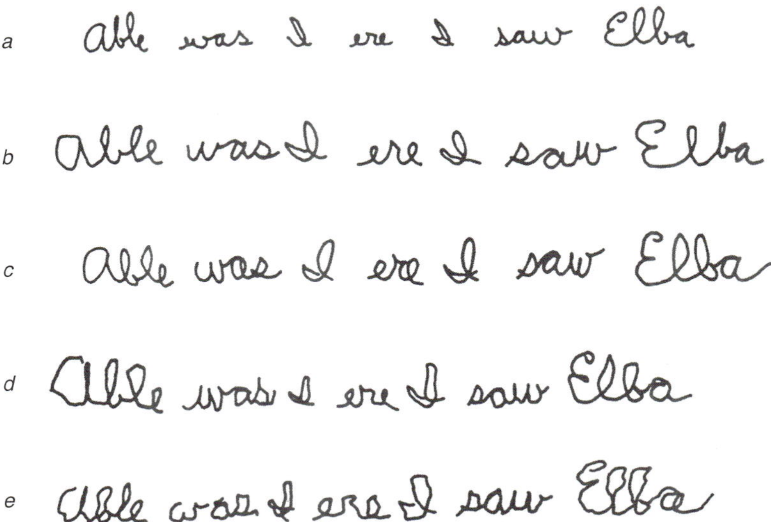

FIGURE 5.9 Five samples of writing a palindrome by the same participant, using *(a)* the dominant hand, *(b)* the dominant hand with the wrist immobilized, *(c)* the nondominant hand, *(d)* the pen gripped by the teeth, and *(e)* the pen taped between toes of the foot.

Summary of GMP Concepts

Some elements of the GMP theory can be summarized as follows:

- A GMP underlies a class of movements that are stored in long-term memory.
- This structure is characterized by its relative timing, which can be measured by a set of ratios among the durations of various events in the movement.
- Variations in movement time, movement amplitude, and the limb used represent the movement's surface structure, achieved by adding different parameters, whereas relative timing represents its deep, fundamental structure.
- Even though a movement may be carried out with different surface features (e.g., duration, amplitude), the relative timing remains invariant.

A good way to understand the invariant features of a GMP with certain added parameters is to consider movement as analogous to the various components of a stereo system (see Focus on Application 5.3).

Revisiting the Storage and Novelty Problems

We started this section on GMPs by expressing dissatisfaction with the simple motor program views as developed earlier in the chapter. Two issues were especially troublesome: the storage problem and the novelty problem. The GMP theory provides solutions to both problems.

For the storage problem, the theory holds that a single GMP can produce an infinite number of movements, so only one program needs to be stored for each class of movements rather than a separate program stored for each movement. Therefore, the storage problem is solved by drastically reducing the long-term memory capacity requirements. For the novelty problem, the theory suggests that since the parameters are not stored as part of the GMP in long-term memory, they can be added as required at the time of movement execution. And since they are not stored as part of the GMP, the movement could be executed by adding parameters that provide for, essentially, an infinite variety of novel movement executions.

However, the GMP portion of the theory does not exactly solve the novelty problem—

FOCUS ON Application 5.3

The Stereo System Analogy

A good analogy for GMPs involves the phonograph stereo system, in which a turntable sends signals from a record into an amplifier, whose output is delivered to speakers. In this analogy, illustrated in the top portion of figure 5.10, the phonograph record represents the GMP, and the speakers are the muscles and limbs. The record has all the features of programs, such as information about the order of events (the guitar solo comes before the harmonica solo), the temporal structure among the events (i.e., the rhythm, or relative timing), and the relative amplitudes of the sounds (the first drumbeat is twice as loud as the second). This information is stored on the record, like the GMP theory's assertion that analogous information is stored in the program. Also, there are many different records to choose from, just as humans have many motor programs to choose from (e.g., throwing, jumping), each stored with different kinds of information.

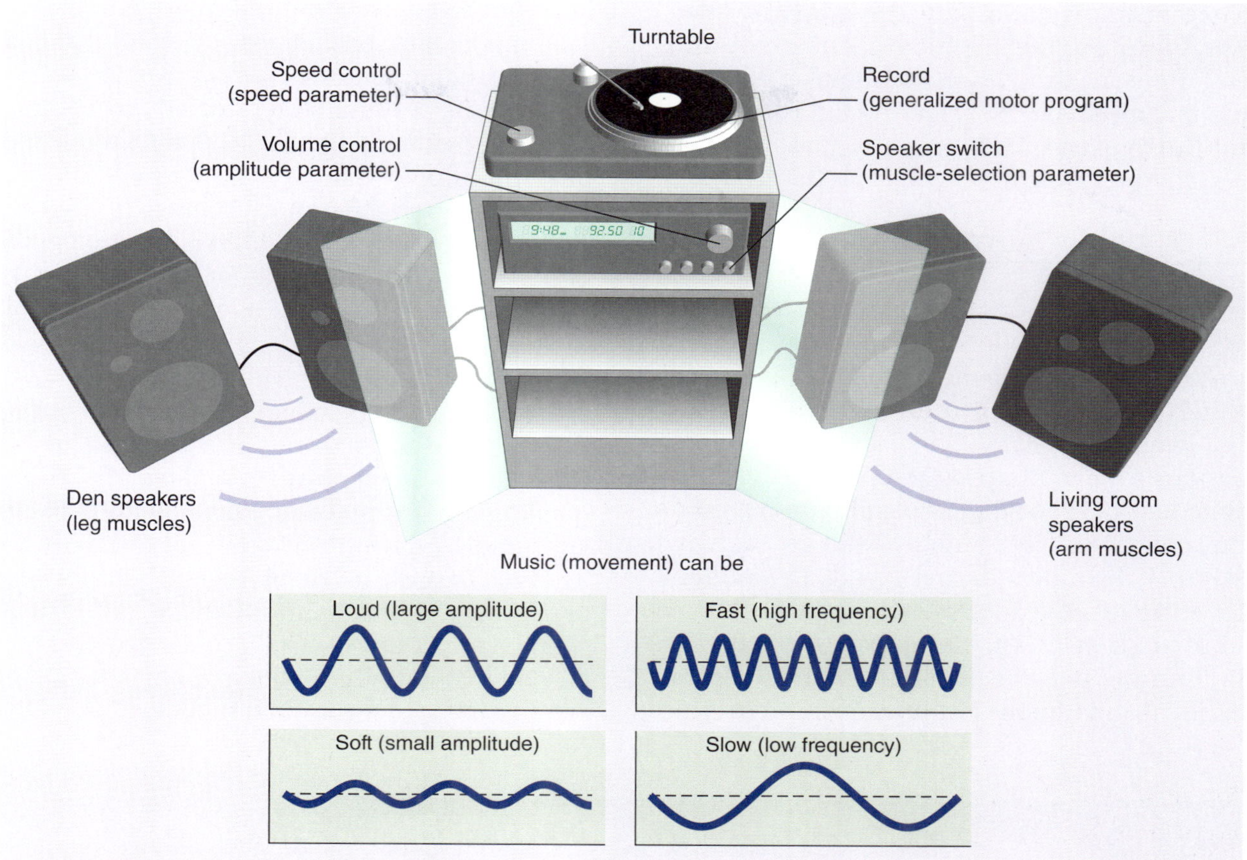

FIGURE 5.10 Illustration of the stereo system analogy.

Notice, though, that the record's output is not fixed (lower portion of figure 5.10): The speed of output can be changed if the speed of the turntable is increased. Note that the relative timing (rhythm) is preserved even though the speed of the music is increased. You can change the amplitude of the output by raising the volume; this increases the amplitudes of all the features of the sounds. Also, you have a choice of which effectors to use: You can switch the output from a set of speakers in the den to a second set of speakers in the living room.

Perhaps if you think of the theory of GMPs in concrete terms, like a stereo system, you can understand most of the important features of the theory more easily. For example, when participants in the study by Shapiro and colleagues (1981) switched from walking to running, they first had to remove the walking "record" and replace it with a running "record." Then they had to parameterize it, like setting the volume, speed, and speaker controls. This analogy of the GMP and its parameters to the characteristics of a stereo system sometimes helps to understand the basic idea.

the problem of deciding what parameters to add remains. In other words, on what basis are parameters supplied, as appropriate, at the time of movement execution? To answer that question, a second representation in long-term memory, called a *schema*, was proposed to work in conjunction with the GMP. The schema is the memory representation responsible for supplying parameters as needed at the time of movement execution.

Chapter 12 discusses how schemas are developed and applied to movement execution. But, for now, think of the schema as a mechanism responsible for selecting the parameters for the chosen GMP.

Summary

In very brief actions, there is no time for the system to process feedback about errors and to correct them. The mechanism that controls this type of behavior is an open loop, called the *motor program*. Considerable evidence supports the motor program idea: (1) Reaction time is longer for more complex movements but can be elicited much faster by startling stimuli; (2) animals deprived of feedback information by deafferentation are capable of strong, relatively effective movements; (3) central pattern generators control some cyclical movements in animals; (4) inhibiting behaviors are demonstrated when one attempts to stop or alter an action after it has been initiated; and (5) a limb's muscle activity patterns are unaffected for 100 to 120 ms when the limb is blocked by a mechanical perturbation.

Even though the motor program is responsible for the major events in the movement pattern, there is considerable interaction with sensory processes, such as the organization of various reflex processes to generate rapid corrections, making the movement flexible in the face of changing environmental demands. Finally, motor programs are thought to be generalized to account for a class of actions (such as throwing), and parameters must be supplied to define how the pattern will be executed (such as throwing either rapidly or slowly). The schema concept and how a schema is acquired with experience are discussed extensively in chapter 12.

HK*PROPEL* ACTIVITIES

HK*Propel* offers these activities to help you build and apply your knowledge of the concepts in this chapter. Additionally, you'll find a key terms flashcard review activity and a key terms quiz, along with audio supplements for selected figures, as indicated by QR codes throughout the chapter.

Interactive Learning

Activity 5.1: Indicate whether each in a list of statements applies to simple motor program theory or general motor program theory.

Activity 5.2: Determine whether motor skills are controlled by open-loop or closed-loop processes, or a combination of both.

Activity 5.3: Review the conceptual model of motor control by identifying which elements are associated with open-loop control processes only, closed-loop control processes only, or with open- and closed-loop processes.

Activity 5.4: Listen to a discussion about anticipation in sport, then consider what parts of a task might serve as advanced cues.

Activity 5.5: Indicate whether several motor program features are invariant or surface in nature.

Principles-to-Application Exercise

Activity 5.6: The principles-to-application exercise for this chapter prompts you to choose a skill and identify components of the movement that a person would control using open-loop and closed-loop processing, as well as situations in which both types of control would be important.

Motor Control in Everyday Actions Narratives

Moving Sidewalks and Beer Glasses

Antilock Brakes

The Point of No Return

Forensic Motor Control

Check Your Understanding

1. Name the two distinct parts of an open-loop control system. How does an open-loop control system differ from a closed-loop control system? Describe how each part of an open-loop control system might function for a child tossing toy blocks into a bin.
2. Research evidence for the existence of motor program control comes from diverse research areas. List the six types of research evidence and discuss how two of these areas provide evidence for movements being planned in advance.
3. Though there were appealing parts of motor program theory, a desire to modify motor program theory to solve the storage and novelty problems arose. What idea emerged from this desire? How does it help to explain novel movements? How does it deal with the storage problem?

Apply Your Knowledge

1. A student is packing her lunch for school. List three movements (or components of movements) involved in packing a lunch that would be controlled using open-loop processes and three that would be controlled using closed-loop processes. Choose one of the open-loop controlled movements and describe a parameter of the generalized motor program that the student could modify.
2. A woodworker is building a piece of furniture that includes large, small, simple, and complex pieces. Describe two GMPs that may be used in building the furniture, and discuss two parameters that the woodworker might need to modify throughout the project for each GMP.

6

Principles of Speed, Accuracy, and Timing

Controlling Simple Movements

CHAPTER OUTLINE

CHAPTER OBJECTIVES

Chapter 6 describes various principles and laws of simple and coordinated actions. This chapter will help you understand

- the speed–accuracy trade-off in simple aiming movements,
- logarithmic and linear relationships between speed and accuracy, and
- the relationship between timing accuracy and movement time.

CHAPTER PREVIEW QUIZ

1. What does it mean to "trade off" speed for accuracy, or vice versa?
2. What is the general form of a linear equation?
3. Why is the duration of the bat swing important when hitting a baseball?

The construction worker is pounding nails, trying to finish an outdoor project, when she notices a storm approaching. She quickens her pace, but in so doing, she notices that her aims are missing the nail more and more often—something that occurs rarely when working at her normal pace. Why is this happening? How does working at a faster pace and swinging her hammer more forcefully contribute to more frequent misses?

This chapter addresses questions such as these about movement control. Some of the most fundamental principles of movement production are shown to govern the relationship between speed, accuracy, and timing. Along the way, we reveal some of the underlying causes of movement errors and discuss ways to minimize them. These laws of movement production apply to the control of relatively simple movements. In the next chapter, we discuss some ideas related to the performance of more complex movements.

One of the fundamental principles of rapid movement concerns the relationships between the speed of a movement, the distance to be covered, and the resulting accuracy. Everybody knows that when you do things too quickly, you tend to do them less accurately or effectively. The old saying "Haste makes waste" suggests that this idea has been around for a long time. Woodworth (1899) studied these phenomena early on, showing that the accuracy of line-drawing movements decreased as their length increased and speed became faster. A major contribution to our understanding of this problem was provided by the psychologist Paul Fitts, who formulated a mathematical principle of speed and accuracy that is now known as **Fitts' Law**.

Fitts' Law

Fitts used a research paradigm in which the participant tapped alternately between two target plates as quickly as possible. The distance between the targets (termed *A*, for movement **amplitude**) and the width of the targets (termed *W*, for target **width**) were varied in different combinations (see figure 6.1). The movement time (MT) to complete

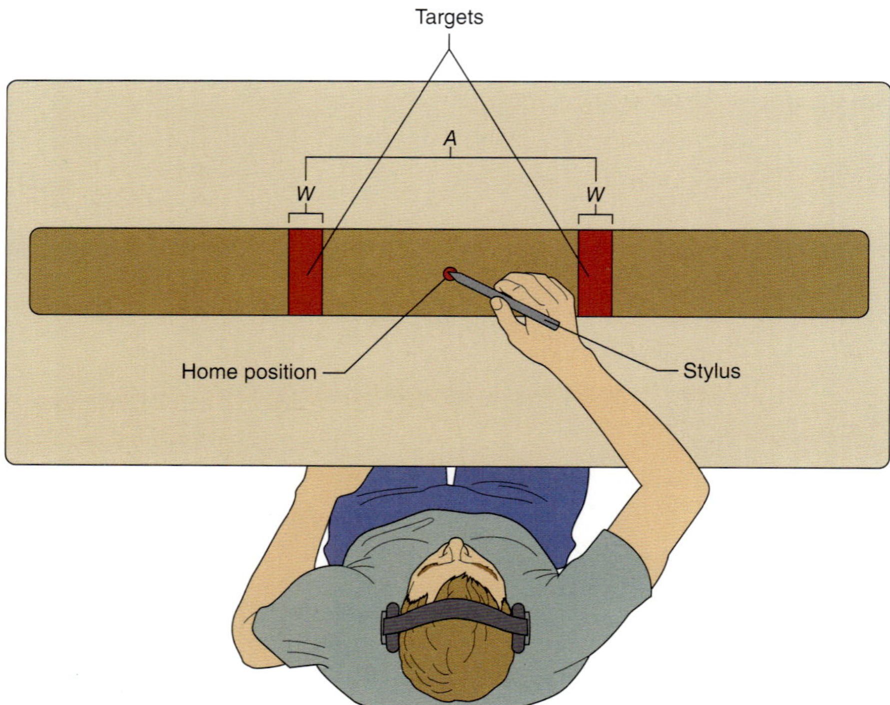

FIGURE 6.1 Illustration of a participant performing a Fitts tapping task. The participant taps between two targets of varying width (*W*) and amplitude (*A*), attempting to move as rapidly as possible while keeping the number of target misses to a minimum.

these rapid taps increased systematically with either increases in the movement amplitude (due to a larger distance between the targets) or decreases in the target width (due to a narrower target-landing area). These relationships were combined into a formal mathematical statement that is now known as Fitts' Law (see Focus on Research 6.1).

FOCUS ON Research 6.1

Fitts' Tasks

In his most well-known experiment, Fitts (1954) asked participants to make movements of a handheld stylus between two target plates. In this task, which is now typically known as the Fitts tapping task (see figure 6.1), the widths (*W*) of two targets and the amplitude (*A*) between them were varied in different combinations. The participant's goal was to alternately tap each target as quickly as possible while making as few errors as possible (missed targets <5%). The experimenter would measure the number of taps completed in, for example, a 20 s trial and then compute the average time per movement, or movement time (MT).

This target-tapping task was just one method that Fitts used to study rapid aiming. Figure 6.2 illustrates two other tasks used in Fitts (1954) research. In figure 6.2*a*, the participant's task was to move small metal disks with holes in the center (like carpenters' washers) from one peg to another. In figure 6.2*b*, the task was to move small pins from one hole to another. In these task variations, Fitts defined target width in terms of the gap, or tolerance, between the disks and target pegs (figure 6.2*a*), or the diameter of the holes in the plate in relation to the diameter of the pin (figure 6.2*b*). With the **index of difficulty (ID)** defined in this manner, Fitts found that the same equation—MT = $a + b$ (ID)—held true in accounting for the effects of the task parameters on movement speed.

How do all these experimental tasks converge to define Fitts' Law? The first part is easy—amplitude is the distance-covering portion of MT and is common to each task. The effect of target size is more complicated. In the aiming task, this is essentially just target width. However, in the disk-transfer (figure 6.2*a*) and pin-transfer

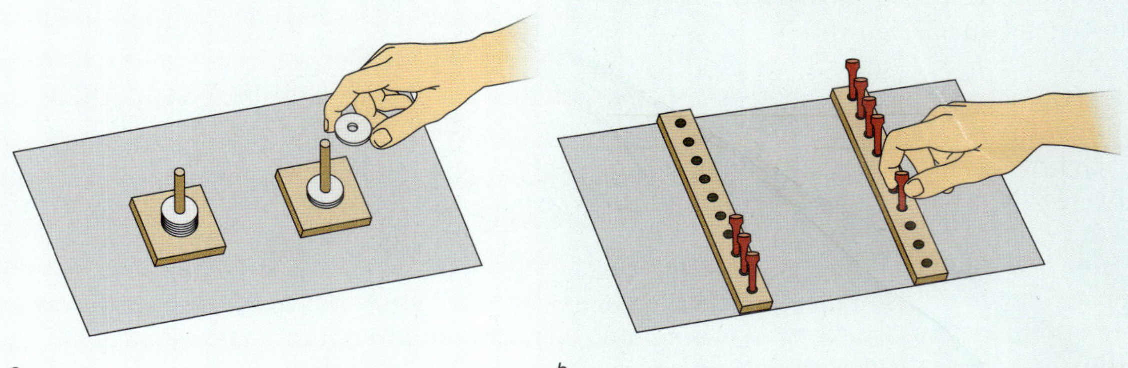

FIGURE 6.2 The two additional movement tasks used by Fitts (1954): *(a)* disk- and *(b)* pin-transfer tasks.

> *continued*

Research 6.1: Fitts' Tasks > *continued*

tasks (figure 6.2*b*), the target size is operationalized as the difference between sizes of the held object and the target object. For example, in the pin-transfer task, a large hole only represents an easy ID if the pin being inserted is relatively narrow. If the pin is wide, the task becomes more difficult because there is a smaller gap, resulting in less tolerance for aiming error. Thus, all three of these tasks converge upon the central problem of the **speed–accuracy trade-off**—how the task parameters cause the participant to vary MT in order to make the aimed movement accurate.

Exploring Further

1. What would the ID be for a tapping task that had $W = 4$ and $A = 16$?
2. What effect on MT would you expect if you doubled the size of one icon on your phone's home screen?

Fitts' Law states that MT remains unchanged when the ratio of *A* to *W* remains constant. In general, very large-amplitude movements to wide targets require about the same time as very short movements to narrow targets. In addition, Fitts found that the MT increased as the ratio of *A* to *W* increased when *A* was made larger, *W* was made smaller, or both. He combined these various effects into a linear equation:

$$MT = a + b\,[\log_2(2A/W)]$$

where *a* (the MT-intercept) and *b* (the slope) are constants, and *A* and *W* are defined as before. The term $\log_2(2A/W)$ is referred to as the *index of difficulty* (ID), which is a measure of the difficulty of the various combinations of *A* and *W*. The relationships between *A*, *W*, and MT are plotted in figure 6.3 for one of Fitts' data sets. From this graph, we can conclude that MT is linearly related to the $\log_2(2A/W)$. More simply, Fitts' Law says that MT is linearly related to ID.

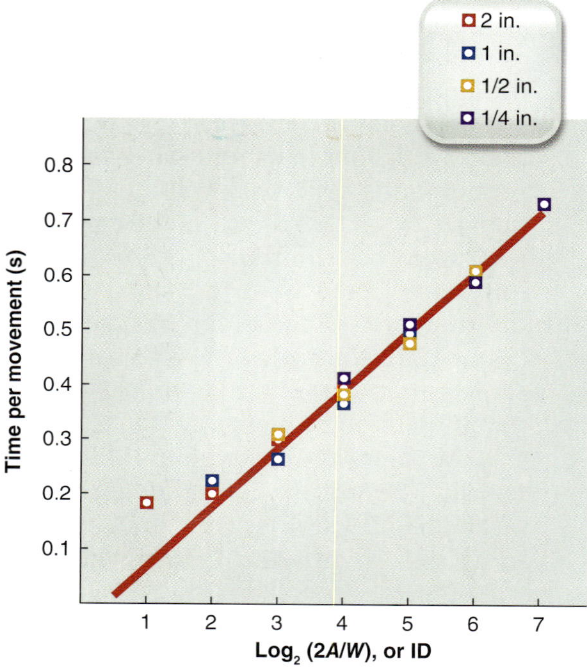

FIGURE 6.3 Average movement time (MT) as a function of the index of difficulty (ID).

In what has now become the typical Fitts tapping task, participants are told to minimize the number of target misses. In other words, they are instructed to adjust MT so that the errors are acceptably small. When the target size is widened, the accuracy requirements are relaxed because a larger area of landed aims still hit the target. Therefore, MTs are smaller than when narrow targets are used. This represents one specific type of speed–accuracy trade-off—the tendency for people to move faster or slower depending on the consequences of being inaccurate (see Focus on Application 6.1). Fitts' Law describes the lawful relation that exists among MT, *A*, and *W* in this specific tapping task.

Fitts' Law has been found to hold under many different environmental conditions (e.g., tapping underwater or in outer space),

FOCUS ON Application 6.1

Trading Off Speed and Accuracy

Research by Fitts and others used a task in which participants were asked to make movements that achieved two goals: 1) moving as quickly as possible, while 2) keeping target misses to a minimum. In other words, accuracy was demanded and speed was traded off (i.e., slowed down or sped up) to achieve these two task goals. This is a rather odd request compared to how speed and accuracy are valued in our normal activities of daily living.

In many activities of daily life, there is no demand to move as quickly as possible. Having perfectly cooked, over-easy eggs in the morning requires that cracking open the shell be done without puncturing the yolk. Nobody wants to put a scratch on their car, so parking it in a tight space requires slow, precise steering. A work of art can be ruined by the slip of a hand. There is no tolerance for error in these instances, so taking it slowly is the golden rule.

But some activities now emphasize speed without regard to accuracy. Spell-checkers and auto-correct functions mean that we can type as rapidly as possible without regard to the increased errors that are likely to occur. Previously, typing errors were onerous and time consuming to detect and correct. These are now automatically fixed by typo correction algorithms. The same goes for drawing a graph on a computer. It is easy and fast to undo a mistake. Accuracy can be sacrificed for increased speed in these examples.

At other times, the speed–accuracy trade-off depends on situational factors. Most Major League Baseball pitchers lower their pitch velocity when they are behind in the count because of the increased need to be accurate to avoid a base on balls. Taking one's time to apply makeup is a general rule of thumb, unless the once-an-hour bus is just minutes away.

In the final analysis, the speed–accuracy trade-offs are not arbitrary human performance decisions. They are determined by the values and anticipated consequences of alternative outcomes.

for many different groups of people (e.g., children, older adults, individuals with neurological impairments), and for movements made with different effectors (e.g., handheld, foot-held, head-mounted pointing devices; see Schmidt et al., 2025; Plamondon & Alimi, 1997). Importantly, Fitts' Law has many different applications in daily life, such as the safety, effectiveness, and productivity of workspaces (see Focus on Application 6.2).

Visit HK*Propel* to read "Pouring Coffee" and "The Calculator" and complete the self-directed learning activities.

The movements studied with the Fitts' tapping task almost always combine programmed actions with feedback corrections to land on the target (discussed in the previous two chapters). That is, the performer generates a programmed initial segment of the action toward the target, processes visual feedback about its accuracy during the movement, and initiates one (or sometimes more) feedback-based corrections to guide the limb to the target area (Elliott & Bennett, 2021).

Finally, it is reasonable to suspect that slower movements are more accurate, at least in part

FOCUS ON **Application 6.2**

Fitts' Law in Daily Activities

Fitts' Law was formulated based on simple experiments involving aimed movements. But the research applies to many different situations in sports, in the design of industrial workspaces, in the organization of controls in automobiles, aircraft, and so on. One example is the design of keyboards and calculators. Look at the keyboard on your computer or cell phone. If the layout uses principles consistent with Fitts' Law, you will notice that some keys are larger than others. For example, the Space and Return keys on my iPhone are three times larger than any of the letter keys. My PC keyboard has a space bar that is five times the width of a letter key, and the Return key is twice the width and length of a regular key. Having larger keys means that we can make the faster movements to more frequently used keys with a reduced risk of aiming errors. In other words, we can sacrifice a considerable amount of precision and still be accurate if we aim at a relatively large key. This feature allows us to move very quickly to these often-used keys. What other keys on your keyboard are given the same privilege? Does the calculator on your cell phone have similar advantages for one or more keys? What about other data-input devices?

Navigating a cursor around a computer monitor also uses the principles of Fitts' Law. For example, the size of an icon affects the time to move a cursor onto it. Making icons larger or having dynamic icons that increase in size as the cursor approaches them reduces MT and aiming errors. Placing icons near the corners or along the borders of the display makes them infinitely large (in the direction of movement) because your cursor automatically stops when reaching the screen edge. And centrally locating the most often-used icons reduces the average movement distance from anywhere on the screen.

Some designs use Fitts' Law for the opposite reason—to encourage you to make errors or slow down. For example, the next time you navigate to a website with a pop-up advertisement that can be closed by clicking the *x* icon, note how small the *x* is, whether it is moving or stationary, and how far it is located from the content of the message. Presumably, the longer it takes for you to get your cursor onto the *x* icon, the longer the information on the screen will have been there for you to see and hear (perhaps unwillingly). The design uses Fitts' Law purposely to increase movement time.

Consider one more example of using Fitts' Law to purposely slow you down. Many urban planners post reduced speed limits in high pedestrian traffic areas. Common methods to encourage drivers to obey the limits include radar traps, automated photo cameras, and the like. Other methods, collectively known as *traffic calming*, work very well too. Some are obvious, such as speed bumps. A lesser-known method simply reduces the lane width—either with permanent curbs or temporary devices such as cones. This method of traffic calming is effective because most drivers will trade off speed to avoid damage to their vehicles.

In this photo, which of Fitts' three experimental conditions (see figures 6.1 and 6.2) relate best to the traffic-calming rationale?

(*a*) How can Fitts' Law help explain the varied sizes of keys on a keyboard? What keys in this photo take advantage of Fitts' Law? (*b*) How would you redesign this calculator to take advantage of Fitts' Law in general? Provide an example of how it might be redesigned.

because there is more time available to detect errors and to make corrections (as discussed in chapter 4), and that MT lengthens when more corrections need to be made. In this way, the main reason MT increases with narrow target widths is that each correction adds time.

Fitts and Peterson (1964) used the same idea and variables as in the reciprocal-tapping task (figure 6.1) but with movements from a starting position to a single target, which are more like everyday aiming movements. These targets varied in size (*W*) and amplitude (*A*) from the starting position and were to be done as rapidly as possible while maintaining a low rate of error. The independent variables *A* and *W* and the dependent variable MT related to each other in essentially the same way as they did in the reciprocal task. That is, the equation for Fitts' Law also applies to the single-movement paradigm, which increases our confidence that Fitts' Law is one of the truly fundamental laws of motor behavior. The finding also adds confidence to the application of Fitts' Law to features of everyday life.

In brief, Fitts' Law tells us the following:

- Movement time (MT) increases as the movement amplitude (*A*) increases.
- MT increases as the aiming accuracy requirement increases—that is, as target width (*W*) decreases.
- MT is essentially constant for a given ratio of *A* to *W*.
- These principles are valid for a wide variety of conditions, participant variables, tasks or paradigms, and effectors.

However, as with most research, the questions that Fitts' research answered raised many other questions. What about movements that are completed in a *very* short period of time, where presumably no feedback is involved during the movement? How can MT depend on the number of corrections when there is not enough time to make even a single correction? The next section answers some of these questions.

Schmidt's Law

Suppose that you made a quick movement of your hand, as in the example of swinging a hammer at the start of this chapter. How would your accuracy change as the distance and movement time of the hammer swing varied? We discussed Fitts' Law in the previous section, which described the effects of target distance and size on MT when errors are kept at a minimum. In this section, we change the variables and describe how MT and distance affect the errors made.

Studies using this alternative method to the Fitts' task have examined aiming movements where the participant directs a handheld stylus from a starting position to a target, with MT and movement distance varied experimentally. The participant is instructed to move in a given MT (e.g., 150 ms) and receives feedback after each movement to help achieve the goal MT. Figure 6.4 shows one set of results from this task, where accuracy is expressed as the amount of spread or inconsistency of the movement end points about the target area. This measure, called **effective target width (W_e)**, is the standard deviation of the target end points (the calculation of W_e is similar to the calculation of variable error [VE] in chapter 1).

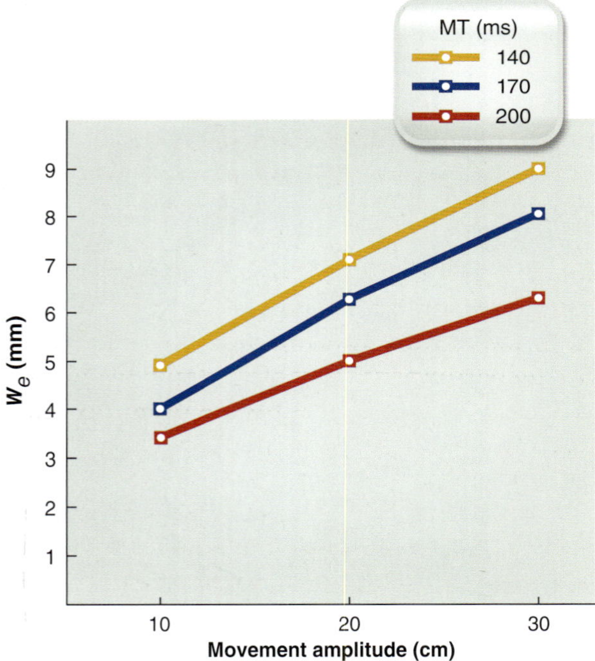

FIGURE 6.4 Variability of movement end points (W_e or effective target width, defined as the standard deviation of the produced movement distances) in a rapid aiming task as a function of MT and distance.

It is important to note from the legend in figure 6.4 that these movements are *very* fast, all with MTs of 200 ms or less. From the previous chapters, you would expect that such actions are controlled primarily by motor programming processes, with essentially no time available to make vision-based feedback corrections. Figure 6.4 illustrates two important findings:

1. W_e increases as the movement amplitude increases for each MT (compare the set of three data points at 10 cm vs. 20 cm vs. 30 cm).
2. W_e increases as the MT is reduced at each of the amplitudes (compare errors for the yellow vs. blue vs. red lines).

The importance of these effects of distance and MT on W_e suggest that the open-loop processes involved in movement control are also subject to the speed–accuracy trade-off. The decreases in accuracy when MTs are short are not due simply to the fact that there is less time to process visual feedback. Decreases in MT also seem to influence the processes that generate the initial parts of the movement—that is, the open-loop processes necessary to produce quick movements.

Note that this finding is consistent with Fitts' Law. In that situation, if the participant tries to make movements of a given distance too quickly, the result will be too many failures to hit the targets (which is unacceptable in terms of the experimenter's instructions). So the participant must slow down to comply with the experimenter's instructions, decreasing the variability in the movements and hitting the target more often.

Schmidt and colleagues (1979) combined these separate effects of movement amplitude (*A*) and MT into a single expression (as Fitts did) and found a linear relationship between W_e and the ratio *A*/*MT*, or average velocity. For example, in figure 6.5, the variability in hitting the target is plotted against the movement's average velocity. The figure illustrates clearly that aiming errors increased almost linearly as movement velocity increased. As in the previous edition of this book, we follow others (e.g., Jagacinski & Flach, 2003) in naming this principle **Schmidt's Law**, which describes the *linear speed–accuracy trade-off for rapid aiming movements.* Schmidt's Law suggests that aiming errors are about the same for various combinations of movement amplitude and MT that have a constant average velocity. Thus, increases in movement amplitude and decreases in MT can be traded off with each other to maintain movement accuracy in these rapid tasks.

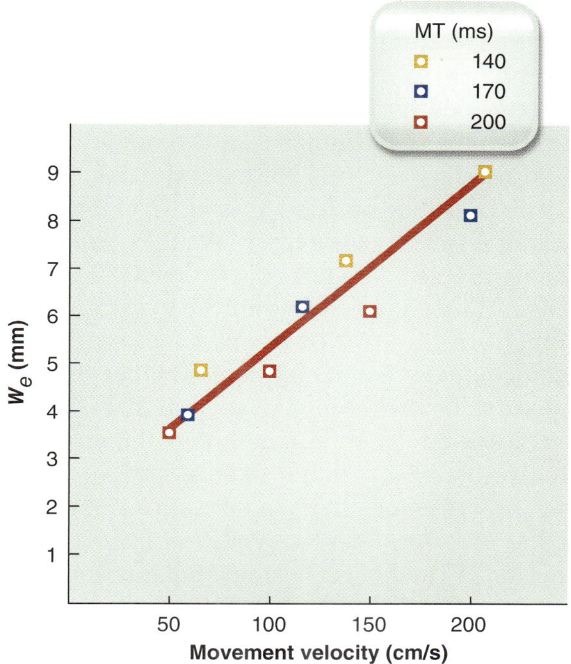

FIGURE 6.5 Variability of movement end points (W_e) increases as a function of average movement velocity (*A*/*MT*) in a rapid aiming task (goal MTs of 140 ms, 170 ms, or 200 ms).

Visit HK*Propel* to read "The Gimme Putt" and complete the self-directed learning activities. 

Understanding Schmidt's Law

Why do very rapid movements, in which there is little time for feedback processing and corrections, produce more errors as the movement distance increases or the time decreases? The answer seems to lie with the processes that translate the motor program's output into movements. In chapter 5, we discussed how motor programs are responsible for determining the ordering of muscle contractions and the amounts of force that must be generated in the participating muscles. How might these processes contribute to movement inaccuracy?

If someone attempts to produce an identical force over and over on successive trials, the actual force produced will be somewhat inconsistent. This variability is thought to be caused by the relatively "noisy" (i.e., inconsistent) processes that convert central nervous system impulses into the activation of muscle motor units (which ultimately exert forces on bones, causing movements). Also, there is variability in the contractions generated by various reflex activities.

The presence of these noisy processes in the system means that the forces actually produced in a contraction are not exactly what the motor program intended. Noise in the system can be thought of in terms of the phonograph record analogy presented in chapter 5. By this analogy, noise can be introduced in several places in the stereo system, such as scratches on the record, quality of the turntable needle and speakers, and imperfections in the electronics and wiring of the system. These deviations from perfect fidelity in the stereo system make the sounds we hear slightly different from the sounds as originally recorded.

In movement control, these noisy processes are not constant; they change as the amount of contraction force changes. This has been studied using tasks in which the participant is asked to produce brief (ballistic) force applications to an apparatus handle; these force applications are such that the peak force produced on any contraction matches a (submaximal) goal force. Figure 6.6 illustrates a typical set of results. Notice that as the contraction force increases, there is more variability in these forces, as if the noisy processes were becoming larger as well. In the figure, the variability in these forces, which is interpreted as the size of the noise component, is shown as a function of the size of the contraction, expressed as a percentage of the performer's maximum force.

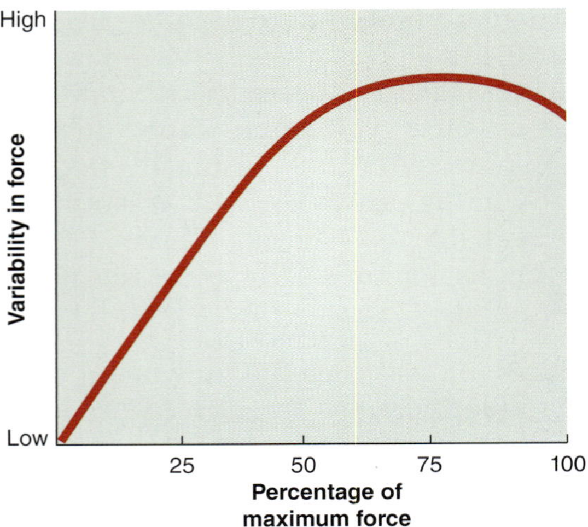

FIGURE 6.6 The relationship between the variability in force produced as a function of the percentage of maximum force used.

The noise component generally increases as the amount of force increases, up to about 70% of the participant's maximum. However, when the contractions are very large, approaching maximal values, the amount of force variability appears to level off again, with perhaps a slight decrease in the force variability in nearly maximal contractions. These findings have been reported in both laboratory tasks (Sherwood et al., 1988) and with real skills, such as an overarm throwing task in which participants threw balls at 40% to 100% of their maximum velocities (Urbin et al., 2012).

In summary, increasing the speed of a rapid movement contributes to its inaccuracy for the following reasons:

- The relative contraction forces of the various participating muscles are a major factor in determining the ultimate trajectory of the limb.
- When MT decreases, more force is required.
- When amplitude increases, more force is required.
- More force generates more variability, which causes the movement to deviate from the intended trajectory, resulting in errors.

Exceptions to Fitts' and Schmidt's Laws

As common as the speed–accuracy trade-off seems to be for movement behavior, there are a few situations in which it does not appear to hold, or at least in cases in which the principles are somewhat different from those indicated in the previous sections. These situations involve cases in which

- extremely rapid and forceful actions are involved,
- targets are embedded in a visual illusion, and
- timing accuracy is the movement goal.

Very Forceful Movements

Many human activities, especially those in sports, require extremely forceful contractions of muscles, leading to nearly maximal movement speeds, as in punting a football or throwing a 100 mph fastball. Making the movement at near-maximal speed is often only part of the problem because these actions often must be performed with great precision in space and time. As it turns out, alterations in movement speed affect these nearly maximal actions somewhat differently from many of the less forceful actions discussed so far.

Consider a rapid, horizontal, straight-arm movement in which a handheld pointer is aimed at a target as if it were a ball to be hit. What would happen to the spatial accuracy if the required MT decreased so the movements would be closer and closer to the performer's maximal force capabilities? This is similar to swinging a hammer harder and harder, with the limit being your own force capabilities. As you might expect from Schmidt's Law, movements with shorter MTs are less spatially variable but only up to a point, as seen in figure 6.7. Participants in this study by Schmidt and Sherwood (1982) produced rapid MTs with goals between 160 ms (slowest) and 80 ms (fastest). When those MT goals resulted in forces between 21% and 50% of maximum, there was a rapid increase in spatial variability (figure 6.7). However, when the MT was reduced further and the percentage of maximum force rose from 50% to 84%, there was a decrease in the variability (similar to the force variability in figure 6.6). Thus, very rapid and very slow movements have the most spatial accuracy, and moderate-speed movements have the least accuracy. This set of data goes against the strict interpretation of Schmidt's Law, in which faster movements are always less spatially accurate.

How can these near-maximally forceful movements be made so rapidly yet be so spatially accurate? Recall that, when the forces are very large, approaching maximum, the force variability levels off and actually decreases slightly, as seen in figure 6.6. Therefore, the nearly maximal movements in figure 6.7 are operating in a range where the forces are becoming more consistent with increases in force. This low force variability allows these very forceful actions to be very consistent spatially.

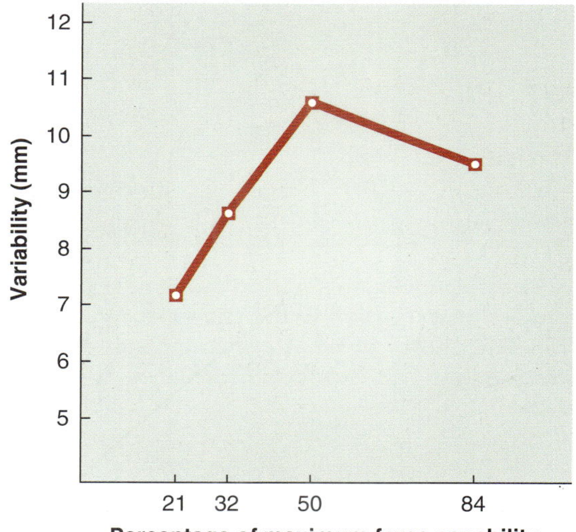

FIGURE 6.7 The effect of force on the positional variability in horizontal arm swing movements. The percentage values on the *x*-axis are the percentages of the participant's maximum force produced and correspond to increasingly smaller MTs (i.e., 21% = 158 ms mean MT; 32% = 130 ms; 50% = 102 ms; 84% = 80 ms).

Very forceful movements performed at nearly maximal speed are an exception to the speed–accuracy trade-off. In this photo, at what percentage of maximum velocity might you expect performance to be most variable?

In summary, here's how the theory attempts to explain what happens when a movement requires very high levels of muscular contractions (greater than about 70% of the participant's capabilities):

- Increasing speed by reducing MT can decrease spatial and timing errors.
- Because a greater muscular force requirement actually increases accuracy in this range, adding inertial load to the movement can decrease error up to a point.
- An inverted relationship exists between spatial accuracy and force requirements, with the least accuracy at moderate levels of force.

Targets Embedded in Visual Illusions

Aiming at targets, such as throwing darts at a bull's-eye, putting a golf ball toward a hole, or kicking a soccer ball toward a goal, can be influenced greatly by its surrounding visual environment. Consider the figures presented in figure 6.8, for example. Figure 6.8*a* illustrates three target circles—one with no surrounding environment (the lone circle in the middle of the figure), one surrounded by a ring of small circles (array on the left), and one surrounded by a ring of large circles (array on the right). Perceptual experiments performed with these stimuli typically find that the target circle surrounded by the ring of small circles is judged to be larger than the target circle surrounded by the ring of large circles. The perceived size of the control target (with no surrounding environment) usually falls in between.

Another visual illusion is the Müller-Lyer illusion (figure 6.8*b*). When participants are asked to judge the length of the line, the figure on the left with the inward-pointing arrows is perceived to be longer than the control line in the middle and much longer than the line on the right with the outward-pointing arrows.

The actual sizes of the targets in figure 6.8 are exactly the same—the middle circles in figure 6.8*a* all have the same diameter, and the lines in figure 6.8*b* are all the same length. Yet when motor control experiments use targets like these, their surrounding visual environments influence the aiming errors. For example, in a study by Elliott and Lee (1995), participants made a ballistic aiming movement from one end of a Müller-Lyer target toward the other end of the line. Consistent with the perceptual illusion, the aiming errors were largely overshoots (positive CE

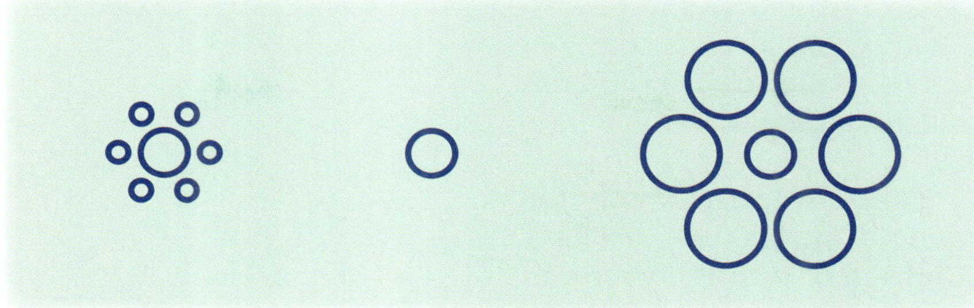

a Ebbinghaus-Titchener illusion: The circle in the middle appears larger when surrounded by smaller circles (far left) than when surrounded by larger circles (far right). Both are the same size as the lone circle in the center.

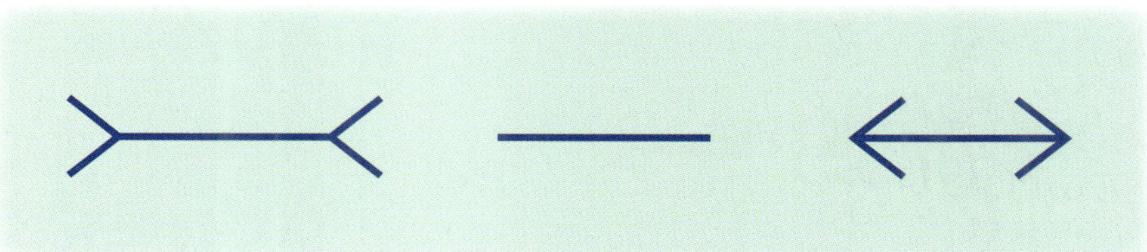

b Müller-Lyer illusion: The line connecting the two inward-pointing arrows (far left) appears to be longer than the line connecting the two outward-pointing arrows (far right) even though the two lines are the same length as the line in the middle.

FIGURE 6.8 Two visual illusions used in aiming studies: *(a)* the Ebbinghaus-Titchener illusion and *(b)* the Müller-Lyer illusion.

[constant error]) in the lines that appeared to be longer (left side of figure 6.8*b*) and mostly undershoots (negative CE) in the lines that appeared to be shorter (right side of figure 6.8*b*).

Similar findings have been shown with the Ebbinghaus-Titchener illusion circles. In studies by Witt and colleagues (2012) and Arexis and Maquestiaux (2023), participants putted golf balls toward circular targets surrounded by rings of smaller or larger circles. Similar to the perceptual judgments, putting was more successful when made toward target holes that appeared to be larger (figure 6.8*a*, left side) than holes that appeared smaller (figure 6.8*a*, right side).

Of special interest with these visual illusions, however, are some potential implications for sport performance. For example, Chauvel and colleagues (2015) found that participants who putted toward a hole surrounded by a ring of small circles (making the hole seem bigger) improved their performance more during a practice session than a group of participants who putted toward a hole surrounded by a ring of large circles. Importantly, when retested a day later, the surrounding circles were no longer present for either group. The group that had previously practiced with the perceptually larger hole maintained an advantage in performance. As we will discuss in later chapters, such differences, when found in tests of retention, are strong evidence for learning effects. In this case, practice with the holes that were perceived to be larger produced better learning than with the smaller-looking holes.

Movement Timing

Previous sections of this chapter were concerned with changes in *spatial accuracy* as movement velocity was systematically altered. However, for some skills, the main goal (or an additional goal) concerns *temporal accuracy* (e.g., batting a baseball). In such skills, a movement must be timed so that some part of it is produced at a particular moment (e.g., the bat must cross the plate coincident with the arrival of the ball). The timing accuracy is as critical to the movement's success as the spatial accuracy. As another example, a perfectly struck chord on the guitar only contributes to the music when its timing is right.

In this section, we are concerned with the temporal component of such skills, discussing the factors that affect timing accuracy. The temporal component can be isolated somewhat in the rapid task in which the performer makes a fast movement, whose goal is to produce a particular MT as accurately as possible. Timing accuracy is studied as a function of changes in MT as well as other variables. As it turns out, skills with purely temporal goals seem to follow somewhat different principles than those with purely spatial goals (Schmidt et al., 1979).

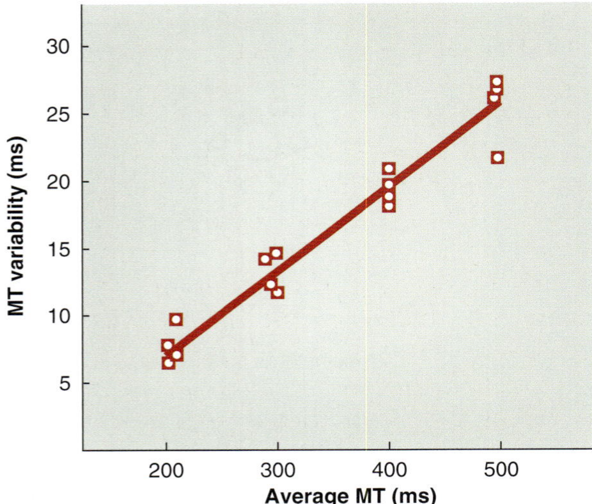

FIGURE 6.9 The effect of average MT duration on the variability of timing. As MT decreases (i.e., movements are made faster), the variability of timing decreases (i.e., becomes more stable).

What happens when participants are asked to produce movements of a given distance with the MT goal reduced from 300 ms to 150 ms? One might expect that because the velocity of the movement is larger, it would have more error, as in figures 6.4 and 6.5 (Schmidt's Law). Not so. Decreasing the MT (i.e., making movements faster) decreases the timing error, making the movement more accurate in time, not less. This can be seen in figure 6.9, in which variability in timed actions increases almost linearly with increases in goal MT (i.e., slower movements). Reducing the goal MT by half reduces the timing errors almost by half. This relationship between MT and timing variability holds not only for discrete, single-action movements but also for repetitive movements (Wing & Kristofferson, 1973).

These findings about timing errors are not as strange as they seem at first, as you will see if you do the following simple experiment using the timer on your cell phone. Without looking at the elapsed time, start the timer and then stop it exactly 10 s later. Do this 10 times in total, and record the amount of error on each trial. Then use the error scores on the individual 10 trials to generate average constant error (CE) and variable error (VE; see chapter 1). Next, do 10 trials of the task again, but this time try to generate 5 s. Then, do 10 trials trying to generate a time of 20 s. Compare the error measures generated for the three tasks. You will likely find that the amount of error (especially VE) you made in estimating 5 s will be considerably less than for 10 s, which in turn will be considerably less than for 20 s. Why? A probable reason is because our internal system that generates these durations (including both the stopwatch and arm movement tasks) is noisy, or variable, and the amount of this noise (variability) increases or accumulates as the duration of the event to be timed increases.

Applying the Principles: Baseball Batting

To help in understanding the principles of rapid aiming movements discussed in the previous section, we apply these principles to a familiar task like batting in baseball. Specifically, we consider how altering the MT of the bat swing is expected to affect performance. In so doing, let's assume that some factors are held constant, such as the nature of the pitch and the game situation.

Figure 6.10 summarizes a few facts about the timelines involved in hitting a baseball. A 90 mph (145 km/h) pitch requires about 460 ms to travel from the pitcher to the plate, and let's assume for now that the MT from start to finish of the bat swing is about 160 ms (Hubbard & Seng, 1954). Evidence presented earlier showed that the internal signal to trigger the swing occurs about 170 ms before the movement starts (Slater-Hammel, 1960; review figure 5.4*b* and Focus on Research 5.2). With these process durations combined, the signal to trigger the action must be given about 330 ms before the ball arrives at the plate—that is, 170 ms to prepare the swing plus 160 ms to carry it out. Therefore, the decision about whether to swing at the ball must be made well before the ball has traveled even halfway to the plate—after only 130 ms of ball travel! Now let's consider how speeding up the bat swing by just 20 ms will help the batter.

An important consideration, given the previous discussion of speed and accuracy processes in the chapter, is this: What would happen if the batter could speed up the swing, for example, from 160 ms to 140 ms? The bat swing's MT could be made shorter to make the movement faster through training, by using a lighter bat, or by changing the biomechanics of the swing. Reducing the bat swing MT by 20 ms would have important implications for several separate factors discussed in the previous few sections.

Visual Processing Time

Figure 6.10 shows that shortening the MT delays the beginning of the swing to a position several feet later in the ball's flight. This provides additional time for viewing the ball's trajectory and determining time to contact, which should allow for more accurate anticipation of where and when the ball will arrive. Therefore, shortening the MT should provide more effective anticipation of the ball's trajectory.

Swing-Initiation Timing Accuracy

If the swing of the bat is speeded up, the decision about when to initiate the movement is made later and is more temporally accurate. In an experiment on a simulated batting task, shortening the MT stabilized the initiation time of the movement, as if the batter were more certain of when to start the swing (Schmidt, 1969). Starting the swing at a more stable time therefore translates into a more stable time for the movement end point at the plate, which yields greater movement timing accuracy.

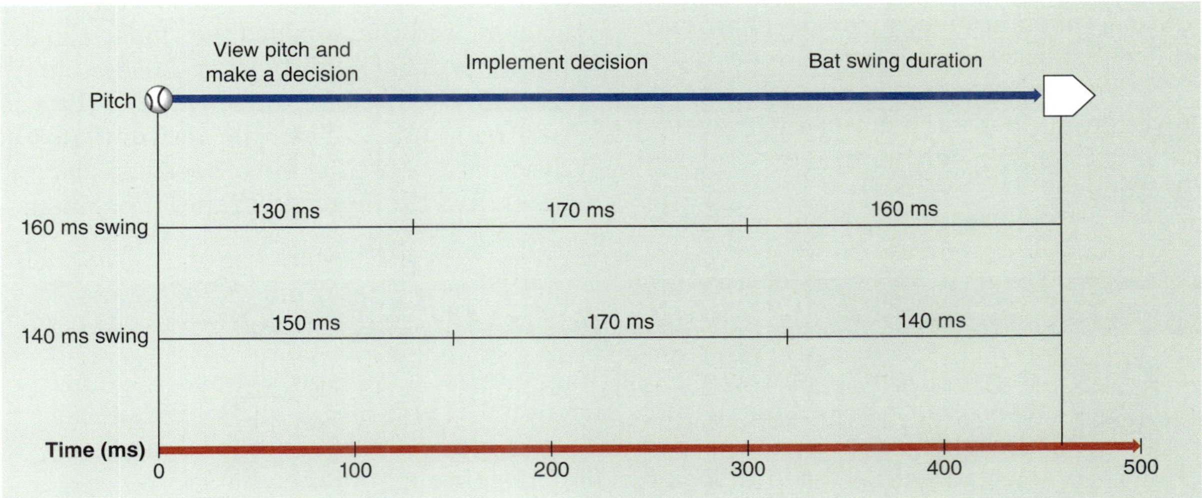

FIGURE 6.10 Timeline of events as a baseball leaves the pitcher's hand and arrives at the plate. The pitch is traveling at a velocity of 90 mph (145 km/h). Working from the right side of the figure to the left, assume that a fast swing (140 ms) has 20 ms less MT than a slow swing (160 ms) and that implementing the decision takes 170 ms for both swings. The additional time gained from swinging faster allows for an additional 20 ms to view the pitch and make a swing decision.

Movement Timing Accuracy

One process the batter must go through in planning the swing is to estimate the duration of his own movement. Poulton (1974) termed this *effector anticipation*. Therefore, the batter selects an MT, then initiates the action so that the middle of the movement coincides with the ball's arrival at the plate. If the actual MT differs from the one predicted, the middle of the movement will be too early or late, causing timing errors in hitting the ball. Because reduced MT increases movement timing consistency, the movement's actual duration will be closer to the batter's estimate. This will result in greater accuracy in hitting the ball, particularly in terms of movement timing (see Schmidt, 1969).

Movement Spatial Accuracy

Making the movement faster also influences spatial accuracy, as discussed earlier. If the movement is already relatively slow, instructions to decrease the MT have a detrimental effect on accuracy in hitting the ball. However, most bat swing movements are already quite fast, near the performer's limits in producing force. Recall that when movements are already very fast and forceful, reducing the MT even further tends to increase—not decrease—accuracy because the force variability decreases in this range with decreases in MT. Therefore, reducing the MT when it is already quite short results in improved spatial accuracy, resulting in more frequent ball contact.

Ball Impact

Finally, of course, a faster swing gives more impact to the ball if it is hit—a critical factor in the game of baseball. Increasing the load by having a heavier bat can improve spatial accuracy (Schmidt & Sherwood, 1982) and would have only minimal negative effects on movement speed. Clearly, both added bat mass and a faster MT contribute to greater impact with the ball if and when it is hit.

Nearly every factor associated with decreased bat swing MT discussed here would be expected to influence the chances of hitting the ball. Perhaps understanding these factors makes it clearer why professional batters seem to swing at near-maximal speeds.

Summary

Speed and amplitude variations influence the accuracy of rapid movements controlled by motor programs, and these actions display a typical speed–accuracy trade-off. Increases in speed (decreases in MT) usually degrade spatial accuracy unless the movements are very rapid and forceful. On the other hand, decreasing the MT usually enhances timing accuracy. These effects are caused by relatively noisy processes in the central nervous system, and the muscles that make the contractions differ slightly from those originally intended. Fitts' Law and Schmidt's Law are two principles of simple movements that describe and predict how speed and accuracy are traded off in making rapid movements.

HK*PROPEL* ACTIVITIES

HK*Propel* offers these activities to help you build and apply your knowledge of the concepts in this chapter. Additionally, you'll find a key terms flashcard review activity and a key terms quiz, along with audio supplements for selected figures, as indicated by QR codes throughout the chapter.

Interactive Learning

Activity 6.1: Identify the correct equation for Fitts' Law.

Activity 6.2: Select the type of movement to which each statement applies to better understand the speed–accuracy trade-off and exceptions to it.

Activity 6.3: Listen to a discussion about Fitts' Law, then apply what you've learned to a skill that has spatial and temporal requirements.

Activity 6.4: Choose labels for a figure depicting timelines involved in hitting a baseball at different speeds.

Principles-to-Application Exercise

Activity 6.5: The principles-to-application exercise for this chapter prompts you to identify a skill that involves rapid movement and requires accuracy, then explore how the speed–accuracy trade-off phenomenon applies to the skill you have chosen and explain the sources of error in rapid movements.

Motor Control in Everyday Actions Narratives

Pouring Coffee

The Calculator

The Gimme Putt

Check Your Understanding

1. Distinguish between temporal and spatial accuracy. Give an example of an activity (e.g., a game of tennis) where both might be important. Describe a situation where temporal accuracy is important and explain why, then do the same for a situation where spatial accuracy is important.
2. Explain what Fitts' Law tells us about motor control and speed–accuracy trade-offs.

Apply Your Knowledge

1. Your friend has come up with a silly competition: At the driving range, you race to see who can go through a bucket of golf balls the fastest while keeping score for accuracy in hitting a middle distance on the range. The winner is determined by a combined score of time and error (distance from the target). Discuss two strategies that you might use to win the competition. Would your strategies change if the winner were determined by time and the combined distance of your shots? What if the competition got even sillier and the accuracy in timing between the shots mattered?

7

Performance of Complex Movements

Differing Approaches to Understanding Coordination

CHAPTER OUTLINE

CHAPTER OBJECTIVES

Chapter 7 describes differing approaches to understanding how complex motor skills are performed. This chapter will help you understand

- the nature of abilities and how they are distinguished from skills,
- the difficulty in predicting future successes in motor performance, and
- action as a problem-solving process.

CHAPTER PREVIEW QUIZ

1. Define what it means to be an all-around athlete, in your opinion.
2. What is the relative-age effect in youth sports?
3. What is an ecological view, and how might it help to understand performance?

The first six chapters of this book have described the study of motor performance by deconstructing the performance process, illustrated by the conceptual model (see figure 5.2). We focused on research concerning the performance of relatively simple skills, such as speeded reactions or aimed limb movements. However, much more complex skills characterize skilled performance in sports, music, performing arts, and indeed, most activities of daily living. Look at the photo on the first page of this chapter, for instance. The person is juggling knives while balancing on a unicycle and playing bagpipes, all at the same time. In this chapter, we consider different ways to think about how complex movement skills like these are performed.

Two different approaches to the study of complex movement are described in this chapter. Early in motor skills research, there was an emphasis on identifying skills and abilities—how the set of skills and abilities individuals possessed could define them, and what predictions could be made for future performance based on this knowledge. A second approach has investigated performance as the product of an individual's interaction with the environment. Both approaches have contributed significantly to an understanding of what it means to be skilled.

The Differential Approach

The approach that dominated motor skills research into the 1960s concerned the performance differences that exist between and among people. This approach used techniques referred to as the **differential method**, concerned with the fact that none of us are the same. The method focused on how and why we differ from one another. Consider the conceptual model presented in figure 5.2 as illustrating all the ways in which individual differences could occur. Essentially, every process we discussed in the earlier parts of the book is a candidate for the study of **individual differences**.

The differential method contrasts markedly with the experimental method, using alternative ways of thinking about and conducting research. As a result, individual-differences research tends to look very different from the type of experimental research that was described in the first six chapters. Two rather distinct emphases characterize the differential approach: the study of *abilities* and the study of *prediction*.

Abilities

A typical question asked by an individual-differences researcher might be this: Why is Bonnie such a standout surgeon? One answer concerns practice and learning (the focus in part II of the book)—the standout surgeon has devoted many hours to practicing her craft, which has made a large contribution to her skilled performance. A different answer is that the surgeon possesses some important abilities—fundamental characteristics that underlie her skills and allow her to perform at a high level. An **ability** is a characteristic that is largely innate and is not modifiable by practice.

Prediction

The second aspect of individual-differences research concerns **prediction**. The car insurance industry charges us rates that are dependent, in part, on the likelihood that we will have an accident and uses historical data to determine these numbers. The insurance company knows that there is a relationship between certain fundamental driver characteristics (e.g., the driver's age, accident record) that are relatively strongly related to (or correlated with) future accident probability. These driver characteristics can be thought of as analogous to abilities—the insurance company is predicting the likelihood of an accident based on some measures about you. Of course, the company cannot accurately predict whether you will have an accident next year. But if you are in a younger age group (16-25), the likelihood of having an accident is greater than that of someone in an older age group, thus your premium rates are higher.

Prediction is all around us. Universities typically use various test measures as estimates of which applicants are most likely to succeed in their programs (e.g., the Law School Admission Test is used as a predictor of success in law school). Some dental schools use various spatial abilities tests to screen applicants for admittance into their programs. The gymnastics coach may screen out people who are not likely to become collegiate gymnasts based on, for example, body configuration. People who are over 6 ft (1.8 m) tall and weigh more than 220 lb (100 kg) are less likely to be successful gymnasts than others with slighter physical dimensions. Others may attempt to predict who will be successful based on more movement-based ability measures, such as National Football League's (NFL) Scouting Combine, which includes various tests of speed, strength, and agility.

Abilities Versus Skills

Of critical importance to individual-differences research is the distinction between the concepts of ability and skill. In common language, these words are used more or less interchangeably, as in "Buddy has good ability (or skill) at guitar." However, as defined earlier, abilities are genetically determined and largely unmodifiable by practice or experience. An ability, therefore, is part of the innate, basic "equipment" people use to perform various tasks. Skill, on the other hand, refers to one's proficiency at a specific task, such as shooting a basketball. Practice, of course, can modify skills, which are countless and represent the person's potential to perform those specific activities. Thus, one could say, "Christone has good visual acuity," implying that he has the ability to see very well. But seeing well does not necessarily make Christone an exceptional middle linebacker. He has developed the specific skill of identifying patterns of motion in football through considerable practice, and this *skill* has Christone's visual acuity as an underlying *ability*.

Think of an ability as something that sets limits on performance. If someone has very poor visual acuity, then developing a skill that requires precise vision will be very difficult. Using an earlier example, people with very large body configurations will be more limited in becoming skilled gymnasts than they will be in becoming defensive linemen in football. The requisite abilities for a particular task act as constraints to limit the level of skill that a particular individual can eventually attain.

In this photo, name two potential visual abilities and perceptual skills demonstrated by a professional wicket keeper.

Be aware, however, that there is a danger in placing too much emphasis on this notion of abilities as constraints to potential skill development. If a novice does not perform very well on a particular task, this might lead to the suspicion that she does not have the requisite ability to develop the skill. However, much of this deficit can often be overcome through effective practice. Notice that even though measures of the skill can change with learning, the ability underlying this skill would not change with practice (because it is stable and enduring). Appreciating the differences between the terms *ability* and *skill* is important in understanding how the differential method applies to issues such as individual differences and prediction.

Defining Individual Differences

Individual differences are defined as stable, enduring differences among people in terms of some measurable characteristic or performance of a task. Two people can differ in at least two distinct ways. First, if the test involves a very stable measure such as body weight, after a single measurement, we might conclude that one person really is heavier than the other. Although the scales might have some small degree of variability, the *repeatability* of the measure is very good. This is an example of a measured characteristic that reveals a stable, enduring difference between two people.

A second difference between people, however, can also occur when no stable, enduring difference is present. For example, if one person rolls a strike in bowling on one attempt and another person rolls a gutter ball, it might not be wise to conclude immediately that the first person is a better bowler than the second person based solely on this one measurement. The reason is that motor performance is highly variable and almost anything can happen on a single performance attempt. The study of individual differences is based on stable, enduring differences. In the first example (weighing people on scales), you are relatively confident of stable, enduring differences in the measured trait, whereas in the second example, you are not.

Understanding the All-Around Athlete

One of the long-lasting controversies in the individual-differences literature concerns the (so-called) all-around athlete. Most of us have known a kid from school who was a star athlete on the football, baseball, and basketball teams and who also won medals in track and field. And then there were those other kids—the all-around *non*-athletes. They seemed to have no proficiency in motor skills whatsoever. How do we understand the underlying basis for these apparent all-around athletes and non-athletes? Two hypotheses, quite different in their approach to answering this question, have been proposed.

Visit HK*Propel* to read "The Babe" and complete the self-directed learning activities.

General Motor Ability Hypothesis

One view of the all-around athlete is that all performances are based on a single ability, called the **general motor ability**. In this view, the all-around athlete is one who possesses a strong general motor ability—a single capability that underlies motor performance. Conversely, the all-around non-athlete is the person who lacks this strong general motor ability and thus succeeds in essentially no skilled physical activities.

The idea of a general motor ability shares many similarities with ideas popular in the early 20th century about the structure of cognitive skills. This kind of thinking was the basis for the idea of general intelligence, which attempted to explain a person's supposed potential for cognitive activities in terms of an overall, unitary value—the IQ (intelligence quotient). Furthermore, some believed that general cognitive ability and general motor ability were relatively separate, with intelligence contributing very little to motor skills and vice versa.

Henry's Specificity Hypothesis

In contrast to the general motor ability hypothesis, Henry (1958/1968) proposed that motor abilities are *specific* to a particular task or skill. This idea had three important assumptions:

1. Henry suggested that humans possess many separate abilities rather than just one.
2. These abilities were assumed to be independent of each other; thus, the strength of one ability was completely unrelated to the strength of any other ability.
3. Any specific skill we learn or task we perform depends on a *set* of abilities, with each skill or task composed of a different set.

The last assumption was the most critical of the **specificity hypothesis**, because it predicted that the performance of any two tasks (such as running speed vs. skating speed) would be unrelated. Since the abilities that underlie any two skills might have few, if any, abilities in common, the specificity view predicted that there is little common basis for similar performance outcomes.

Predictions made by the general motor ability and specificity views were often evaluated using a correlation analysis (see chapter 1). The idea was straightforward. To find support for the general motor ability view, measures of performance on various tasks for a large sample of individuals should reveal that exceptional athletes score well on all tasks, weak athletes should score poorly on all tasks, and mediocre athletes should score moderately on all tasks. The general motor ability view predicted that since a common underlying ability was responsible for performance on all tasks, a high correlation should exist between the performances of any two tasks, as shown in figure 1.4*a* and 1.4*b*. In contrast, the specificity view would predict that, because there is no overall ability that underlies performance on different tasks, performance on any two tasks should reveal a very low correlation, as shown in figure 1.4*c*. That is, an individual's performance on one task should be unrelated to their performance on a different task. Researchers used this strategy to examine both field and laboratory data to determine whether high or low correlations among movement tasks would be found.

There are numerous data sets in the literature, but one by Drowatzky and Zuccato (1967) makes the point particularly well (see Marteniuk, 1974, for a full review). Drowatzky and Zuccato examined a large group of participants on six balance tests and computed the correlations between all combinations of pairs of tests (15 correlations in all). Table 7.1 shows these values and contains the correlation between every test and every other test. The highest correlation in the entire matrix was between the tests named *bass stand* and *sideward stand* (r = .31). All the other correlations were numerically lower than this, ranging from .03 to .26. Even the highest correlation of .31 is low from a statistical viewpoint (r = .31 means that there was only $.31^2 \times 100 = 9.6\%$ of shared variance between these two tests; over 90% of the abilities underlying the two tests were different). Based on these data, it is impossible to argue that there was some single, underlying general motor ability that accounted for individual differences in all these tests. Rather, these findings, plus many other studies, provided strong support for the specificity view.

TABLE 7.1 Correlations Among Six Tests of Balance

	Diver's stand	Stick stand	Sideward stand	Bass stand	Balance stand
Stork stand	.14	−.12	.26	.20	.03
Diver's stand		−.12	−.03	−.07	−.14
Stick stand			−.04	.22	−.19
Sideward stand				.31	.19
Bass stand					.18

Abilities as a Basis for Prediction

As mentioned earlier, a large part of the traditional work on complex movement concerned predicting future performance or skill. In many movement-based skills, attempts to predict the potential for future performance have often been based on the measurement of current abilities. In baseball, for example, it would save considerable time if individuals could be reliably identified as future elite pitchers and then given specialized training.

As promising as this idea sounds, however, the prediction of success in movement skills is not very effective. There are two important reasons why this is so. First, effective prediction for the desired activity (e.g., pitching) would require a full understanding of the requisite abilities, which are poorly understood. Research underscoring Henry's specificity hypothesis showed quite clearly that the single general ability was untenable. But how many abilities are there, and how specific might they be? The Drowatzky and Zuccato study (1967; table 7.1) showed that six separate tests of balance ability were uncorrelated, suggesting that, at the very least, there could be many abilities that underlie balancing alone. There is no way to know which of these might be most important for pitching, for example, or how they would be identified in tests.

Even if the underlying abilities for the desired activity were known, there is the further problem that the contribution of relative abilities for a task shifts with practice. At one level, this is obvious. For beginners learning a new motor skill, considerable cognitive activity is involved in deciding what to do, remembering what comes after what, and trying to understand the instructions, rules, task scoring, and the like. Therefore, someone with strong cognitive abilities (*if* these could be accurately identified and measured) might be a good candidate for selection for some task. But with some experience, as one learns the intellectual parts of the task, abilities related more to movement control and perception might replace the role of these cognitive abilities in performance. Therefore, the strong abilities identified among novice performers for early skill development might not be the same as those required in later stages of expertise.

Prediction for future success in sports sounds wonderful in principle but faces many difficulties in reality. For example, selecting individuals who would become successful pilots was an important goal for the Allied powers during World War II. Participants were measured on a large number of predictor tests, which were presumed to underlie various abilities. At best, the test battery identified only about 50% of the abilities the criterion pilotry task measured; the remaining abilities underlying pilotry remained unknown (Adams, 1953, 1956; Fleishman, 1956). The situation is even more dismal in sports because this problem has received little systematic study and claims by some to successfully predict expert performance (e.g., the NFL's Scouting Combine) lack scientific support.

Nevertheless, research on individual differences and prediction has received renewed support in recent years (Anderson et al., 2021; Raganathan et al., 2022). This resurgence has emerged because of advances in statistical methods that can uncover nuances in individual differences, especially as people interact with various tasks and environments. This emphasis on individuals interacting with their environment serves as an excellent departure point for discussing an alternative view for the study of complex skills.

Visit HK*Propel* to read "Websites and Silly Walks" and complete the self-directed learning activities.

The Ecological Approach

The differential approach to the study of complex motor performance focuses on the measurement of abilities and individual differences—how abilities combine to define an individual and how a set of abilities makes us different from each other. The process-oriented approach, as we have described in chapters 1 through 6, treats individuals as basically the same in terms of how movements are performed. The remainder of this chapter now shifts to examining performance using the **ecological approach**.

FOCUS ON Application 7.1

The Relative-Age Effect

An interesting phenomenon was discovered when examining the statistics on high-level hockey players in Canada (i.e., those playing on elite junior teams). These statistics, used mostly for promotional purposes, include such things as each player's height, weight, position played, hometown, and birthday. It turns out that few players on the team were born in the late months of the year, and that many were born in January, February, and March. Why should it be that a disproportionate number of high-level hockey players were born early in the year? Could it be that being born early in the year leads to better general hockey ability?

Beginning with the research of Barnsley and colleagues (1992), popularized in the mainstream press by Gladwell (2008), and found to occur in many other sports as well (reviewed by Cobley et al., 2009; Smith et al., 2018), there is one very compelling and reasonable explanation. And it is not a "better general ability" explanation.

Nearly everyone knows that in Canada, hockey is a very special and traditional sport. Seemingly, most kids would like to see themselves succeed at the highest level possible in hockey. As a result, Canadian hockey is structured so that there are many age-group teams available to join, starting at a very early age. In those leagues, players are typically assigned to teams based on calendar-year age groupings. This procedure creates a very interesting bias because a child born on January 1 would play on a younger calendar-age team than a child born just one day earlier, on December 31.

We know, of course, that, especially in young boys and girls, one year makes a big difference in terms of maturation, body size, and so on. Older boys and girls (i.e., those with a birth date early in the calendar year) tend to be bigger, faster, and stronger, other things being equal. In some cases, coaches of these age-group teams focus more attention on the most effective players, setting the stage for a "rich-get-richer" phenomenon. As a result, these relatively older kids improve more than teammates born later in the year, which carries over to the next age-group team. Now they have an advantage because (1) they are still older than the kids born late in the year, and (2) they had the extra coaching and attention during the previous year because they were older—and so forth.

This phenomenon has been labeled the **relative-age effect** because the players who are born early in the calendar year are relatively older than the players born late in that year, even though, by traditional methods, they are categorized as the same age and play in the same league. In a way, this argument goes against the idea that champion players are born with the best abilities. Rather, this argument suggests that those players who were lucky enough to be born early in the year have an advantage over their late-in-the-year counterparts because of the enriched coaching, playing time, and so on.

The fundamental idea of the ecological approach is that complex skilled behavior occurs as a function of how we interact with the world around us. The ecological approach examines human movement by studying it in a changing, or dynamic, environment. The ideas presented in the remainder of this chapter have been influenced by many researchers, often working in different disciplines, such as psychology, kinesiology, and the physical sciences. We present ideas that represent a broad range of experimental methods that share a common perspective: the environment presents us with problems to be solved, and studying how movement solutions are achieved provides insights about how we perform complex actions. The discussion here is designed to provide a basic understanding of how the world around us shapes movement; not to provide an exhaustive review of the topic. The reader is encouraged to read Button and colleagues (2021) for a more complete discussion.

We have organized the remainder of the chapter into sections that describe movement behavior in a number of dynamic situations:

- Coordination of moving body parts with other moving body parts
- Coordination of one person's movements with other individuals
- Performance of movements under changing speeds
- Performance of movements in changing physical environments
- Coordination of movements with changing perceptual contexts

Within-Individual Coordination

In chapter 6, we presented various factors related to the speed and accuracy of making rapid, mainly single-limb, aiming movements. Much of that discussion focused on actions such as moving a limb to a target (e.g., positioning a cursor on an icon or a foot on the brake pedal) or using two limbs together to move a single object (e.g., swinging a baseball bat to hit a ball or an axe to split a block of wood). The principles discussed in chapter 6, such as Fitts' Law and Schmidt's Law, appear to describe speed–accuracy trade-offs very well for these types of movements.

But consider what happens when we coordinate limbs not with the purpose of moving a single object (e.g., a bat or an axe) but with distinct goals for each limb. For example, a guitarist presses on specific strings at specific locations with the left hand while the right hand strums all or some of the strings; a typist presses the Ctrl and Alt keys with the left hand and presses the Delete key with the right; and a carpenter holds a nail with two fingers on one hand while swinging a hammer with the other. Are these types of actions adequately explained by the same principles as before, or are unique principles required to explain them? Various methods have been devised to explore this question, which we describe in the next sections.

Bimanual Fitts' Task

The **bimanual Fitts' task** is a variation of the discrete single-limb task, whereby each limb moves to a separate target. For example, the limbs could be assigned to identical but separate tasks, both with either low IDs (figure 7.1*a*) or high IDs (figure 7.1*b*). Or each limb could be assigned to a different (incongruent) ID, for example, one with a low ID and one with a high ID (figure 7.1*c*). Recall that, according to Fitts' Law, the task parameters, width (W) and amplitude (A), govern MT. If this were to always hold true, then the MT for any combination of tasks should be determined solely by its ID. Therefore, a strict prediction of Fitts' Law would be that each limb should arrive at its target in a time consistent with that task's ID. Specifically, the following predictions should hold true:

- For congruent low-ID tasks (figure 7.1*a*), MTs for both limbs should be relatively short.
- For congruent high-ID tasks (figure 7.1*b*), MTs for both limbs should be relatively long.
- For incongruent tasks (figure 7.1*c*), MT for the limb moving to the low-ID task should be short and MT for the limb moving to the high-ID task should be long.

The studies by Kelso and colleagues (1979) found that, in general, when both limbs moved to targets of the same ID (congruent low- and high-ID tasks), the MTs were within the expected values as predicted by Fitts' Law. However, for limbs moving to targets with incongruent IDs, the results failed to

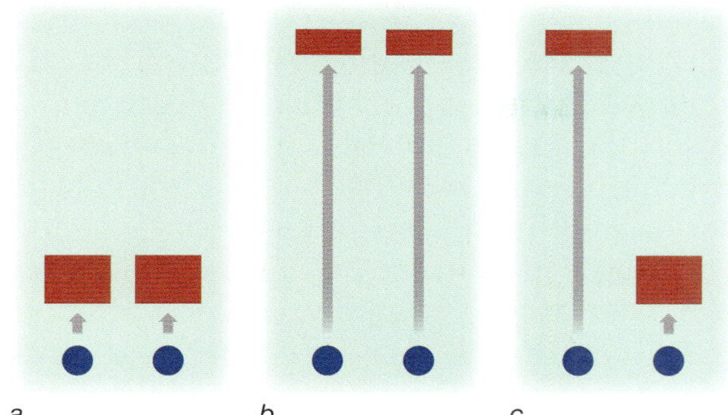

FIGURE 7.1 Three variants of the bimanual Fitts' task: *(a)* Both limbs perform a low-ID task (large target, small amplitude); *(b)* both limbs perform a high-ID task (small target, large amplitude); and *(c)* incongruent limb-ID assignment, the right hand performs a low-ID task and the left hand performs a high-ID task.

support the strict predictions of Fitts' Law. For example, when paired with a limb moving to a high ID, the MT of the limb moving to a low-ID task was considerably longer than would be expected. Fitts' Law failed to accurately predict the MTs when two limbs were moving to targets with incongruent IDs. Results from bimanual experiments such as these represent an additional exception to Fitts' Law as discussed in chapter 6.

The γ–V Experiment

Here is another experiment that illustrates how the motor system attempts to coordinate incongruent movements. Try this yourself. Draw small figures that represent the Greek letter gamma (γ) on a touchscreen, whiteboard, or sheet of paper taped to your desk. Draw the γ relatively quickly, without stopping. The figure must loop over itself near the center and have a rounded bottom. When you can do this effectively, use the other hand to draw capital Vs—that is, two opposing slashes (\ /) connected at the bottom. The procedure is the same as before except that now the figure must not cross over itself and must have a pointed bottom. Most people do not have any trouble producing these figures when each is drawn on its own, as shown in figure 7.2*a*.

Now try to produce these two figures simultaneously, using the same hands as before. You will find, as Bender (1987) did, that doing both tasks at the same time is very difficult, with results such as those shown in figure 7.2*b*. Most people make the same figure with both hands, or at least they produce certain features of one of the different figures with both hands (e.g., a rounded bottom). The implication here is that even though individuals have the capability of producing γ's and Vs perfectly well when performed separately, the joint production of both symbols results in something unique. Combining multiple degrees of freedom to produce incongruent actions is not simply the product of two independent processes. Instead, the result is a coordinated action that uniquely expresses an adaptable movement system.

FIGURE 7.2 The γ–V task. Participants are asked to produce the capital letter V with the left hand and the Greek letter gamma (γ) with the right hand. *(a)* In unimanual trials, only one letter is written at a time; *(b)* in bimanual trials, both letters (V and γ) are written simultaneously.

Analysis of the head movements of novice and expert golfers during a putt showed different coordination patterns between the movements of the golfer's head and the putter.

This unique expression of independently moving parts is also subject to individual differences. For example, Focus on Research 7.1 describes a skill (golf putting) in which the development of expertise changes the **coordination** pattern of limb and head movements. Learning is just one factor that plays a key role in how individual differences alter movement coordination. Age, gender effects, and physical limitations all influence how individual differences in movement are expressed.

Between-Individual Factors

People often coordinate their actions with others to achieve a common goal. The interplay among musicians in an orchestra results in a dynamic interaction that produces music that is greater than the sum of the individual parts. Rowing, dancing, cheerleading, and tugs-of-war are a few more examples where people must work together as a unit to maximize group output—be that maximum force, velocity, or some other end result.

These natural, interpersonal coordination patterns are fascinating, for they suggest that humans tend to synchronize motor behaviors as functional units in social contexts. This finding has been documented in situations

Rowing involves a team effort where forces are timed to maximize output.

FOCUS ON Research 7.1

Head–Arm Coordination in Golf Putting

Almost every golf instructor will tell you that body sway during the golf putt is detrimental to accuracy—the golfer should keep the lower body, torso, and, most importantly, the head as still as possible and simply rotate the shoulders to move the putter and strike the ball. But, for a number of reasons, this is very difficult to do. For example, a putting study by Lee and colleagues (2008) showed that both novice and expert golfers moved their heads considerably during a putt. However, they did so in fundamentally different ways.

Figure 7.3*a* illustrates 60 putts taken by one of the novices in the study, and figure 7.3*b* shows 60 putts by one of the experts (note that the same trends were shown by the other experts and novices in the study). The blue lines are traces of the movement velocities of the head during a putt, and the red lines are velocity profiles of the putter during the same time period. Note that although both the novice and expert moved their heads during each and every putt, the novice moved the head in the *same* direction as the movement of the putter, while the expert moved the head in the *opposite* direction of the putter.

Regardless of the direction of head movement, have another look at both graphs. Do you notice some similarities between the two? The point at which the velocity traces of the putter reversed direction in the graphs coincided generally with the reversal of the head velocity (the areas inside the gray boxes in each figure). Since it was not possible to keep the head still during the putt, novices dealt with the problem by moving their heads in the same direction as the motion of the putter; experts dealt with it by moving their heads in the opposite direction as the movement of the putter.

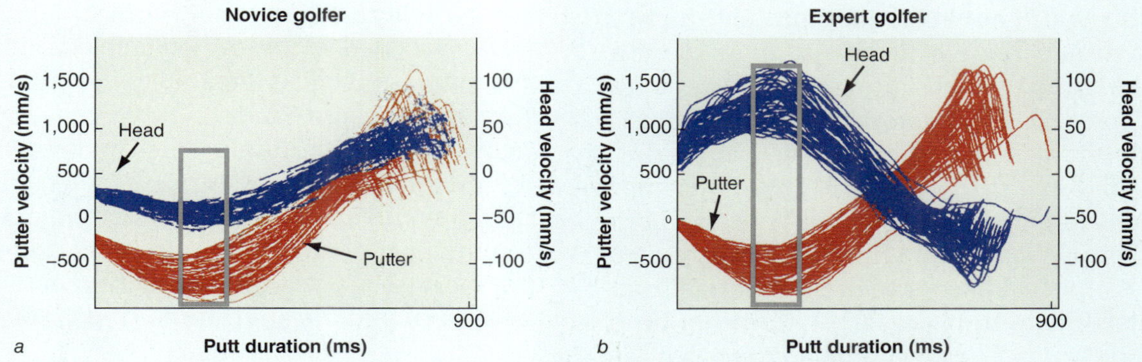

FIGURE 7.3 Velocity profiles of 60 putts made *(a)* by a novice golfer and *(b)* by an expert golfer. Each line represents the kinematic timeline of one putt (blue lines are head velocities, red lines are putter velocities). Both novices and experts moved their heads during the putts, but with different coordination patterns. The novices moved their heads and putters in the same direction; the experts moved them in the opposite direction.

as simple as two people walking side by side (van Ulzen et al., 2008) and as complex as the spontaneous coordinated clapping by an audience at the end of a concert (Néda et al., 2000; see Oullier & Kelso, 2009, for a review). Note that instances of interpersonal coordination do not imply that people are walking or clapping in unison throughout the entire episode. Rather, they exemplify cases where periods of coordinated behavior far exceed what would be anticipated if the individual actions were completely independent, as exemplified very clearly in Focus on Application 7.2.

Environmental Interactions

The ecological approach uses a more contextualized way to understand principles of movement control than is typically achieved with a reductionist, process-oriented approach. In the previous section, we saw that simultaneously coordinating the movements of two limbs does not follow the same principles as performing the two movements independently. Coordination is more than the sum of the individual parts. In this section, we discuss how movement is altered when the immediate environment is changed.

Bimanual Fitts' Task Revisited

We saw in previous sections that the ID in Fitts' Law did not accurately predict the MT of an aimed limb when it was paired with another limb that was moving to a target with a different ID. This "compensation" in adjusting the movement was seen even more dramatically in a study by Kelso and colleagues (1983). Here, both limbs moved to congruent task IDs. However, one limb was forced to go over a physical barrier in order to move from the starting point to the target; the other limb had no barrier. The researchers found that the unimpeded limb, even though not physically required to do so, elevated as if it were going over a barrier. The physical presence of the barrier for one limb was sufficient to change the trajectories of both limbs.

Locomotion Studies

Bipedal animals, like humans, typically use one of two gaits to move around—walking or running. Although we can hop, skip, and locomote using other types of gaits, walking and running are the two most common. Sometimes we voluntarily make the decision. But at other times, this decision is influenced very strongly by the environment. In the next few sections, we describe situations where there is an advantage to changing gaits or a cost for not doing so.

Gait Transitions in Horses Why, when you are on a treadmill, do you choose to walk at some speeds yet run at other speeds? Researchers who studied the **gait transition** in horses on a treadmill provided one answer to this question.

Horses, being quadrupeds, have more gait options than bipeds (Alexander, 2003). When allowed to freely choose a gait, horses typically walk at speeds between 1 and 2 m/s (4-7 km/h), trot at speeds of 3 to 4 m/s (11-14 km/h), and gallop at speeds greater than 5 m/s (>18 km/h). So what happens when a horse is put on a treadmill that is sped up or slowed down? Hoyt and Taylor (1981) found that horses naturally changed gaits at speeds that corresponded to optimal energy expenditure. And when trained to extend gaits to non-normal speeds, horses did so at an energy cost. For example, trotting at slow speeds, where horses would naturally walk, and at high speeds, where they would naturally gallop, were associated with elevated levels of energy consumption when compared to the preferred gaits at the same speeds. Hoyt and Taylor suggested that minimizing energy costs was a likely explanation for why horses selected the gaits they did and when transitions occurred from one gait to another. In this case, energy costs drive the dynamic interaction between the animal and the environment. But there is an alternative explanation.

Gait Transitions in Humans Consider the findings of a study of gait transitions in humans by Diedrich and Warren (1995). Their participants walked on a treadmill at speeds that were above and below what is considered normal and comfortable (which is ~ 3.6 km/h, or 2.2 mph). They also ran at speeds that were normal for running and at speeds much slower than normal for running.

FOCUS ON Application 7.2

Usain Bolt Versus Tyson Gay

A fascinating example of spontaneous, unintentional interpersonal coordination occurred in the men's 100 m sprint final in 2009 (Varlet & Richardson, 2015). The much-anticipated showdown between Usain Bolt and Tyson Gay resulted in a world record performance by Bolt, who ran the race in 9.58 s, shaving an incredible 1.1 tenths of a second off the world record—a record that, historically, is typically bettered by hundreds of a second, not by over a tenth of a second! But would Bolt have achieved such a remarkable time without Gay beside him? An analysis of the race by Varlet and Richardson revealed that it may have been the interpersonal coordination of their behavior that facilitated this remarkable performance.

Figure 7.4 illustrates the relative phase for each pair of strides taken by the two sprinters (see Focus on Research 7.2 for a discussion on relative phase as a measure of within- and between-individual coordination). Because Bolt is much taller than Gay, his stride is longer and less frequent. As a result, there is a continuous "drift" of the relative phase of the two sprinters' stride cycles during the race. The continuous drift is shown clearly in their semifinal races (in which they competed in separate heats), as shown in figure 7.4*a*. The drift is also apparent for portions of the final race (figure 7.4*b*). However, there were four periods during the final when Bolt's and Gay's strides locked at a 0° relative phase for three to four strides at a time. These periods of phase locking were not an accident and revealed spontaneous interpersonal coordination that likely benefited both sprinters, because they both posted personal best race times.

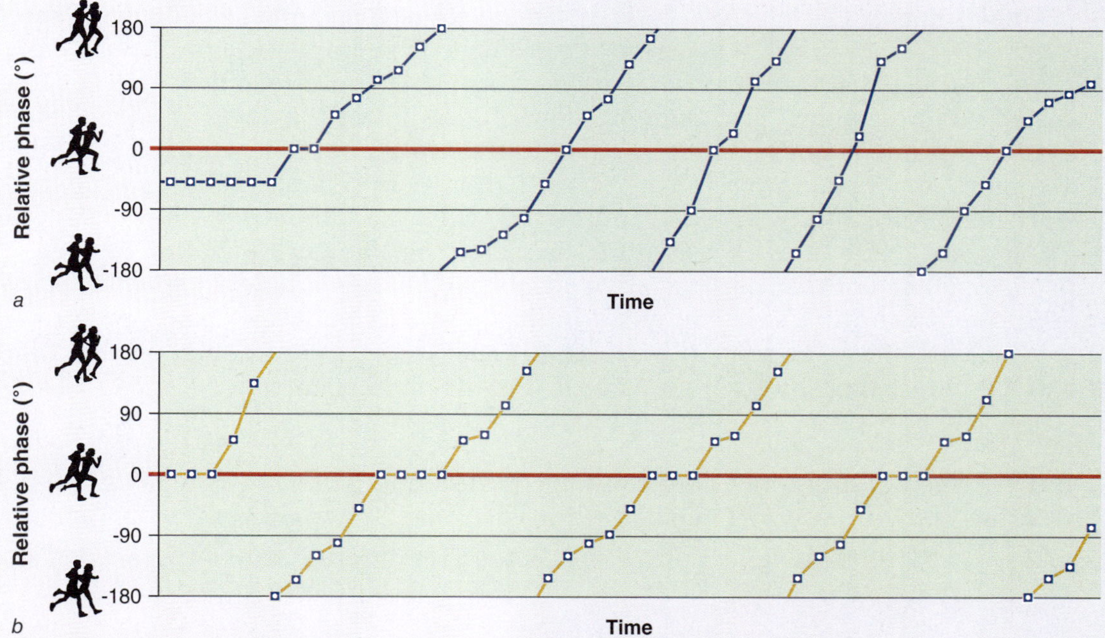

FIGURE 7.4 Analysis of the Usain Bolt–Tyson Gay relative phase drifts during their *(a)* semifinal and *(b)* final 100 m races. Each blue dot represents a relative phase value of the stride cycle each time Bolt's right foot touched down. The semifinal (in which they raced in separate heats) shows no evidence of phase locking, whereas in the final (in which they ran in adjacent lanes), Bolt and Gay phase locked in synchronous timing (0° relative phase) for three to four strides at regular intervals throughout the race. Both sprinters performed personal best times in the final, with Bolt shaving an incredible .11 s off the world record.

FOCUS ON Research 7.2

Relative Phase: An Index of Coordination

An oscillating object, such as a pendulum, can be characterized as a repeating cycle with 360° of phase angles. Any single point for the oscillating object within its trajectory can be identified as a specific phase angle. When two oscillating objects are compared, a measure of how much they are synced together can be described in terms of **relative phase**. In coordination experiments, the oscillating objects may be two fingers, two legs, or even two limbs of different people.

In the two-finger example, relative phase provides a single value that describes the position of one finger within its 360° oscillation cycle relative to the position of the other finger within its cycle. In performing an **in-phase** pattern, for example, the goal is to maintain the same relative position of both fingers within their own respective cycles. For example, if at some point both fingers are at 120° through the oscillation cycle, then the relative phase is the difference between the right finger's phase angle (120°) and the left finger's phase angle (120°). Therefore, the in-phase relative phase goal is a relative phase of 0° (i.e., 120 – 120 = 0). For an **anti-phase** pattern, the goal is to coordinate the fingers to be in opposite positions within their cycle (e.g., 300° vs. 120°), always offset by a relative phase of 180° (300 – 120 = 180).

An average (or mean) relative phase is calculated by summing the relative phase values throughout a trial and dividing by the total number of measures taken. An in-phase pattern usually has a mean of 0° relative phase, and an anti-phase pattern has a mean near 180° relative phase when performed accurately. However, since movement is never perfect, a measure of variability is an important additional statistic. The relative phase standard deviation is calculated similarly to the variable error, as described in chapter 1. The standard deviation captures the degree to which each individual sample is unlike the mean of all the samples. In other words, it describes how reliably the mean describes the coordination performance. When all the individual samples are tightly arranged around the mean, the standard deviation is small; when they are scattered widely around the mean, the standard deviation is large.

Taken together, both the mean relative phase and the standard deviation are important indices of coordination. The mean indicates which pattern is being performed (in-phase, anti-phase, or some other pattern), and the standard deviation describes how reliably (or consistently) that pattern is being performed.

Exploring Further

1. Describe the difference between the coordination patterns made by the upper arms in the front crawl versus the breaststroke in swimming.
2. How would fatigue affect the performance of swimming strokes in terms of the relative phase measures?

Figure 7.5 illustrates some very interesting results of this experiment but needs some explanation. First, locomotion speed is expressed on the horizontal axis as a Froude number, which is a dimensionless scale that accounts for individual differences in a person's size and stride length. In general, the range of Froude numbers represents walking speeds ranging from 3.2 to 9.0 km/h (2.0-5.6 mph) and running speeds ranging from 5.4 to 13.0 km/h (3.4-8.1 mph). The vertical axis expresses the standard deviation of the relative phase of the ankle and knee angles—a measure of the stability of the gait pattern's relative phase (see Focus on Research 7.2). The shaded vertical box in the figure represents the average speeds at which the participants freely chose to change from a walking to a running gait (or from a run to a walk) as the experimenter sped up or slowed down the treadmill. These transitions occurred at speeds ranging from 6.8 to 8.4 km/h (4.2-5.2 mph).

What is most interesting to note in figure 7.5 is that the stability of the walking gait's relative phase became weakened when walking slower or faster than the preferred speed. Similarly, the running gait was destabilized when participants ran at speeds where they would normally walk (i.e., to the left of the shaded box).

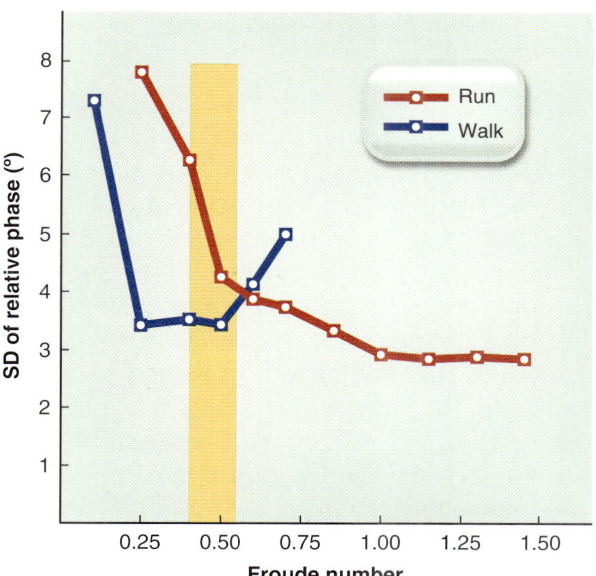

FIGURE 7.5 The stability (standard deviation) in the ankle–knee relative phase at various walking and running speeds (Froude number). The shaded area illustrates the normal transition speeds for changing gaits. Walking was more variable both above and below the preferred speed; running was more variable below the preferred speed.

The Diedrich and Warren (1995) findings are critically important, for they suggest that we choose to change from walking to running and from running to walking not because of energetic reasons but to achieve a more efficient and effective coordination pattern for the current locomotion speed. In this case, the standard deviation in the relative phase of the pattern was the key impetus for deciding to change gaits. Here is an instance of an interaction between the individual and the environment being driven by a desire for movement efficiency, with voluntary gait changes designed to maximize efficiency and involuntarily imposed gaits occurring at a cost.

Split-Belt Treadmill Walking A novel approach to locomotor adaptation has been studied using a **split-belt treadmill**, in which the left and right legs step on separate belts with each stride. When both belts move at the same speed, walking and running occur normally with a symmetrical gait. The locomotion pattern must be adapted quickly when the two belts move at different speeds, resulting in an asymmetrical stride. Remarkably, the new asymmetrical pattern persists well after the treadmill belts return to a symmetrical speed (Torres-Oviedo et al., 2011). This is a wonderful demonstration of how the environment can be altered to create changes in movement dynamics. The finding has applications for treating impaired nervous systems, such as following a stroke, in which an asymmetrical gait might be present—a split-belt treadmill could help the patient change an asymmetrical gait to a more symmetrical one (Helm & Reisman, 2015).

Bimanual Timing

Try this simple experiment: Point your index fingers on both hands straight ahead of you, as if you were pointing two pistols at a target, then oscillate both fingers. Even with these very simple instructions, most people spontaneously do this task by oscillating each finger toward their midline, then away, oscillating back and forth using an in-phase mode of coordination. Here, in-phase means that right-finger flexion and the correspond-

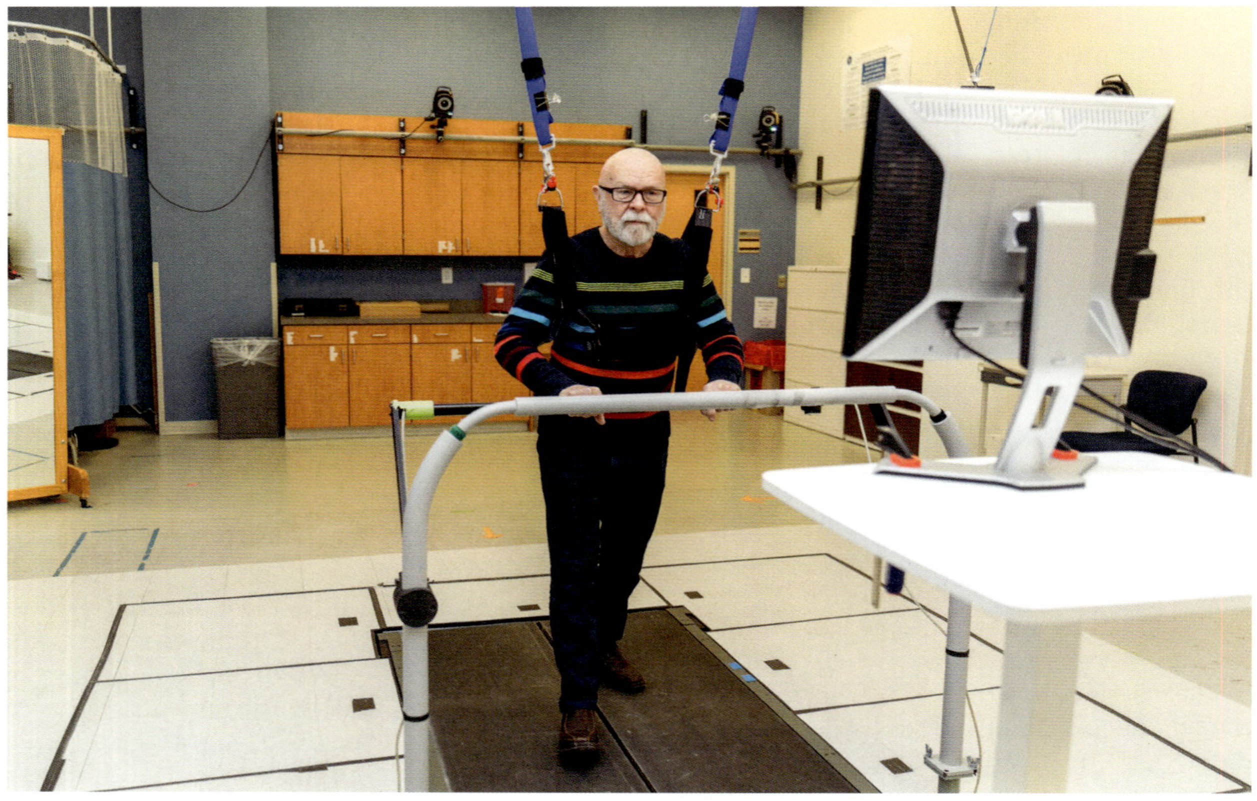

Split-belt treadmills can aid in the physical rehabilitation of gait disorders following neurological impairment.

ing left-finger flexion occur at the same time within their cycles and with relatively consistent timing (i.e., a mean relative phase of 0° with a low relative phase standard deviation). Some people might also choose a coordination pattern like most car windshield wipers move—in alternation (called *anti-phase*, or a *180° relative phase*).

But what happens when these movements are synchronized with a perceptual input that increases in frequency? As we saw in the Diedrich and Warren (1995) study described in the previous section, this environmental influence has a disruptive but peculiar effect on the stability of these coordination patterns. In a landmark study by Kelso (1984; Kelso et al., 1986), participants moved their fingers in either an in-phase or an anti-phase pattern by keeping pace with a metronome that began at a low speed (1.25 Hz; slightly faster than one complete cycle per second), then increased in speed at regular intervals. Figure 7.6 illustrates the results of their study.

Figure 7.6 looks rather complicated, but the results are straightforward. Means (figure 7.6*a*) and standard deviations of relative phase (figure 7.6*b*; see Focus on Research 7.2) illustrate how the in-phase and anti-phase patterns were performed as the metronome speed increased. As expected, the in-phase pattern started near a mean of 0° and remained there as speed increased. Also, as expected, the anti-phase pattern started near a mean of 180°. However, with increased speed, the fingers originally coordinating in the anti-phase pattern had completely switched to an in-phase pattern by the time the metronome reached a speed of 2.75 Hz. The standard deviation data help us understand why this happened. Although the in-phase pattern remained stable as speed increased, the anti-phase pattern became increasingly destabilized with increasing speed. Normal stability was regained by the time the pattern had completely switched to an in-phase relative phase.

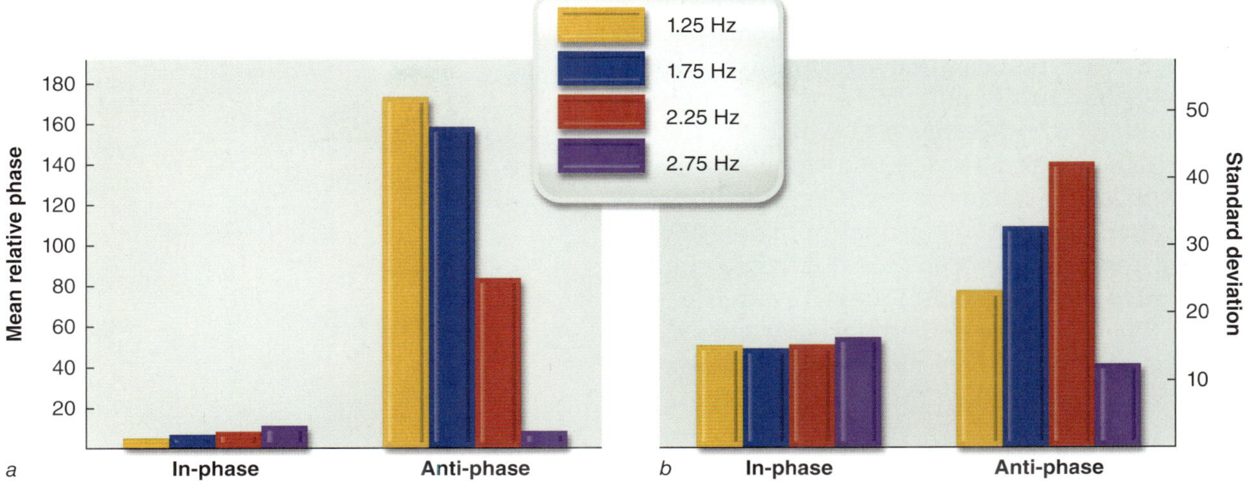

FIGURE 7.6 *(a)* Mean relative phase and *(b)* standard deviation of relative phase for coordination patterns starting in-phase or anti-phase as a function of movement speed.

Like the work of Diedrich and Warren, Kelso's bimanual finger paradigm revealed that different coordination patterns had different levels of stability when responding to environmental changes (in this case, the metronome frequency). Here, though, the change was asymmetrical—both coordination patterns were stable at low frequencies, but only the anti-phase pattern destabilized at higher frequencies.

Some have criticized the oscillating, two-finger research as too experimental or lab oriented to relate to real or complex motor skills. But as we have discussed throughout the book and will continue to do in the chapters that follow, the importance of these studies is not what they say about performing these simple tasks per se. Rather, their importance is what is revealed about the processes that underlie human motor performance and learning. The initial work on the **coordination dynamics** of two oscillating fingers and the theory development that followed (Haken et al., 1985; Kelso, 1995, 2022) has led to new perspectives, research, and theorizing about activities such as drumming (e.g., Fujii et al., 2010), swimming (e.g., Seifert et al., 2014), and cross-country skiing (Cignetti et al., 2009), among many other real skills and activities. We wonder (or doubt) whether these advances could have been made without the empirical and theoretical groundwork laid with experiments using these simple, lab-based tasks.

Visit HK*Propel* to read "Party Tricks" and "Disappearing Act" and complete the self-directed learning activities.

Perception and Bimanual Coordination

We saw in the previous section that bimanual coordination pattern stability was asymmetrical—that in-phase patterns appeared to be more stable in response to environmental challenges (i.e., changes in metronome frequency) than anti-phase patterns. However, this apparent biological dynamic can be altered under different environmental conditions. Next, consider how changes in the perceptual environment can alter coordination stability.

Participants in one study reported by Mechsner and colleagues (2001) moved rotational cranks with each hand in the horizontal plane. Normally, bimanual coordination is stable only for phase-locked frequencies, where the two hand cranks are moving at the same speed. Coordinating the limbs to move in nonharmonic frequencies such as 4:3 is difficult and unstable. However, Mechsner and colleagues devised a system where the participants could not see their limbs—only the flags attached to the cranks that their limbs were moving. The participants were unaware that a gear system had been attached to the movement of one crank, which altered the frequency at which the flag moved. They found that a 1:1 movement of the *flags* was easy to achieve, even though the *limbs* were moving at a 4:3 coordination frequency. Similar results have been found using altered augmented feedback techniques (Kovacs et al., 2010). By altering the perceptual environment, researchers created new movement coordination stability that had previously been quite unstable.

Environmental End-State Goals

A casual observation led David Rosenbaum on a journey to describe why individuals choose flexible movement plans based on end-state goals (e.g., Rosenbaum, 2010). He observed that servers in outdoor cafes (where unused glasses sit upside down on tables) would grasp a glass using an inverted (thumb-down) posture in order to pick it up, invert it, and pour water into it. A series of experiments later confirmed that end-state comfort ruled the grasp choice decision—initial awkward postures are adopted in order to achieve an anticipated measure of comfort when using or placing the object. For servers, it was simply a decision that foreshadowed later efficiency and effectiveness by predicting levels of end comfort during the movement planning stage.

As a further demonstration of the role of environmental goals and anticipated end-state comfort, imagine how you would turn over an hourglass, as illustrated in figure 7.7*a*. As predicted by Rosenbaum's end-state comfort ideas, you would likely grasp the hourglass in the middle using an inverted, palm-up posture so that you would place it on the table with the hand in a comfortable posture. Now imagine inverting two hourglasses, as illustrated in figure 7.7*b*. Here, the likely initial posture for each limb would be thumbs (or palms) down, but symmetrical, with the back of each hand facing the other. Here, the symmetry of the hand movement achieves a coordinated effort that ends in a comfortable state for both.

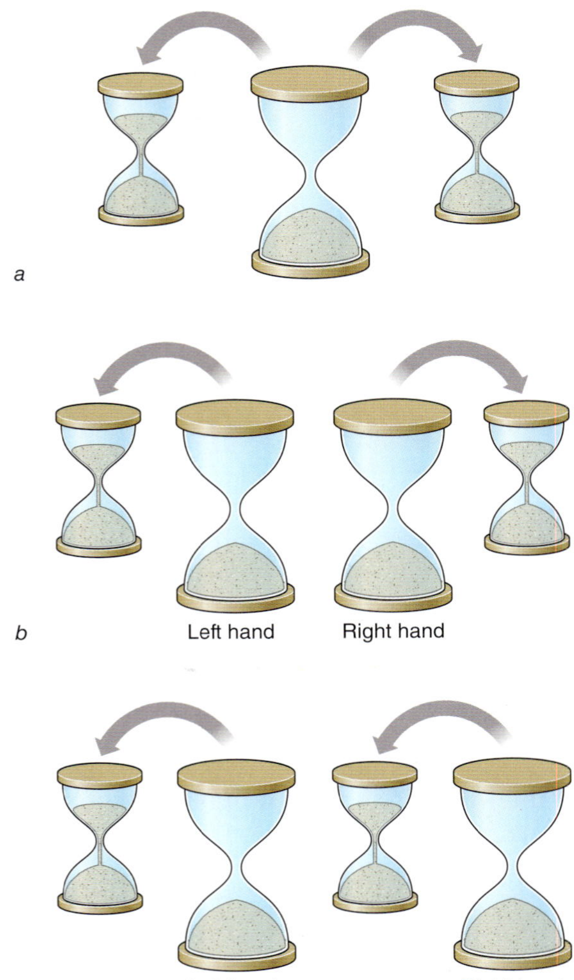

FIGURE 7.7 *(a)* How would you orient your hand to turn over the glass? *(b* and *c)* Then, consider how you would orient your hands to simultaneously turn over both glasses to achieve the results as shown. In all cases, initial awkward grips and coordination modes would be chosen to maximize an anticipated comfortable end position when placing the object.

Now consider the action required in figure 7.7*c*. Here, the initial postures of the two hands would be asymmetrical—the left hand adopting a thumb-down posture and the right hand adopting a palm-up posture so that both achieve end-state comfort (e.g., Janssen et al., 2010; Kunde & Weigelt, 2005). An asymmetrical coordination of the initial posture of the hands is chosen to satisfy the combined influence of the environmental goal and the expected, or predicted, comfort levels resulting from the action.

Summary of the Ecological Approach

In the previous section, we described a number of ideas, concepts, and experimental results that exemplify some examples of research from an ecological-approach perspective. In each case, the movement system was required to adapt to the environmental features, which sometimes changed during the movement. The ecological view can be summarized as a dynamic, problem-solving process resulting in movement that evolves over time. The environment presents the problem to be solved, and movement represents the solution to the problem.

The bimanual Fitts' task presented a problem in which two limbs were assigned targets that sometimes differed in task IDs. The solution was an interdependent action that allowed each limb to achieve its goal, but with some shared features of movement (speed, trajectory). Locomotion studies revealed that changing speeds of one or both legs presents a problem for the movement system that gait changes resolve. Continuously moving one finger on each hand is an easy problem to solve at a slow speed by coordinating them in one of two innately stable patterns. However, when the movements are made faster, only one pattern remains stable to provide a solution. The study with the rotating flags demonstrated the power of our perceptual system to solve a polyrhythmic coordination problem. The server can overturn glasses using a variety of solutions, depending on the desired end state. In all these cases, the problem presented by the environment resulted in an adaptation of movement to solve the problem by more efficient, effective, and sometimes novel means.

Some researchers consider the ecological approach to be inconsistent with the information-processing view that we have discussed in the previous chapters. The argument is that environmental information directly specifies, or constrains, how movements are organized without the requirement of a command center in the brain. We disagree, obviously, and believe that the environment provides information that we process and act upon, using the approach specified by the conceptual model developed to this point in the book. In the end, it is likely that neither theoretical approach will be correct in all aspects, which should lead to the development of new theories with stronger predictive powers. And this is a good thing, because such is the fate of a healthy science.

Summary

There are many interesting aspects of understanding complex skills in people and approaches to their study. Ability is a critical concept that is defined as a stable, enduring trait that underlies the performance of various tasks. An ability is distinguished from a skill, which is proficiency in some particular task. Henry's (1968) research tells us that the old concept of a general motor ability, with one ability thought to underlie all motor proficiency, is incorrect. Generally, the relationships between skills are low, suggesting that abilities are very specific to particular tasks. Predicting success in some future activity is a critical individual-difference consideration and is based on the notion of abilities. However, prediction is not very effective, probably because of the incomplete understanding of the fundamental abilities that underlie performance, and this is particularly so in sports.

A different approach to the study of complex skills is the ecological approach. In this view, the environment poses problems for movement that are solved by the dynamics of the motor system. Various research issues exemplify the ecological approach. For example, in the bimanual Fitts' task, the two limbs must reach their intended goal, but the movements of one have a strong influence on the kinematics of the other. Locomotion studies reveal that we tend to change gaits in response to environmental changes in order to preserve movement efficiency. The ecological view challenges the conventional understanding of complex skills by reconsidering how movement adapts in response to a changing world.

HKPROPEL ACTIVITIES

HK*Propel* offers these activities to help you build and apply your knowledge of the concepts in this chapter. Additionally, you'll find a key terms flashcard review activity and a key terms quiz, along with audio supplements for selected figures, as indicated by QR codes throughout the chapter.

Interactive Learning

Activity 7.1: Explore the distinction between an ability and a skill by indicating which in a list of descriptions applies to each.

Activity 7.2: Test your understanding of the correlations between skills by interpreting two correlation graphs and how the performance skills would most likely correlate.

Activity 7.3: Test your understanding of how movements made with two or more degrees of freedom are performed at the same time.

Activity 7.4: Listen to a podcast about the relative-age effect in sport, then consider links to abilities versus skills.

Principles-to-Application Exercise

Activity 7.5: The principles-to-application exercise for this chapter prompts you to identify a sport or activity and analyze the abilities and skills that would affect its performance, as well as consider the issues that would arise when predicting who would be successful in the sport or activity.

Motor Control in Everyday Actions Narratives

The Babe

Websites and Silly Walks

Party Tricks

Disappearing Act

Check Your Understanding

1. How were statistical correlations used to examine abilities? What did researchers find out about correlations among skills? What does this tell you about the concept of a general motor ability?
2. Describe three components involved in attempts at predicting a future skill level on a criterion task. How effective is skill prediction in a sport setting?
3. Describe both a single-limb and a bimanual Fitts' task. Explain, in general terms, how findings using the bimanual Fitts' task were different from those using the single-limb task.

Apply Your Knowledge

1. Explain the differences between an ability and a skill. How would you illustrate these differences to a friend who has told you that she would like to train quickness

in her young field hockey team? What might you suggest including in practice to improve skills requiring speed?

2. What difficulties might a talent scout for a high-level swim team encounter when predicting which young children at a swim camp are likely to do well at an elite level? How might the abilities needed to perform well as a novice differ from those needed after several years of training?
3. Your band is trying a new song in which a critical guitar part comes in off the beat of the drummer. Why might the guitarist find this difficult to do?

PART II

Principles of Skill Learning

To this point in the text, our focus has been on understanding some of the factors that underlie performance, such as the principles of movement control and information processing. Most of the major variables that determine the quality of movement output have been introduced and discussed. In addition, we have developed a conceptual model of motor behavior that illustrates most of the important factors that influence movement. At this point, you should have a reasonably good overall concept of how skills are performed and what some of the limiting factors might be.

The concepts and terminology in part II should be familiar, because they are mainly the same as those used in part I. A major focus in part II concerns how the components of the conceptual model change with practice and experience, as well as the research-based principles that govern such changes. As in part I, a major emphasis is on research indicating how certain features in practice contribute to the future capability for movement. As you will see, many of these features of practice are available to the coach or instructor to use directly with learners; hence, this discussion includes many ways in which practice can be varied in real-world settings to optimize learning. Another related issue concerns the extent to which skills are retained over time so they can be helpful to the performer in the future. Part II concludes with a discussion of some of the theories and theoretical constructs that have been proposed to explain the motor learning process. As you will see, none are correct in every respect; however, each contributes a significant understanding about the principles that underlie the process.

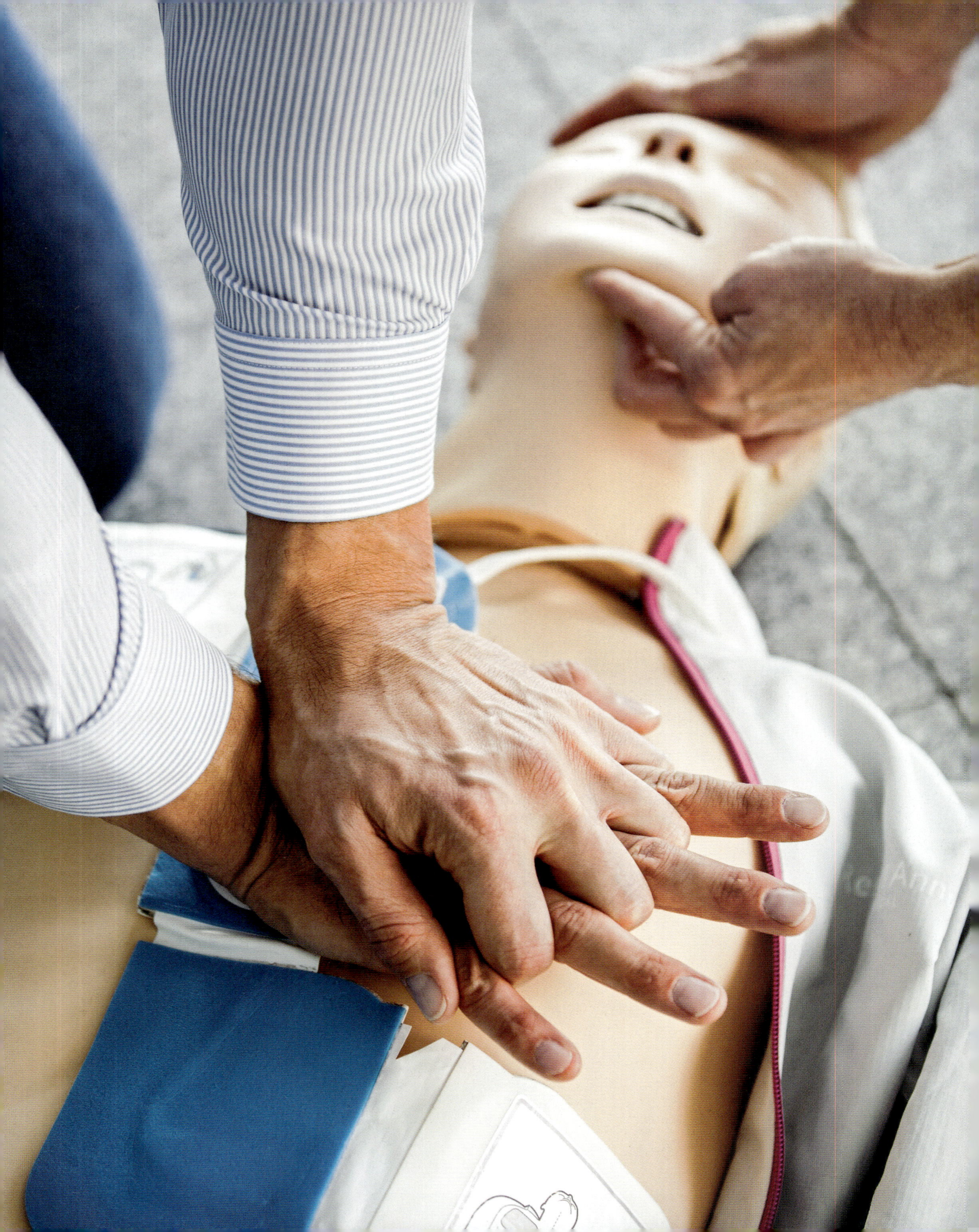

8

Introduction to Motor Learning

Concepts and Methods in Research and Application

CHAPTER OUTLINE

CHAPTER OBJECTIVES

Chapter 8 introduces the concept of motor learning and describes fundamental principles regarding how it is studied. This chapter will help you understand

- a clear definition of motor learning and how it differs from motor performance,
- temporary and relatively permanent effects of practice variables,
- transfer designs and their importance in learning research, and
- the measurement of transfer of motor skills.

CHAPTER PREVIEW QUIZ

1. In your own words, describe the difference between learning and performance.
2. How do retention tests differ from transfer tests?
3. Provide an example of how musical skill can be transferred.

Imagine that you are an instructor in a two-day cardiopulmonary resuscitation (CPR) course, teaching a set of skills to a group of adults. For grading, you want to measure skill improvements but are puzzled about how to do it. Would the best measure of skill take into account the students' levels of proficiency at the start of the class? Would you measure the amount learned at the conclusion of the course, when fatigue might influence the results? Or would you measure skill at some time later, after the course has finished, by which time some forgetting might have occurred? What skills should you ask learners to perform in the test—the same as practiced earlier or slight variations of them? And under what conditions would the test be conducted—in the stress-free conditions in which the skills were taught, the heightened anxiety levels that would put the skills to the test in a real emergency, or some other context?

This chapter concerns motor skill learning, the set of processes through which practice and experience can generate large, nearly permanent gains in human performance. The initial focus of the chapter is understanding the concept of learning and establishing some basic ideas about how learning is defined and conceptualized. Then we turn to how one can evaluate the effectiveness of practice in both laboratory and practical settings with relevance to instruction. Finally, we discuss the **transfer of learning**, in which the skills acquired in one situation are applied to another.

The capability to learn is critical to biological existence because it allows organisms to adapt to the features of their environments and gain from experience. For humans, this learning is the most critical of all. Think how it would be to go through life equipped only with the capabilities inherited at birth. Humans would be relatively simple beings indeed without the capability to talk, write, or read, and certainly without the capability to perform the complex movement skills seen in sports, music, or industry. Although learning occurs for all kinds of human performances—cognitive, verbal, interpersonal, and so on—the focus here is on the processes that underlie learning the cognitive and motor capabilities that lead to skills as defined earlier.

Learning seems to occur nearly continuously, almost as if everything you do today generates knowledge or experience that affects how you do other things tomorrow and beyond. However, this book takes a more restricted view of learning, in which the focus is on situations involving practice (or training)—deliberate attempts to improve performance of a particular skill or action.

In this photo, describe one fundamental difference between performance and learning for the basketball player practicing a free throw.

Practice, of course, often takes place in classes or lessons, either in groups, as might be seen in the CPR example provided earlier, or individually, as in private ski lessons or physical therapy sessions. Usually, but certainly not always, there is an instructor, therapist, or coach to guide this practice, to evaluate the learner's progress and give feedback, and to decide about future activities to foster progress. This focus on practice defines an important class of human activities and involves many factors—such as the nature of instructions, evaluation, and scheduling—that collectively determine the effectiveness of practice.

Instructors are in an important position to influence learning if they have a solid understanding of the fundamental processes underlying practice settings. A critical starting point is understanding the nature and definition of learning.

Motor Learning Defined

When a person practices, the usual (or expected) result is an improved performance level, which is often measured as a global outcome score, such as a lower golf score, reduced time to complete a simple surgical operation, or a larger number of roofing shingles nailed in a 20 min period. But there is more to learning than just improved performance outcomes. Researchers have found it useful to define learning in terms of the gain in the underlying capability for skilled performance developed during practice, with the improved capability being specifically responsible for improved performance.

But be aware that improved performance does not by itself define learning. Rather, improved performance is an indication that learning *may* have occurred, which represents a very important distinction. This idea can be formalized by a definition:

> **Motor learning** is a set of processes associated with practice or experience leading to relatively permanent gains in the capability for skilled performance.

There are several important aspects to this definition, which are discussed in the next sections:

- Learning affects capability.
- Learning results from practice or experience.
- Learning is not directly observable.
- Learning requires relatively permanent changes.

Learning Affects Capability

The term **capability** for performance may seem odd, but it simply reflects the fact that any single performance may not accurately reflect the underlying skill level. Just as the fastest runner does not always win the race and the more skilled tennis player does not always win the game, any performance may exceed or fall short of its theoretical true capability. So we are interested in measuring the underlying capability for performance, being mindful that on any given occasion, the learner might not, for various reasons, perform up to her capability.

Learning Results From Practice or Experience

Many factors can improve the capability for skilled performance. However, learning is concerned with only some of these factors—those related to practice or experience. For example, the performance capabilities of children increase as they mature and grow. However, growth factors alone are not evidence of learning because they are not related to practice. Similarly, gains in cardiovascular endurance or strength could occur in training programs, leading to more effective performance in activities like soccer, but these changes are not related to skill improvement.

Learning Is Not Directly Observable

Practice results in alterations to the central nervous system. Many researchers refer to these alterations as *brain plasticity*, which refers to changes as the result of experience (Kantak & Winstein, 2012). Some of these changes result in relatively permanent improvements in movement capability. These processes are not directly observable in general, so their existence must be inferred from the changes in performance they presumably support.

The changes underlying learning occur to the fundamental decision-making and movement-control processes discussed in the previous chapters that are brought together in the conceptual model of human performance. Figure 8.1 shows the conceptual model again, this time highlighting some processes that are influenced by practice.

Some examples of changes to these processes include the following:

- Improving analysis of environmental and movement feedback information (during stimulus identification)
- Improving action selection (during response selection) and parameterization (in movement programming)
- Creating more effective generalized motor programs
- Generating more accurate and precise anticipated feedback
- Establishing more accurate references of correctness

Learning can occur at all levels of the central nervous system, but the levels highlighted in figure 8.1 account for the biggest changes. Of course, we have discussed all these processes before; we now simply add the notion that they can be improved in various ways through practice, leading to more effective performance.

Even though the underlying processes are not directly observable, we can usually observe and measure the products of the learning process by measuring changes in skill. Changes in underlying processes lead to more effective capability for skill, which underlies more skillful performances. Therefore, evidence about the development of these processes can be gained by examining carefully chosen performance tests. The performance gains on these tests are usually assumed to result from gains in skill.

Learning Requires Relatively Permanent Changes

One important qualification must be added to the previous section. In order for a change in skilled performance level to be regarded as due to learning, the change must be *relatively permanent*. Many factors affect a momentary level of skilled performance, some of which are temporary and transient. For example, skills can be affected by drugs, sleep loss, mood, stress, motivation, and many other factors. Most of these variables have only a temporary effect, with performance levels returning to normal when their effects disappear. Consider caffeine, for example; the performance gains from the caffeinated state to the decaffeinated state are not due to learning because the changes are transient and reversible by adding caffeine again. These changes were clearly not relatively permanent.

In studying learning, it is important to understand those practice variables that affect performance in a relatively permanent way. This changed capability is then a relatively permanent part of the person's makeup and is available at some future time when the given skill is required.

An analogy might be useful to drive home this concept. Changes occur when a pot of water is put on a hot stove, the most obvious being that the water temperature rises. Moving the pot from the stove to the table will eventually return the water temperature to its original state. The changes to the water, therefore, would not be analogous to learning because the internal (temperature) change is not relatively permanent. However, when an egg is put into boiling water, its internal state is forever changed. This change is relatively permanent because removing the egg from the boiling water and allowing it to cool does not reverse its internal state.

The relatively permanent changes in the egg are analogous to changes in humans due to learning. When people learn, relatively permanent changes occur that survive the shift

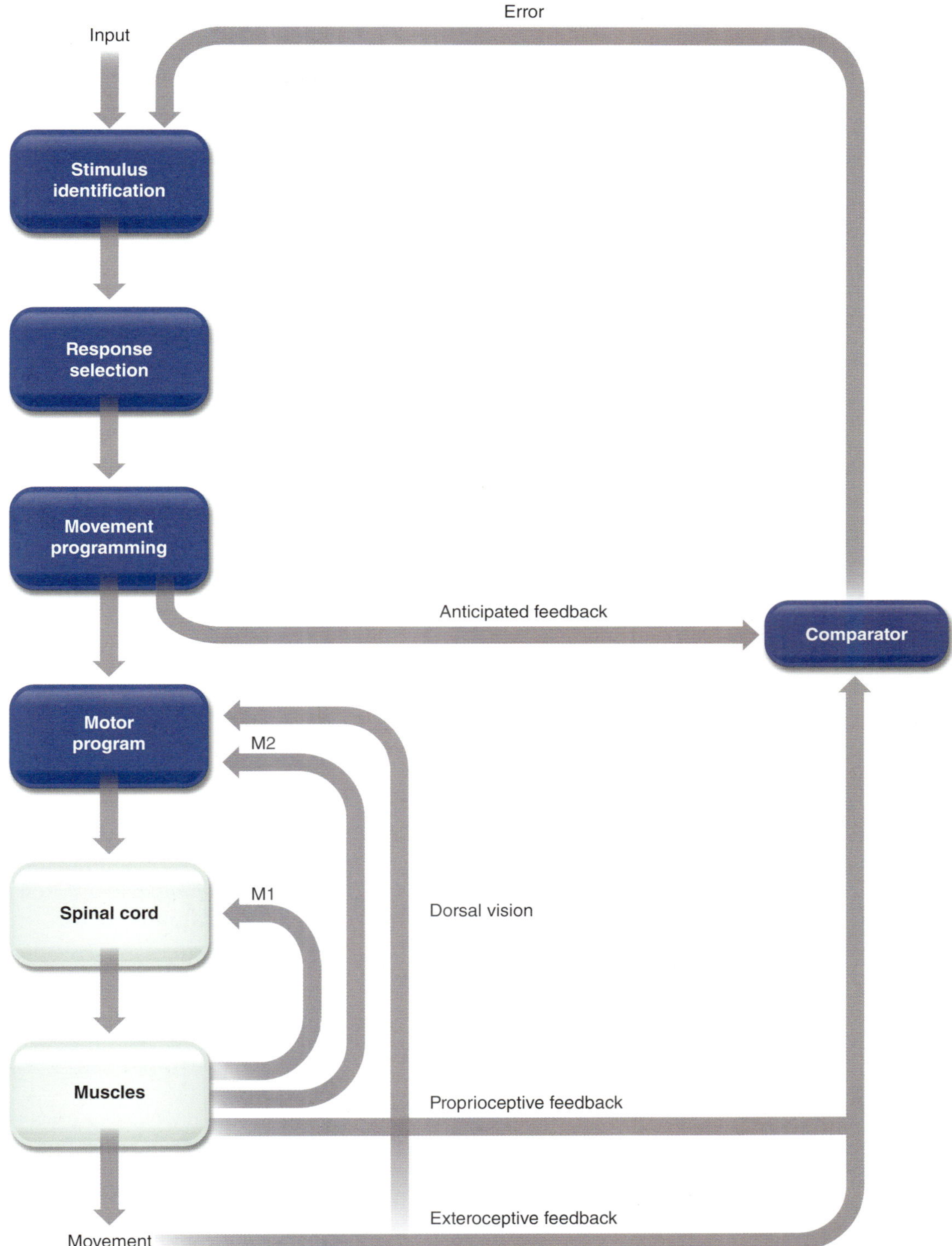

FIGURE 8.1 Conceptual model with the processes that improve with practice highlighted in dark blue.

to other conditions or the passage of time. After learning, you are not the same person you were before, just as the state of the egg is not the same as before.

The realization that performance alterations due to learning must be relatively permanent has led to special methods for measuring learning and evaluating the effects of practice variations. Essentially, these methods allow scientists to separate relatively permanent changes (due to learning) from temporary changes (due to transient factors). We return to this idea in a subsequent section.

To emphasize the features of the definition of learning, the following statements are important to keep in mind:

- Learning results from practice or experience.
- Learning is not directly observable.
- Learning changes are inferred from certain performance changes.
- Learning involves a set of processes in the central nervous system.
- Learning is not the cause of all changes in performance.
- Learning produces an acquired capability for skilled performance.
- Learning changes are relatively permanent, not transitory.

Visit HK*Propel* to read "How You Get to Carnegie Hall" and complete the self-directed learning activities.

How Is Motor Learning Measured?

Measuring learning and evaluating progress are conducted similarly and with the same general principles for both the experimental effects studied in the laboratory and the practical effects in applications of daily living. Some of these are presented in this section.

Performance Curves

By far the most common and traditional way to visualize and evaluate learning progress during practice is through **performance curves**. Suppose that a large number of people are practicing some task and performance measures on each of their attempts (or trials) have been collected. From these data, a graph of the average performance for each trial can be drawn, as shown in figure 8.2.

The difference in the performance curves shown in figure 8.2 simply reflects the scoring measures. In figure 8.2*a*, these data could be some measure of success in which a higher score on the vertical axis reflects better performance, such as the percentage of shots made in basketball or a score given by a judge for a gymnastics routine. Figure 8.2*b* could represent a measure of success in which a lower score on the vertical axis reflects better performance, such as the number of errors made or the time taken to complete a task. The shape of each curve is essentially the same and illustrates what is classically known as a *typical* performance curve—illustrating that the largest gains in performance occur early in practice, with smaller improvements occurring later on.

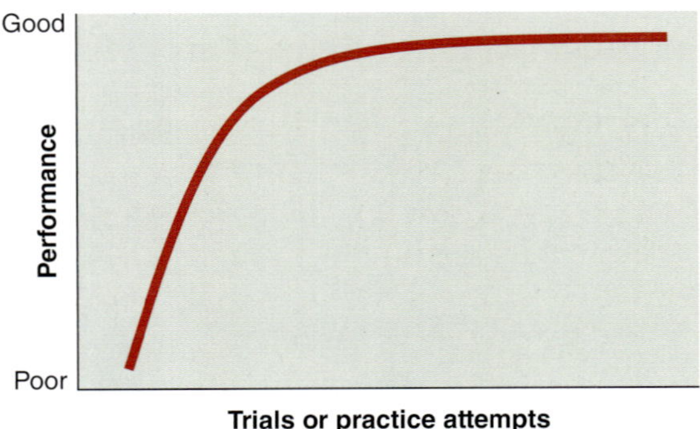

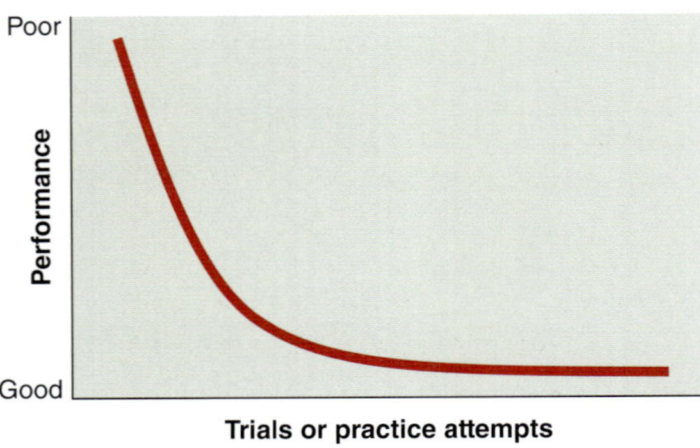

FIGURE 8.2 The typical performance curve when practicing a motor task. Performance improves rapidly early in practice and more gradually later on. The curve *(a)* will rise if the performance measure increases on the *y*-axis, such as free-throw percentage, or *(b)* will fall if the measure decreases on the *y*-axis, such as frequency of errors.

The typical performance curve has been seen many times in research, under many different types of practice conditions, and for many different tasks. An example from research can be seen in figure 8.3. These data were generated in an experiment using a rotary-pursuit tracking task in which participants attempted to keep a handheld stylus in contact with a constantly moving target (Ammons & Willig, 1956). The measure of performance, percent time-on-target (or TOT), is the proportion of time in contact with the target during a 1 min trial. This figure is interesting for a number of reasons, illustrating several details about performance changes during practice. However, basically, it reveals an underlying performance curve similar to figure 8.2*a*.

The data plotted in figure 8.3 illustrate the performance of one group of participants (who were part of a larger experiment). This group performed nine blocks of trials in a massed-practice format (see chapter 10 for more on massed practice). Each participant practiced the tracking task for 90 trials, with each trial lasting 1 min. This group performed 10 consecutive trials in a block. After performing the 10th trial in each block, the participants rested for 20 min.

Although, figure 8.3 does not look at all like the typical performance curve that was defined in figure 8.2*a*, looks can be deceiving. As you might expect, 10 min of continuous performance would result in the accumulation of considerable fatigue, both physically and mentally. The data illustrated in figure 8.3 are a classic example of the effects that massed practice has on performance: (1) During each block of 10 trials, there was considerable deterioration in performance due to fatigue, and (2) following each 20 min rest period, there was a considerable boost in performance (e.g., from trial 10 to 11, from 20 to 21) due to recovery from fatigue. In other words, across the entire practice period, there were instances of dramatic losses in performance followed by dramatic improvements in performance.

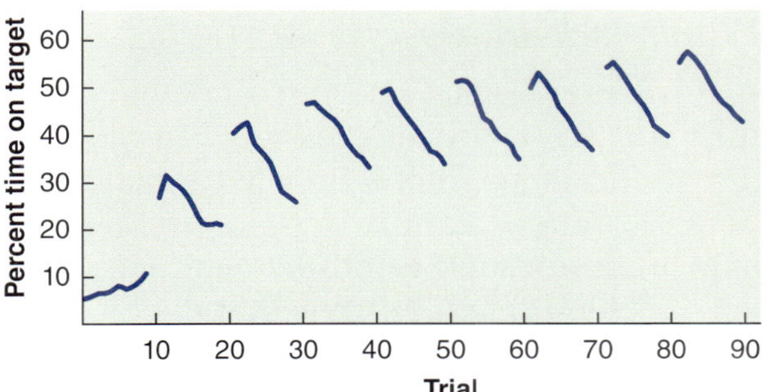

FIGURE 8.3 Performance curve for a group of participants practicing a rotary-pursuit tracking task. The score reflects the proportional time in contact with the object to be tracked during a 1 min trial. Participants in this experimental group performed 10 consecutive trials without rest (i.e., 10 min of continuous tracking), followed by a 20 min rest period, then 10 more consecutive trials, followed by a 20 min rest, and so on until 90 total trials had been practiced.

But notice two other trends that these data illustrate. The fact that performance deteriorated due to accumulating fatigue within each 10-trial block does not overshadow the fact that steady improvements were achieved throughout. Figure 8.4 shows two curves created by connecting critical data points that represent these improvements. One curve (the red dashes) connects the data points from the first trial in each of the nine 10-trial blocks. The other curve (the yellow dots) connects the data points from the last trial in each block. The shape of each of these curves resembles the shape of the graph in figure 8.2*a*—both curves showing the typical, rapid rise in performance gains early on, followed by slower improvements later.

The general form of performance curves—steep at first and more gradual later—is one of the most common features of learning in most motor tasks and reflects a fundamental principle, sometimes called the *law of practice* (Snoddy, 1926). The mathematical form of these curves and how they change with various features of the task and the nature of the learners have been discussed in some detail by numerous writers in the skill area (e.g., Newell et al., 2001).

The major points so far about performance curves can be summarized as follows:

- Performance curves are plots of individual or average performance against practice trials.

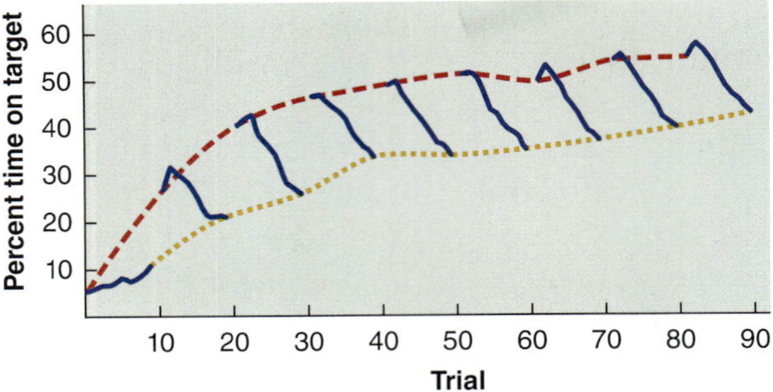

FIGURE 8.4 This figure illustrates the same data as figure 8.3 but with two performance curves added. The red dashed curve connects the data points from the first trial in each 10-trial block. The yellow dotted curve connects the data points from the last trial in each block. Despite the changes that occur within each block trial, both curves demonstrate the typical performance curve when practicing a new motor task—that rapid gains in performance occur early in practice, with more gradual gains occurring later.

- Such curves can either increase or decrease with practice, depending on the particular way the task is scored.
- Improvements are typically rapid at first and much slower later—a nearly universal principle of practice.

Limitations of Performance Curves

There are many ways to use performance curves, such as to display a single individual's performance gains or to chart the progress of a group of individuals. However, several potential difficulties require caution in drawing interpretations from these curves.

Performance Curves Are Not Learning Curves

As useful as performance curves are for illustrating learners' progress, their usefulness is limited for several reasons. Performance curves are not **learning curves**—that is, they do not chart the progress of learning. These curves are simply plots of performance (usually the average of many participants' performance) over practice trials, which, as seen in the next sections, do not necessarily indicate much about progress in the relatively permanent capability for performance, as learning was defined earlier (see Focus on Research 8.1).

Performance Curves Mask Differences Between Individuals

One of the main reasons in favor of using performance curves is that they average or "smooth out" the variability that exists among different learners. By averaging a large group of people, performance changes in the (hypothetical) average participant can be seen, and, it is hoped, inferences can be made about changes in general proficiency. This is particularly useful in research settings where the difference between two groups of participants is studied as a function of different practice methods, for example. This will be an important concept in issues presented in later chapters.

The drawback of using performance curves is that the averaging process hides differences that exist between people, termed *individual differences* in chapter 7. Because of this, the averaging method gives the impression that all participants improve at the same rate or in the same way, which we know is not correct in most cases.

Performance Curves Mask Differences Within Individuals

A third drawback to performance curves is that averaging procedures tend to obscure the performance fluctuations within a single person. When examining smooth performance curves, such as those in figures 8.4 and 8.5, it is tempting to assume that the individual learners' performances contributing to the curves progressed smoothly and gradually as well. We will often see figures in which performance plots represent not just a single trial but a block of trials, especially in later chapters. What this means is that multiple separate trials for any single participant are averaged to produce a single score, which is then averaged over the group of participants in an experimental condition. Thus, the averaging

FOCUS ON Research 8.1

Learning Curves: Facts or Artifacts?

In an important early article, Bahrick and colleagues (1957) identified problems in the interpretation of so-called learning curves. Participants practiced a tracking task in which hand movements of a lever were used to follow a cursor presented on a screen. The researchers recorded the performances for analysis and later scored them in three different ways. First, they defined performance accuracy in terms of a very narrow band of correctness around the track (5% of the screen's width) and counted the number of seconds out of each 90 s trial that the participant was on target (TOT). Next, Bahrick and colleagues estimated TOT using a band of correctness that was somewhat larger or more lenient (15% of the screen's width), and then they scored the data once again using a very large target band of correctness (30% of the screen's width). The plots of these various TOT scores for each trial resulted in the three curves shown in figure 8.5.

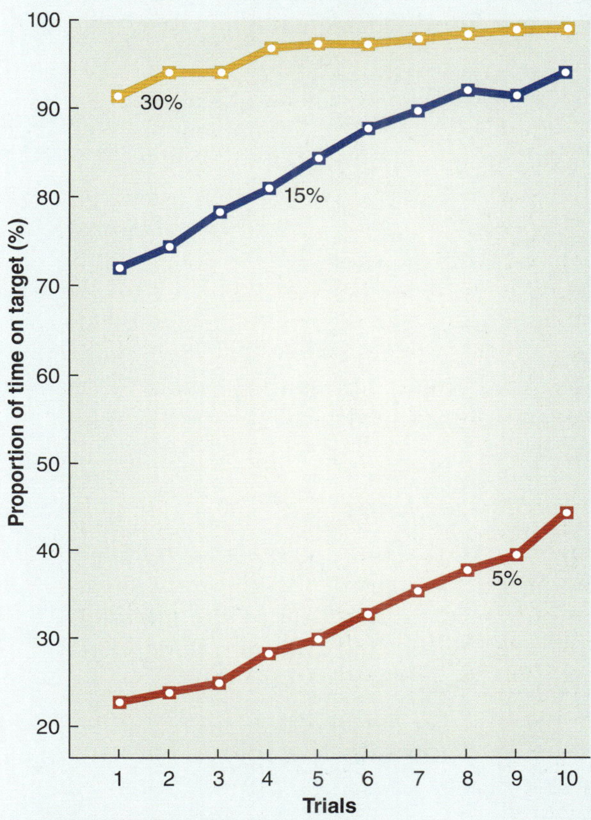

FIGURE 8.5 Proportion of time-on-target for a group of participants practicing a tracking task, scored with three different bandwidth criteria. Performance was on target when the participant's tracking was within 5%, 15%, or 30% of the screen's width near the cursor.

While viewing figure 8.5, keep in mind that these curves came from the same performances by the same participants who were not aware of the scoring that Bahrick and colleagues did afterward. If you were to consider the shapes of these curves as indicators of learning, you would be forced to draw three contradictory conclusions: (1) The learning gains were rapid at first and slower later (30% curve); (2) the learning gains were linear across practice (15% curve); or (3) the learning gains were slow at first and more rapid later (5% curve). In fact, each participant experienced only one improvement rate, but it was estimated in three different ways, which led to three different conclusions about how performance changed with practice. Scoring artifacts caused these differences.

One type of scoring artifact occurs when a performance maximum is reached. This is called a *ceiling effect* because a higher performance score is not possible. In this study, 100% time-on-target represents the ceiling (literally, the curve has reached

> *continued*

Research 8.1: Learning Curves: Facts or Artifacts? *> continued*

the "ceiling" of the graph) and is clearly influencing what the 30% scoring criterion implies about the improvement rate. Performance minima can also represent a scoring artifact. If tracking error had been measured in this study (e.g., using root-mean-square error, or RMSE), then zero error would be the minimum score possible and would be called a *floor effect*, because a lower performance score than this is not possible (again, literally, the curve has reached the "floor" of the graph).

Exploring Further

1. Think of another motor learning task and describe how changes in the criterion for success could be made and how these changes might affect the shape of the performance curve over practice trials.
2. Provide an example of a floor effect and a ceiling effect for your answer to question 1.

process produces a curve that masks both within-participant and between-participant variability.

Learning Never Ends

Perhaps one of the most visually appealing yet illusional features of the typical performance curve is the leveling of the curve as practice progresses. This plateau leaves one with the impression that learning is complete, leaving no room for improvement. Two classic studies in the motor learning literature reveal that this impression is a myth.

Bryan and Harter (1897, 1899) studied the perceptual–motor skill of telegraphy—the language of sending and receiving Morse code. They studied telegraphers of varying levels of experience and discovered many important findings. For example, the perceptual skill of receiving Morse code became faster and more efficient with practice. However, this was achieved not only through quantitative improvements (speed of letter detection) but also through qualitative changes. As skill developed, telegraphers progressed by first perceiving individual letters, then groupings of letters, then whole words, and finally, common phrases or groupings of words. The timing of dots and dashes is a critical component of sending Morse code, and Bryan and Harter found that the consistency in movement timing continued to improve over many years of experience (see Lee & Swinnen, 1993, for more analysis). In sum, there was no evidence that improvements stopped being made in either the perceptual or motor components of telegraphy skill. Rather, performance became more efficient and less variable with continued practice.

Crossman (1959) presented a very different type of analysis of a motor skill. He tracked the performance of cigar rollers who used a machine to combine leaves of tobacco into a finished product. Crossman found that improvements in performance time leveled off after seven years of experience (or 10 million cigars!) had accumulated. However, the plateau in performance was not due to a limitation in human performance. Rather, performance leveled off because the machine had reached the limits of its cycle time. Presumably, the cigar rollers would have continued to improve if they had not reached the machine's limit.

Reaching the limits of the measurement tool's sensitivity to reveal further changes is almost always the cause of the illusion that learning has ended. More sensitive measures of performance, including methods to document brain plasticity, would provide clearer evidence that learning continues to evolve over time.

Distinguishing Learning From Performance

The distinction between learning and performance is critically important, not only for the experimental study of learning but also for evaluating learning in practical settings. According to this view, practice can have two different kinds of influences on performance—one that is relatively permanent and due to learning and another that is short term and due to factors that are temporary and transient.

Temporary Versus Relatively Permanent Effects of Practice

One product of practice is learning—the establishment of a relatively permanent improvement in the capability to perform. Keep in mind that a relatively permanent change in the person would result from changes in one or more of the processes illustrated in figure 8.1. This change allows the individual to perform with more certainty, more precision, more adaptability, and potentially many other improved features. The change endures over many days or even many years. Essentially, the concern of researchers who study motor learning is the discovery of methods to maximize the development of these relatively permanent changes so that these methods can be used in various practical settings to enhance learning effectiveness and efficiency.

It is important to remember, however, that many practice conditions have both temporary effects and relatively permanent ones. Some have positive effects on performance (e.g., motivation), whereas other effects are negative and degrade performance (e.g., fatigue). A key concern is identifying what these effects are and distinguishing their effect on performance versus their effect on learning. This is a critically important concept not only for instructors but also for learners who are self-evaluating their progress (see Focus on Application 8.1).

FOCUS ON Application 8.1

Self-Assessments of Learning

In most activities of daily life, the learner is responsible for making decisions about how to practice, such as scheduling the frequency and duration of sessions. Practice for a motor skills competition is no different from studying, for example—you determine how and how much to practice, and you stop when you feel competent or confident in your predicted capability to perform, just as one does in preparing for an exam. The critical question is this: On what basis do you predict you are fully prepared for the competition or test?

A common problem is that most learners interpret temporary indicators of performance as predictors of learning or remembering. This is especially problematic when a temporary boost to performance is (mistakenly) used to assess learning. One factor addressed in chapter 10 concerns repetitive (blocked) versus interleaved (random) practice scheduling. Blocked practice generally produces better performance during practice than interleaved practice. And, when asked to predict their performance in a delayed **retention test**, participants engaged in blocked practice predicted that they learned much better than participants engaged in random practice (Simon & Bjork, 2001). However, the reality is much different (the opposite, in fact; see chapter 10 for details). This research illustrates that self-assessed judgments of learning can be quite unreliable, especially when they are based on current indicators of performance during practice. Soderstrom and Bjork (2015) provide a good review of the research and the applied nature of memory and learning issues.

Various kinds of instructions or encouragement during practice elevate performance due to a motivating or energizing effect. Providing guidance in the form of physical assistance or verbal directions during practice can benefit performance. Various mood states can elevate performance temporarily, as can certain drugs. Other temporary practice factors can be negative, degrading performance temporarily. For example, sometimes practice generates physical or mental fatigue, which can depress performance relative to rested conditions (e.g., see figure 8.3). Lethargic performances can result if practice is boring or if learners become discouraged by their lack of progress. Numerous other factors associated with practice could exert similar effects.

Practice can have numerous important effects on the learner:

- Temporary effects that vanish with time or a change in conditions
- Relatively permanent effects that persist across many days, even years
- Simultaneous temporary and relatively permanent effects that influence both performance and learning

Separating Temporary and Relatively Permanent Effects

Suppose that you are interested in trying a new teaching aid for improving a golfer's alignment skills when putting. Since such a device is not legal for actual competition and can be used only during practice, your evaluation of the benefit of this new alignment aid must be based on whether it enhances performance in a relatively permanent way—that is, after the device has been removed (in an actual golf game). After all, if the positive effects of the alignment aid disappear as soon as it is removed, the aid cannot have provided much advantage as a learning tool.

Whenever learners practice, and especially when instructors intervene to enhance learning (e.g., by giving instructions and feedback), it is important to have a way to separate the relatively permanent effects from the temporary effects. Frequently, in research settings and sometimes in practical settings as well, learners are divided into two or more separate classes or groups. For example, suppose that one group of golfers practices by attempting to make 6 ft (1.8 m) putts with the alignment aid, and another group practices without the aid. The two groups might practice under these two different conditions for a period of time, perhaps over 10 sessions, with records kept of the percentage of putts made. You might average all the golfers' scores for each group separately and plot performance curves. Such a plot might look like the one in figure 8.6, where the average percentage of putts made from 6 ft (1.8 m) is plotted across the 10 sessions.

Which condition is more effective for learning—practice with the alignment aid or without it? The answer looks obvious from a quick glance at the graph in figure 8.6. The figure reveals that the group of golfers who used the alignment aid improved their performance in practice considerably more than the group who practiced without the aid. It is obvious that practice performance with the alignment aid was more beneficial than without it, and the difference might be due to learning, which would be most interesting

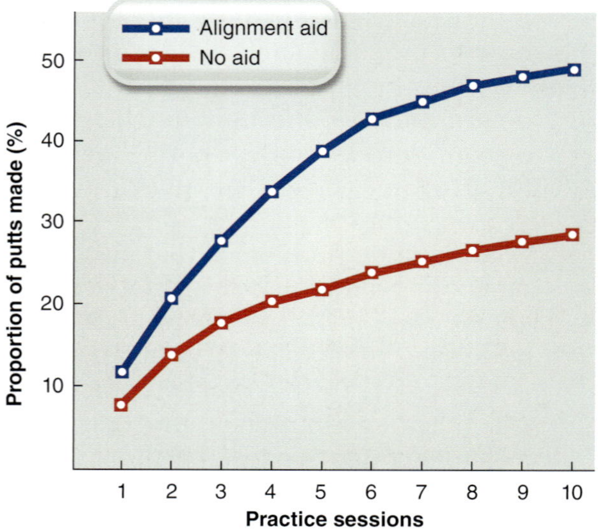

FIGURE 8.6 Hypothetical performance curves across 10 practice sessions for two groups practicing the golf putt with or without an alignment aid.

In this photo, identify one positive and one negative result that might occur when practicing using this training aid that physically constrains movement.

and valuable to know. As argued in the previous section, however, the difference between these two groups might be only a temporary performance effect, which could disappear as soon as the alignment aid was removed.

The problem can be posed more systematically in the form of three hypotheses about the two conditions:

Hypothesis 1: The group that practiced with the alignment aid learned *more* than the group that practiced without it. (They developed a stronger relatively permanent capability for performance.)

Hypothesis 2: The group that practiced with the alignment aid and the group that practiced without it were *equal* in their relatively permanent capability for performance.

Hypothesis 3: The group that practiced with the alignment aid learned *less* than the group that practiced without it. (They developed a weaker relatively permanent capability for performance.)

Which of these three hypotheses is correct? The answer, based only on the data in figure 8.6, is unknown. The information presented in the performance curves says nothing about whether the advantage of the alignment-aid group is due to some relatively permanent (learning) effect or to some temporary (performance) effect that disappears once the alignment aid is no longer available. This is a critical problem because there is no real basis for deciding which learning method is better. Fortunately, additional procedures are available that permit separation of learning and performance effects.

Transfer Designs

A transfer design can answer whether a change that improves performance in practice also improves learning by separating the relatively permanent and temporary effects of a variable. There are two important features of transfer designs.

1. Any temporary effects of the variable must be allowed to dissipate. In our golf example, the temporary effects of the alignment aid (if any) might be informational or physical (a type of guidance), operating mainly during actual performance, so very little time for dissipation would be needed. As a result, any other temporary effects (such as increased motivation) would dissipate relatively quickly and certainly would dissipate before the next session.
2. The learners in both groups must be tested again under common conditions in what is often called a *transfer* (or *retention*) *test*. In our example, both groups would perform either with or without the alignment aid to equalize any temporary effects that the test conditions themselves might have on retention performance. Otherwise, the results would be difficult to interpret.

In general, the terms **transfer test** and **retention test** tend to be used interchangeably. Sometimes a test is called a *transfer test* if there is a change of task conditions, but called a *retention test* if given under the relatively same conditions or after a rest period. Be aware that these definitions are not used consistently in research. The critically important issue, however, is that the various participant groups that had initially practiced under different experimental conditions are now examined under identical (common) test conditions. The tests could be given a day or more after the last practice session or several minutes after the last session. In our golf alignment-aid example, the primary interest would be in the potential benefit of the aid in later performance on the golf course. So, both groups would perform the test when the aid is no longer available (analogous to a game situation).

The logic that underlies a transfer or retention test is this: Assuming that all the temporary effects have dissipated by the time the test is administered, any differences observed in the test should be due to the relatively permanent effects that were acquired through training. In our example, the learning effects of the alignment aid are not evaluated during practice but in the transfer or retention test, after any temporary effects have disappeared, leaving the relatively permanent effects to be revealed on the test.

The essential features of a transfer design can be summarized as follows:

- Allow sufficient time (rest) for any temporary effects of practice to dissipate. The amount will vary depending on the nature of the temporary effects.
- Evaluate learners again in a transfer or retention test, with all groups performing under identical conditions.
- Observe any differences, which, in this transfer test, are due to a difference in the relatively permanent capability for performance acquired during earlier practice—that is, due to learning.

Let's now consider the possible transfer test outcomes of the hypothetical alignment-aid experiment just described and associate each outcome with one of the three hypotheses described earlier. Figure 8.7 shows four possible outcomes. In the first outcome (figure 8.7*a*), the performances of the two groups are different by approximately the same amount as were present at the end of the practice sessions (compare performance on session 10 with the transfer test result). In this case, the appropriate conclusion would be that the difference between groups achieved during practice was due to a relatively permanent effect because allowing the temporary effects (if any) to dissipate did not change the groups' relative status at all. Conclusion: Practice with the alignment aid was more effective for learning than practice without the aid, supporting hypothesis 1.

Now consider the outcome in figure 8.7*b*, where the transfer performance of the group practicing with the alignment aid is better than that of the other group, but the difference is smaller than in the last practice session (10). From these test results, one could argue that some of the performance difference between these groups in the practice session was due to temporary effects because dissipation reduced the magnitude of the difference between the groups. However, not all of the practice session difference was temporary because some of it remained in the transfer test after the temporary effects dissipated. Conclusion: Practice with the alignment aid elevated performance temporarily, but it also produced some lasting benefits for learning compared to practice without the aid, also supporting hypothesis 1.

Next, examine the outcome in figure 8.7*c*, where the transfer performances of the two groups are essentially the same as the level of the no-aid group at the end of practice. Here, when the temporary effects have dissipated, all the differences that had appeared between the groups during practice have been eliminated. This leads to the conclusion that the beneficial effect of the alignment aid was entirely due to some temporary elevating change, and none of it was due to learning. Conclusion: Practice with the alignment aid elevated performance compared to perfor-

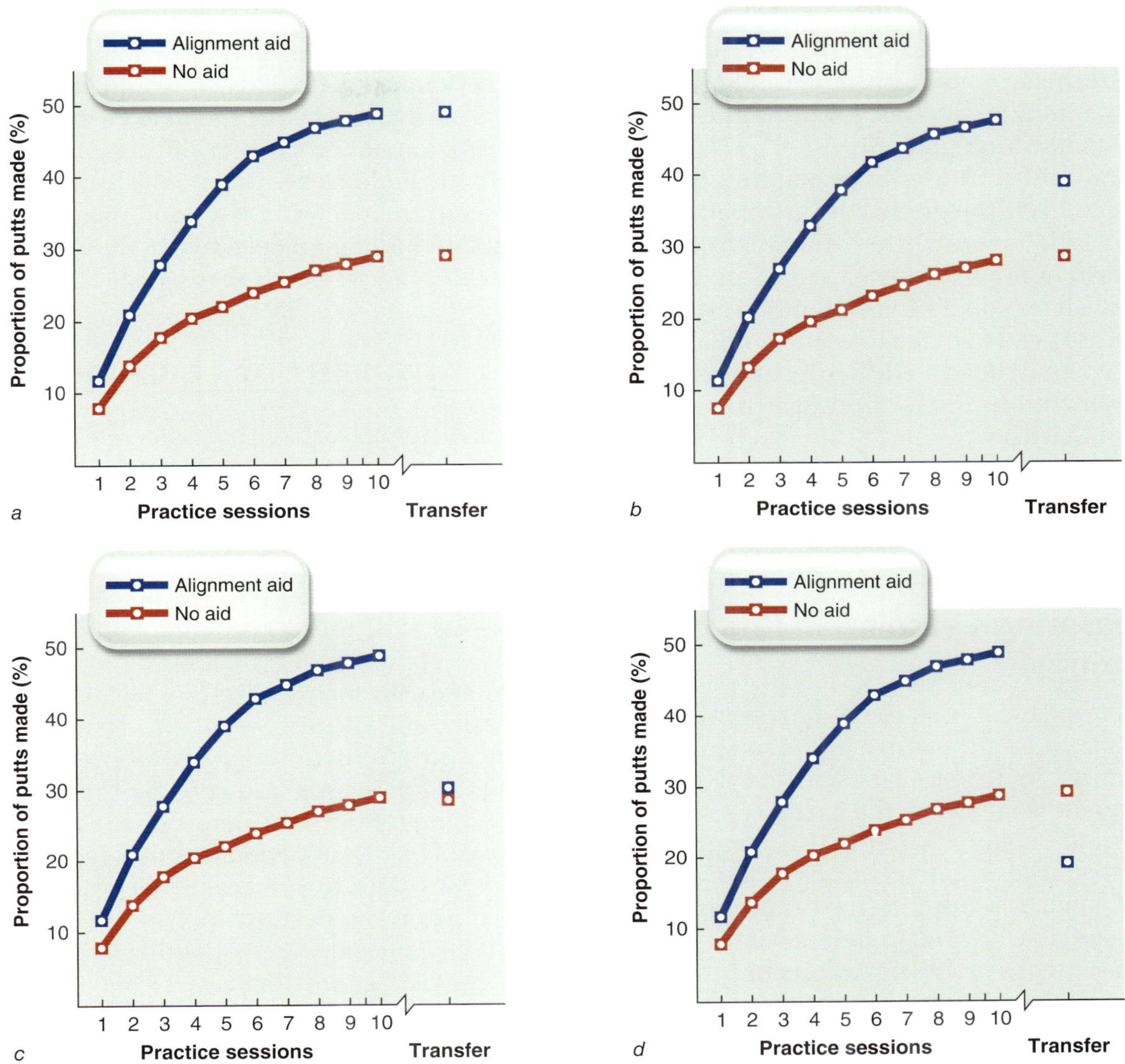

FIGURE 8.7 Hypothetical effects on transfer tests of two groups practicing the golf putt with or without an alignment aid. Four possible outcomes on the transfer test are illustrated: *(a)* The alignment aid resulted in transfer that was equal to the advantage over unaided practice found in the last practice session, supporting hypothesis 1; *(b)* the alignment aid resulted in transfer that was better than unaided practice, although the advantage was lower than found in the last practice session, also supporting hypothesis 1; *(c)* the alignment aid resulted in transfer that was no better than unaided practice, supporting hypothesis 2; and *(d)* the alignment aid resulted in transfer that was worse than unaided practice, supporting hypothesis 3.

mance without the aid, but it had no effect on learning, supporting hypothesis 2.

Finally, examine the outcome in figure 8.7*d*, where the transfer performance of the group that had practiced with the alignment aid was less accurate than that of the group that had practiced without the aid. This is an important yet seemingly rather odd and counterintuitive result, for it reveals that not only did all performance advantages of the alignment aid disappear when the temporary effects dissipated but that the alignment aid resulted in a learning effect that was worse than practice without it. Conclusion: Practice with the alignment aid elevated performance during practice but had a degrading effect on learning compared to the group that practiced without the aid, supporting hypothesis 3. (We will see some results that look like this in chapters 10 and 11, including the actual effects of training aids.)

You will find graphs resembling those in figures 8.7*a* through *d* in the coming chapters. Each will look a little different from these generic figures. However, if you understand the basic rationale that retention or transfer tests are used to make inferences about learning, you will have no difficulty understanding how to interpret the findings presented in these figures.

Visit HK*Propel* to read "Learning to Win From Losing" and complete the self-directed learning activities.

Measuring Learning in Practical Settings

The issues just discussed may seem, at first glance, to relate mainly to the evaluation of learning in research situations. However, transfer designs form the basis for evaluating learning in many teaching situations as well. For example, when a learner practices some skill, such as producing the proper amount of pressure in CPR, the proficiency level reached at the end of a practice session may not reflect the actual performance capability achieved. Because various factors involved in practice also affect performance temporarily, they may mask or inflate the underlying acquired skill capability.

Practice conditions may also not reflect the emotional conditions under which some skills are required. For example, skills needed by police and firefighters are often performed in emergency or other highly charged situations, where the emotional stress may be elevated quite dramatically compared to the situations under which practice is typically conducted. Therefore, retention and transfer tests that include emotional stress may be required to assess the true underlying skill capability acquired during practice.

A related issue concerns evaluation for the purpose of grading. If a learner's grade in some activity is related to the amount learned, then basing the grade on performance toward the end of some practice session would be unwise. The learning level would tend to be masked by various temporary practice effects. A far better method would be to evaluate the learner's performance in a delayed test administered sufficiently long after practice so that the temporary effects of practice have dissipated.

Transfer of Learning

As mentioned earlier, the terms *retention test* and *transfer test* are often used interchangeably. The difference between the two terms usually refers to the relationship between the conditions under which practice and testing are conducted. A retention test usually assesses skill under the same conditions as those in practice. A transfer test requires performance under conditions that differ from practice conditions.

A similar difference exists concerning the terms *retention* and *transfer* themselves. *Retention* refers to the persistence or maintenance of a skill following practice. In contrast, *transfer* refers to the influence of previous learning on the performance of either a new skill or the same skill under previously unpracticed conditions.

The similarity of the new skill to the previously learned skill can also influence transfer. Researchers use the terms **near transfer** and **far transfer** to refer to performing new skills that share either many features (near) or few features (far) in common with the previously learned skill. As you might expect, the amount of near transfer is usually greater than the amount of far transfer.

The influence of previous learning can either degrade or enhance performance on a new skill, referred to as *negative transfer* and *positive transfer*, respectively. Be careful in your thinking about these terms, however. A decline in performance of a new task is often attributed as evidence of negative transfer, which could be a mistake. Positive or negative transfer is assessed by comparing it to a no-practice control group. Negative transfer rarely occurs—when performance of a new task following a previously learned skill is worse than performance of the task without having previously learned a related skill.

The Role of Transfer

Transfer is assumed when the skills learned in one task are applied successfully to the performance of a skill in a new situation or to the learning of a new skill. Consider the skill of typing. Almost everyone has learned to type at one time or another. But now consider the variety of applications of that skill that one might encounter every day. You send text messages using the virtual keyboard display on your phone. You type an email on your laptop or tablet using a physical keyboard. You use a device at work or school that has a slightly different size, shape, feel, and so on compared to your device at home. Keys on a screen layout make no movement, whereas the keys on a physical keyboard depress when touched. Different physical keyboards have unique resistances and amounts of depression. The list of ways in which you transfer your typing skills daily is endless. Yet your typing skill transfer is relatively seamless.

Transfer also becomes important when switching from one task to another. For example, those who have learned to drive using a standard transmission find it quite easy to transfer driving skill to an automatic transition. The reverse, switching from an automatic to a standard transmission, is obviously more difficult because of the additional steps involved in accelerating and stopping a vehicle. Nevertheless, we would expect positive transfer in both cases, relative to someone who has never having learned to drive at all.

Visit HK*Propel* to read "Zero-Sum Training" and complete the self-directed learning activities.

Transfer is also assumed when instructors modify skills to make them easier to practice. For example, relatively long-duration serial skills, such as doing a gymnastics routine, can be broken down into their elements for practice. Practicing the stunts in isolation must benefit the performance of the whole routine, which is made up of the individual stunts. However, in more rapid skills, such as a tennis serve, it is usually not so clear that breaking down the skill into ball-toss and ball-strike portions for part practice will be effective for transfer to the whole task. The principles of transfer applicable to such situations will be the focus of more discussion in chapter 9.

How Is Transfer Measured?

Issues concerning the measurement of transfer closely relate to the learning measurement issues discussed earlier. Essentially, we want to understand how previous experience or learning influences performance or learning on the transfer task.

The first author experienced a good example of learning transfer during a research leave in Belgium. Raised in Canada, he learned to type using a standard QWERTY keyboard layout, so the experience of using the AZERTY layout on the computers in Belgium fascinated him. (The keyboard names reflect the six letters appearing in the top left row of the layout.) Figure 8.8 illustrates the two layouts—the A, Z, Q, W, and M keys are in different locations on the two keyboards. Although only the location of five keys was

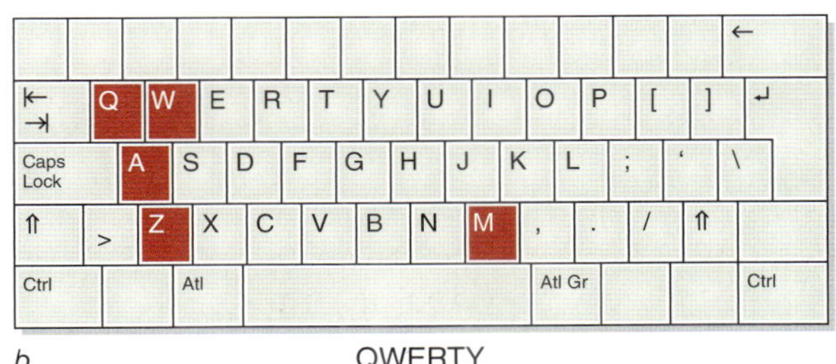

FIGURE 8.8 Standard layouts for the *(a)* AZERTY and *(b)* QWERTY keyboards.

different, he found that this seemingly small difference seemed to make a large difference in his typing performance.

How could one measure the effect on transfer of switching from one keyboard layout to another? One way to do this experiment would be to have groups of people who are just learning to type. Suppose that two groups of learners practiced typing text on a QWERTY keyboard—one group received, say, 100 h of practice and another group received 20 h of practice. A third group (control) would have had no previous typing experience. All groups would then be examined by typing for 5 h on the AZERTY layout (transfer task).

The only reason for the groups to differ on the first (and subsequent) tests with the transfer (AZERTY) layout is that previous experience with the QWERTY layout somehow influenced performance. Therefore, the focus of the results would be the relative differences between the groups on the transfer task.

The set of results in figure 8.9 shows one potential outcome for these three experimental groups. The study might use a combined score as the dependent measure, summing the time to complete a passage of text and the number of incorrectly typed keys. The figure presents hypothetical scores for illustrative purposes. Figure 8.9 shows that the group with 100 h of experience on the QWERTY keyboard performed better on the transfer keyboard than the group that had only 20 h of practice. In turn, that 20 h group was better than the group with no previous typing experience. The conclusion would be that having previous typing experience transferred positively to performance on the new keyboard. Additionally, the number of hours of previous experience was positively related to the amount of positive transfer.

But suppose the results of this experiment had turned out a little differently. Instead, let's suppose that having considerable (100 h) previous experience with the QWERTY layout resulted in positive transfer but having relatively little previous experience (20 h) resulted in negative transfer when switched to the AZERTY layout. Such a result might resemble the transfer performance results shown in figure 8.10. In this case, the qualitative nature of the transfer performance (positive or negative) was related to the amount of previous experience with the original keyboard layout.

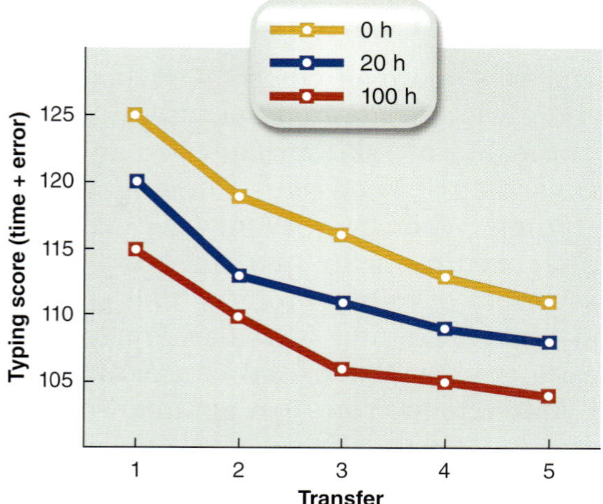

FIGURE 8.9 Hypothetical typing scores on a transfer (AZERTY) keyboard layout following either 100, 20, or 0 h of previous experience with a QWERTY keyboard layout. Both the 100 h and 20 h groups show positive transfer to the new layout when compared to the control (0 h) group.

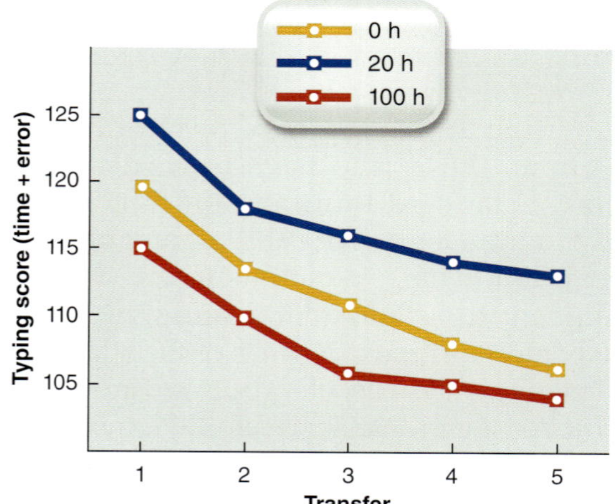

FIGURE 8.10 Hypothetical typing scores on a transfer (AZERTY) keyboard layout following either 100, 20, or 0 h of previous experience with a QWERTY keyboard layout. The 100 h group shows positive transfer when compared to the performance of the control group. However, in these hypothetical results, the 20 h group shows negative transfer because their previous experience with the QWERTY layout resulted in performance on the AZERTY layout that was worse than the control group, which had no previous typing experience.

Specific Versus Generalized Transfer

The previous sections on measuring learning have perhaps left the impression that the only way to measure the relative amount learned is by performance on some delayed retention test. This is probably the most important way to estimate learning, but other ways are possible, and some are even preferable in some situations.

The essential issue is what we want learners to be able to do after training. In some cases, learners are trained to be proficient at a specific task with a limited range of variations. For example, basketball players take foul shots using a set shot from a distance of 15 ft (4.6 m) to the basket (i.e., from the free-throw line). So, it seems perfectly reasonable to devote considerable set-shot practice from the free-throw line because the set shot is a specific type of basketball skill that is normally not performed at any other location on the court. Many closed tasks share these characteristics.

On the other hand, many training settings are designed to promote transfer to different yet very similar settings in the real world. This is an example of near transfer, defined earlier, in which the training task is relatively similar to the learning goal. A good example that contrasts nicely with the free throw is the jump shot in basketball. The jump shot can be taken from an infinite number of places on the court and in a variety of game situations. Being able to perform in such varied and unpredictable conditions is one mark of a highly skilled performer. Therefore, tests of transfer in which performance is measured on some variant of the task that is similar yet different from those in the practice conditions would be a reasonable test of generalized transfer.

Sometimes instructors want to train learners to develop more general capabilities for a wide variety of skills, only a few of which are actually experienced in practice. In far transfer, the eventual goal is quite different from that in the original practice setting. For example, elementary school children are taught to throw, jump, and run; the main concern is the extent to which these activities transfer to future activities involving throwing, jumping, and running but occurring in very different settings.

In all these situations, the evaluation of training effectiveness is not based exclusively on how well the learners master the skills during actual practice. Rather, if transfer to relatively different activities is the goal, the most effective training program will be the one that produces the best performance on some transfer test performed in the future—one that may involve quite different skills from those actually practiced. Here, the effectiveness of a training program is measured by the amount of transfer to some different activity.

Summary

Motor learning is defined as a set of processes associated with practice. As such, the emphasis is on the determinants of this capability, which support or underlie the performance. Hence, factors that affect performance only temporarily need to be distinguished from the factors affecting this underlying capability, which makes the use of learning curves somewhat risky for evaluating learning.

However, temporary and learning effects can be separated through the use of retention and transfer tests. In some experiments on learning, groups of learners practice under different acquisition conditions; after a delay, they are tested on the same task but under conditions that are identical for all the groups. This procedure focuses attention on the learners' relative performance in the retention tests as the true measure of learning.

HK*PROPEL* ACTIVITIES

HK*Propel* offers these activities to help you build and apply your knowledge of the concepts in this chapter. Additionally, you'll find a key terms flashcard review activity and a key terms quiz, along with audio supplements for selected figures, as indicated by QR codes throughout the chapter.

Interactive Learning

Activity 8.1: Using a figure from the text, interpret the findings of a transfer design study to understand the effects of a mechanical aid on learning.

Activity 8.2: Review the types of learning transfer by matching terms with their definitions.

Activity 8.3: Check your understanding of the definition of motor learning through a fill-in-the-blanks exercise.

Activity 8.4: Watch a video explaining the distinction between performance and learning; consider where this distinction may not have been recognized in your previous experiences.

Activity 8.5: Test your understanding of performance curves and their limitations.

Principles-to-Application Exercise

Activity 8.6: The principles-to-application exercise for this chapter prompts you to choose a skill and examine the effects of practice on a person learning that skill. You will identify the possible temporary and permanent effects of practice and consider how you could collect evidence to distinguish temporary from permanent effects.

Motor Control in Everyday Actions Narratives

How You Get to Carnegie Hall

Learning to Win From Losing

Zero-Sum Training

Check Your Understanding

1. Define motor learning and indicate why each of the following terms is important to that definition.
   - Capability
   - Practice and experience
   - Performance
2. Distinguish between near transfer and far transfer and between positive transfer and negative transfer. Give one example of each.
3. List and describe two limitations of using performance curves to evaluate learning progress.

Apply Your Knowledge

1. List three essential features of a transfer design. How would these features be included in an experiment to examine if using a pole to aid balance during a one-foot stance task is beneficial to learning to perform the one-foot stance task without the pole?
2. Describe one practical setting where the proficiency level reached at the end of a practice session may not reflect the actual performance capability achieved under the conditions where the skill will eventually be required. How could you assess the true level of skills learned during practice?

9

The Motor Learning Process

Practice, Retention, and Transfer

CHAPTER OUTLINE

CHAPTER OBJECTIVES

Chapter 9 describes the processes that influence motor learning—practice, retention, and transfer. This chapter will help you understand

- basic principles of practice,
- processes of human performance that benefit from practice,
- factors that influence the retention of skills after periods of no practice, and
- factors that influence the transfer of skills to new tasks or situations.

CHAPTER PREVIEW QUIZ

1. What is the so-called 10,000-hour rule of practice?
2. How do discrete and continuous skills differ in lengths of retention?
3. What is the difference between physical versus psychological simulator fidelity?

Playing the guitar provides a good example of how practice leads to the development of motor skill. Consider the beginning chords of the classic rock song "Rumble" by Link Wray. The first three chords are D, D, and E. For a right-handed guitarist, the D chord involves holding down the second fret of the third string with the index finger, the second fret of the first string with the middle finger, and the third fret of the second string with the ring finger of the left hand while strumming the first four strings with the right hand. This D chord is played twice; then the fingers on the left hand shift to make an E chord, which requires putting the index finger on the first fret of the third string and the middle and ring fingers on the second fret of the fourth and fifth strings, while the right hand now strums all six strings.

The beginner guitarist faces a number of problems simultaneously, such as knowing which fingers to place where, avoiding strings that should not be touched, remembering what positions compose what chords, determining which strings the right hand should strum, and quickly moving the hand and fingers to new positions on different strings to create a whole new chord. And this does not even consider the timing structure that must underlie these chords or that for right-handers, the left hand is doing the more difficult job. It is very impressive, indeed, that anyone can learn to play the guitar given what we've just described, yet many people do it very, very well.

Learning to play the guitar is a good example of the topics presented in this and the next three chapters. Performance starts out hesitantly, with many errors being made. Practice, both physical and nonphysical, typically leads to improvements in performance, which are reflected by changes within the individual and in how movements are made. Time away from playing the guitar affects future performance because the retention of skills is expected to be different for different types of tasks, so classifying guitar playing as a member of one of several classes of skills is important. Motor learning would be very inefficient if we had to progress through the entire skill acquisition process for each and every guitar that we might play and under different circumstances in which we find ourselves (e.g., standing vs. sitting). We expect our playing skills to generalize (or transfer) to different guitars, situations, and environments; therefore, information about the factors expected to affect transfer constitutes a critical component of any discussion of the learning process.

Two Principles of Practice

Quite simply, *practice* is the single most important factor leading to the acquisition of motor skill. However, the term is also one of the most poorly understood and misused terms when applied to the concept of learning. In this section, we describe two principles of practice, how they affect learning, and what occurs as the result of practice.

Quite simply, as a general rule, more practice produces more learning. However, practice is much more than time spent "going through the motions." Attempts to attach a specific number to the time required to attain expertise have impeded a better understanding of the skill acquisition process (see Focus on Research 9.1). In this section, we describe two basic principles of practice and what might and might not lead to effective and efficient skill acquisition.

Practice Specificity

Although transfer is a hallmark of learning (discussed in more detail later in this chapter), a consistent finding in the literature is that motor learning is quite specific. In general, **practice specificity** suggests that what you learn depends largely on what you practice.

Specificity effects are wide ranging. For example, practicing in a particular environment or workspace often leads to better performance mainly (sometimes only) in that workspace compared to a different or altered workspace (one basis for the so-called home-field advantage; Carron et al., 2005). Another

FOCUS ON Research 9.1

The 10,000-Hour Myth

The book *Outliers* by Malcolm Gladwell generated a considerable amount of interest in practice and learning. Gladwell claims that acquiring expertise requires a minimum of 10,000 hours of practice—a concept that had arisen from research conducted by Anders Ericsson and his colleagues (read Ericsson & Pool, 2016, for a great overview). Unfortunately, this so-called 10,000-hour rule misrepresented Ericsson's work. The *quantity* of practice was not Ericsson's main concern because not all practice methods are equal in their impact on learning. Instead, Ericsson's focus was on the *quality* of practice.

Ericsson used the term **deliberate practice** to represent how **expertise** is attained. Deliberate practice is effortful, directed specifically toward goal attainment, and requires augmented feedback to improve performance. Research has shown, for example, that skilled athletes engage in more of the behaviors typified by the term *deliberate practice* than do less-skilled athletes (Coughlan et al., 2014). The idea has been a useful construct in many different fields of training, including the development of expertise in music, sports, and medicine. The myth of the 10,000-hour rule underscores the fundamental idea, discussed in this chapter and in chapters 10 and 11, that motor learning is more about practice quality than practice quantity.

important finding is that the sensory feedback (e.g., visual, auditory, tactile) resulting from performance becomes part of the learned skill, such that later performance is more skillful when that same sensory information is available, compared to situations in which one or more of these feedback channels is altered (Proteau, 1992).

While an important goal of practice is to facilitate transfer (i.e., performance in unpracticed situations or contexts), it is important to recognize that practice specificity is the dominant characteristic. A concrete example of research in practical situations makes this point vividly clear. Law enforcement officers are sometimes required to use a service weapon in encounters with dangerous offenders—situations in which the encounter is highly stressful and rapidly evolving. Although officers undergo considerable training to improve shooting accuracy, training often involves range practice, in which shots are fired at static targets under nonstressful conditions. A literature review by Cooper and colleagues (2024) revealed that shooting accuracy declined considerably when officers performed under pressure. However, adding stressful conditions to the training context mitigated the decline. Thus, contextualizing training in anticipation of specificity effects is an important consideration for organizing practice.

Practice Is Not Simply Repetition

The term *repetition* is often incorrectly equated with the term *practice*, and many well-intentioned instructors and coaches confuse the two concepts. To us, **repetition** invokes the idea of going over something again and again. The implication is that repetition somehow "grooves" or "stamps in" a memory, with more repetitions leading to a deeper, more durable memory. The metaphor causes one to think (incorrectly, in our view) of learning as a concept like muscle hypertrophy, which results from repetitious exercise.

Police officer weapons training often involves firing at static targets under nonstressful conditions.

Consider the following quote from Bernstein in counterpoint to the traditional view of practice as repetition.

> **Bernstein:** The process of practice towards the achievement of new motor habits essentially consists in the gradual success of a search for optimal motor solutions to the appropriate problems. Because of this, practice, when properly undertaken, does not consist in repeating the *means of* solution of a motor problem time after time, but in the *process of solving* this problem again and again by techniques which we changed and perfected from repetition to repetition. It is already apparent here that, in many cases, "practice is a particular type of repetition without repetition" and that motor training, if this position is ignored, is merely mechanical repetition by rote, a method which has been discredited in pedagogy for some time. (Bernstein, 1967, p. 134)

The conceptual model that we have developed throughout the book highlights the most important components of the human information-processing system that are involved in movement control. These components fluctuate due to temporary factors, improve with development, and regress with advancing age. Importantly, though, the processing system components become more effective and efficient with learning. In our view, the most effective learning occurs when practice activates as many of the individual components of the processing system as possible. In this way, practice is successful to the degree that it engages the entire conceptual model presented in figure 8.1. Practice should focus on optimizing learning, not necessarily performance (see Focus on Application 9.1). The next section describes how the conceptual model's individual components either improve with practice or are shown to have improved when experts are studied.

FOCUS ON Application 9.1

Learning Versus Performance During Practice

When learners acquire a new skill, they are obviously doing something different from what they had done earlier. The processes leading to learning require that something change, usually resulting in performance that becomes more effective and efficient. Yet, when assisting learners during practice, many instructors encourage them to do their best on each practice attempt. This generates two, sometimes conflicting, practice goals: performing as well as possible in practice versus exploring new techniques, strategies, and movement patterning that often lead to suboptimal performance.

In our assessment of the research literature, the old adage that "if you make errors in practice, you will learn to make errors" could not be farther from the truth. The learner who attempts to always perform as well as possible in practice may try avoid experimenting from attempt to attempt, which detracts from learning. The approach for maximizing performance ("do your best") that repeats the most effective pattern discovered so far is not effective for learning in part because it discourages experimentation.

One way to separate these conflicting practice goals is to provide two fundamentally different activities during practice—practice sessions and test sessions. First, provide practice sessions in which you instruct the learners simply to avoid repeating what they did earlier. Tell the learner to explore different strategies to discover a more effective pattern of action. Self-discovery of new skill techniques is a hallmark of motor learning, and the effective instructor can use various means to help the learner make these discoveries (Button et al., 2021; Newell, 1986). The learner should know that performance quality is not critical during this practice period and that the only goal is to discover some new way to execute the skill that may be more effective in the long term.

Of course, the measure of the effectiveness of this learning progress is a test of some kind (as discussed in the previous chapter). After some time in the practice session, the instructor could announce a switch to a test session, in which the next period of time is treated as a test. In the test session, the learner tries to perform as well as possible. After the test session, the learner has some idea of his progress and can return to the discovery practice mode to continue searching for more effective movement patterning and skill technique. Such tests could be formally evaluated and graded, but they can also be effective if given only for the learner's information. Evaluating progress by asking learners to compile their own test scores is an excellent method to help them assess their own progress; it is both motivating and educational (we will have much more to say about feedback and evaluation in chapter 11).

Benefits of Practice

Obviously, improved performance is a major goal of practice, which can be thought of as developing the capability to perform some skill on demand. However, there are several other benefits of practice that leave the learner with capabilities that are not so obvious. Actually, the term *motor learning* is a bit of a misnomer, because what results from practice is much more than just *motor* learning. In this section, we describe some benefits to expect from practice.

Perception

Perceptual expertise is the hallmark of many open skills, although you might be surprised to learn that *chess* provides an unlikely framework for one method of its study. DeGroot (1946) and Chase and Simon (1973) studied the memory of chess experts and nonexperts after showing them brief glimpses of chessboards. In one condition, the chess pieces of a partially played game were shown to all participants; in another condition, the same number of chess pieces were arranged randomly on the board (i.e., a grouping of chess pieces that was unlikely to occur in an actual game). After viewing the board for about 5 s, the participants used a blank chessboard to re-create the scene they had just viewed. As expected, the experts were much better than the nonexperts at re-creating the partially played game board. Surprisingly, though, the experts were no better than the nonexperts at re-creating the randomly arranged board. What these studies showed was that the experts did not simply have a better general memory for remembering the location of chess pieces. Rather, the experts' capability to remember the information was specific to their attained skill—they could acquire the information very quickly if, and only if, the chess pieces were organized in a way that was relevant to their expertise. Remembering the randomly placed pieces was inconsistent with their expertise, rendering the experts' memory for the layout no better than the nonexperts.

The chess studies provided a framework for studying the perceptual advantage that is gained with motor skill practice and experience. For example, expert and nonexpert indoor rock climbers were shown a wall that outlined a difficult but climbable route and another wall with the same number of handholds and footholds but that was impossible to climb. When trying to remember each, the experts remembered the difficult route better than the nonexperts but were no better at remembering the impossible route (Pezzulo et al., 2010). Like the chess experts, the memory advantage for experienced rock climbers was specific to the nature of the skill they had attained.

Experts were better at remembering briefly shown rock-wall layouts than nonexperts but only if a climbing route was possible.

Perceptual specificity in sports is also true with respect to using vision—expertise in many ball sports is not due to some general visual superiority that allows one to see better. One method that researchers have used to study expertise involves using contact lenses that blur vision. In closed tasks such as basketball shooting and golf putting, performance only deteriorated when vision was blurred to the point of near-legal blindness. Even in dynamic, open tasks, such as cricket batting, performance deteriorated only under substantially blurred conditions (see reviews by Farrow & Abernethy, 2015; Limballe et al., 2022). In these cases, the perceptual expertise remained intact despite degraded vision.

The fact that performance does not deteriorate as vision is degraded means that other factors must account for the superior perceptual and anticipatory skills of experts. A few methods have been used to assess the expertise advantage, such as studying a performer's gaze or using occlusion methods that either stop a video at a critical time or edit a video so that it blocks critical perceptual information from view (see Focus on Research 2.2 and Williams & Jackson, 2019). Using these methods, several important discoveries about practice and skill development have been uncovered (see reviews by Abernethy et al., 2012; Williams, 2020):

- Skilled performers are better at seeing patterns of movement among opponents and their own teammates (e.g., detecting a run vs. pass play in football).
- Skilled performers are better at using opponents' postural information to predict future events (e.g., a goalkeeper predicting the direction of a penalty kick).

Traceurs and traceuses, who are skilled in the activity of parkour, see obstacles in the environment as challenges to act upon. In this photo, describe a different parkour activity in which the object is viewed as something different from how it might normally be viewed.

- Skilled performers are better at using situational contexts to make probabilistic judgments about what will happen next (e.g., likelihood of a pass or shoot in basketball).
- Skilled performers direct their gaze more efficiently and effectively to gain the most important information in the visual environment (e.g., a baseball batter focusing on the pitcher's hand and ball grip).
- Skilled performers are better at avoiding deceptive moves by their opponents (e.g., head fakes).

In sum, experts use their expertise to identify, predict, anticipate, and otherwise gain spatial and temporal advantages from available environmental information.

Visit HK*Propel* to read "Wayne Gretzky" and complete the self-directed learning activities.

Attention

In chapter 3, we presented several concepts about attention, which we now consider from a learning perspective. This section describes the effect of practice on three attention concepts.

Reduced Capacity Demands

One fundamental concept from chapter 3 was that most tasks demand some attention, and performance suffers when the overall demand exceeds the available capacity (e.g., see the discussion on distracted driving in Focus on Research 3.2). One benefit of practice is that the attention a task demands reduces as learning progresses.

An important study by Leavitt (1979) illustrates this concept well. In his study, Leavitt compared hockey players of different ages and of different playing abilities within each age on the performance of a skating task (which was the main task), done either without a stick and puck or when stickhandling a puck. (Ice skating without controlling a puck simultaneously is much less attention-demanding compared to skating and stickhandling a puck simultaneously.) The time required to skate a fixed distance was measured.

Figure 9.1 illustrates Leavitt's results. The graph is somewhat complex, so we will highlight a few key points. First, as expected, skating times when stickhandling the puck, in general, are longer than when skating without moving the puck (compare the *no-puck* vs. *puck* data points as a whole). Second, also as expected, the time when skating with the puck becomes progressively shorter as children become older (i.e., as they advance from the Novice to Atom to Peewee to Bantam age groups). Last, within each age group, average-skilled players suffered less decrement in time when skating with the puck than did the poorly skilled players (as indicated by the slopes of the red lines, which are flatter than the slopes of the blue lines). Together, these findings point to the conclusion that as hockey skill improved, there was less attention demanded by either the skating or stickhandling (or both), allowing them to be performed together with reduced performance decrements.

Schaefer and Scornaienchi (2020) later replicated the Leavitt (1979) study's conclusions in adults performing a table tennis task. Experts showed considerably less decrement in shot-return accuracy than novices when simultaneously performing a cognitively demanding memory task. Again, these findings suggest that less attention to the task is required as skill develops, leaving more resources available to engage in other concurrent activities without a severe cost to performance.

Driving an automobile while using a cell phone was another topic that we discussed in chapter 3. A large amount of research evidence has concluded that multitasking is hazardous to driving performance (see Ishigami & Klein, 2009; Caird et al., 2018, for reviews). But, given the findings just discussed, one might wonder if the decrement is the same for all drivers or more pronounced for individuals who have less experience (or skill) in either driving or using their phone. The research findings are mixed, however. In one study, for example, practice that involved both simulated driving and a secondary

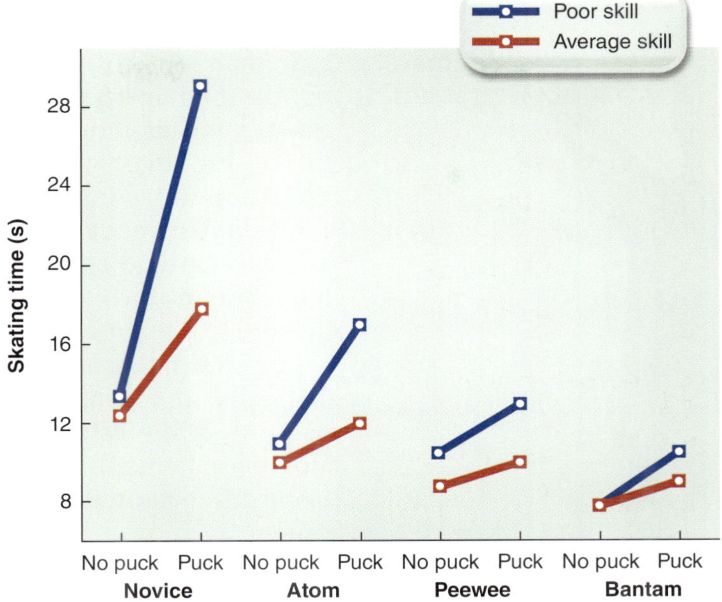

FIGURE 9.1 Skating times measured when participants were skating alone (the no-puck condition) and when they were skating and stickhandling (the puck condition) simultaneously. (Novice = 7.9 years old on average; Atom = 10.1 years; Peewee = 11.3 years; Bantam = 14.1 years)

task improved performance but failed to eliminate the distraction deficit (Cooper & Strayer, 2008). But in another study, 2.5% of the participants examined were identified as *supertaskers*, showing no deficit to driving performance while engaged in various secondary tasks (Watson & Strayer, 2010). How and why these skills emerged and how (or if) they can be learned is a focus of research.

Reduced Effector Competition

Another important concept of attention is that interference can arise when a task requires moving two or more effectors simultaneously. The classic example of patting your head and rubbing your stomach simultaneously illustrates the problem (see figure 9.2). The issue shares some similarities with the attention-demand concept, as discussed in the previous section and in chapter 3, but is unique in the sense that one has no trouble rubbing (or patting) both the head and the stomach simultaneously. The interference is not a matter of doing two things simultaneously but of doing two *different* things simultaneously.

Interference arises when one effector has a movement pattern or timing that differs from the other effector. Bender's (1987) research, discussed in chapter 7, illustrates nicely both the problem and the benefits that result from practice. She found that producing the English letter V with one hand and the Greek letter γ with the other hand was nearly impossible when these actions were performed simultaneously. Effector competition was reduced (but not eliminated) with considerable practice, perhaps due to the development of a single motor program that was responsible for controlling the two limbs as if they were a single limb (i.e., with a single motor program; see Schmidt et al., 1998).

Multi-effector timing is easy to do if the limbs produce a synchronous rhythm (e.g., 1:1, 2:1) but very difficult if the timing is more complex (e.g., 3:2, 4:3). But we know from expert drummers, for example, that complex polyrhythms can be learned. A review of the evidence by Maslovat and Klapp (2024) suggests that whole-task training is critical in establishing an integrated timing representation, which we discuss later in this chapter.

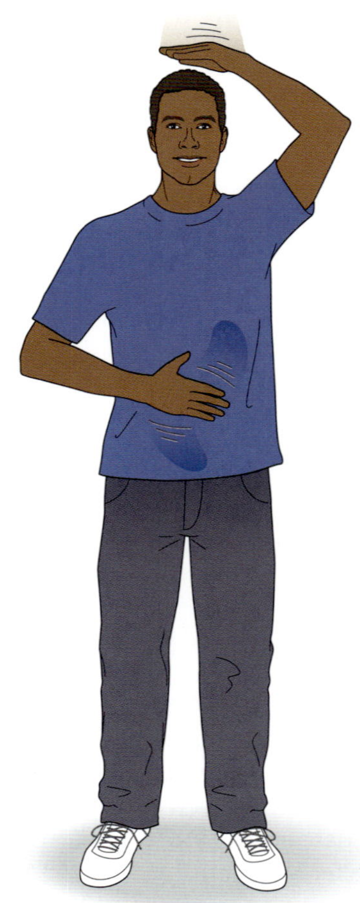

FIGURE 9.2 A typical coordination problem that practice can solve.

Attentional Focus

In chapter 3, we discussed the performance effects of directing a performer's attentional focus through verbal instructions. For most performers and activities, focusing on the intended result of an action (an external focus) produces better performance than focusing on the movement itself (an internal focus; see reviews in Chua et al., 2021; Herrebrøden, 2023). However, analyses of experts' use of focus suggest a more nuanced role of attentional focus.

Expert golfers, for example, tend to focus their attention differently depending on situational factors. 1) They use a more internalized focus during training sessions but a more externalized focus in competition, and 2) they shift from an internal focus during the preparation stage to an external focus during execution (Bernier et al., 2011). Experts also shift their focus of attention while performing continuous tasks, such as running, or serial tasks, such as figure skating (Bernier et al., 2016). Frequent shifts between a focus on environmental cues and monitoring body focus cues become critical when factors such as fatigue require that athletes make adjustments during an extended performance period.

An external focus of attention appears to be critically important at the time of execution of most skills (especially in discrete tasks). However, focusing on internal cues appears to be important when making adjustments during training and while performing endurance tasks.

Motor Programs

A prominent theme in the motor learning literature suggests that many motor skills, especially discrete skills, are learned through developing motor programs. The hypothesized process involves combining smaller motor programs (responsible for very brief movements) with larger programs (controlling longer periods of movement). The **gearshift analogy** provides a useful way to consider how this process works.

When first learning to shift the gears of a standard-transmission car, the beginning driver goes through each of the seven steps illustrated in figure 9.3, the movement for each of these steps presumably being controlled by a separate motor program. As proficiency is gained, some steps are combined into larger motor programs that control two or more of the individual steps. At the highest skill level, a single motor program controls the movement for all seven steps.

Correlation analyses are one method to identify whether one or more motor programs control a sequence of actions (see chapter 1). All movements result in certain kinematic landmarks (e.g., time to reach peak acceleration, peak velocity). When correlations are performed (over many trials within a participant) the result is a matrix of many pairs

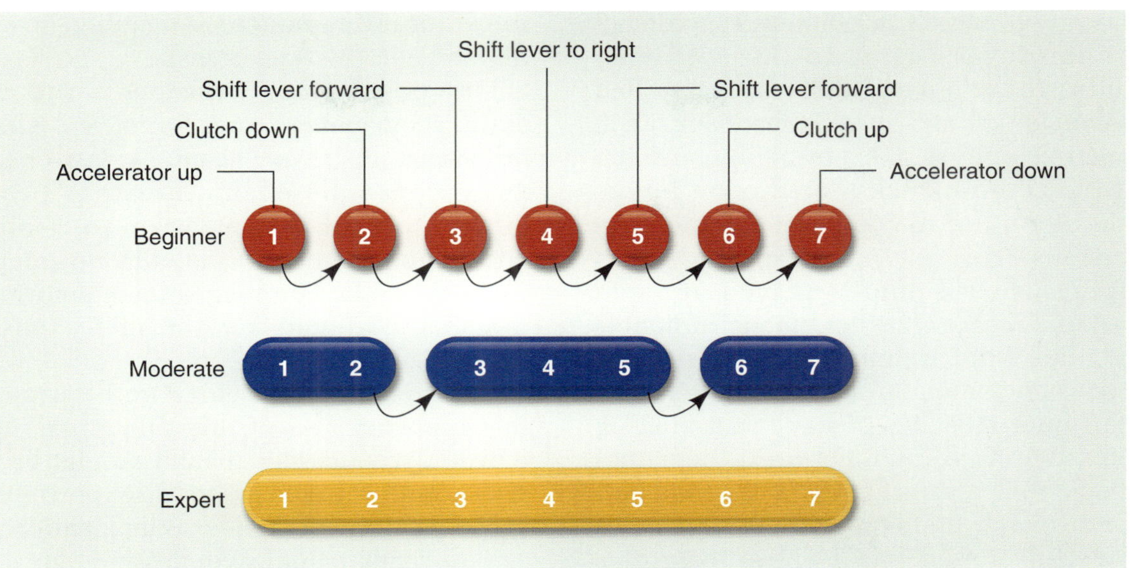

FIGURE 9.3 The gearshift analogy—using the example of shifting a standard-transmission car from second to third gear. Development of expertise results in the reorganization of seven individual motor programs into one program.

of correlations between all the landmarks. A single motor program is assumed to exist if all the pairs are highly correlated. A low correlation between any pair of landmarks is evidence either that there is no motor program involved or that there are two or more separate programs (Schneider & Schmidt, 1995). This type of research has many applications. For example, using this rationale, researchers analyzed childproof butane lighters and provided evidence that more than one motor program was required to complete all the steps of igniting the lighter (Schmidt et al., 1996), confirming the effectiveness of the intended safety feature that it required two distinct actions.

Error Detection and Anticipation

The capability for an individual to self-detect an error when it is made represents another benefit of practice. For example, the instructor is usually present during practice when a student is learning cardiopulmonary resuscitation (CPR) skills. Therefore, self-detection of errors is not important because the instructor is there to point out mistakes and suggest corrections (termed *augmented feedback* and discussed in detail in chapter 11). The problem, though, is that the instructor will not be available to detect and correct errors when the learner attempts to perform this skill in an actual emergency. The learner who can analyze her errors independently and make corrections in the moment will be far more skilled at providing CPR. This **error-detection** and correction capability tends to make the learner self-sufficient, which is one overall goal of practice. We will have much more to say in chapter 11 about how error-detection skills development is promoted (or discouraged) by the way augmented feedback is provided.

Tasks differ with respect to sensory information. The sound of the engine is particularly important to the race car driver, and the sound of the instrument is obviously important to the musician. Visual information is critical to the dentist, although when provided by a mirror, that information requires special translation skills. People who have lost their eyesight can become quite adept at using tactile feedback to read (e.g., Braille) and auditory feedback for echolocation. Detecting and using sensory information is a process that accompanies skill development.

One way in which the capability to detect errors improves is due to the enhanced capability to anticipate feedback. The skilled physician anticipates specific feedback when conducting a physical examination, and the failure to confirm such a prediction immediately alerts her to a potential issue. The skilled musician anticipates a specific sound emerging when a note is played and can immediately recognize that the instrument is out of tune if the anticipated auditory feedback does not match the actual feedback. The football quarterback will have that sinking anticipation of an interception if the actual feedback that accompanies a thrown ball does not match the expected consequences of a well-executed pass. These examples highlight the fundamental importance of skill development as a process of learning to analyze feedforward information, anticipate outcomes, and make corrections if time permits (Wolpert & Flanagan, 2001).

Retention of Skill

There are many factors to consider regarding the retention of motor skills. For example, how practice is organized and when augmented feedback is provided have such profound effects on skill retention that the next two chapters are devoted entirely to these topics. This section concerns the fate of motor skills after a *retention interval*—a period of time during which no further practice is undertaken. As we will discuss, the absence of practice is often, but not always, detrimental to skilled performance.

Recall from chapter 2 that *warm-up decrement* represents a situation where we fail to perform up to expectations at the start of an activity following a rest period or break. The first of a series of throws in darts or free throws in basketball are good examples of warm-up decrement. Performance is often underachieved unless the factors that support it are reinstated prior to movement initiation. The implication of warm-up decrement is that motor skills, or the factors that support optimal performance of them, are prone to forgetting. The amount of forgetting, however, depends on the type of task.

One puzzle about learning is that some skills seem never to be forgotten, whereas others are lost rather quickly. An often-repeated example of the former is riding a bicycle, a skill that we seem to retain for very long periods of time with no intervening practice. In contrast, some memories are forgotten quite quickly, especially those for discrete skills.

Consider the following two early studies that are examples of this difference. In the first study, conducted many years ago by Neumann and Ammons (1957), experimenters asked participants to learn the locations of a series of eight paired switches and lights. This task seemed to have a relatively heavy verbal memory component in that participants had to learn and remember which switch went with which light. Practice continued until participants performed two consecutive, errorless trials, which, as illustrated in figure 9.4, required about 63 trials on average. At that point, the entire participant pool was split into five subgroups, each defined by the length of time before a retention test would be performed—retention intervals of 1 min, 20 min, two days, seven weeks, or a full year. The results illustrated in figure 9.4 are very clear. The length of the retention interval dramatically affected retention performance, with one year of no practice producing the least skilled performance on the first retention trial and returning this group essentially to the level at which they started 12 months earlier. This group required the largest number of trials (as compared to the other groups) to regain the criterion of two errorless trials. Be careful to note here that reattainment of the criterion (36 trials) for this group was less than in original practice, indicating that not all skill had been lost during this retention interval.

Now contrast the results from the Neumann and Ammons study (figure 9.4) with the findings reported by Fleishman and Parker (1962), presented in figure 9.5. The task required producing complex tracking movements involving coordination of the hands (in both the left–right and forward–backward dimensions) and the feet (in the left–right dimension), using an aircraft-type stick and rudder controls. Retention tests were performed after nine months, one year, or two years. As illustrated in figure 9.5, the retention loss was remarkably small, even after two years of no practice.

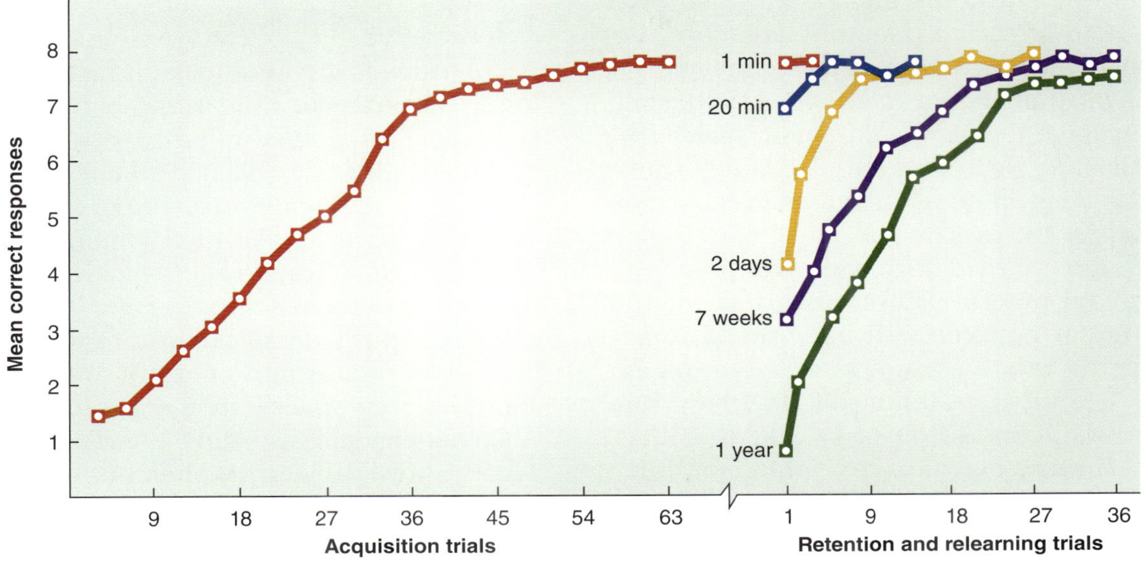

FIGURE 9.4 Forgetting a discrete task, as indexed by first trial performance and the number of practice trials to reacquire the original criterion, was related to the length of the retention interval (1 min, 20 min, two days, seven weeks, or one year).

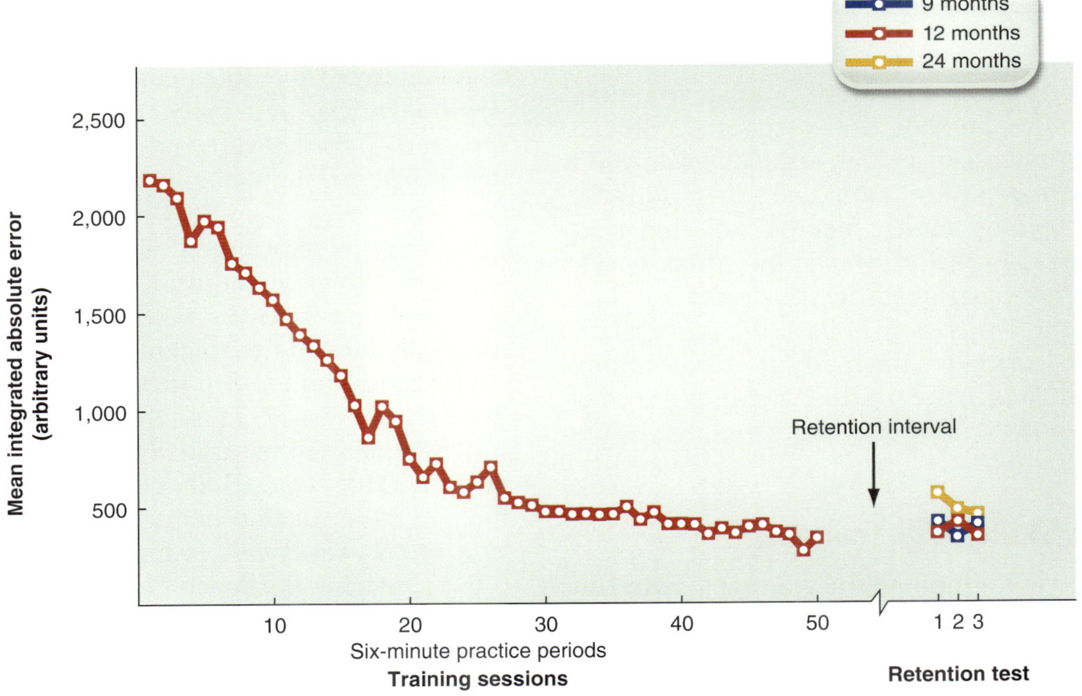

FIGURE 9.5 Motor skill tracking performance was retained well for retention intervals of up to two years following original practice.

Visit HK*Propel* to read "Like Riding a Bicycle" and complete the self-directed learning activities.

What does the difference in the results of these two studies mean? We argue that long-term retention depends largely on the nature of the task—discrete tasks are forgotten relatively quickly, especially those with a relatively large cognitive component such as the one used in Neumann and Ammons' study. On the other hand, continuous tasks, exemplified by the task in the Fleishman-Parker study, are retained very well over long periods of no practice. Of course, the amount of original practice will have much to say about the relative amount of retention for these tasks (e.g., Ammons et al., 1958). But, in general, continuous tasks, like the adage about riding a bicycle, are retained for much longer periods of time than discrete tasks.

Visit HK*Propel* to read "The Keypad" and complete the self-directed learning activities.

Transfer of Skill

Transfer, which is sometimes called *generalization*, is an important goal of practice. It refers to the idea that learning acquired during practice of a given task can be applied to, or *transferred* to, other tasks or situations. An instructor should not be satisfied that students can perform only those task variations they have specifically practiced. The instructor wants them to be able to generalize specific learning to the many novel variations they will face in the future. An important concern is how to conduct practice to maximize generalization.

What Skills Will Transfer?

Transfer is defined as the gain or loss in the capability to perform one task following practice or experience on another task. Transfer is positive if it enhances performance in the other skill, negative if it degrades it, and zero if it has no effect at all (see discussion in chapter 8, as well as figures 8.9 and 8.10). The issues surrounding transfer, and particularly maximizing transfer by adjusting teaching methods and styles, are far-ranging and discussed briefly here.

Transfer and Similarity

An old idea in psychology and motor learning is that transfer of learning between two tasks increases as the similarity between them increases. One idea was *identical elements* (Thorndike & Woodworth, 1901), according to which learning certain elements in one situation transferred to another skill because the second skill used the same elements. This concept should sound familiar to the reader because it relates quite closely to the ideas about practice specificity discussed earlier.

Consider a classic study published years ago by Lordahl and Archer (1958). They asked three groups of participants to practice a rotary-pursuit tracking task (discussed earlier) on two consecutive days. On the first day, the three groups practiced their trials on a turntable that rotated at either 40, 60, or 80 rpm. Day two was considered the transfer day, in which all groups performed their trials at 60 rpm. The results, illustrated in figure 9.6, revealed that transfer performance on day two favored the group that had practiced day one at the same speed (60 rpm). In fact, only the 40 rpm group could catch up to this group's performance level by the end of day two practice.

In a second experiment with the same task and similar experimental design, Lordahl and Archer varied the size of the turntable disk (distance of the tracking target from the center) and again found that day two transfer performance was best for the group that had practiced using the same task dimensions on day one. These specificity of transfer findings have been replicated many times, including in a recent study by Huang and colleagues (2021), varying the speed of a bimanual coordination task.

Transfer in Early Stages of Learning

What underlies transfer, and why do some skills show more or less specificity of trans-

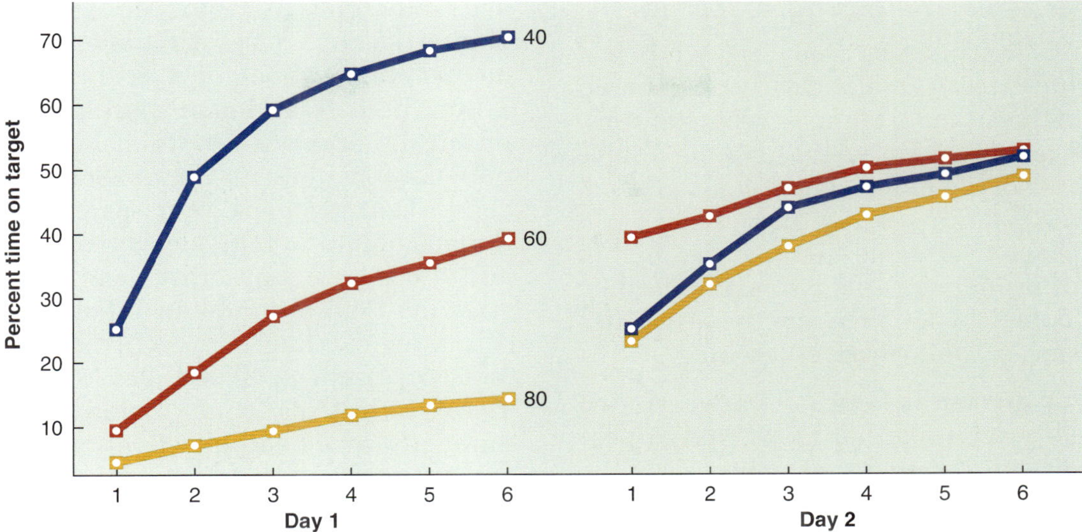

FIGURE 9.6 Specificity of pursuit-rotor transfer. Three groups practiced 30 trials (six blocks of five trials each) on two consecutive days. On day one, the groups practiced at speeds of either 40, 60, or 80 rpm. On day two, all groups transferred to practice at 60 rpm.

fer? The following sections offer some possible reasons in the early stages of learning.

Fundamental Movement Patterning Many have suggested that the so-called overarm pattern underlies many skills, such as throwing a baseball, serving in tennis, spiking a volleyball, and other actions that require forceful overarm movements to strike or throw an object. All these involve rotation of the hips and shoulders and ballistic actions of the shoulder–arm–wrist, ending finally with wrist–hand action to accomplish the particular goal. An analogous idea common among gymnasts is that certain fundamental actions (e.g., the sharp hip extension in a kip) can be applied to many apparatus events. In both these examples, if practice is given at one variant of the class of movements sharing the same general pattern, then the learner should be able to transfer the learning to any other variant using this same pattern. Of course, practicing a kipping action would not transfer to an overarm action or vice versa, because these skills use very different patterns from separate movement classes.

Perceptual Elements Similarity is also evident in the numerous perceptual elements underlying many tasks. For example, learning to intercept flying balls of various kinds (baseballs, footballs, tennis balls, and so on) depends on learning the common features of ball flight, which are based on the principles of physics. In a similar way, police trainees must be attuned to the perceptual cues that alert them to a dangerous situation. Learning to anticipate and react appropriately to such cues in one situation should facilitate transfer to other situations in which the perceptual elements are similar.

Strategic and Conceptual Similarities Similar strategies, rules, guidelines, or concepts are present in many different activities. For example, driving behaviors, signs, traffic lights, and general rules of the road are common within a restricted population or community, which facilitates driving performance when you travel to parts of the country that are new to you. However, one would expect much less transfer, or perhaps even some negative transfer, when the rules of the road differ dramatically, as when tourists drive on the opposite side of the road in a foreign country (e.g., North Americans driving in Australia).

Transfer as Learning Progresses

The transfer principles apply best when just beginning to learn a skill. In early practice, an overarm throw and a tennis serve seem similar, and relating them might help the novice get an idea of the movement that is required. However, a tennis serve and an overarm throw are not the same thing, and at higher levels of proficiency, the two skills become more distinct. What, then, are the principles of transfer for later stages of learning?

Motor Transfer Is Small Between two reasonably well-learned tasks that appear somewhat similar, there is usually very little transfer. The transfer that occurs is usually low and positive—the skills generally facilitate each other to some small extent. But the amount of transfer is generally so low that it ceases to be a major factor. Contrast this with the earliest practice stages, where transfer was a major goal. Therefore, teaching a particular skill A (which is not of major interest) simply because you would like it to transfer to skill B (which *is* of major interest) is not very effective, especially when one considers the time spent on skill A that could have been spent on skill B. Transfer is fine when received "for free" in early practice, but it usually requires too much time in later practice.

The principle just mentioned also applies to using various **lead-up activities**. These actions are usually not of interest in themselves but are only a means to another goal—the transfer to another skill. For example, learning to suture wounds by starting with grapes is a cost-effective lead-up activity to working with more realistic simulators or patients. In general, however, learning such preliminary activities tends to transfer to the degree that they are effectively similar to the goal conditions, which we will discuss in more detail shortly.

No Transfer of Basic Abilities A common misconception is that a fundamental ability (see chapter 7) can be trained through various drills or other activities. The thinking is that with some stronger ability, the learner will see gains in performance for tasks with this underlying ability. For example, athletes sometimes use "quickening" exercises, hoping these exercises will train some fundamental ability to be quick, allowing quicker actions in their particular sport. Coaches and physical therapists may use balancing drills with the goal of increasing general balancing ability; eye movement exercises are used with the goal of improving general visual abilities; and there are many other examples. Such attempts to train fundamental abilities may sound logical, but they simply do not work (e.g., Abernethy & Wood, 2001; Lindeburg, 1949). Resources (time, money) would be more efficiently and effectively allocated to practicing the specific goal skills.

There are two correct ways to think of these principles. First, there is no general ability to be quick, to balance, or to use vision, as discussed in chapter 7. Rather, quickness, balance, and vision in various tasks are each based on many diverse abilities, so there is no single quickness ability, for example, even if it could be trained. Second, even if there were such general abilities, they are, by definition, essentially innate and not subject to modification through practice. Therefore, attempts to modify an ability with a nonspecific drill are usually ineffective (e.g., see Giboin et al., 2018). A learner may improve their skill at performing the drill itself, but this learning does not transfer effectively to the goal skill.

Visit HK*Propel* to read "Sport Snake Oils" and complete the self-directed learning activities. 

Transfer of Part Practice to Whole Performance

Some skills are enormously complex, such as playing a musical instrument or performing a gymnast's routine. In such situations, the instructor cannot present all aspects of the skill at once for practice because the student would be overwhelmed and would likely grasp almost none of it. A frequent approach is to divide the task into meaningful units that can be practiced separately in isolated parts. The eventual goal is to integrate these practiced units into the whole skill for later performance. This is not as simple as it may sound because there are several factors that make integrating the learned units back into the whole skill somewhat difficult.

The question is how to create subunits of skills and how they can be practiced for maximum transfer to the whole skill. It is a simple matter to divide skills into parts. For example, you could separate a gymnastics routine into the component stunts, or you could divide the left and right hands of piano practice into separate components for practice. And each subpart could be divided even further. But the real question is whether these parts, practiced in isolation, will be effective for learning the whole skill, which is the end goal. Thus, **part practice** is based on the transfer-of-learning principles defined earlier. Will practice on the subunits transfer to the whole task that contains them? How much (if any) time should be spent on part practice, and would this time be more effectively spent practicing the whole task?

At first glance, the answers to these questions seem obvious. Because the part of the task practiced in isolation seems to be the same as that part in the whole task, the transfer from the part to the whole task would seem to be almost perfect. This may be so in certain cases, but there are many other situations in which transfer is far from perfect. These differences in part-practice effectiveness depend on the nature of the skill.

Serial Skills of Long Duration

In many serial skills, the learner's problem is to organize a set of activities into the proper order, as with the gymnast who assembles a routine of stunts. Practicing the specific subtasks is usually effective in transferring them to whole sequences. Part transfer works best in serial tasks of very long duration, where one part's actions (or errors) do not influence the next part's actions. That is, part practice is most effective for skills in which the parts are performed relatively independently. The learner can devote more practice time to the troublesome parts without practicing the easier (or mastered) elements, making practice time more efficient.

However, in many serial skills in sports, performance on one part frequently determines the movement that must be made on the next part. If the ski racer comes out of a turn too low and fast, this affects the approach for the next turn. Small positioning errors on the beam in one move determine how the gymnast must perform the next one. If a part-to-part transition is critical, as it might be if the sequence is run off quickly, modifying a given action as a function of performance on a previous action is an important component of the skill. These transitions between parts of the whole skill cannot be practiced and learned in isolated part practice; **whole practice** is necessary. The gymnast might be able to do all the individual stunts in her routine, but she still might not be able to perform an effective routine in a meet because she has not learned to modify each component movement based on the previous one.

Discrete Skills of Short Duration

Any skill is, in some sense, serial because certain pieces of it come before other pieces, such as hitting a baseball, which contains step, hip turn, and swing elements. At some point, though, these individual parts, when viewed separately, cease to be parts of the whole skill. Dividing a golf swing into smaller and smaller arbitrary parts destroys a critical aspect that allows the parts to be characterized as components of a swing—that is, the division seems to disrupt the essential features of the action. Practice at these subparts could be ineffective, even detrimental, to learning the whole task.

Several experiments suggest that practicing parts of a discrete task in isolation transfers little, if at all, to the whole task, especially if the task is rapid and ballistic (e.g., Lersten, 1968; Schmidt & Young, 1987). This absence of transfer is probably related to the fact that the components in rapid tasks usually interact strongly. In fact, transfer from the part to the whole can even be negative in certain cases, so practicing the part in isolation could be worse for the whole task than not practicing at all!

A gymnast putting together a routine (coauthor Richard Schmidt, pictured here when he was an NCAA gymnast at Cal) must become skilled at performing the routine as a whole, because each movement must be modified in response to the previous movement. In this photo, describe another serial task in which discrete parts are put together into a whole.

This evidence suggests that when very rapid skills are broken down into arbitrary parts, these parts change compared to the same parts in the whole task. Part practice contributes very little to learning the whole task because the parts that are practiced are not the same when performed separately compared to when performed in the whole task. In tasks like the slap shot in ice hockey, for example, practicing the backswing separately from the downswing changes the dynamics of the action at the top of the backswing, which is dominated by actively lengthening muscles whose spring-like properties allow the downswing to be smooth and powerful. Therefore, practicing the backswing in isolation, which eliminates the role of these spring-like muscle properties, is quite different from performing the same backswing in the context of the whole skill.

The principles of part practice can be summarized as follows:

- For prolonged, serial tasks with no component interaction, part practice on the difficult elements is very efficient.
- For very brief, programmed actions, part practice is seldom useful and can even be detrimental to learning.
- For tasks that have interacting components, the more the components interact with each other, the less effective part practice is.

Simulation, Virtual Reality, and Transfer

Creating and using mockups that simulate the real world has been a training staple for years. In general, these mockups come in two forms: **simulators**, which are physical replicas of real-world environments, and **virtual reality (VR)**, which uses computer-generated immersive technology to replicate a real-world experience. Each has strengths and weaknesses but is similar in that transfer principles are commonly used to assess their value.

Simulator and VR environments can be very elaborate, sophisticated, and expensive, such as simulators to train pilots to fly aircraft and sea captains to navigate marine vessels (figure 9.7). But some simulators are not elaborate at all, such as wireless video game consoles (e.g., Levac et al., 2012). Simulation can be an important part of an instructional program, especially when the skill to be learned is expensive or dangerous (e.g., learning to fly a jetliner or navigate a ship), where facilities are limited (e.g., cycling on a treadmill instead of in a velodrome), or where real practice is not feasible (e.g., practicing golf outdoors in the winter in Minnesota).

Evaluating Simulator Effectiveness

A simulator or VR environment must provide positive results to justify its use. Therefore, the amount of transfer resulting from the time spent is an important consideration in determining its effectiveness and efficiency.

FIGURE 9.7 A maritime simulator for training ship navigational skills.

Consider figure 9.8, showing the hypothetical performances on a novel motor learning task for two groups of participants. The experimental group began practice on the transfer task after 3 h of practice on a simulator or VR task. The control group received no prior practice on the simulator or VR.

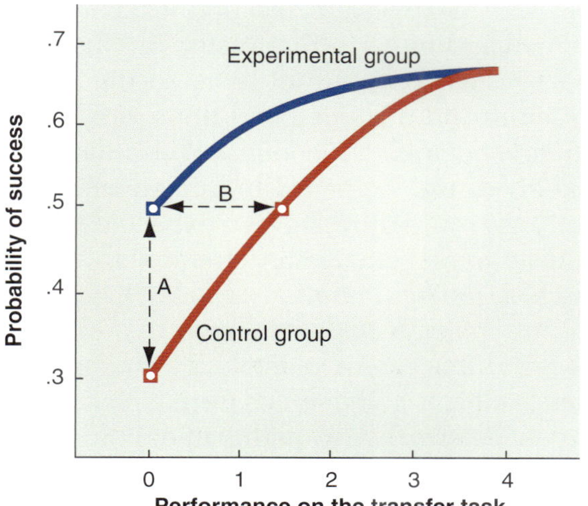

FIGURE 9.8 Hypothetical performances of two groups of learners on a novel motor learning task. The experimental group practiced a simulation task for 3 h before initial practice on the transfer task, whereas the control group had no previous practice.

Figure 9.8 illustrates the performance of both groups on the transfer task. Note that the point on the axis corresponding to 0 h of practice refers to the first trial on the transfer task for both groups (this point occurs after 3 h of practice on the simulator task for the experimental group and 0 h for the control group). From figure 9.8, we can see that there is considerable positive transfer from the simulator to the transfer task, seen as the gain in probability of success from .30 to .50 (the difference labeled A in figure 9.8). Now look at the difference labeled B in figure 9.8. This difference suggests that the simulator group started at a level (.50) that took the control group 1.5 h to achieve on the transfer task. So, from one perspective, the simulator experience saved about 1.5 h of practice on the transfer task.

However, there is another way to look at this result. Remember that the experimental group had already spent 3 h of practice on the simulator. Since this group spent 3 h of practice on the simulator, but the control group "caught up" in 1.5 h, the simulation actually *cost* 1.5 h of real (sometimes very expensive) simulator time. Viewed in this way, the simulator was not effective at all in reducing the time of training.

Time is not the only relevant factor here, though. The effectiveness of simulation must also be judged in relation to factors such as cost, availability, safety, and other considerations of training on the transfer task. For example, relative to practice costs in a VR or flight simulator, the cost of training in an actual jetliner would be staggering, as would the obvious concerns for the safety of people and equipment. Thus, the evaluation of simulation training in an instructional setting can be complicated, because it must take into account a number of important factors in making decisions about its effectiveness.

Simulator Fidelity

Remember that the overall goal of simulation is to facilitate transfer—performance or learning of the transfer task. Scientists who conduct research in this area refer to the quality of the simulation in terms of *fidelity*—the degree to which the simulator mimics or is faithful to the transfer task. Two different types of fidelity constructs are often considered: 1) **Physical fidelity** refers to the degree to which the features of the simulation and transfer tasks themselves are identical, and 2) **psychological fidelity** refers to the degree to which the behaviors and processes produced in the simulator replicate those required by the transfer task. Although these seem like similar constructs, in fact they are quite different and have the potential to result in quite different effects on transfer (e.g., Kozlowski & DeShon, 2004).

Because transfer is expected to increase with task similarity, this idea has naturally led to the notion that physical fidelity should be as high as possible. Aircraft cockpit simulators replicate the cockpit of a real aircraft very closely (although doing so is often very expensive). Another example is CPR mannequins, which are designed to be as anatomically correct as possible for the purpose of training lifesaving skills. Physical fidelity refers to the degree to which the simulator replicates the physical features of the transfer task—possessing as much of the look, sound, and feel of the transfer task as possible.

Psychological fidelity is less concerned with the physical similarity between the simulator and transfer tasks and more concerned with the target skills and behaviors required to perform the transfer task. In the case of CPR mannequins, for example, simulator training might emphasize the perceptual and decision-making processes present in an emergency situation, under high levels of stress, and perhaps under environmental challenges (e.g., extreme heat or cold). Psychological fidelity is concerned with training the skills that will be required of the end user in the transfer task.

Achieving physical and psychological fidelity are complementary, not competing, goals when designing simulation environments (Kozlowski & DeShon, 2004). Still, situations can arise in which too much faith is placed in physical fidelity without enough attention devoted to psychological processes. Returning to our CPR example, some mannequins provide very realistic physical fidelity—the sights, sounds, and proprioceptive feedback that would appear to promote excellent perceptual and motor skill transfer. But just using the mannequin without considering how to structure the practice conditions and how to provide augmented feedback would be a mistake, because the behaviors practiced during training would ultimately be expected to affect transfer to real emergency situations.

These issues of training motor skill behaviors are the major focus of the next two chapters. As we will see, how practice is structured and how feedback is augmented during practice will largely determine the quality of motor learning that results from practice.

VR Fidelity

There is no question that VR's entertainment value and potential transfer effectiveness have captured the imagination of many. One need look no further than Enzo Bonito (see

Focus on Application 9.2) to get excited about the potential successes offered by training in simulated environments.

VR is an immersive technology in which the user moves within a computer-generated environment to perform a task. Sometimes the improvement in performing the VR task represents the ultimate goal, such as in esports. But, for other applications, the VR task serves as a training opportunity to improve skills needed to perform the transfer task.

Virtual reality can be particularly creative for psychological fidelity. Computer-generated situations in which a trainee is performing surgery, for example, can be programmed to produce unexpected events (bleeds, cardiac arrest, etc.) that require decision-making skills and taking appropriate

FOCUS ON Application 9.2

From Esports to Real Sports

On a weekend in late January 2019, the potential for simulation to provide a valuable training ground reached a whole new level. Until that weekend, Enzo Bonito, a 23-year-old with a passion for race car driving, had had very limited experience driving a real race car. Most of his experience had been esports racing—basically sitting in a chair at home racing on a video console (see figure 9.9). The game changer came when Enzo won a real race in a real race car against two professional race car drivers.

FIGURE 9.9 Racing simulator.

Under most circumstances, amateurs are at a severe disadvantage when competing against professional athletes. A top-level amateur would be hard-pressed to return a Novak Djokovic tennis serve or make bat contact with a Shohei Ohtani fastball or

> continued

Application 9.2: From Esports to Real Sports *> continued*

curveball. Tiger Woods once claimed that a good amateur golfer with a 10 handicap would have very little chance of scoring under 100 at a U.S. Open golf tournament. Professional athletes who make a living out of sports are frequently battle-tested, face intense scrutiny by fans (and nonfans), and perform under severe conditions that most amateurs have never experienced. Clearly, the odds were stacked against Enzo.

The critical moments came in a Race of Champions series in Mexico City, in which electric cars were raced around a winding circuit in pursuit style, each race lasting approximately 1 min. To the shock and surprise of many (especially the race play-by-play commentators in videos available online), Enzo beat former F1 driver Lucas di Grassi by about a half second. Later in the weekend, he also beat former Indianapolis 500 winner Ryan Hunter-Reay.

Should we be surprised? Yes, and no. Driving a simulated race car shares many features with driving a real race car, perhaps most importantly the almost identical hand-held units that control direction, braking, and acceleration. So, good transfer might be expected. However, driving a race car produces inherent feedback information, such as visual cues and haptic feedback, that is impossible to simulate precisely.

In many respects, Enzo's success was a complete surprise. Of no surprise to anyone, however, is that the result provided a boost of confidence not only to esports participants but also to those who consider simulation an indispensable training tool.

actions. Though VR technology has created some very impressive replicas of real environments, they often lack inherent sources of feedback from hands-on tools that other simulators provide (e.g., surgical simulation environments), resulting in movement characteristics that are unlike the performance of real skills (Harris et al., 2019).

The emergence of **mixed-reality** environments merges the technological advantages of both VR and simulators. These mixed reality devices combine the computer-generated context of the transfer task (e.g., an operating room) with the tools (e.g., laparoscopic instruments) and target task (e.g., removing and suturing within the body cavity). Often, the result is a virtual environment with high psychological and physical fidelity, in which procedural and motor skills are acquired with real-time augmented and inherent feedback. Though these mixed reality systems will only improve in the years ahead, the skills learned in many mixed reality training environments have already been shown to transfer well to the performance of the transfer task (e.g., Alaker et al., 2016; Levac et al., 2019; Savir et al., 2023).

Summary

Motor learning is a fundamental necessity that we often take for granted, yet it is required for just about every facet of our daily existence. Practice is the single most important factor leading to motor learning, although confusion exists regarding how it should be undertaken. Learning results in improvement of all the information-processing elements that comprise the conceptual model developed in the previous chapters.

Periods of no practice are a fact of life, and the retention of learned skills after a lengthy time away from them represents a critical area of research. Retention of skills is affected greatly by their classification; continuous skills are generally retained much more completely and for longer periods of time than discrete skills. Warm-up decrement refers to a specific type of retention deficit due to the loss of an activity set. Being able to perform a learned activity in a new situation concerns the issue of skill transfer. Simulators of various kinds can efficiently mimic important elements of a skill when practicing the actual skill would be too costly, dangerous, or impractical.

HK*PROPEL* ACTIVITIES

HK*Propel* offers these activities to help you build and apply your knowledge of the concepts in this chapter. Additionally, you'll find a key terms flash-card review activity and a key terms quiz, along with audio supplements for selected figures, as indicated by QR codes throughout the chapter.

Interactive Learning

Activity 9.1: Distinguish the goals of practice and test sessions by indicating whether each in a series of statements applies to practice or testing.

Activity 9.2: Review the terminology of skill acquisition, retention, and transfer through a matching exercise.

Activity 9.3: Listen to a podcast discussing specificity of learning in sport, then consider how you might create specificity in the environment and in cognitive processes during practice.

Activity 9.4: Test your understanding of characteristics of skilled performers in comparison to novices.

Principles-to-Application Exercise

Activity 9.5: The principles-to-application exercise for this chapter prompts you to choose a movement skill, identify the goal of practice for this skill, and explore additional ways that practice might affect performance of this skill.

Motor Control in Everyday Actions Narratives

Wayne Gretzky

Like Riding a Bicycle

The Keypad

Sport Snake Oils

Check Your Understanding

1. Distinguish between performance and learning during practice. How can they have conflicting goals, and how might this be overcome?

Apply Your Knowledge

1. List four benefits of practice discussed in this chapter and provide an example of how each might be illustrated by a karate student and a truck driver.
2. Your neighbor tells you that he will be learning to lead climb at a local rock-climbing gym. He says that lead climbing can be difficult because there are many parts to placing the safety gear properly while climbing, and the decisions made can influence the next movement. From what he tells you about the lessons, it seems the instructor will use part practice. Why might the instructor have chosen this method? What alternatives would the instructor likely have considered, and why were these not chosen?

10

Organizing and Scheduling Practice

How the Structure of Practice Influences Learning

CHAPTER OUTLINE

Distribution of Practice
Variability in Practice
Motivation for Learning
Observational Learning and Mental Practice
Summary

CHAPTER OBJECTIVES

Chapter 10 describes the influence of how practice is structured and the various conditions under which practice is conducted. This chapter will help you understand

- basic concepts regarding the nature of practice,
- practice schedule organizations and their effect on performance and learning,
- the role of practice variability in motor learning, and
- the influence on learning of nonphysical factors, such as motivation, observation, and mental practice.

CHAPTER PREVIEW QUIZ

1. What does practice *distribution* refer to?
2. Which is a better practice order for learning: drill-type practice or random interleaving?
3. How might motor learning occur without any movement at all?

Imagine that you are in charge of designing a plan for teaching skills to a group of learners. They may be prospective chiropractors learning different manipulation techniques, a high school woodworking class learning to use different tools, or perhaps a physical education class learning a set of tumbling exercises.

Or maybe there is no teacher involved, and you, the learner, are wondering how best to structure your music practice. How would you organize your time? How would you intersperse physical practice with periods of rest? In what order would you practice various skills, how much variation in skills would you introduce into your practice, and how much practice would you allow on one task variation before moving to the next? The answers to questions like these determine, to a very large degree, the effectiveness of practice on learning. This chapter presents the principles that help you solve these problems concerning how to maximize practice quality.

In motor learning experiments, many features of practice settings can be varied systematically, and these factors have been found to make practice more or less effective. Of course, being armed with principles of learning will facilitate such decisions, equipping you to make wise choices about structuring practice to produce the most effective outcomes—usually the maximization of learning. In this chapter, we describe some of the most important factors that researchers have investigated regarding maximizing the retention and transfer of the capabilities improved as a result of practice.

Distribution of Practice

Scheduling practice is a major concern in designing any training program. For example, the schedule must consider how many days per week skills should be practiced, whether to provide layoff days, how much to practice on each day, and how much rest to provide during the practice period on each day so fatigue does not become a problem. These questions have been studied in the laboratory and in applied settings, revealing interesting and useful implications for skill learning.

Two general terms have been used in the literature to define practice distribution: massed (or concentrated) practice and distributed (or spaced) practice. Be aware that these terms do not have a simple definition because they are determined relative to the overall duration for which the skills are practiced. Many studies in the early research on distribution of practice conducted all the practice trials within a single session. In these studies, **massed practice** was defined as providing very little rest between trials. For example, if the study provided practice trials that lasted 30 s, a massed-practice schedule might call for rest periods of only 5 s between trials, or perhaps no rest at all between trials. Conversely, a **distributed practice** schedule might have much longer between-trial rests, perhaps as long as the trial itself (30 s in this example), or even longer in some experiments (a study by Ammons [1950], for example, included a condition where only one trial was conducted per day with a 24 h rest period between trials).

Other studies have defined practice distribution relative to longer time scales. For example, suppose a trainee was provided with four training sessions each lasting three hours. A massed practice might have all four sessions conducted on a single weekend (i.e., across two days), while a distributed practice group might have the four sessions spread across four consecutive weekends (i.e., across 22 days). Therefore, the terms *massed* and *distributed* refer, in general, to practice that is either compressed or spaced in time relative to the overall duration of training.

Distributing Practice Sessions

One of the first scheduling decisions concerns how long the learners will practice in a session and for how many sessions. Since a major goal is usually to facilitate maximal learning in a real situation, most training schedules provide a limited period of time in which certain skills are practiced (e.g., a fixed number of weeks).

One frequent solution to the problem is to organize practice into as concentrated a schedule as possible to maximize the time spent improving the skills. However, as shown by Baddeley and Longman (1978) with keyboard skills, there is likely some upper limit to the amount of practice time per day that will be effective for learning. In their study, postal workers were trained for 60 to 80 h of practice time. The practice was varied in terms of the amount of practice time per session (1 or 2 h) and the number of sessions per day (once or twice per day). Among the three groups that received a total of 80 h of training, one group completed the training in 20 days (with two, 2-h sessions per day), and two groups completed the training in 40 days (distributed either as two, 1-h sessions per day or one, 2-h session per day). A fourth group received 60 h of training in 60 days (one, 1-h session per day).

The data in figure 10.1 show the results for the last part of the training period for all four groups, plus the results for three retention tests conducted months later. (Note that one peculiarity of this study was that the group having the most distributed practice [1 h once per day] received 20 h less total practice time than the other three groups.)

A consistent finding in figure 10.1 throughout practice and in retention was the relatively poor performance of the most concentrated practice group—the individuals who practiced for 4 h a day (2 h sessions twice per day, purple trace) over just 20 days. Distributing

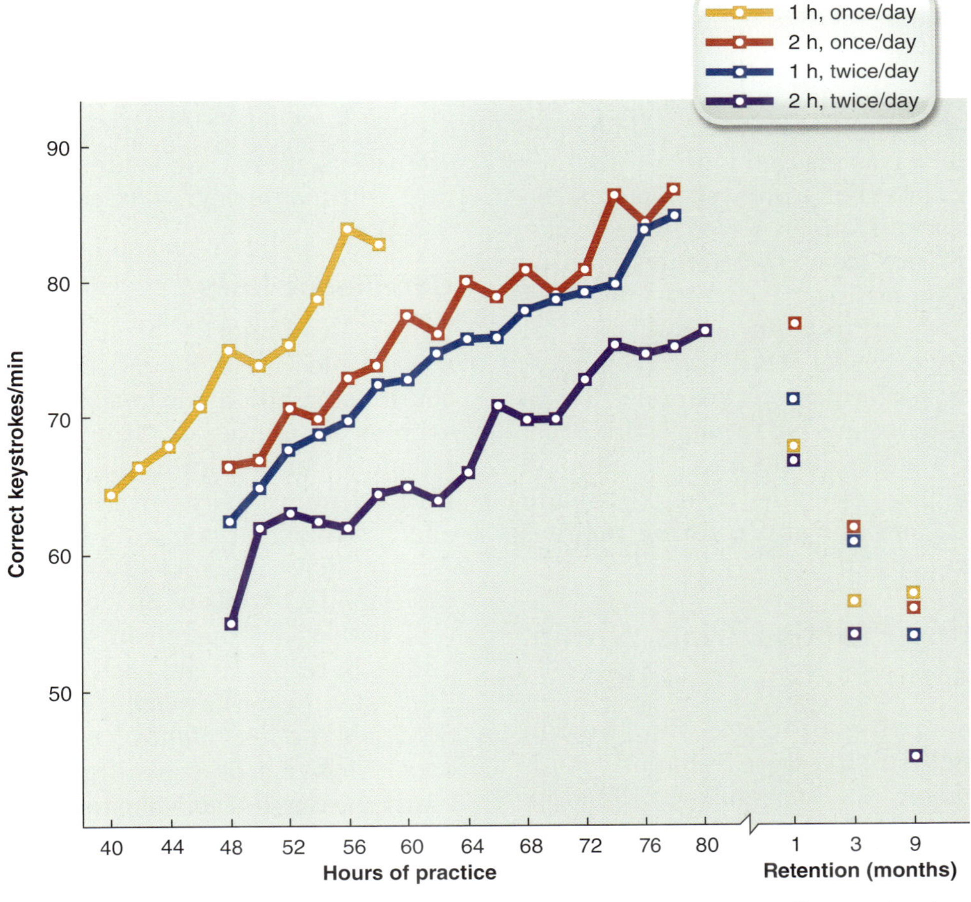

FIGURE 10.1 Retraining postal workers on keyboard tasks under different distribution-of-practice conditions. Four groups of learners practiced for either one or two sessions per day, for 1 or 2 h per session. The group performing in the most concentrated schedule (2h twice per day) generally performed the poorest throughout practice and in retention.

practice over longer periods (40 or 60 days) produced superior performance over the practice periods and in all the retention tests.

But one other interesting finding in the Baddeley and Longman (1978) study must also be noted. The practice schedule that produced the poorest performance during practice as well as the least learning (2 h twice per day, purple trace) was voted as the most popular practice condition among the trainees. This finding illustrates an important consideration: Learners do not always know which procedures work most effectively in terms of retention of learning. We will see more evidence of this poor understanding of the learning process later in this chapter.

Another practice distribution study confirms the importance of spacing practice across longer time periods. Laparoscopic surgery skills are often practiced in a single day using box simulators or mixed VR (see chapter 9). Spruit and colleagues (2015) compared the training of several laparoscopic tasks across three 75 min sessions. For one group, practice was massed with all sessions on one day. The other group received spaced practice—sessions spread across three weeks. The results were clear: Distributed training resulted in superior performance measures at the end of training, in a retention test conducted two weeks later, and in another retention test performed one year later. These and other studies have led to suggestions that distributed practice be adopted in surgical training (Cecilio-Fernandes et al., 2018) and in many educational and training regimes (Brown et al., 2014).

Distributing Practice Trials Within a Session

Issues concerning practice distribution during a single session were frequently studied in the laboratory, especially in the early years of the research. Researchers interested in massed and distributed practice were concerned with the effects of physical and mental fatigue-like states on learning effectiveness (see Lee & Genovese, 1988, for a review). For a given number of practice trials, decreasing the amount of rest between trials reduced the time available for dissipation of both mental and physical fatigue, degrading performance on the next practice trial and perhaps interfering with learning. Many experimenters used a fixed number of practice trials in an acquisition session, varied the amount of rest between these trials, and then measured learning in a retention test. These work and rest schedules have different effects on performance and learning for discrete and continuous tasks.

Discrete Tasks

Only a few distribution-of-practice experiments have used discrete tasks. Generally, when the task involves performance trials that are only a few tenths of a second, as in a throw or a kick, it is very difficult to make the rest periods short enough to affect performance. In the laboratory, with rest periods as short as 300 ms, seemingly far shorter than for any real-world practice session, the result has been no decrement in performance (see Carron, 1967; Lee & Genovese, 1989). For discrete tasks, there is no evidence that reducing the rest time through massed practice affects learning.

Continuous Tasks

By far, the majority of studies comparing massed and distributed practice have involved continuous skills analogous to real-world tasks such as swimming or typing. In these tasks, fatigue states can build up within a trial, so varying the rest between trials has very large effects. An example is a study by Bourne and Archer (1956), in which groups of participants performed 21 trials of 30 s on a pursuit-rotor task, with each group given either 0, 15, 30, 45, or 60 s of rest between each trial. Figure 10.2 illustrates the performance results in the practice trials and in a retention test. Three general conclusions can be drawn from this figure and typify the results seen generally with distribution-of-practice experiments using continuous tasks (Lee & Genovese, 1988):

1. Longer rest periods lead to better performance during practice (i.e., distributing practice has a positive effect on performance).

2. The positive effect of longer rest intervals on performance remains large in a retention test (i.e., distributing practice has a positive effect on learning).
3. The size of the differences between distribution groups is reduced (but not eliminated) after a retention interval (i.e., the magnitude of the learning effect is generally smaller than the magnitude of the performance effect).

Costs and Benefits of Practice Distribution

The effects of lengthy rest periods between trials within a session or by distributing sessions over days have considerable importance when viewed from the standpoint of practice effectiveness versus practice efficiency. Clearly, longer rest periods have positive effects on both performance and learning. However, these effects come with a cost, because essentially, the rest periods represent "lost time." In economic terms, the cost of introducing rest periods into a training application (e.g., in an airplane cockpit simulator) might outweigh the benefits to learning.

Fortunately, there are alternatives to resting that can make the time between physical practice trials more effective *and* efficient from a learning standpoint. We will return to this issue later in the chapter. For now, think about what other activities could be undertaken instead of resting and what effect the performance of these other activities would have on performance and learning.

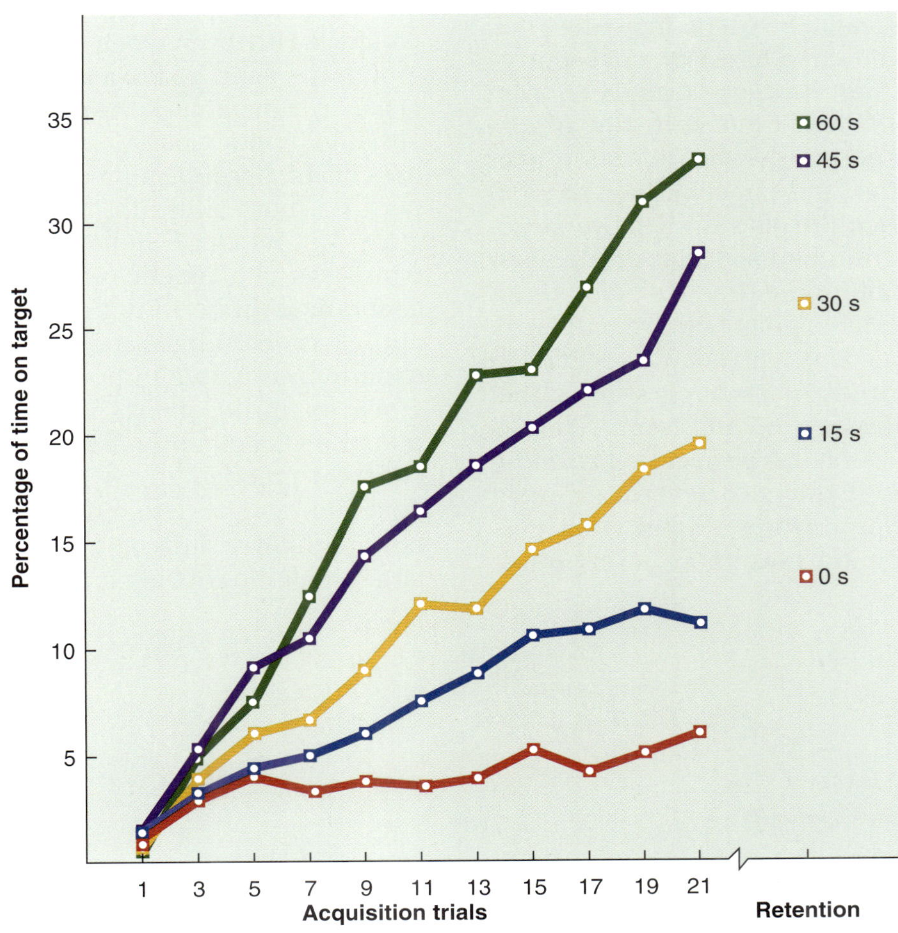

FIGURE 10.2 Examining the effects of rest intervals of differing length, inserted between 30 s periods of practice on a pursuit-rotor task. Graph labels (0 s, 15 s, etc.) refer to rest periods between acquisition trials given to different groups of participants. Longer rest periods resulted in better performance during practice and in a retention test.

Variability in Practice

One of the most important practice scheduling areas of research to emerge in motor learning concerns the organization of variability in practice. Consider the practice of chipping to a target in golf. Suppose the learner strikes, for example, 80 balls in the chipping portion of a practice session. How should practice be structured? Should all 80 chips be struck from the same location, toward the same target (termed **constant practice**)? Or should 20 shots each be directed to, for example, four different locations and distances (termed **variable practice**)? If one chooses variable practice, should the variability be ordered with 20 shots directed at target A, then 20 at target B, and so on. (termed *blocked* variable practice)? Or should the practice at the four targets be interleaved, with no more than one shot taken at the same target on consecutive attempts? Further, if interleaving is chosen, should it be unstructured with the simple provision that no two consecutive shots ever be directed at the same target (termed *random* variable practice), or should a more structured organization be used that creates systematic variation to the practice (sometimes called *serial* variable practice)? We will break down these questions with answers generated from the hundreds of research studies that have been published on the topic. Though this area of research has been called *variability in practice*, it refers to several different concepts and procedures. Figure 10.3 may help to understand how these terms relate to each other.

Constant Versus Variable Practice

Evidence suggests that variable practice can be effective for learning in many situations. A basic research paradigm contrasts at least two groups of learners: One is a constant-practice (nonvariable) group that performs acquisition trials on only a single variation of a skill; the other is a variable-practice group that has acquisition trials on several (usually three or more) variations of a skill. The two groups have the same amount of practice (i.e., the same number of total practice attempts) and differ only in the amount of variability involved.

The constant group usually outperforms the variable group during the practice trials of an acquisition phase. Typically, a learner can produce repeated instances of a single version of a movement more effectively than multiple versions. However, when participants in both groups are switched to a novel version of the task in a transfer test, the group that received variable practice performs at least as well as the constant group, and in many studies they perform more skillfully (e.g., Kerr & Booth, 1978; McCracken & Stelmach, 1977). In other words, variable practice enhances transfer (or generalizability), allowing the performer to apply past learning to actions not specifically experienced before in practice.

An example of this research was published by Catalano and Kleiner (1984). The constant-practice group practiced a coincident-timing task (coinciding the arrival of a moving light with a hand movement) using target velocities of only one speed (subgroups

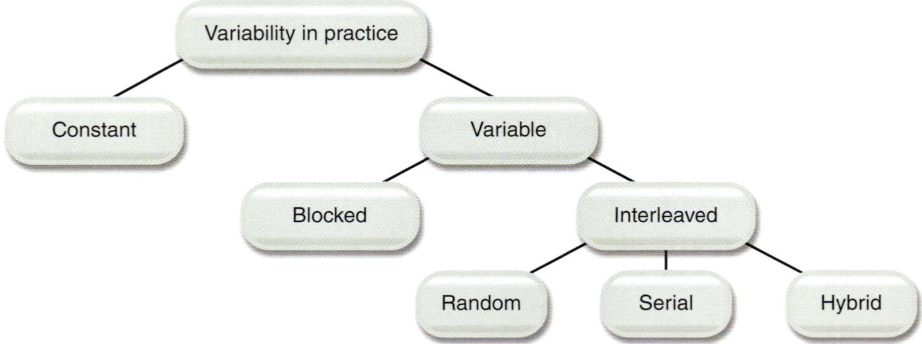

FIGURE 10.3 Different terms used to describe variability in practice.

of constant practice at either 5, 7, 9, *or* 11 mph). The variable-practice group received the same number of total acquisition trials but spread across all speeds (5, 7, 9, *and* 11 mph). Transfer tests were then given on task versions that were not experienced previously by either group (1, 3, 13, *and* 15 mph). Figure 10.4 illustrates that in three of the four transfer velocity tests, variable practice led to much smaller timing errors than constant practice; hence, variable practice produced generalization. Many skills require us to produce variations that have never been produced before, and variable practice is one means of maximizing the capability to move effectively in this way.

But there are two additional issues to mention regarding this research. One concerns generalization. Suppose, for example, that the goal of practice is not generalization of the skill but rather to perform the skill exactly as practiced. An example of this is the game of horseshoe pitching, in which the distance to the stake is always 40 ft (12.2 m). Another example is the basketball free throw, in which a specialized skill (the set shot) is practiced and performed almost exclusively from the same location on the court. The result of this

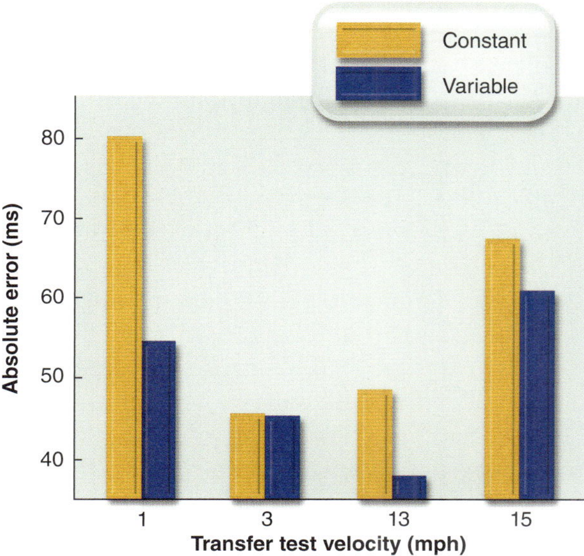

FIGURE 10.4 Mean absolute timing errors at four coincident-timing transfer target speeds following practice in either a constant (yellow) or variable (blue) practice condition.

specialized practice is what has been called an **especial skill**—a skill that is especially effective for that location on the court. Focus on Research 10.1 describes this effect in more detail.

The other concern regarding variability-in-practice research is an important methodological issue. In their review of the research, Lee and colleagues (1985) discovered that studies with variable practice structured in an interleaved order generally found beneficial transfer effects (i.e., variable practice outperforming constant practice). However, variable practice performed in a blocked order had little advantage over constant practice. Was this discovery more than simply a methodological quirk in the research? Apparently not, considering the results of a landmark study by Shea and Morgan (1979), discussed in the next sections.

Blocked Versus Random Practice

In many, if not most, real-world settings, the learner's goal is to acquire multiple skills in a limited practice period, sometimes even in a single practice period. For example, physicians practice different skills related to surgery (such as suturing and knot-tying skills), musicians practice multiple songs in rehearsal, tennis players practice serving and various ground strokes during a single session, and so on. An important question confronting the learner or instructor is how to sequence the practice of these various tasks during the practice session to maximize learning. Two variations have powerful effects on performance and learning: **blocked practice** (sometimes called *drilled* or *repetitive* practice) and **interleaved practice** (sometimes undertaken randomly or in some other nonblocked format). Their effects on learning have been termed the **contextual-interference** effect (Battig, 1979).

Suppose that your student has three tasks to learn in a practice session (tasks A, B, and C). A commonsense method of scheduling such tasks would be to practice all trials of one task before shifting to the second, then to finish practice on the second before switching

FOCUS ON **Research 10.1**

Especial Skills: An Exception to Variable Practice?

The research literature suggests using variable practice when faced with learning that needs to be generalizable. But how would practice be structured best if only one variation of the **criterion task** would ever be performed?

This question was addressed in a series of experiments involving skilled basketball players (Keetch et al., 2005, 2008), skilled archers (Nabavinik et al., 2018), and skilled baseball pitchers (Simons et al., 2009). For example, in basketball, there are shots in which the player's feet leave the ground (jump shots) and shots in which the player does not jump (set shots). Jump shots are taken anywhere on the court and are used in most game situations; set shots are typically taken only at the foul (or free-throw) line.

Keetch and colleagues (2005) predicted that if variable (jump-shot) practice results in the development of a generalizable skill, then performance at one location should be highly related to performance at all other locations, including shots at the free-throw line. In contrast, constant practice of the set shot, practiced only at the free-throw line, might result in a specific advantage for performance at just that one location. Moreover, this prediction should be particularly strong for highly experienced players who have taken thousands of set-shot practice shots in the development of their expertise.

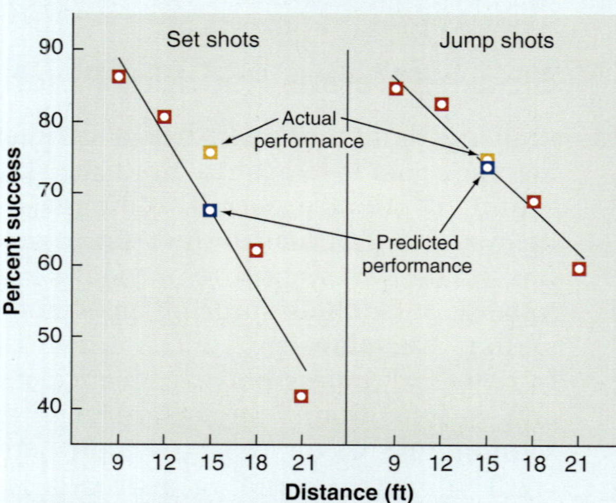

FIGURE 10.5 Performance of set and jump shots from five different locations. The blue data points represent the predicted performances for the set and jump shots at the free throw line (15 ft) based on linear regression analyses from the four other locations. The yellow data points represent the actual performance scores. Set-shot performance shows an advantage at the free throw line (yellow data point much higher than predicted), whereas no specific advantage is seen for jump shots at the free throw line (yellow and blue data points overlap).

Figure 10.5 presents data from college basketball players shooting set shots and jump shots from five locations perpendicular to the basket (including one from 15 ft —the free throw line). Performance at locations closer to (9 ft and 12 ft) and further from the free throw line (18 ft and 21 ft) was used to predict performance at the free throw line (15 ft). As you can see in figure 10.5, jump-shot accuracy was almost exactly as predicted when taken at the free throw line (compare the yellow [actual] and blue [predicted] data points). In contrast, set-shot performance at the free low line was much more accurate than predicted.

These findings have some interesting implications for learning, because they seem to suggest structuring practice according to the criterion demands of the task—how the skills will be performed in the test situation. If generalization is the goal, then it makes sense to use variable practice. However, if only one version of the task will ever be performed, then concentrating practice from just that one location appears to have practical merit (Breslin et al., 2012).

Exploring Further

1. Name another skill usually performed from only one location that might show an effect similar to the set shot in basketball.
2. The Keetch and colleagues (2005) study used college-level players as research participants. What results would you expect for professional basketball players and for high-school players?

to the third. This is called *blocked* practice, in which all the trials of a given task (for that day) are completed before moving on to the next task. Blocked practice is typical of some drills in which a skill is repeated over and over with minimal interruption by other activities. This kind of practice seems to make sense because it concentrates practice on one task at a time, allowing the learner to refine and correct it with no interference from the practice of the other tasks. Unfortunately (in our opinion), a blocked schedule has been and continues to be the dominant practice strategy used in skills training across many disciplines.

An alternative practice scheduling variation is called *interleaved* practice, where frequent switches occur in the order of tasks practiced—the tasks are randomly or systematically interleaved across the practice period. Learners switch practice attempts among the three tasks so that, in the more extreme cases, they never (or rarely) practice the same task on two consecutive attempts. From a commonsense perspective, the random method, with its high level of trial-to-trial variability and its high level of interference between tasks, might seem to be disruptive to the learning process. At least, that is what many believed until the publication of an experiment that has had enormous impact on our understanding of motor learning (see Focus on Research 10.2).

The Shea and Morgan Experiment

John Shea and Robyn Morgan (1979) conducted a groundbreaking experiment that revolutionized the way researchers think about practice. Building on some ideas of William Battig (1966, 1979), Shea and Morgan had participants practice three different tasks (A, B, and C) that involved responding to a stimulus light with a series of rapid arm movements. Each task paired a specific-colored light with a different movement sequence. One group of participants practiced the three tasks in a blocked order, completing all trials of task A before moving to task B trials, which they completed before completing all the trials of task C. A second group practiced in a random order; no more than two consecutive trials could occur for any one task. A key point to remember is that the two groups had exactly the same amount of practice on each task and the same amount of total practice—the two groups differed only in the order in which they practiced the tasks.

Figure 10.6 presents the results. Lower times illustrate better performance because the goal was to respond to the stimulus and complete the movements as quickly as possible. During acquisition, notice that the blocked order was far more effective for performance (with shorter times) than the random order. But recall also from chapter 8 that differences during acquisition cannot

FOCUS ON Research 10.2

Impact of Shea and Morgan (1979)

The impact of Shea and Morgan's (1979) findings on research and application has been monumental. Hundreds of studies have been conducted on blocked and interleaved practice effects since their research was published. Researchers have studied these effects not only using laboratory motor skills but also using sport and occupational motor skills, perceptual skills, various cognitive skills, and in educational settings. Many reviews of this work have been published, focusing on behavioral findings in motor skills (e.g., Lee, 2012), neural correlates (e.g., Lage et al., 2015; Wright & Kim, 2019), and cognition and education (e.g., Bjork & Bjork, 2019; Firth et al., 2021).

The research has also influenced how researchers, instructors, and educators view the broader picture of the distinction between performance and learning. The surprising impact of how augmented feedback is provided (Salmoni et al., 1984; see chapter 11) might not have been discovered had the Shea and Morgan findings not shifted the authors' opinion about how to view the role of errors in practice. The very influential concept of *desirable difficulties* in training cognitive operations can be largely attributed to the lasting impact of Shea and Morgan's research (Bjork & Bjork, 2020). Importantly, the research findings have now influenced recommendations about how to conduct practice in a vast array of everyday activities, such as music practice (Carter, 2020), studying (Carpenter et al., 2022; Samani & Pan, 2021), and practicing various sport skills (e.g., Lee & Schmidt, 2014; Williams & Hodges, 2023).

be interpreted as differences in learning; rather, delayed retention (or transfer) tests are needed to evaluate learning.

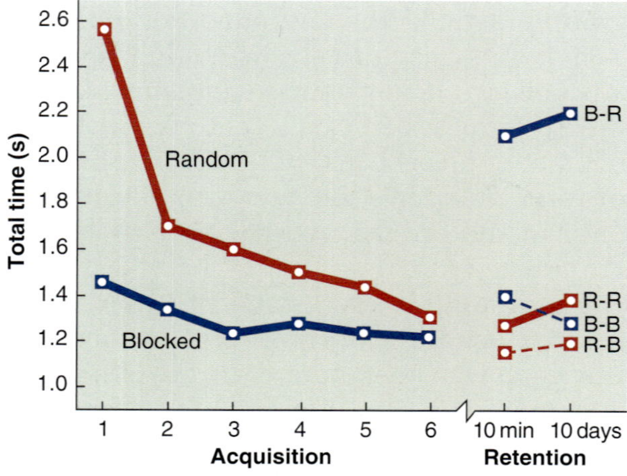

FIGURE 10.6 Performance under random- and blocked-practice orders during acquisition, and in random-ordered and blocked-ordered retention tests.

Shea and Morgan tested for learning by conducting retention tests after 10 min and 10 days; these tests were conducted under either random or blocked orders, which produced four subgroups. The following abbreviations indicate the order in acquisition and the order in retention, respectively: R-B, R-R, B-R, and B-B. For example, R-B denotes **random practice** during acquisition and a blocked order of retention trials.

The retention results are a bit complicated, so let's break them down. When the retention tests were performed in a random order, the group that had random practice in acquisition (R-R, solid red line) greatly outperformed the group that had blocked practice in acquisition (B-R, solid blue line). When the retention tests were performed in a blocked order, again, the random condition in acquisition (R-B, dotted red line) outperformed the group that had blocked practice in acquisition (B-B, dotted blue line).

Note that the difference for the blocked order retention test was smaller than for the randomly ordered retention test. In sum, the random conditions in acquisition produced more effective retention (learning), although the magnitude of this benefit was dependent on the trial order of the retention test.

Variability-in-Practice Research Reconsidered

Earlier, we alluded to an issue about variable-practice research concerning how variable practice is scheduled. Considering the Shea and Morgan (1979) results, the issue now becomes clear. Studies that scheduled variable practice in a trial-by-trial random order tended to show large advantages compared to constant practice (e.g., Catalano & Kleiner, 1984; Pigott & Shapiro, 1984). When variable practice was performed in a blocked order, the advantage, compared to constant practice, was eliminated or greatly reduced (Lee et al., 1985). Though variable practice is considered important for learning, the Shea and Morgan findings suggest that scheduling *how* variable practice is ordered greatly determines its effectiveness.

Visit HK*Propel* to read "But I Was Great on the Practice Range" and complete the self-directed learning activities.

Why Random Practice Is So Effective

The Shea and Morgan (1979) findings surprised many researchers by showing that random practice produced better learning even though performance in acquisition was much poorer than blocked practice. The findings were a large surprise because most theoretical and practical viewpoints suggested that conditions that make learners most proficient *during* practice should maximize learning. At the time, there was no motor learning theory that could explain this opposite result (keep this idea in mind as you read chapter 12). As a result, some interesting new hypotheses were offered to explain the findings.

Shea and Morgan (1979; Shea & Zimny, 1983) suggested that changing the task on every random-practice trial made the tasks more distinct from each other and more meaningful, resulting in more elaborate memory representations. As revealed in participant interviews after the experiment, random-practice participants tended to relate the tasks being practiced to concepts already in memory (creating meaningfulness), such as discovering that the arm movement pattern for task B essentially had the shape of an upside-down Z. Also, they made distinctions between tasks, such as "Task A is essentially like task C, except that the first part is reversed" (creating distinctiveness). The blocked-practice participants, on the other hand, tended not to make such statements. Instead, they talked of running off the performances more or less automatically, without thinking much about the movements or how the tasks related to each other. Blocked practice did not induce the kind of comparative and contrastive efforts in practice that were experienced during random practice. According to this **elaboration hypothesis**, increased meaningfulness and distinctiveness produced more durable memories for the tasks and thus increased performance capabilities in tests of retention and transfer.

An alternative hypothesis explained the beneficial effects of random practice somewhat differently. Lee and Magill (1983) suggested that switching from one task to another (e.g., from A to B) requires that a new movement plan be generated to perform the new task (B). Doing so causes the movement plan for the previous task (A) to be forgotten. When task A is encountered again a few trials later, the learner must generate the movement plan again, which is effortful, attention-demanding and error prone, resulting in poorer performance compared to blocked practice (Monsell, 2003). However, this plan-generating process is beneficial for learning. In blocked practice, on the other hand, the performer remembers the plan generated on a given trial and simply applies it to the next trial, which minimizes the frequency and effort that the learner must use to generate new plans. Learning is poor because the learner is not required to generate a new plan for the task on every trial. In this way, the key focus of the **forgetting hypothesis** is the repeated generation, forgetting, and regeneration of movement plans during practice. This hypothesis promotes a somewhat counterintuitive idea that forgetting benefits learning (Cuddy & Jacoby, 1982).

Research studies have provided support for both hypotheses. For example, in a study by Wright (1991), members of a blocked-practice group were encouraged to make explicit verbal comparisons of the task currently practiced with one of the other tasks to be learned—essentially inducing this group to mentally practice the tasks with meaningful and distinctive processing, even though the tasks were physically practiced in a blocked order. This special blocked-practice group outperformed the other practice groups that had a similar intervention but without the benefits of explicit comparative and contrastive processing. The results supported the elaboration hypothesis because of the benefit gained by inserting these specific elaborative and distinctive processing activities into blocked practice.

A key prediction of the forgetting hypothesis was that random practice forces more extensive planning operations on each trial compared to blocked practice. A study by Lee and colleagues (1997) attempted to reduce or eliminate the need for these planning operations during random practice by presenting a powerful model just before each practice trial. This model provided extremely strong guidance for the upcoming trial, essentially preventing or blocking the learner from undertaking the planning process. In the experiment, the presence of the model combined with random practice was compared with blocked and random practice as normally conducted.

The model had an extremely potent effect on performance during acquisition (when the model was present), as seen on the left side of figure 10.7. In fact, the random + model group's performance was not only far better than the group that had normal random practice, but it was also equal to

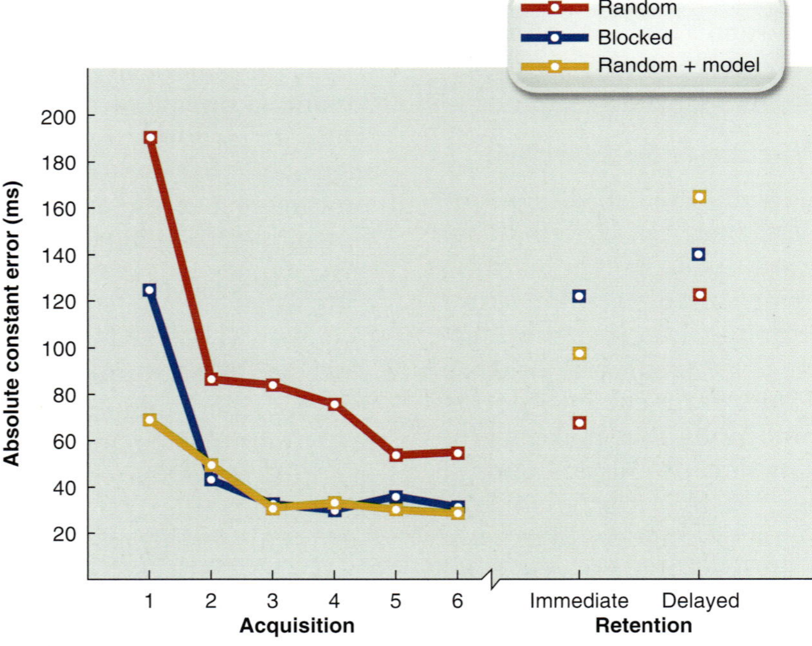

FIGURE 10.7 Providing a powerful guiding model eliminated both the detrimental acquisition performance effects and the learning benefits of random practice.

the performance of the blocked group. However, in the retention tests, when the model was withdrawn, the random + model group regressed considerably, to the point that this condition led to the most error in the delayed retention test. Providing the powerful model before each practice trial, while beneficial for performance when it was present, was disastrous for learning. The model obliterated the beneficial advantages of random practice by preventing the planning process that would normally occur. These findings not only support the forgetting hypothesis but also show that simply conducting physical practice in a random order is not a "magic bullet" for effective motor learning—the underlying cognitive activities that accompany random practice to boost learning must be performed as well.

A number of studies have provided evidence supporting the elaboration hypothesis, and a number have supported the forgetting hypothesis. As a result, it is perhaps best to consider these hypotheses as complementary rather than competing explanations of contextual-interference effects. Other explanations have been provided as well (e.g., Broadbent et al., 2017; Schöllhorn, 2016; Wright et al., 2016), and as more research emerges, these important theoretical debates should become clearer.

Random Practice Versus Other Interleaved Orders

We have seen that for variable practice to be effective, it should be interleaved. But must interleaving be random? Or can other interleaving orders be as effective or even better?

Random Versus Serial Practice

One potentially important factor in random practice is its disarray—the practice order is unpredictable other than the learner know-

This walking garden allows rehabilitation patients to practice walking with crutches over many surfaces, allowing for variable and random practice.

ing not to expect multiple repeated trials on the same task. Would a more predictable order, one that is more structured but still nonblocked, be as effective as or even more effective than random practice?

Lee and Magill (1983) assessed this idea, replicating the Shea and Morgan (1979) task using what they termed a *serial* practice order. A **serial practice** order (ABCABCABC. . .) is nonblocked, like random practice (ACBABCBCA. . .), yet perfectly predictable, like blocked practice (AAA. . .BBB. . .CCC). Their findings, illustrated in figure 10.8, revealed that serial practice had the same effect as random practice—both serial and random groups' performance was worse than blocked practice in the acquisition trials but better in retention. Subsequent studies (Lage et al., 2022) have found similar results.

Hybrid Schedules

Blocked and interleaved practice orders represent extreme ends of the practice schedule continuum—interleaved practice involves very little (or no) repetition of the same task from one practice trial to the next, and blocked practice involves almost no interleaving of practice on other tasks. These scheduling extremes might be responsible for the rather dramatic contrast seen, especially during acquisition, when interleaving greatly reduces performance compared with blocked practice. Thus, one reason for seeking an alternative schedule concerns the fact that neither interleaved nor blocked practice optimizes both performance and learning.

There is another important reason for seeking an alternative schedule to either blocking or interleaving—the learners' perception of their own learning progress. Simon and Bjork (2001, 2002) asked their participants to make predictions about the success of their practice schedule just before a retention test. The results, presented in figure 10.9, revealed that participants in both blocked and interleaved groups had obtained rather stark false impressions about the efficacy of their practice condition. When asked to predict how they would do in a retention test, blocked practice had fooled the participants into thinking that they had learned much *more* than they really had. In contrast, random practice had led the participants to believe that they had learned *less* than they really had. Thus, another reason to seek an alternative to blocked and interleaved practice would be to give learners (and their instructors) a more realistic understanding of how their learning is progressing. Various forms of hybrid schedules seem to satisfy that goal.

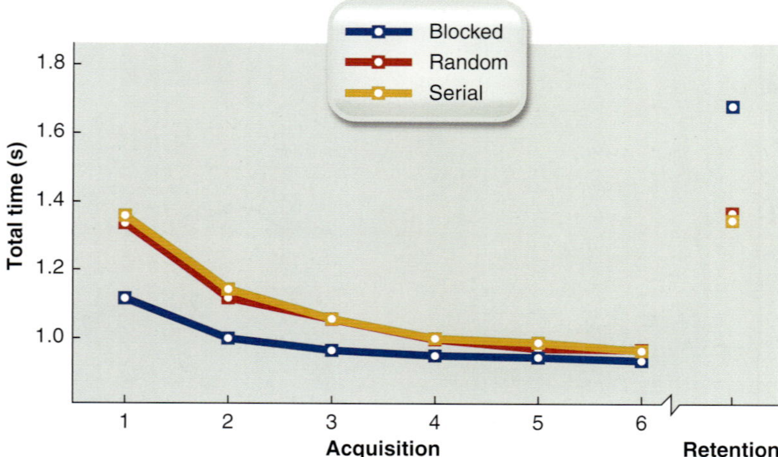

FIGURE 10.8 Serial practice produced similar performance and retention effects as random practice (from data presented in Experiment 2).

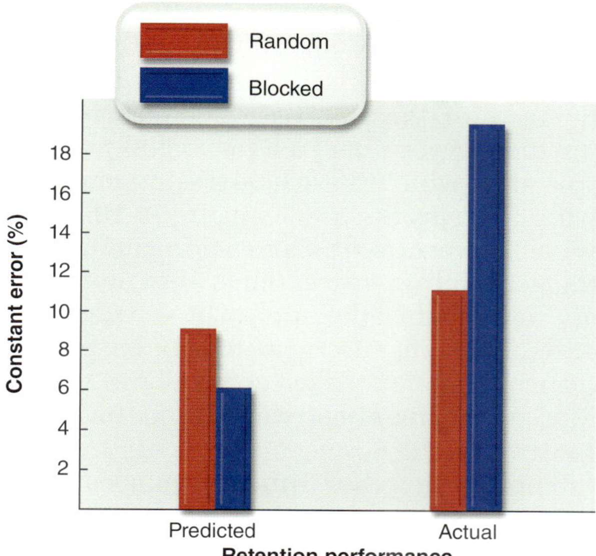

FIGURE 10.9 At the end of acquisition practice, all individuals were asked to predict how they would perform in a retention test. Those who had practiced in a blocked order (blue bar on the left side of the figure) predicted that they would perform very well in retention. Those who practiced in a random order (red bar) thought they would perform more poorly. In actual retention performance, the blocked group (blue bar on the right side of the figure) performed very poorly and much less skillfully than the random group (red bar).

Interleaved Blocks Some researchers have found that moderate amounts of interleaving are beneficial for performance *and* learning, with the practice schedule including interleaved short strings of blocked practice. For example, in a study by Landin and Hebert (1997), novices practiced a basketball shooting task from different locations on the court in either a blocked order, a quasi-random order, or a hybrid order in which practice rotated from task to task after performing mini blocks of three attempts from the same distance. This hybrid practice format was successful in reducing the performance deficit normally seen during purely random practice and facilitating learning as measured in both blocked- and random-ordered retention tests (see Pigott & Shapiro, 1984; Porter & Magill, 2010).

Practice Contingencies Although interleaving blocks of practice might appear to represent a good compromise for lessening the detrimental effects on acquisition performance while retaining the learning benefit, one disadvantage is that it is not sensitive to individual differences. Three blocked trials at a time might be optimal for one person, for example. But five blocked trials, or no task repetitions at all, might be better for another person.

A type of schedule more sensitive to individual differences is a **contingency schedule**, whereby the decision to repeat the same task or switch to an easier or more difficult task depends on the individual's performance success (Choi et al., 2008; Simon et al., 2008). For example, if someone is having considerable difficulty performing a task, an instructor might consider some blocked repetitions until the difficulties are overcome. The obvious problem with this approach, however, is that performance change (or lack of change) does not necessarily reflect learning (as discussed in chapter 8). Approaches to better understand these contingencies and their effects on performance versus learning represent an intriguing theoretical challenge for researchers, as well as an exciting new practical approach to practice scheduling.

Motivation for Learning

At this point in the chapter, we significantly shift focus. Until now, we have discussed how factors related to the organization of practice influence performance and learning—factors that determine how practice is conducted. We now shift to a focus on the learner and consider other practice-related factors that affect learning.

Instructors often have the impression that the learner's motivation is not a problem—that a student would obviously want to learn a particular skill. However, students do not always share their instructors' enthusiasm for learning. An unmotivated learner is not likely to practice, and the result can be little or no learning. A motivated student tends to devote greater effort to the task, with more serious practice and longer practice periods, leading to more effective learning. How can instructors influence this motivation to learn?

Intrinsic motivation for learning concerns the learner's internalized drive—here, a drive to learn a skill. Considerable research has been conducted to understand how intrinsic motivation affects the learner in a wide variety of situations and skills, resulting in important advances in theory (e.g., Deci & Ryan, 2000) and application (e.g., Weinberg & Gould, 2024). For our purposes, however, we restrict the discussion to the tools and techniques that may influence a learner's intrinsic motivation.

Deci and Ryan (2000) suggest that three basic needs largely determine an individual's intrinsic motivation: autonomy (control of one's own destiny), competence (mastery of the skill), and relatedness (being accepted within a social context). Of course, the importance of each of these basic needs will differ for each individual. Therefore, as an instructor, determining how best to respond in a learning context involves becoming familiar with the individual and understanding how the acquisition of a motor skill fits into the individual's needs. The following sections discuss how specific factors that influence motivation may affect motor learning.

Goal Setting

An important motivational method is **goal setting**, whereby learners are encouraged to adopt specific performance goals. This method has had numerous applications, particularly in industry, and it has strong implications for learning in sport and physical education (Locke & Latham, 1985). In an experiment involving learning to shoot a firearm, Boyce (1992) set specific goals for some participants, instructed others to set their own specific goals, or simply told participants to "do your best." Performance of the three groups over a five-session practice period in which these goal-setting methods were given is presented in figure 10.10, along with the results in a retention test where the goal-setting instructions were no longer applied. The findings clearly showed that adopting a specific goal improved performance compared to the "do your best" group. Moreover, this effect was maintained in a retention test.

These and other findings suggest that instructors should encourage learners to set realistic goals—ones that can be reasonably achieved with practice and effort. The learner can become discouraged by not approaching goal levels that are set too high. Yet goals that are too easily met can result in boredom and reduced motivation. Encouragement to commit to a specific, challenging (but not impossible) goal is strongly motivating and has positive benefits for performance and learning.

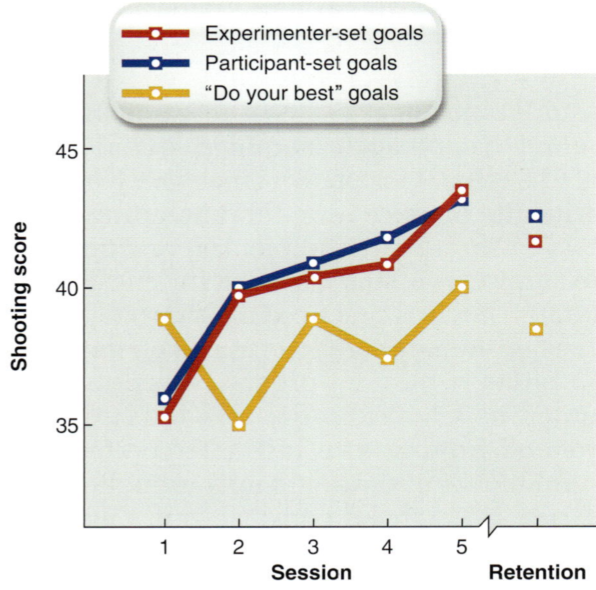

FIGURE 10.10 Learners practiced a shooting task after different goal-setting assignments.

Self-Regulated Practice

Although Boyce's (1992) participant-set-goal group described in the previous section did not outperform the experimenter-set-goal group, there is ample evidence that providing at least some control over the learning environment influences motivation and enhances learning. Researchers call this **self-regulation**, which refers to giving learners ownership over some components of practice. In studies of this type, learners are typically told that they can control factors such as how much practice to undertake, when augmented feedback will be provided, or how to organize the practice schedule (reviewed by Sanli et al., 2013).

An important consideration in the experimental design of self-regulation studies is the inclusion of a **yoked group** that receive the same conditions of practice as the experimental groups. Practice conditions for a yoked group are determined entirely in advance and are not under the control of the learner, but in all other ways, they are identical to the conditions of the self-regulated practice group. For example, Wulf and Toole (1999) allowed some participants to choose the exact trials when they would use ski poles as assistance devices in a simulated skiing task. Each participant in the yoked group was paired with a participant in the self-regulated group and used the poles on the same trials as their self-regulated counterpart. The key difference was that the yoked participant had not made the decision regarding whether to use poles. Following two days of practice, performance in retention was far superior for the self-regulated group compared to the control group, even though both groups had received exactly the same schedule of practice. The inclusion of the yoked group, therefore, allowed the researchers to be confident in their conclusion that self-regulation—giving the learners ownership of their practice regime—had positively influenced the quality of learning.

Social-Comparative Information

Although augmented feedback—information that is provided to the learner from an external source—is the focus of the next chapter, it also serves an important role as a motivator. Feedback from a coach or instructor in the form of praise or positive evaluation can have a positive impact on learning. In fact, evidence suggests that positive augmented feedback can boost motor learning even when that feedback is not entirely true (Lewthwaite & Wulf, 2012; Wulf & Lewthwaite, 2016).

In one study involving a balance task (Lewthwaite & Wulf, 2010), participants in the false-positive normative feedback group (red bars in figure 10.11) were told that their performance was 20% more accurate than the average performance of others who had participated in the experiment. Another group (blue bars in figure 10.11) was given **false-negative normative feedback**—they were told that their performance was 20% worse than the average participant. A third (control) group (yellow bars) was provided only their actual results, with no mention of normative standing. The results of these feedback conditions illustrate clear benefits for the **false-positive normative feedback** group by the end of the first day of practice, throughout the second day of practice, and in retention. Interestingly, there were no meaningful differences between the false-negative group and the control group, suggesting that the normative feedback provided a boost to learning when it was positive but did not degrade learning when it was negative.

These findings have been replicated in an applied setting. Eliasz (2016), using a similar experimental protocol with first-year medical students, found that providing false-positive normative feedback benefited learning a surgical task—again, even though the feedback itself was untrue.

In all, the collective findings from studies on goal setting, self-regulation, and positive normative feedback are very persuasive evidence favoring the beneficial role of motivation in motor learning. According to Wulf and Lewthwaite (2016), motivating experiences increase an individual's confidence and expectations for future performances. When applied in practice, these motivational experiences contribute to enhanced

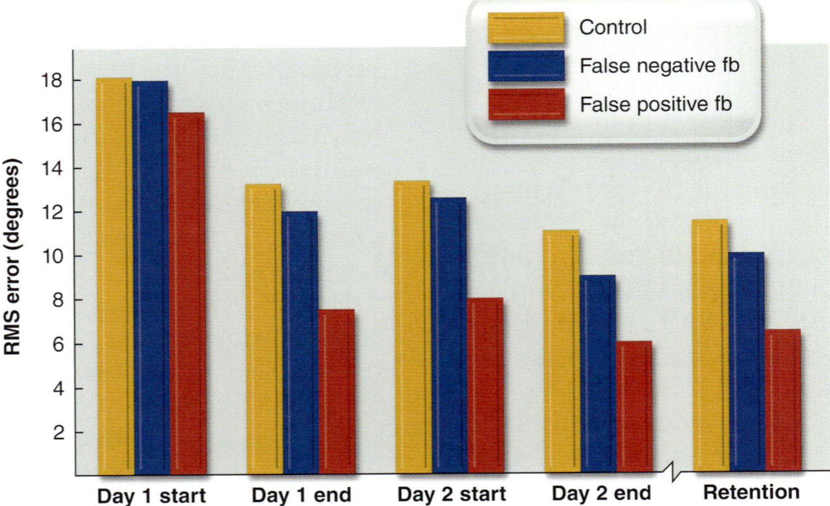

FIGURE 10.11 Lewthwaite & Wulf (2010) balance task results. One group received false-positive normative feedback about their performance (red bars), another received false-negative normative feedback (blue bars), and a control group received only true feedback (yellow bars).

learning. We will have more to say about the role of motivation in motor learning theory in chapter 12.

Observational Learning and Mental Practice

Not all prepractice instructions are best provided verbally. Actions, strategies, and anticipated perceptual experiences are sometimes more effectively illustrated in a visual modality than described in words. In such cases, visual aids, such as images, videos, and live **demonstrations** by an instructor or by the learners themselves (sometimes called **modeling**), are often used. This procedure comes under the general heading of **observational learning**, in which the learner gains information by watching another's performance.

Researchers have studied the observational learning process quite intensely over the past several decades. The result is a complex set of moderating variables that influence the process. The decision about how to maximize the effectiveness of a model seems to depend on a number of factors, which Ste-Marie and colleagues (2012) summarize well. How observational learning works without active movement on the part of the learner is a question that has raised plenty of debate. But there is little doubt that a considerable amount of learning, particularly early in practice, comes from scrutinizing others' actions. Important questions such as who the model should be (e.g., another learner vs. a skilled performer), when observation should be scheduled relative to physical practice, and what additional information should be provided during the observational process have drawn considerable attention among researchers. The recommendations provided by Ste-Marie and Hancock (2015) are excellent starting points for the interested reader.

Visit HK*Propel* to read "Bend It Like Becker" and complete the self-directed learning activities.

Another useful addition to the collection of activities in a practice session is to ask the learner to mentally rehearse skills to be learned without overt physical practice. In **mental practice** (or mental imagery), the

Mental practice contributes positively to learning, though the exact way it does this is still unclear. One way may be by allowing the learner to practice decision-making, such as mentally simulating the turns that a slalom skier will make during a run.

learner might think about the skills being learned, rehearse each of the steps sequentially, imagine doing the actions that would result in achieving the goal, or anticipate the sensations (e.g., auditory or proprioceptive) that may occur as a result of performing an action.

Can this method actually contribute to learning? For many years, scientists and educators in the motor learning field had very much doubted that motor learning could be accomplished through mental practice. The understanding of practice and learning at the time held that some cognitive aspects of a skill could be learned through mental practice but that overt physical action was essential for the motor aspects of learning. Many believed that motor learning could not occur without movement, active practice, and feedback from the movement to signal errors.

However, evidence from various experiments has demonstrated convincingly that mental-practice procedures actually generate motor learning. Although mental practice does not result in as much learning as the same amount of physical practice, mental practice does result in far more improvement than in no-practice control groups (see Feltz & Landers, 1983, for a review). Figure 10.12, from Hird and colleagues (1991), provides results from two separate tasks, the pegboard and pursuit-rotor tasks. The fact that mental practice generated learning in the pursuit-rotor task (for example), which does not seem to have a high cognitive component beyond the first few trials, suggests strongly that the learning of motor control is likely involved with mental practice.

How Does Mental Practice Work?

There are several views regarding how mental practice generates new task learning. One idea focuses on the cognitive aspects of the task—that mental practice facilitates learning what to do (Heuer, 1985). For example, a tennis player could decide what shot to make and where to direct it; a skier could rehearse the sequence of turns in the ski run; and a surgeon might consider the steps to take in a delicate operation. These cognitive elements are thought to be present only in the early stages of learning (the cognitive stage discussed in chapter 8). Thus, according to this view, mental-practice effects are predicted to apply only to early learning since these cognitive components of learning drop out after being acquired in the first stage (see chapter 12).

Although learning cognitive elements is undoubtedly a major factor in mental practice, evidence such as that illustrated in figure 10.12 (and in Focus on Application 10.1) suggests that there is more to mental practice than just this. Beyond these early

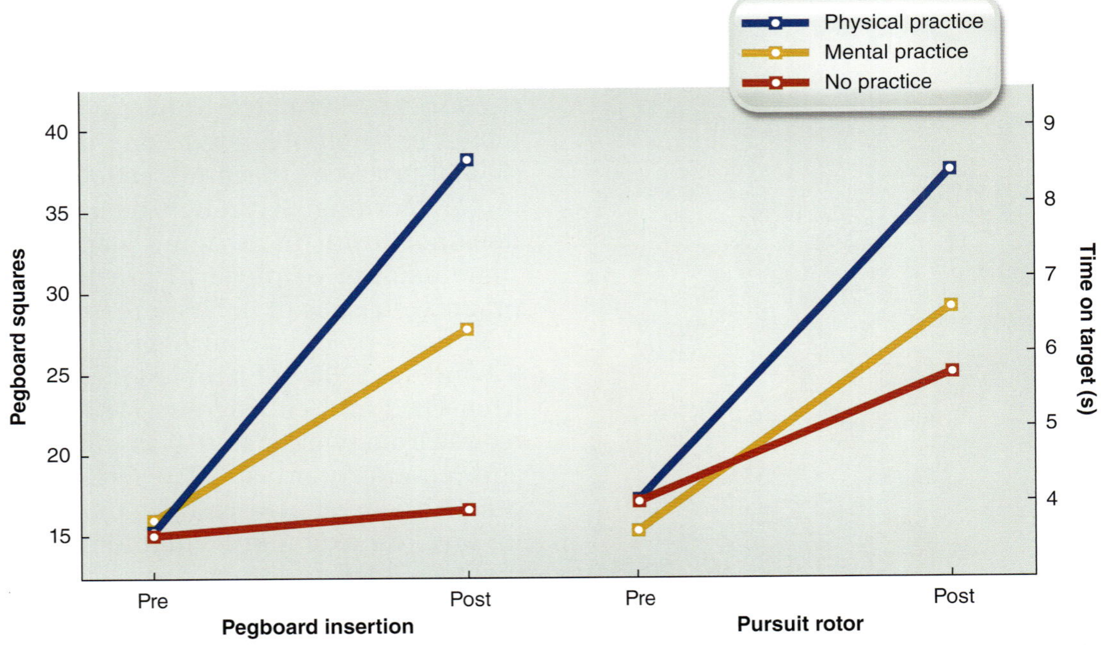

FIGURE 10.12 Effects of physical practice (blue) and mental practice (yellow) compared to no-practice control conditions (red) on groups learning a pegboard-insertion task (left) and a pursuit-rotor task (right).

stages of practice, both the pegboard-insertion task and the pursuit-rotor task involve considerable learning of movement control, because these tasks seem largely devoid of cognitive or conceptual components. Clearly, mental practice is not just cognitive or symbolic learning.

One account for the role of mental practice in acquiring the motor aspects of skill learning has origins that can be traced back to the 1800s. Mental practice, according to this older view, causes the motor system to produce minute contractions of the participating musculature, with these contractions being far smaller in amplitude than those necessary to produce action. In this view, the central nervous system carries out the movement, providing practice even without overt body movement. Although EMGs (electromyograph recordings of the muscles' electrical signals) show some evidence of weak activities during mental practice, the patterning of these EMGs does not resemble that of the actual movements very closely, making it difficult to understand how these electrical activities alone could be the basis for enhanced learning. The idea that motor learning from mental practice occurs from minute muscular contractions has not generated much research support.

However, a more recent view of this account of mental practice holds promise. In this view, mental practice (or imaging) produces anticipated sensory consequences of an action (also called *feedforward information*). As discussed earlier (see chapter 4), feedforward information is a critical component of movement control, allowing one to anticipate the results of an action if it was performed as expected and to make rapid corrections if the feedback information does not match the feedforward (expected) signals. The idea here is that by producing those anticipated sensations during mental practice, the learner

FOCUS ON Application 10.1

Mental Practice in Stroke Rehabilitation

The application of mental practice as a method to improve motor skills has been a part of sports for years. In some sports, the facilities are restricted to certain seasons of the year; therefore, mental practice would be a perfect fit for practicing the sport in the off-season when facilities are not available. When research on mental practice began to reveal positive effects on motor learning, instructors and therapists began to use these methods in their teaching and therapies, respectively—notably, they were justified in using these methods in stroke rehabilitation.

Stroke is a medical condition that results in damage to the brain. Often the damage is to one side (hemisphere) of the brain, resulting in motor control impairments to the opposite side of the body. One goal of rehabilitation is to regain function by repairing the brain as the result of goal-directed movements. Active physical practice can lead to partial or full restoration and compensation.

But there are limitations to the amount and frequency of rehabilitation treatments involving a therapist. Active movement outside therapy times may be encouraged but, unless specified and monitored, may not always be wise (for various reasons). Fortunately, recent research has shown that mental practice (and imagery) generates neural activations of the brain that are similar to actual movement (Garrison et al., 2010). Although mental practice cannot replace physical rehabilitation, the combination of the two forms of practice may be more effective than either form alone (Cha et al., 2012; Dickstein & Deutsch, 2007; Nilsen et al., 2010). There appears to be little doubt that mental practice serves as an effective addition to occupational and physical therapists' arsenal of rehabilitation tools.

builds what some have called a *forward model* of the action in memory. In this way, some motor learning can occur in the absence of movement, but further refinements require physical practice to learn how the forward model compares with actual sensory feedback resulting from movement (e.g., Gentili et al., 2010; Kim et al., 2022).

When and How to Use Mental Practice

The learner needs to be instructed carefully in the methods of mental practice. It is not enough simply to suggest that the learner go somewhere and "practice mentally"—systematic procedures are necessary. Weinberg and Gould (2024) provide additional tips for maximizing the use of imagery and mental practice, such as performing imagery and mental-practice activities in as many different settings as possible. Because mental practice and imagery require no apparatus, large groups of learners can practice at the same time. The clever instructor will find ways to interleave the two practice modes to provide maximal gains, for example, by urging mental practice during the rest phase between trials of a fatiguing task or to break up a long string of repetitious physical practice trials (see Focus on Application 10.2).

FOCUS ON Application 10.2

Practice Distribution Revisited

An important practical issue arose at the beginning of this chapter concerning the costs versus benefits of distributed practice. Although relatively long rest periods are effective for performance and learning, they are inefficient from a time-management perspective. For example, in the Baddeley and Longman (1978) postal worker retraining study, the most extremely distributed practice group would have required four times longer to complete the same amount of practice as the most extremely massed group (20 vs. 80 days).

To increase both effectiveness and efficiency, it would make sense from a theoretical and a practical viewpoint to substitute other activities for rest. The research on interleaving tells us that taking a break from performing the same task by performing a different task has a positive effect on learning. So, replacing rest with physical practice on alternative tasks would be one way to enhance the effectiveness–efficiency tradeoff of distributed practice.

Another method, based on the research we have discussed in the latter parts of this chapter, would be to intersperse physical practice with periods of mental practice, imagery, or observation during the rest between trials or sessions. Rather than seeing rest as lost or wasted time, one can use these intervals productively to enhance motor learning during the fatigue recovery period. In effect, this strategy would make distributed practice both effective and efficient compared to massed practice because both intervals of physical practice and mental practice or demonstrations would contribute positive effects to learning.

A third perspective concerns how rest periods can be used to encourage self-evaluation of performance, which would contribute to learning. One principle that we discuss in the next chapter concerns how using augmented feedback allows learners to become self-sufficient in their capability to assess their own performance and to learn to help themselves through error correction. Replacing rest with periods of introspection and self-evaluation between periods of physical practice encourages learners to assess and better understand what makes their own performance more or less effective.

All these factors (see figure 10.13) contribute positively to learning. Inserting them into otherwise empty rest intervals would benefit both training effectiveness and efficiency (see Ong & Hodges, 2012).

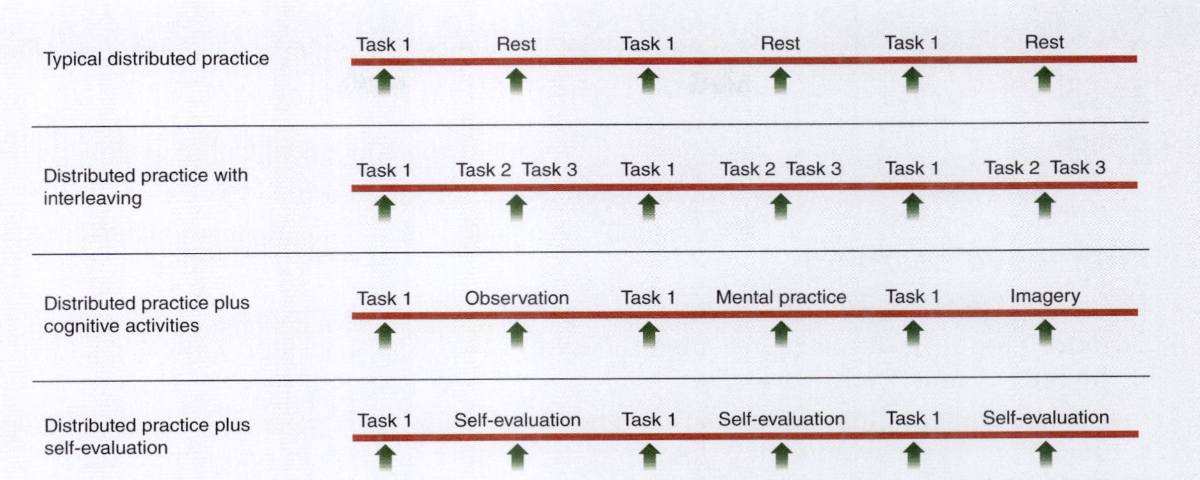

FIGURE 10.13 Alternatives to resting in a distributed practice schedule. Replacing rest periods with either cognitive or other physical activities would have beneficial effects on learning, making distributed practice both effective and efficient.

Summary

Rest periods during physical practice (relative to no-rest conditions) produce gains in learning, especially for continuous tasks. However, long rest periods have the disadvantage of making practice less time efficient. Research suggests that these rest periods can be used more efficiently if combined with periods of physical practice on other tasks, observation or mental practice, or self-evaluation.

Compared to constant practice, in which only a single variant is practiced, varied practice facilitates retention and generalizability to a novel situation whose specific variant has not received prior practice. Large learning gains can be made through effective practice organization and scheduling. An important concept is random (or interleaved) practice, which interleaves the practice order of trials of several tasks during acquisition. Relative to blocked practice, in which trials of a single task are practiced repeatedly, interleaving produces far more skilled performance at retention (i.e., more learning). Interleaving prevents the learner from repeating the same movement plan on successive trials and from gaining experience from performing different activities on adjacent trials.

Physical practice is just one way to rehearse a task. Several methods not involving physical rehearsals have also been shown to enhance learning. Observation of a human model provides objective information that learners can use to organize their thinking about the task. Mental practice and imagery reflect important methods for undertaking this organization of thoughts.

HK*PROPEL* ACTIVITIES

HK*Propel* offers these activities to help you build and apply your knowledge of the concepts in this chapter. Additionally, you'll find a key terms flashcard review activity and a key terms quiz, along with audio supplements for selected figures, as indicated by QR codes throughout the chapter.

Interactive Learning

Activity 10.1: Better conceptualize the possible ways of organizing practice by identifying the pattern represented by each of five graphical representations and the type of practice illustrated.

Activity 10.2: Explore the ways that random practice leads to better learning than blocked practice by matching descriptions to either the elaboration hypothesis or the forgetting hypothesis.

Activity 10.3: Answer a series of questions on how instructors can influence learners' levels of motivation.

Activity 10.4: Listen to a podcast discussing motivation and learning in sport, then consider ways you might implement choices in practice sessions.

Activity 10.5: Match statements regarding mental practice and observational learning to the appropriate headings.

Principles-to-Application Exercise

Activity 10.6: The principles-to-application exercise for this chapter prompts you to choose an activity that involves several motor skills, identify a specific learner, design a practice session that would include blocked practice and random practice, and explain why these types of practices are used for each skill.

Motor Control in Everyday Actions Narratives

But I Was Great on the Practice Range

Bend It Like Becker

Check Your Understanding

1. Explain how rest and cognitive activities between periods of practice influence motor learning.
2. Explain why including variable and random practice when teaching a person to play volleyball can be beneficial to learning. Are there any volleyball skills for which this type of practice would not be beneficial? Why or why not?
3. Discuss the differences between internal-focus and external-focus instructions. Give an example of each for someone learning to play the piano. Which of your examples would be more beneficial to learning for an intermediate student?

Apply Your Knowledge

1. Discuss three motivational tools or techniques that a physical therapist could use to help ensure a client is motivated during a recovery program. What factors would you consider in order to integrate observational learning or mental practice into the client's schedule?
2. You have volunteered to coach your nephew's soccer team for the summer. Two skills that you would like to work on with your team are penalty kicks and dribbling the ball down the field. How might you organize work and rest periods during practice for each of these skills? How might you include an amount of task variability appropriate to each skill? Are there any characteristics of your players that you would need to consider when organizing practice? Why?

11

Augmented Feedback

How Supplemental Feedback Influences Learning

CHAPTER OUTLINE

CHAPTER OBJECTIVES

Chapter 11 describes the influence of augmented feedback on motor performance and learning. This chapter will help you understand

- the types of augmented feedback,
- the way augmented feedback functions to influence performance and learning,
- the various properties of augmented feedback, and
- the influence of the various ways in which augmented feedback can be delivered.

CHAPTER PREVIEW QUIZ

1. What is the difference between augmented feedback and inherent feedback?
2. What is the difference between knowledge of performance and knowledge of results?
3. Is physically restricted guidance a good technique for improving a motor skill?

One of the most important learning processes concerns the use of feedback. As discussed in chapter 4, feedback may be a natural consequence of the movement, such as seeing a hammered nail become flush with a block of wood or feeling and hearing the tap of a keyboard. It is information that is picked up by our senses. Feedback can also come in various artificial forms that are not so obvious to the learner, such as the performer's score in a rifle range test or a comment about a swimmer's leg kick when performing the breaststroke. This type of feedback is also information, but it is not picked up directly by our senses. Instead, it is supplemented (or augmented) by an external source. Often, this feedback is under the instructor's direct control and represents an important component of practice.

This chapter complements chapters 9 and 10 because it also concerns practice and learning. This chapter focuses on how learners receive and use information about performance to make future corrections. Here, we discuss some principles of how supplemental feedback influences learning, examining questions about its frequency, timing, and the most effective kinds for learning.

Feedback Classifications

The term *feedback* originally emerged from the analysis of closed-loop control systems, referring to information about the difference between performance and some desired goal state (see chapter 4). In closed-loop system terminology, *feedback* refers to information about error. In human performance systems, the term is used to refer to information about movement and movement outcomes, not just errors.

It is helpful to form a clear feedback classification system because the terms and what they refer to can be confusing. One classification appears in figure 11.1, which divides all movement-related sensory information available to the learner into several subclasses. First, it is useful to categorize the information as either naturally available to us in our environment, which is termed *inherent feedback* (sometimes called *intrinsic feedback*, discussed in chapter 4), or information that is supplemented to the learning environment, called **augmented feedback** (sometimes called **extrinsic feedback**). It is also useful to distinguish between three types of augmented information in terms of

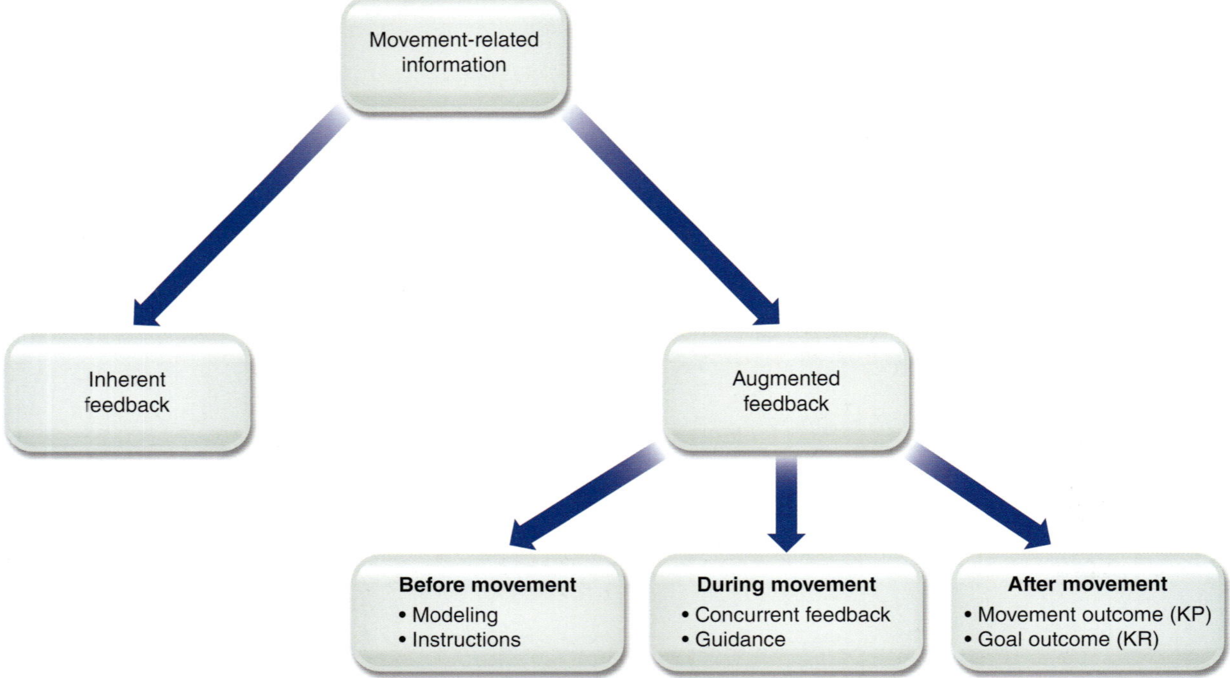

FIGURE 11.1 A feedback classification scheme.

when it has been supplemented to the learner: before, during, or after the movement. (Strictly speaking, only information provided during or after the movement fits the strict definition as feedback, because it is information arising from moving or having moved that is being "fed back" to the learner. But we will consider supplemental information provided before movement in this discussion as well, because learners often use it to reflect on what they have done.)

Inherent Feedback

As discussed in chapter 4, **inherent feedback** is information arising as a natural consequence of action. When you take a swing at a tennis ball, you feel your hips, shoulders, and arms moving; you see, hear, and feel the ball's contact; and you see where the ball travels. These types of information are inherent to the task, and most performers can perceive them more or less directly, without special methods or devices. Other kinds of inherent information might be the sounds or smells made by a race car engine or seeing and hearing the progress of a saw blade as a carpenter cuts through a piece of wood or as a surgeon drills into a bone. This general class of feedback has been discussed throughout the text during the development of the conceptual model of human performance.

Augmented Feedback

Augmented feedback is information supplied to the learner in addition to inherent feedback. As the name suggests, augmented feedback serves to supplement the inherent (naturally available) information. Most importantly, augmented feedback is information that the instructor controls; thus, it can be given (or not given) in different forms. In addition, augmented feedback can be given at different times to influence learning—before, during, or after movement.

Before Movement

Information provided by an instructor or coach to the learner before a movement begins was discussed in chapter 10 using terms such as *modeling* and *instructions*. This type of information is supplemental to the learner's practice experience and is provided to augment the way the learner thinks about or conceptualizes how to approach the task. This type of information is not feedback in the strict sense because it is not usually information about what the learner has done but, instead, what could be done.

During Movement

Information provided during movement often occurs when the learner is performing a continuous task, such as walking, in which the augmented feedback can be used to alter an ongoing movement. This type of information has been termed *concurrent feedback* because it is augmented information provided to the learner concurrently with ongoing movement. Visual, auditory, and haptic feedback about gait in stroke rehabilitation are all types of concurrent feedback. *Guidance devices*, which provide feedback in the form of physical restriction during movement execution, also provide concurrent augmented feedback because they usually help to restrain movement within prescribed limits of motion, and attempts to move beyond these restraints result in various forms of inherent feedback.

Many cars are equipped with the capability to provide both types of augmented feedback while driving. For example, the car's lane departure feature can provide visual, auditory, and haptic concurrent feedback when a line on the road is unexpectedly crossed. It can also provide a type of physical guidance by nudging the steering wheel in the opposite direction of the departure.

After Movement

The most common use of augmented feedback occurs when provided after a movement. Post-movement feedback can be provided about the results of the movement or about the movement itself. It has been a research focus for many years and, due to its significance in motor learning, has been added as an integral part of our conceptual model, completing the bottom-line feedback loop in figure 11.2.

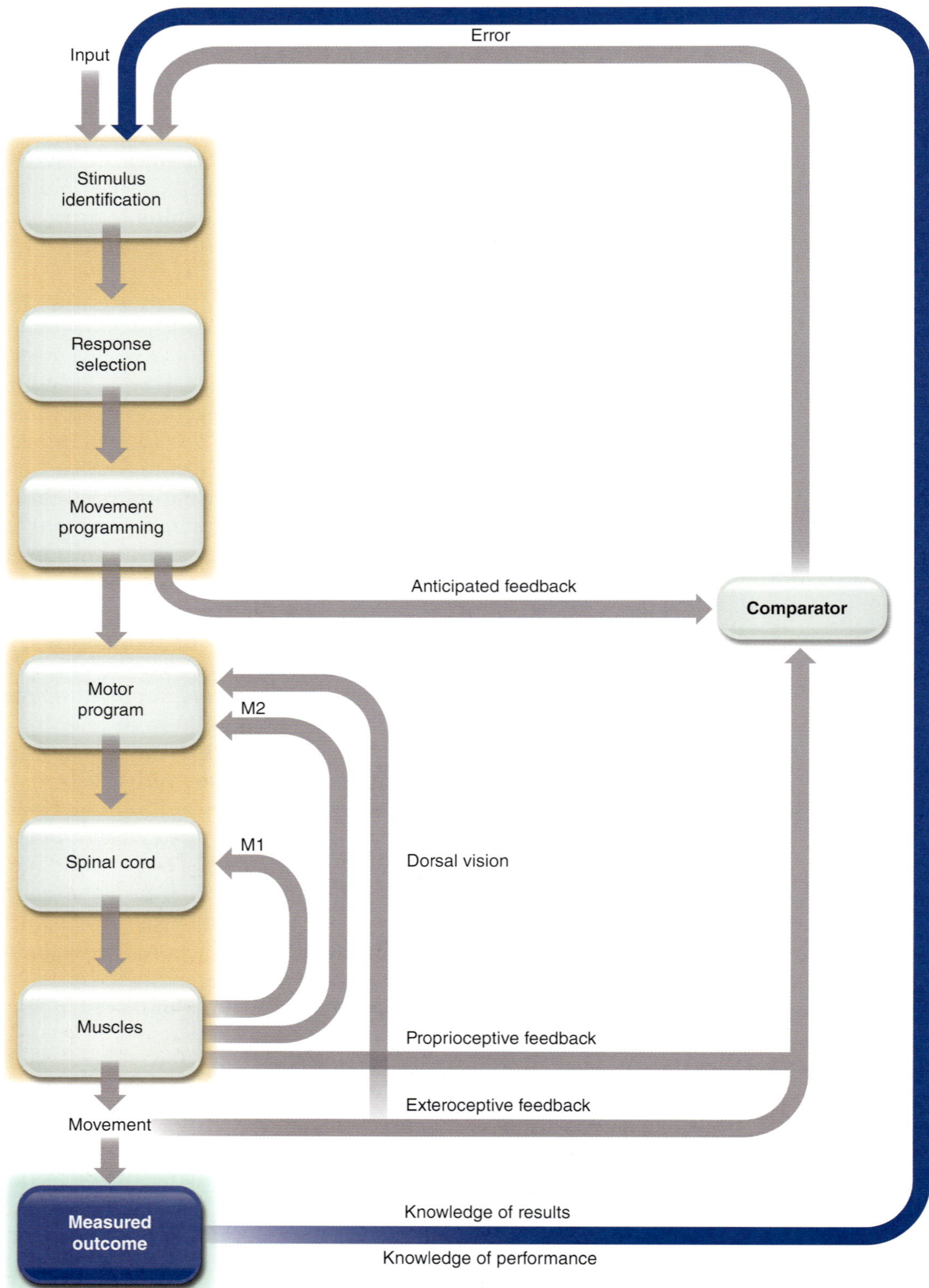

FIGURE 11.2 Conceptual model with the addition of augmented feedback.

Knowledge of results (KR) represents one category of post-movement augmented feedback. KR is usually verbal information (or at least information that can be verbalized) about the success of an action with respect to the environmental goal. In many daily activities, KR merely confirms what is known from inherent feedback. Telling someone he missed the nail with the hammer or telling a basketball player she missed the free throw are examples of when KR (the verbal information) is redundant with the information supplied by inherent feedback.

However, KR is not always redundant with inherent feedback. Surgical residents, springboard divers, and dancers must wait for subjective assessment scores to know the success of their performances. In riflery and archery, it is not always possible to see where the projectile hits the target area, so augmented KR information must be received from a coach or a scoring device. In these cases, KR is important for performance and learning because learners would not know the outcomes of their actions without it.

KR is frequently used in research, where specific aspects regarding how information is given to learners can be controlled. Researchers use this general method to examine how augmented feedback influences learning. Early research was often conducted with very simple tasks, such as blindfolded limb-positioning tasks. By removing the most important source of inherent feedback (vision), the experimenter made KR critical to learning the task. These experiments generally showed that, without KR, there was no learning at all (e.g., Thorndike, 1927; Trowbridge & Cason, 1932). On the other hand, providing KR about errors facilitated improvements in practice that remained in retention tests even when KR was no longer given.

These results suggest that, when learners cannot detect their own performance errors through inherent feedback, no learning occurs unless some form of augmented feedback is provided. This is one reason feedback is considered the single most important variable for learning except for practice itself (Bilodeau, 1966). Thus, a key principle for learning is

For a gymnast, augmented feedback could be provided as either KR or KP. In this photo, identify an example of gymnast KR and KP.

as follows: *Some information relative to goal achievement must be received through either inherent sources or augmented sources for learning to occur.*

Knowledge of performance (KP), sometimes referred to as *kinematic feedback*, is augmented information about the movement the learner has just made. It is frequently used by instructors in real-world settings. For example, you often hear coaches say things like "Your tuck was not tight enough" in a springboard dive or "Your backswing was too short" in golf. These forms of KP tell the learner something about the kinematics of the movement or about the movement pattern itself. Note that KP information, unlike KR, does not necessarily inform the learner about success in terms of meeting the environmental goal. Rather, kinematic feedback provides information about the nature of the movement that the learner actually produced.

Functions of Augmented Feedback

After a movement attempt, a music instructor says to the learner, "The rhythm was pretty good, but try to slow everything down a little next time." Think of all the meanings that such a simple statement could have for the learner. First, the feedback could have a motivating or discouraging function: It could make the learner more enthusiastic about the activity and encourage her to try harder, or it might be construed in a negative way, which could have a detrimental impact. Second, the feedback can help direct the learner's attention either toward the production of the movement (an internal focus of attention) or toward the effect of the movement (an external focus). Third, the feedback can provide information about the rhythm and absolute timing of the movements, which can be combined with other information (e.g., how the movement felt) to generate new knowledge and take corrective actions. Finally, feedback can also produce a kind of dependency in the learner, such that performance is enhanced when feedback is present because of its influence on the next attempt, but performance deteriorates when it is no longer available.

Generally, in real-world settings, augmented feedback operates in four interdependent ways simultaneously. To summarize, augmented feedback can do these four things:

- Motivate or discourage the learner
- Direct the learner's focus of attention
- Provide information about errors to correct
- Create a dependency, potentially leading to problems later

Motivational Properties

The music instructor tells the struggling piano student, "Keep it up; you're doing fine." Such a casual comment can go a long way toward motivating a student to continue practicing. Early research revealed that if performance was deteriorating in so-called vigilance or sustained-attention tasks (chapter 3), when given positive feedback, performers showed an immediate increase in proficiency, as if the feedback acted as a kind of stimulant to energize them (Arps, 1920). Learners who are given positive feedback say they like the task more, try harder, and are willing to practice longer.

The just-discussed effects of feedback as a motivating tool are primarily *indirect* in their influence. That is, KR encourages the learner to keep practicing, and the results of this additional practice influence learning. However, feedback can also have a *direct* motivational effect on learning. Consider the study by Chiviacowsky and Wulf (2007), for example. Learners in this study practiced a beanbag-tossing task in which their vision of the end-result accuracy was obstructed, making feedback from the experimenter (KR) critical for improving performance. Participants in one group were provided with feedback about their three *best* performances out of the previous six trials over repeated blocks of practice. Participants in another group received information about their three *worst* performances over these same practice periods. When assessed later in a retention test, the group that had received KR on their best performances showed superior learning compared to the other group, suggesting that this feedback had a direct motivational effect on learning.

The implications of motivational effects of augmented feedback have also been investigated in other experimental paradigms. As discussed in chapter 10, feedback can benefit

FOCUS ON **Research 11.1**

Early Views on How Augmented Feedback Works

Research traditions established in animal-learning research early in the 20th century strongly influenced theorizing about how feedback might work in motor learning. In one example, a food reward was given if a hungry animal pressed a lever within 5 s of hearing a tone. Over trials, the animal learned to press the lever quite reliably when the sound occurred. Your new puppy quickly learns to sit on command if you give a treat or a friendly pat when the puppy performs the action. In this case, the food reward serves as feedback for correctly responding to the stimulus (to sit on command).

Scientists realized that the nature and timing of the feedback had a marked influence on learning the desired behavior. Thorndike's (1927) Law of Effect summarized some of the early research. Associations (or bonds) between the stimulus and the correct behavior were presumably strengthened (or reinforced) by feedback. Learning was enhanced by the immediacy or frequency of feedback, presumably by strengthening these bonds. Conversely, if feedback was withheld entirely, there could be no bond strengthening, rendering that practice trial essentially useless for enhancing learning. These basic notions gave rise to the general idea that any feedback variation during practice that makes the information more immediate, more precise, more frequent, more informationally rich, or generally more useful would benefit learning (including motor learning). Such a view made good common sense—it just seems logical that giving more information to the learner should benefit learning—and this view became widely adopted as a result. The principle had strong implications for the structure of practice, encouraging just about anything that would provide more information to the learner.

As you will see throughout this chapter, however, this generalization is probably wrong in several ways. Some of the key feedback variables, such as feedback frequency, feedback delay, feedback summaries, and bandwidth feedback, failed to operate in ways predicted by Thorndike's views. In the end, these early theoretical beginnings were important because they led to more research, new ideas, and a better understanding of feedback processes in motor learning. Important reviews of the feedback literature by Salmoni and colleagues (1984) and Adams (1987) provide much more on the historical context of this work.

Exploring Further

1. Why does the typical experiment in animal conditioning provide an *extinction* period?
2. In what ways does augmented feedback in motor learning work similarly to the provision of feedback in animal conditioning studies? In what ways do the principles differ?

learning when it informs learners that they are doing well compared to their peers or to their performances earlier in practice (Chiviacowsky, 2021). Moreover, simply having the option or control over when, how, or what feedback will be provided appears to have a beneficial effect on motor learning (e.g., Janelle et al., 1997; see review by Sanli et al., 2013). Wulf and Lewthwaite (2016) summarized these and other findings in a theory that further develops the motivational roles of feedback (discussed in chapter 12; see also Schmidt et al., 2025).

Attentional-Focusing Properties

Important discussions earlier in the book addressed the role of attentional focus on performance (chapter 3) and learning (chapter 9). In many situations, performance and learning are enhanced when the learner's attention is directed to the end product of movement (or the effect of the movement on the environment)—typically referred to as an external focus of attention. In contrast, an attentional focus that is directed toward the movement itself (an internal focus) usually leads to poor performance and learning.

Now consider the effects of KR and KP on attentional focus. By its very nature, KR provides information about performance success relative to the movement goal. Put differently, KR directs the learner to think about externally directed information (the movement goal). The informational content of KP, on the other hand, concerns the nature of the movement that was produced, such as the spatial or temporal form of the action. Thus, the informational content of KP directs the learner to think about movement-related information—an internally focused process.

The attentional-focusing properties of KR and KP set up the learner for a potential conflict in practice goals. Since KP is often provided for making changes in movement kinematics or kinetics (e.g., Newell & Walter, 1981), how can it be used without the detrimental impact of directing the learner to internally focus attention? One solution has been to reduce the frequency of providing feedback that induces an internal focus (e.g., Wulf et al., 2002). Another solution is to provide a combination of KR and KP—a strategy that appears to be more effective than providing either one by itself (Oppici et al., 2021). The sections that follow discuss these and other issues regarding scheduling and providing feedback.

Informational Properties

Consider the example mentioned earlier, in which the music instructor tells the student that the rhythm is fine but that the speed could be slower overall. This information provides the basis for making corrections on the next attempt, hopefully bringing the performance closer to the goal of a more skilled performance. Augmented feedback helps the learner to problem solve the process of detecting and correcting errors while learning a more skilled movement pattern.

Recognizing that augmented feedback has a critical informational role raises many important questions for the instructor. For example, in what form is the information best provided (e.g., verbally, in video replays, graphically), how often should it be provided (on every trial, only some trials), and when is it best provided (immediately after an action, delayed somewhat)? These questions about feedback timing are addressed in detail later in this chapter.

Dependency-Producing Properties

When augmented feedback is given frequently, it tends to guide the learner toward the goal movement. In a sense, this process operates in very much the same way as guidance procedures. Physical **guidance** acts very powerfully to reduce and sometimes prevent errors from occurring. This process is fine as long as the guidance is present, but the learner can also become dependent on the guidance, resulting in performance that deteriorates markedly when the guidance is removed and the learner attempts to perform without it (Salmoni et al., 1984).

Just as with physical guidance, augmented feedback can have a powerful role in allowing the learner to correct errors quickly. This becomes problematic, however, if the learner becomes dependent on the augmented source of information instead of internally generated processes to keep the movement on target. Like physical guidance, when augmented feedback is no longer available in a retention test, performance is likely to suffer markedly if the learner has not developed the capability to produce the movement independent of the augmented source of information. Various ways have been developed to minimize dependency-producing effects, as discussed in the sections that follow.

Visit HK*Propel* to read "The Coach as a Dictionary" and complete the self-directed learning activities.

What Feedback to Give

In theory, an instructor could give feedback about countless features of the action. Information-processing and memory capabilities are limited, so it is doubtful that the learner can take in and retain very much during an onslaught of feedback. The learner would simply be overloaded with too much information. Providing too much feedback could lead to an abundance of thought processes during action, leading to an internal focus of attention, as depicted in figure 11.3. The following sections describe various decisions to make regarding what augmented feedback is best to provide.

Precision of Feedback

Augmented feedback about movement errors can be provided in terms of the direction of the error, the magnitude of the error, or both, with varying levels of precision. The following are some of the principles involved.

Qualitative information about the direction of the learner's error (early vs. late, high vs. low, left vs. right, and so on) is generally beneficial for correcting errors. In addition, it is generally helpful to report some of the quantitative magnitude of the errors as part of the feedback. **Precision of feedback** refers to the exactness of detail with which the feedback describes the movement or outcome. You can imagine feedback that only roughly approximates the movement feature, as in learning to do partial weight bearing on crutches. Feedback such as "You put a little too much weight through your left leg that time" would be considered less precise than "You put 4.3 pounds too much weight through your left leg that time."

FIGURE 11.3 Providing more feedback than can be processed effectively can lead to an abundance of thoughts during movement, many of which are internally focused.

Technology has made providing video feedback to athletes easier than ever, but it is more effective when accompanied by cues to help the learner focus on the relevant details. In this photo, name two important cues that might be important to the runner receiving feedback.

How much feedback precision to provide depends on the learner's skill. Early in practice, when the learner's errors are very large, precise information about the magnitude of the errors does not matter. The learner does not have the movement-control precision to match the precision of correction specified by the feedback. By the same argument, more exact feedback would be effective for higher-skilled performers due to their more precise movement-control capabilities.

Video Feedback

The history of motor learning research with respect to providing knowledge of performance (KP) generally follows a timeline of technological developments. Early pioneers recorded force–time tracings in sprint starts on strip-chart paper (Howell, 1956). The recordings were then displayed to the learner as KP feedback together with an optimal tracing superimposed over the learner's tracing. Tiffin and Rogers (1943) used similar methods with industrial tasks.

Films were popular in the 1960s and 1970s, particularly among professional sport teams. These films were used as feedback so that a player could analyze mistakes and determine more effective actions to use next time. As learning tools, though, films were limited because the time required for developing film was usually quite long, troublesome, and costly. Videotape solved many of the problems with film: Feedback about whole performances could be viewed after only a few seconds of tape rewind, and these replays would capture the details of the movement very well. And, of course, digital imagery has taken video feedback to a whole new level. Crisp, clear, high-definition videos can be recorded with a cell phone and instantly distributed to others around the world. Providing immediate video feedback to a learner has never been easier, cheaper, or more informative.

But an important question remains for all these video forms: Is replaying a video of the performance an effective method of providing augmented feedback? Early on, Rothstein and Arnold (1976) reviewed the evidence about film and videotape replays and, surprisingly, found that this feedback was not always useful for learning. One explanation is that because a video provides so *much* information, the learner may not know what information is important and what is not. This led to the suggestion that *cuing*, in which the instructor directs the learner to attend to specific aspects of the performance, should accompany the video to enhance its effectiveness.

Kernodle and Carlton (1992) provided more evidence to support Rothstein and Arnold's suggestions. Participants in each of four groups practiced a throwing task (with inherent feedback blocked) using their nondominant limb and were given retention tests for learning immediately before each of the five practice sessions. One group received only KR about the distance of the throw. The other three groups all received videotape replays of their performances—one group with no additional feedback, another group cued to direct attention to certain parts of the video, and a third group cued to make specific error corrections. The results, illustrated in figure 11.4, were quite clear. Providing video feedback without additional information was no more effective than just providing KR. However, video feedback given with the addition of attention-directing cues was better, and cues about what errors to correct facilitated learning even more.

KP Versus KR?

On the surface, whether to provide KP or KR to a learner seems like an easy question to answer. Since KP provides more precise information about the movement itself, it would seem to be the preferred choice. However, as we have seen in previous sections, the answer is not so simple or obvious. KP can lead to an internal focus of attention, which could be detrimental to learning. And because KP

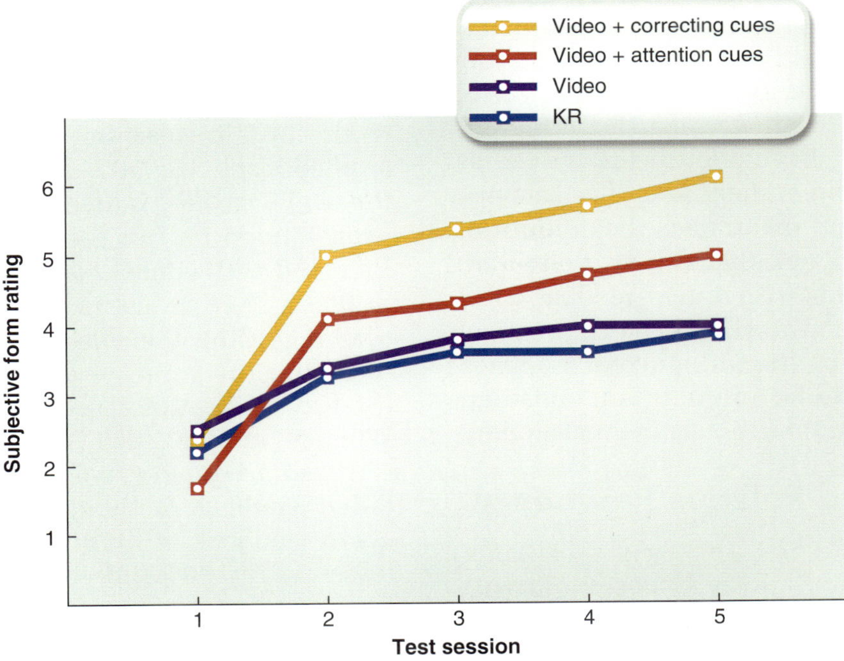

FIGURE 11.4 Providing video feedback facilitated learning only if supplemented with attention-directing cues or correcting cues, as revealed in retention tests conducted before practice on sessions 2 through 5.

is so informative, research suggests that an expert is needed who provides additional information to focus the learner on specific information in order for the feedback to be effective (Oppici et al., 2021).

Some additional evidence suggests another potential downside of KP. Since it is so directive in content, KP removes some of the problem-solving efforts that would otherwise be engaged if only KR was provided (Swinnen et al., 1993). For example, in learning to use a limb prosthesis in a virtual ball-throwing task, participants transferred more effectively to a novel force-production task following KR-feedback training than following KP-feedback training (Bouwsema et al., 2014). Perhaps the information content provided by the KR in this task was sufficient to engage the problem-solving analyses during practice, which then enabled later transfer performance. Whether using augmented feedback *assists* the learning process without *guiding* the process is often not fully revealed until learning is examined in retention or transfer tests.

How Much Feedback to Give

One challenge faced in education and skills instruction is the student–teacher ratio. Small student–teacher ratios (e.g., one-on-one instruction) have often been viewed as ideal because the student gets the teacher's full attention and maximizes the amount of augmented feedback that can be delivered. But do the effects of frequent feedback last beyond the lesson itself? For very practical reasons, assessing the influence of feedback frequency should be an important consideration in designing skills-learning instruction.

Absolute and Relative Frequency of Feedback

The research literature has defined two general descriptors for feedback frequency. **Absolute frequency of feedback** refers to the *total number* of times that feedback is given to a learner across a set of trials in practice. If there are 400 trials and the instructor gives feedback on 100 of them, then the absolute frequency is 100—simply, the total number of feedback presentations. **Relative frequency of feedback**, on the other hand, refers to the *percentage* of trials receiving feedback. In this example, the relative frequency of feedback is 25% (100 feedback trials out of 400 trials).

Consider this situation: A learner practices a task such as rifle shooting at a distant target, where errors cannot be detected without augmented feedback. Because the instructor is busy giving feedback to other students, information about the performances can be given only occasionally. We have discussed the learning benefits of the trials that actually receive feedback, but what about the trials in between for which feedback is not provided? Are they useful for learning?

Perhaps of some surprise, research has shown that so-called "blank" trials can be beneficial for learning, even though participants receive no feedback on them (Winstein & Schmidt, 1990). This can be seen in figure 11.5. Using a limb-patterning task, the 100% group received feedback after every trial (100% relative frequency), and the 50% group received feedback after only half of the trials (50% relative frequency), with the same total number of trials. The groups improved at about the same rate in acquisition. However, in the tests of learning performed without any feedback, the 50% group outperformed the 100% group, indicating better learning even though half of the 50% group's trials involved no feedback.

There is some controversy in the literature regarding the effectiveness of simply reducing the relative feedback frequency (McKay et al., 2022). A key feature in the Winstein and Schmidt (1990) study was that reduced frequency was achieved using a **faded feedback** method. Here, the learner is given feedback at high relative frequencies (essentially 100%) in early practice, which has the effect of guiding the learner toward the movement goal. The experimenter then gradually reduces the relative frequency as skill develops, such that presentation of feedback is infrequent when higher skill levels

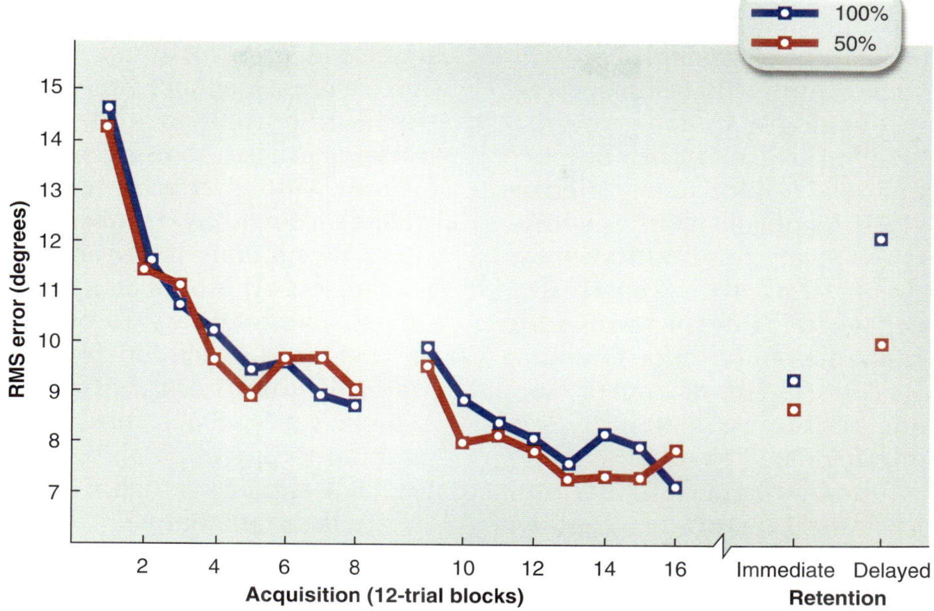

FIGURE 11.5 Reducing the relative frequency of feedback from 100% to 50% over the course of acquisition trials had no detrimental effect on performance and a beneficial effect on learning.

have been achieved. With advanced skill, the performance does not deteriorate much when feedback is totally withdrawn for a few trials. If performance begins to decline, the instructor can give feedback again to bring performance behavior back on target, then withdraw the feedback again. The instructor can adjust feedback scheduling to the proficiency level and improvement rate of each learner separately, thus tailoring feedback to individual differences in capabilities.

The ultimate goal is to generate the capability for the learner to perform without depending on feedback. Even though feedback is critical for developing the movement into a skilled pattern, it appears that it must eventually be removed to accomplish permanent skill learning. The faded feedback idea is both a practical and theoretically sound method to prevent the learner from developing a feedback dependency (Krause et al., 2018).

Bandwidth Feedback

Bandwidth feedback (Sherwood, 1988) is a method that naturally blends qualitative and quantitative types of augmented feedback together with a fading procedure. In this method, the decision about what feedback to provide is based on an acceptability level. For example, if a resident is suturing a wound after a surgery, the instructing physician might say, "Good job" if the stitches were performed satisfactorily or if the time to perform the surgery was acceptable. If either the accuracy or time was not acceptable, the physician might provide precise feedback about the nature of the errors made and what aspects of the performance needed to be improved. Of course, the decision about what feedback to provide depends entirely on what levels of acceptability are set. The term *bandwidth* refers to how the limits of acceptability are defined.

There are two general rules in using the bandwidth method (Sherwood, 1988). First, precise feedback indicating the amount and direction of the error is given only when performance falls outside the bounds of what is defined as acceptable. Second, if performance lies within the bounds of acceptability, then no feedback is given—the learner having been told ahead of time to interpret the absence of feedback as meaning that performance was essentially correct (or acceptable).

Suppose, for example, that chiropractic students were learning a spinal manipulation task for which the goal was to produce a quick burst of 500 N of force on a mannequin. Bandwidth feedback would involve providing precise error information when outside the tolerance limits of the bandwidth and no feedback when inside the bandwidth. Figure 11.6 illustrates how these tolerance limits would apply. The dark orange band in figure 11.6*a* represents a tolerance of ±5% relative to the 500 N goal (475-525 N). The larger, light orange band in figure 11.6*b* illustrates a tolerance of ±10% (450-550 N). Representative results for one student over 10 force-production attempts are shown as data points in the figure.

If the student had been in a 10% bandwidth condition (figure 11.6*b*), she would have received precise error feedback on three trials (1, 6, 7) and no feedback on the other seven trials (2, 3, 4, 5, 8, 9, 10). If the student had been in the 5% bandwidth condition (figure 11.6*a*), she would have received precise error feedback on six trials (1, 2, 3, 4, 6, 7) and no feedback on the four other trials (5, 8, 9, 10). A student in a control condition would receive precise error feedback on all ten trials.

It is important to understand how this feedback procedure works because the size of the bandwidth produces some very important effects on learning. For example, Sherwood (1988) found that a larger bandwidth (10% of the target goal) produced more learning than smaller bandwidths (5% or 1%). Moreover, the feedback provided by the bandwidth method (combining both error feedback and correct feedback) has a larger effect on learning than comparable amounts of error feedback alone (Agethen & Krause, 2016; Lee & Carnahan, 1990).

The effects of the bandwidth method are consistent with several well-established principles for learning. First, the method produces a natural way of fading the frequency of augmented feedback (see the Winstein & Schmidt, 1990, study described in the previous section). When the learner is just beginning, performances tend to be very large and outside the normal tolerance limits, leading to frequent feedback from the instructor. As

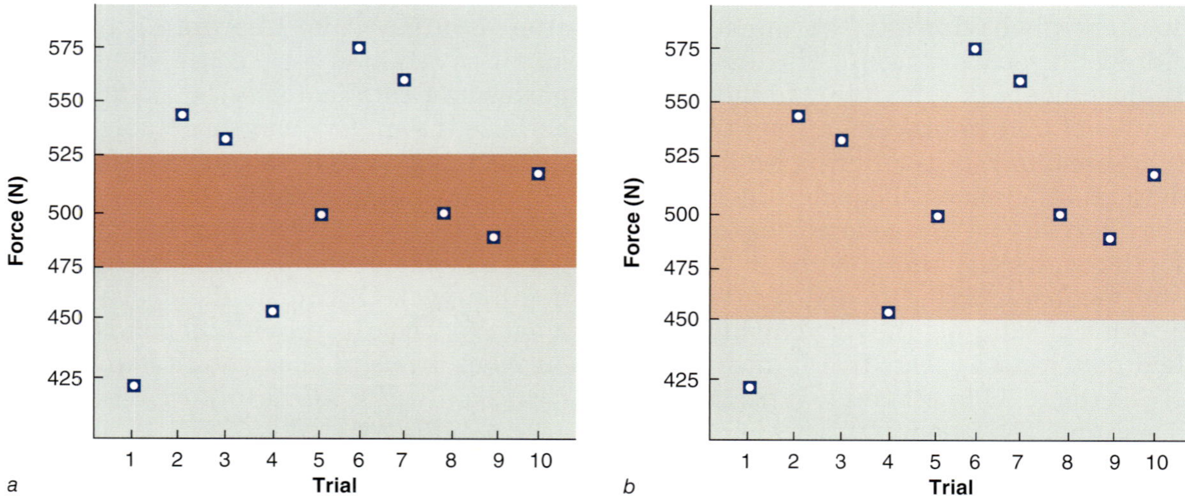

FIGURE 11.6 An illustration of the bandwidth method in a force-production task. Two bands of correctness are shown here. In figure 11.6*a*, the dark orange area represents a ±5% band around the 500 N target goal (475-525 N). In figure 11.6*b*, the light orange region represents a ±10% area around the target goal (450-550 N). Augmented feedback is given only when performance falls outside the predetermined tolerance bands. Performance that falls within the predetermined bands results in no feedback, which the learner has been cued to interpret as a correct performance.

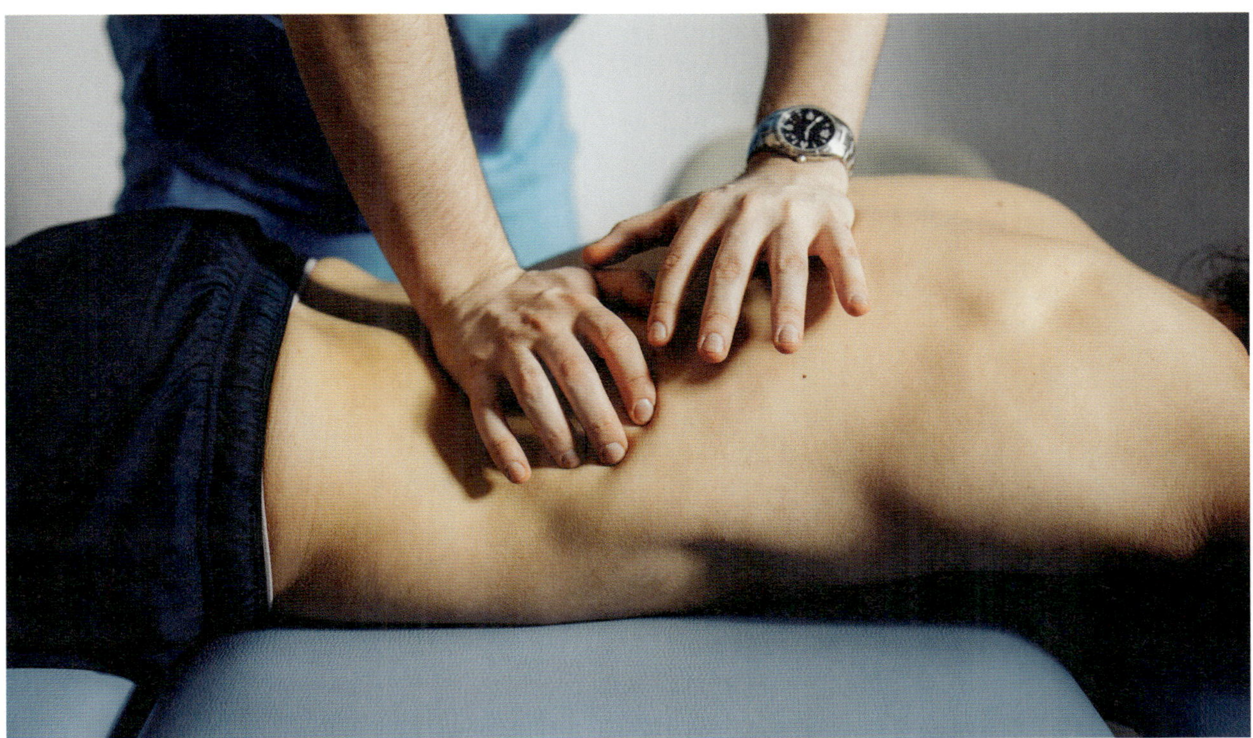

In this photo, describe at least three different ways in which augmented feedback could be provided to a learner in this spinal pressure task.

skill improves, more performances fall within the bandwidth, leading to less frequent error feedback. Therefore, the bandwidth creates a natural fading of error feedback frequency because it is sensitive to the performance levels and improvement progression of the learner.

Second, the method provides for increased motivational influences. With improvements in performance (resulting in more performances inside the bandwidth), the frequency of error feedback decreases, and the frequency of feedback that indicates to the learner that performance has been accurate increases. As we have discussed previously, providing learners with motivating feedback has a strong learning function.

Finally, withholding information on trials that fall within the bandwidth fosters more stable, consistent actions. Eliminating these small trial-to-trial corrections has a stabilizing influence on performance, because the learner is not encouraged to change the action on every trial. This seems especially important when the movement had been essentially correct on the previous attempt.

Summary Feedback

Another method that positively influences learning is summary feedback. In this method, feedback is withheld for a series of trials—for example, following a series of 5, 10, or 20 performance attempts—after which feedback for the entire series is summarized for the learner, perhaps by providing a graph of all the previous performance attempts in that block of trials. On the surface, summary feedback would not seem to be particularly effective for learning. The informational content of the feedback would be seriously degraded because the learner would be unlikely to remember and associate the feedback with any specific practice attempt, and thus would have no basis for making trial-to-trial corrections to improve performance.

But research has shown that **summary feedback** is very effective for learning (e.g., Lavery, 1962; Schmidt et al., 1989). Even though summary feedback is less effective than every-trial feedback for performance during practice, when feedback was not available in retention tests, participants who had received summary feedback performed more skillfully than participants who had received every-trial feedback. Of course, this leads to several questions regarding the use of summary feedback, which we will examine in the next sections.

Summary Size

Evidence suggests that there may be an optimal number of trials to include in summary-feedback reports, with either too few or too many trials being less effective for learning. With every-trial feedback (a one-trial summary), the learner is guided strongly to the goal, but this also maximizes the dependency-producing effects. However, if the feedback summarizes too many trials (e.g., 100), the dependency-producing effects are greatly reduced, but the learner also loses some of the error-correction benefits of directive feedback. This rationale suggests the existence of an optimal number of summary-feedback trials in which the benefits from being directed to the goal are balanced with the costs of the dependency-producing properties.

Support for this rationale was confirmed in experiments by Schmidt and colleagues (1990) and Guadagnoli and colleagues (1996). These findings are important because they reveal that the optimal summary size depends on a combination of learner experience and task complexity. For example, the retention results of Guadagnoli and colleagues, illustrated in figure 11.7, revealed that for experienced learners, larger (15-trial) summaries produced more learning than small (one-trial) summaries, regardless of the task complexity. However, for novice learners, large summaries produced more learning for simple tasks, while small summaries enhanced learning for complex tasks. The finding makes sense: experienced performers can gather and benefit from larger summaries regardless of the task difficulty; however, novices require smaller feedback summaries, especially for more complex tasks.

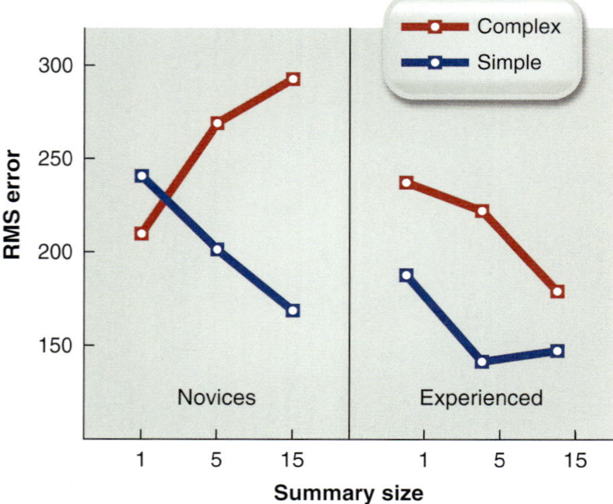

FIGURE 11.7 Retention performance of an optimal summary size was a function of learner experience and task complexity. Experienced learners benefited from larger summaries for both simple and complex tasks. However, novices only benefited from larger summaries for the simple task—they learned the complex task better when given smaller summaries.

Average Feedback

In a statistical variation of summary feedback, called **average feedback**, the learners wait for a series of trials before receiving an average of the trial scores instead of a trial-by-trial (e.g., graphical) summary. For example, the golf instructor might watch the learner make 10 swings before commenting, "Your backswing tended to be a few inches too short on those last 10 shots."

Results from studies by Young and Schmidt (1992) and Yao and colleagues (1994) showed that both average feedback and feedback summaries were far more effective for learning (i.e., retention) than every-trial feedback. The retention results in the study by Yao and colleagues, shown in figure 11.8, revealed an optimal summary size of five trials, with average-feedback conditions (the two yellow bars) slightly more effective for learning than summary-feedback conditions (the two red bars).

Average feedback allows the instructor to report a more complete idea of what the learner's error tendency happens to be. On any one

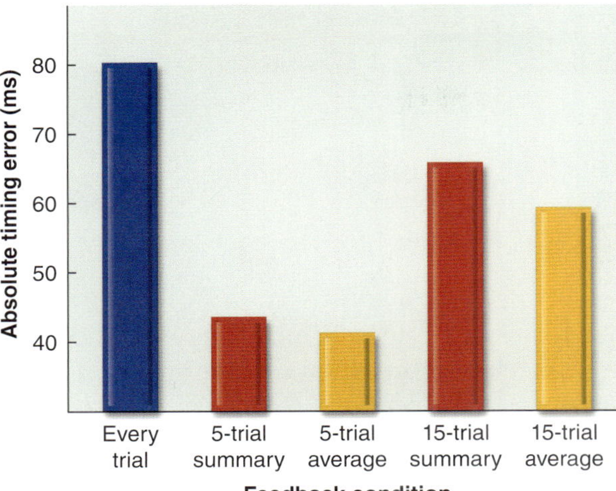

FIGURE 11.8 Retention performance (over two retention intervals) for various feedback conditions. In this study (Yao et al., 1994), average-feedback conditions produced slightly better retention than summary-feedback conditions (the two yellow vs. the two red bars), and five-trial summary or average conditions were better than 15-trial or every-trial conditions.

attempt, many things can occur by chance alone (because performances vary from trial to trial). However, by watching the learner over several performances, the instructor can filter out the variability (i.e., by averaging) to detect the error that a learner typically (i.e., on average) makes. Thus, average feedback gives the learner more reliable information about what needs to change.

How Does Summary Feedback Work?

What are the processes underlying the benefits of summary feedback? The following are three ways summary feedback could function to aid learning:

1. Summary feedback might prevent the dependency-producing effects of frequent feedback because it causes the learner to perform independently for several trials before finally receiving feedback. Then the learner can make corrections to the general error tendencies produced in the earlier trials.
2. Summary feedback might produce more stable performance because feedback is withdrawn for several trials, giving the learner no basis for a change in the movement from trial to trial. Single-trial feedback, on the other hand, encourages the learner to change the movement frequently, which prevents the movement from achieving the stability needed for subsequent performance.
3. Summary feedback appears to encourage learners to analyze their inherent movement-produced feedback to learn to detect their own errors (a concept discussed in chapter 9). Frequent feedback tells learners about errors, eliminating the need to process inherent feedback. The learners do not need to process information about their errors because augmented feedback provides this for them.

Feedback Timing

An important question that remains is *when* should augmented feedback be given? A common myth is that feedback should be given immediately after a performance is completed in order to maximize learning. As we will discuss, however, that advice is undesirable for several reasons.

Augmented feedback timing can be described in terms of three intervals, as illustrated in figure 11.9. When delivered during the ongoing movement, it is typically called **concurrent feedback**. Note that *physical guidance* falls within this definition since it consists of augmented information that serves to signal errors to the learner and is provided during an ongoing movement. (As mentioned earlier, concurrent feedback most often occurs for continuous tasks in which there is sufficient time to use the augmented feedback to correct an ongoing performance.) The interval of time after the completion of movement until augmented feedback is presented is called the **feedback delay interval**. And the interval after the provision of augmented feedback until the next movement starts is the **post-feedback delay** interval.

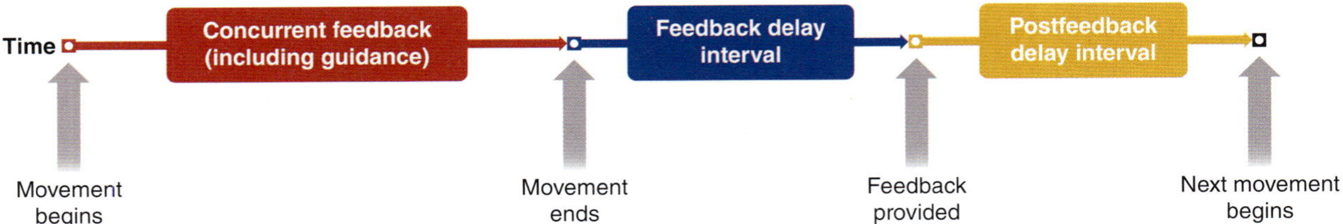

FIGURE 11.9 Terms used to describe the various time intervals when augmented feedback can be delivered.

Feedback During the Movement

One of the most powerful ways to deliver feedback is to provide it while the movement is ongoing. The concurrent augmented information can be used to regulate ongoing actions by giving a basis for correcting errors and directing the movement closer to the action goals. Two methods are typically used to provide ongoing information: (1) concurrent feedback, in which augmented information about the movement error (or the correct movement) is provided by verbal, visual, or auditory means and (2) concurrent physical guidance, in which haptic or kinesthetic information is signaled to the learner by a guidance device (e.g., a robot) or a person (e.g., a therapist) who physically restricts the movement. Despite their apparent differences, the two methods influence motor learning in similar ways.

Concurrent Feedback

An experiment by Annett (1959) provides insight into some processes involved in practicing with concurrent feedback. He asked participants to learn to produce a specific amount of pressure against a hand-operated lever. During the movement, one group of participants received concurrent visual feedback on a display showing the amount of pressure they were exerting relative to the goal pressure. Another group received feedback after the movement. As expected, the concurrent feedback facilitated performance greatly during practice. However, in a retention test with the feedback removed, this group performed very poorly, with some participants pressing so hard that they damaged the apparatus! Participants who had learned the task with concurrent feedback were unable to perform without it. Similar results, showing enhanced performance with concurrent feedback present but poor retention, were found by Schmidt and Wulf (1997) and, as part of a larger study, by Armstrong (1970).

Physically Restrictive Guidance

Concurrent feedback provides information that helps the learner avoid making errors, correct errors quickly, or both. Guidance techniques often work in a more direct way—to prevent the learner from making errors by physical means (e.g., see Focus on Application 11.1).

Physical guidance techniques represent a large class of methods whereby the learner is "forced" to produce the correct movement. Guidance devices have several goals; the main one is to reduce or eliminate errors and ensure that the learner performs the ideal or proper movement pattern. Another goal of guidance devices is to provide a measure of safety when the movement is dangerous, as in gymnastics, where various spotting methods can prevent harmful falls, or in swimming, where fearful beginners can use flotation devices. Guidance is also useful for training with expensive equipment, where mistakes can be costly as well as dangerous, as with learning to drive a car or fly an airplane.

Guidance methods vary widely across settings. Some forms of guidance are very loose, giving the learner only slight assistance in performance. An example is the instructor who provides very light hand pressure to guide the learner or talks the learner through the action. Other forms of guidance are far more powerful and invasive. An instructor can constrain the learner's movements physically, as when the physical therapist forces the patient's movements into the proper

FOCUS ON Application 11.1

Physical Guidance in Stroke Rehabilitation

The effects of acute stroke are often devastating, and many individuals who experience a stroke never fully regain the motor capability that was lost due to brain damage. But many individuals do recover. Some of this recovery is spontaneous, because the brain heals itself following the trauma. And some of the recovery can also be attributed to intense therapeutic interventions involving movement.

Physical guidance is a frequently used technique in rehabilitation and is typically based on two basic fundamental assumptions: (1) that learning is a process of repetition and (2) that repeating an optimal (or correct) movement pattern results in more learning than repeating a movement that is suboptimal, incorrect, or erroneous. Physical guidance techniques are designed with both assumptions in mind. Unfortunately, both assumptions have questionable validity, which we will cover in a later section.

Patients who have had a stroke often tire easily because of their extreme weakness. One advantage of upper limb guidance techniques, for example, is that they can be used to move the limb for the patient (passive movement) or to support the weight of the limb at least partially so that active movement can be done with minimized effort. An advantage, therefore, is that much less fatigue occurs during a therapy session with a guidance device, and more repetitions can be performed as a result, satisfying the first principle.

The second principle is more contentious. The view of optimizing learning as a process of repeating a correct or desirable movement pattern is basically an extension of Thorndike's Law of Effect (see Focus on Research 11.1). This view characterizes learning as a process of strengthening the association between a goal (e.g., to move correctly) and a response (e.g., moving correctly). For Thorndike, augmented feedback, in the form of reward, was the agent that served to increase the repetition of this association. So, in theory, physically restricting the response so that *only* the correct movement can be performed should optimize the Law of Effect.

As we discuss in this chapter, however, the evidence from studies with healthy adults suggests that physical guidance is an ineffective method of practice for several important reasons. Moreover, the use of physical guidance as a therapy intervention in stroke rehabilitation has come under increasing criticism (Mehrholz et al., 2008; Timmermans et al., 2009). The result is that new techniques are now being devised that aim to maximize the positive benefits conferred by guidance devices that provide assistance only when needed, allowing the patient to make and experience some errors in movement but not those that would lead to injury (Banala et al., 2009).

path, preventing a serious fall. Physically restrictive guidance devices are particularly popular in sports such as golf, where swing aids constrain the movement pattern physically in several ways, with the hope that participants will experience and remember the ideal movement pattern.

Each method provides the learner with some kind of temporary aid during practice. The desire, of course, is that learning will be enhanced, as measured by performance in the future without the aid. But the research suggests that while small amounts of guidance might facilitate learning, perhaps in the very early stages of practice, the negative impact on learning accumulates quickly (Hodges & Campagnaro, 2012).

A study by Armstrong (1970) provides important evidence about the effects of guidance relative to the contributions of concurrent feedback and terminal feedback. Over three days of practice, participants learned to move a lever with elbow extension and flexion movements to produce a specific, timed kinematic pattern (illustrated by the blue line in figure 5.6). Figure 11.10 illustrates the three experimental groups' performance on the three days of practice and in retention tests (with no augmented feedback). Movement error was mostly absent through the entire practice period in a guidance group—the physical restriction essentially forced the participants to produce the correct movement pattern. Movement error was not prevented entirely but was eliminated quickly in a concurrent-feedback group, whose participants were able to see the ongoing movement's kinematic trace on a computer screen, overlaid on the target template. And error was eliminated gradually over practice in a group that received terminal KP feedback after the completion of a trial. Figure 11.10 shows that, even after three days of practice, participants in the terminal-feedback group never achieved the level of performance of the other groups. Clearly, the guidance and concurrent-feedback procedures did their job, ensuring that the learners remained on target.

Now consider the respective performances of these groups in retention, in which all groups performed a test condition without the benefit of any guidance or augmented feedback (far right side of figure 11.10). Several things are of interest here. First, the terminal-feedback group, which had been the most erroneous of the three groups during practice, clearly showed the most learning as measured in these retention trials. Second, in the absence of augmented feedback, the terminal-feedback group maintained the level of performance it had achieved at the end of the practice trials. Finally, both the guidance and concurrent-feedback groups' retention performance deteriorated considerably following the removal of their respective augmented information. In fact, both groups' performance deteriorated almost to the level displayed by the terminal-feedback group on its very first block of practice, suggesting that guidance and concurrent feedback were almost completely ineffective for learning. Guidance and concurrent feedback had produced a strong performance effect but essentially no effect on learning.

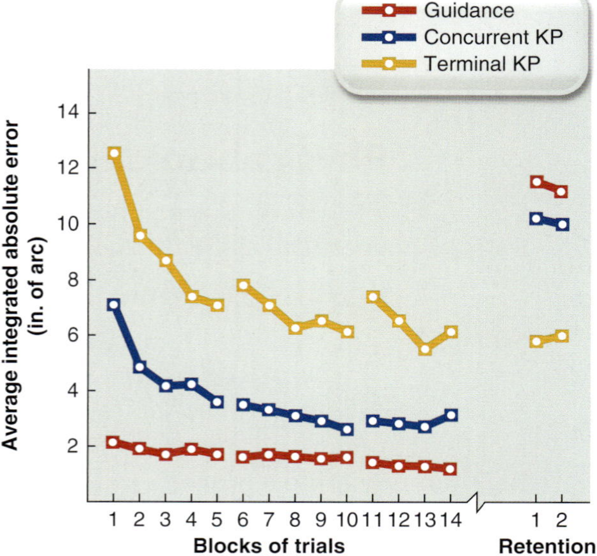

FIGURE 11.10 Effects of physically restrictive guidance (red), concurrent feedback (blue), and terminal feedback (yellow) on over three days of practice and in a no-feedback retention test (from data in Armstrong, 1970).

Visit HK*Propel* to read "The Golfer's Little Helper" and complete the self-directed learning activities.

Error Amplification

If the findings about the negative effects of physical guidance were not surprising enough, more recent research on the effects of **error amplification** might be even more surprising. In this research, computer-controlled robots use restrictive guidance devices to pull and push movements *away* from the intended movement goal rather than toward it. The idea is simple: Rather than restricting the error made in performing a movement, error amplification methods serve to *increase* the magnitude of the error. The intent is to increase the salience of the inherent feedback, making the learner more aware of the error and how to correct it. These methods have provided some provocative results that show benefits to learning that outweigh many traditional methods and are certainly much better than error-restriction methods (reviewed in Heuer & Lüttgen, 2016), despite their unpopularity with participants (Marchal-Crespo et al., 2017). Application of error augmentation methods to learning sport skills (Milanese et al., 2016, 2017) and stroke rehabilitation (Park et al., 2021) has shown promising results.

Common Processes in Concurrent Feedback and Physical Guidance

The evidence discussed in the previous sections points to an important principle. Guidance and concurrent feedback, almost by definition, are effective for performance when present during practice. After all, these informational supplements are designed to help the performer make the correct action, to prevent errors, to aid confidence, and so on, so there is little surprise that performance benefits from them. But the real test of guidance effectiveness is how well participants do when the intervention is removed, and this is where these procedures often fail. When the ongoing information source is removed for retention tests, performance usually falls to the level of, or sometimes below, that of learners who had no guidance at all. That is, guidance is not a very effective variable for learning if it is not used wisely.

How can these principles of guidance be understood? Probably the best interpretation is that, during practice where guidance is present, the learner relies too strongly on its powerful performance-enhancing properties, which actually change the task in several ways. Physical guidance can modify the feel of the task. Decision-making processes are not challenged when the instructor or the guidance device tells the learner what to do. Furthermore, the learner does not have the opportunity to experience or correct errors during the guided movement or the next movement. Therefore, the learner will fail to acquire the capability necessary to perform in a retention test or when the guidance is no longer available.

Notice that this interpretation is really a statement of the specificity view discussed in chapter 9. If guided practice changes the task markedly (as it does), it is not really the same task it was under the unguided conditions. If these modifications are large (as in very strong physical guidance procedures), then practice on the guided version can be thought of as involving practice on a different task rather than practice on the unguided version. Perhaps this was seen most clearly in the Armstrong (1970) study, in which the guided and concurrent-feedback groups' retention performance reverted to the level of the terminal KP group's first block of trials—essentially, these two groups had not practiced the task that was tested in retention.

Feedback After the Movement

In early animal conditioning experiments, a common finding was that laboratory rats learning to press a bar after a tone was presented suffered a decrement to learning if the reward (feedback) was delayed. In fact, if the delay was long enough, there was no learning at all. Some researchers believed that the same finding would apply to human motor learning. But what does the evidence say?

Length of Feedback Delays

First, consider simply lengthening the feedback delay interval (time between movement completion and augmented feedback), with the interval free of other attention-demanding activities (conversations, other trials, and so on). The information-processing view would expect longer intervals to interfere with learning (see the section Short-Term Memory in chapter 2 and figure 2.13). Yet when empty feedback delays, ranging from several seconds to several minutes, have been examined in human research, scientists have almost never found detrimental effects on learning (Salmoni et al., 1984). The lack of any degraded learning when the feedback delays are lengthened is surprising. The evidence seems to suggest that, without other activities in the interval between a movement and its feedback, the instructor need not worry about the delay in giving feedback.

Instantaneous Feedback

There is one exception to the generalization that the length of the feedback delay interval has no effect on motor learning—situations in which feedback is presented very soon after the completion of a movement. Under

FOCUS ON Application 11.2

Physical Guidance in Learning to Swim

As mentioned previously, not all physical guidance is detrimental to learning. Guidance certainly plays an important role in dangerous or frightening situations in which it would be undesirable to continue practice in the absence of guidance. And guidance may also serve a useful function in the beginning stages of learning a skill. Here is an example from personal experience. When one of us (RAS) was a graduate student, he taught a course in beginning swimming. This course should have been called "Teaching the Persistent Nonswimmer to Swim," because many of these students could not swim a stroke and were truly terrified of the water.

After a week or so of learning to become familiar with water (e.g., in the shallow end of the pool, blowing bubbles, and so on), the next task was for the students to learn the elementary backstroke as a lifesaving stroke in case they were to fall into the water somewhere. This process involved the usual techniques (in the shallow end of the pool): learning to float on the back, gliding on the back after a push off from the side of the pool, then adding a frog kick, and eventually adding an arm stroke.

Then came the terrifying part: swimming with the elementary backstroke in the deep end of the pool. Naturally, most of the students were quite apprehensive about this task, so we developed various methods to alleviate their fear. One of these involved the use of long wooden poles. On the first attempt, the instructor would walk along the poolside adjacent to the swimmer in the water, just lightly touching the pole against the swimmer's far-side hip. This did two things: First, it provided a measure of assurance for the swimmer, since all he had to do in an emergency was grasp the pole, and the instructor could pull him to the pool edge. Second, the pole did not interfere with the swimmer's own strokes, allowing him to gain confidence and learn the stroke unimpeded by the guide.

This method was enormously successful. By the end of the course, most students had been weaned from the assistance of the wooden pole and were quite capable of swimming relatively long distances. Over the course of about 10 years in which this course was taught, the average percentage of students who completed the 1 mi (1.6 km) swim was over 70%! The look of pride on these students' faces was impossible to describe.

These were the two major keys to this procedure's success:

1. Nearly completely alleviating the students' fear so that they could learn the stroke
2. Providing support in a noninvasive way so that the guidance did not interfere with the students' movements

the belief that feedback given quickly will be beneficial for learning, many instructors have tried to minimize feedback delays, essentially giving feedback that is almost simultaneous with the completion of movement. Instantaneous feedback is common in many simulators, for example, such as medical mannequins, in which feedback about pressure is displayed immediately after a chest compression is performed.

Note that **instantaneous feedback** is not, technically, the same as concurrent feedback, because feedback is delivered after the movement has finished (especially for discrete tasks because the movement is completed too quickly for concurrent feedback to be useful). But the effects on performance and learning are remarkably similar to those for concurrent feedback. Research shows that giving feedback instantaneously, as opposed to delaying it even by a few seconds, is actually *detrimental* to learning (Swinnen et al., 1990). This can be seen in figure 11.11. Participants in an instantaneous-feedback condition performed a simulated batting task more poorly than the delayed group on the second day of practice and on retention tests given up to four months later. One interpretation is

Golf swing monitors provide the learner with instantaneous augmented feedback about many different parameters of the just-completed swing.

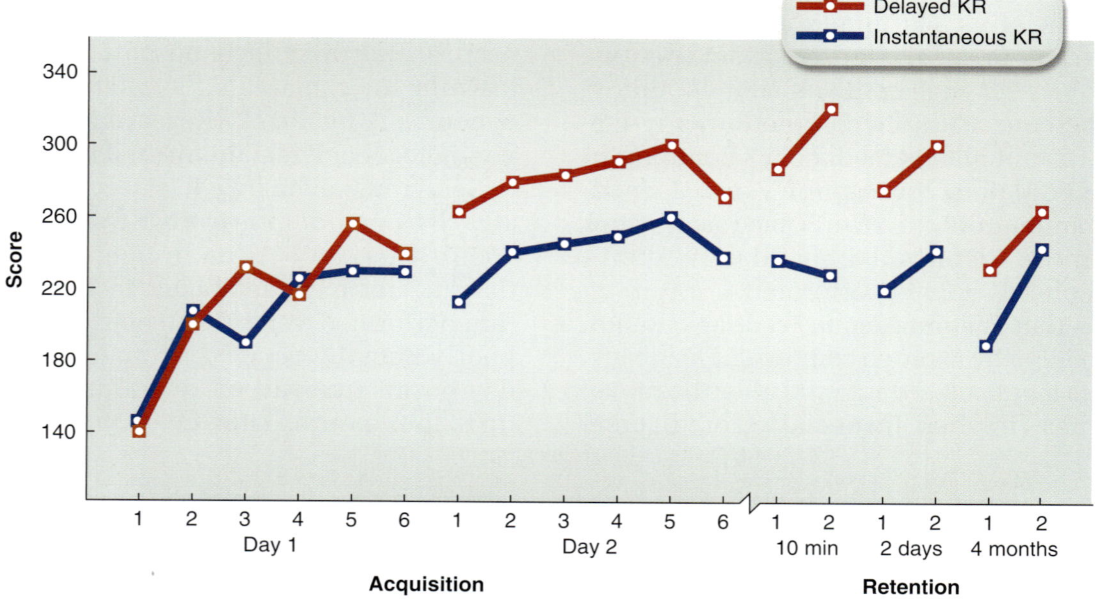

FIGURE 11.11 Instantaneous augmented feedback degraded learning compared to delayed augmented feedback.

that feedback given instantaneously blocks or prevents the participant from processing inherent feedback (i.e., how the movement felt, sounded, looked), thereby restricting the learning of error-detection capabilities, as discussed in chapter 9.

Filled-Feedback Delay Intervals

In many real-world settings, there can be a delay in the delivery of augmented feedback following a movement, during which other attention-demanding activities can occur. These intervening activities may include conversing with a friend, performing some other task, or even attempting other trials of the same task (the summary- and average-feedback methods discussed earlier can be seen as filled-feedback intervals, essentially). The effects of these activities during the feedback delay interval fall into two classes, depending on the nature of the intervening task.

Intervening Activities of a Different Task Imagine that the activity occurring between a given movement and its feedback is a different task. This activity could be a trial of a different motor task or even a task involving mental operations, such as recording one's scores or giving feedback to a friend. Performing these events during the feedback delay interval generally degrades learning as measured on retention tests (Marteniuk, 1986; Swinnen, 1990).

Trials-Delay Technique But what if the intervening activity involves additional trials of the same task? For example, the instructor might give the learner several minutes to practice a skill, then give feedback about the first movement after the learner has completed several more attempts in the interim. For instance, feedback from a therapist to a patient when practicing standing from a seated position might include statements such as "On your first attempt, you started to stand before your feet were properly positioned under your knees," but this is provided after several more attempts at the sit-to-stand have already been completed. This has been called **trials-delay of feedback** technique.

Although the trials-delay procedure would seem to prevent the learner from benefiting from the augmented feedback, the evidence says that it is not detrimental at all, and it may be more effective for learning than presenting feedback after each trial (Lavery & Suddon, 1962). In fact, researchers have suggested that the performance of intervening trials before the delivery of feedback has the effect of raising awareness about the inherent feedback available after performing the task, perhaps making the augmented feedback more important or valuable when it is then presented to the learner (Anderson et al., 2005).

Intervening Subjective Estimations The conclusions of Anderson and colleagues (2005) support the view that learning is enhanced when processing the inherent feedback occurs before augmented feedback is provided. This idea has been examined directly in studies that promoted subjective estimation of task performance during the KR-delay period. For example, learners who practiced a throwing task with their nondominant limb performed more skillfully in retention tests if they made subjective estimates of their throwing technique before receiving augmented feedback during practice (Liu & Wrisberg, 1997). A study by Guadagnoli and Kohl (2001) further revealed the impact of making subjective estimations. They found that the negative effects of 100% KR frequency (see earlier discussion) were eliminated in retention if learners had made subjective estimates of error before the delivery of the feedback on each trial (see figure 11.12). In contrast, the benefit of reduced relative frequency of feedback was not further enhanced by error estimation, perhaps because this 20% group was estimating spontaneously on the no-feedback trials.

Together with the results of the trials-delay studies, these subject-estimation findings support a strong role for learning to process inherent feedback information. Remember that retention tests in all these studies were performed without augmented feedback. Thus, the only information that a learner could use to check on performance accuracy in retention was the inherent feedback, which was always available. Practice conditions that encourage the attention to and processing of inherent feedback tend to promote learning, especially when that is the only source of feedback information available in a retention or transfer situation.

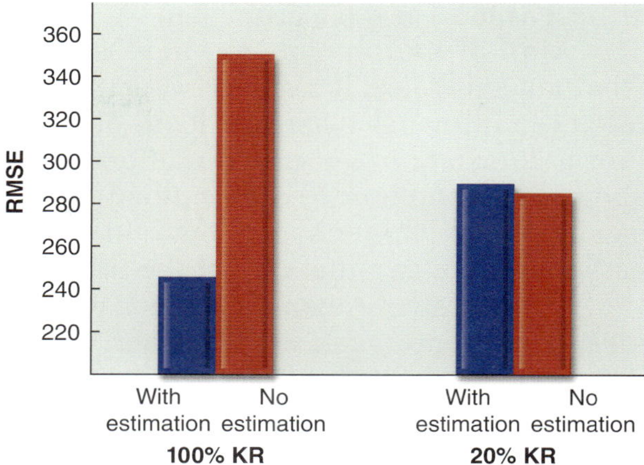

FIGURE 11.12 The negative effects on retention of presenting feedback on every trial (100% KR) were reversed when participants performed an error-estimation procedure. There were no effects on groups that received only 20% relative feedback. RMSE = root-mean-square error.

Post-Feedback Delay Intervals

After receiving feedback for one movement, in the post-feedback delay, the learner attempts to create another movement that is at least somewhat different from the previous one—a movement that will eliminate the errors signaled by feedback. How much time is required for processing this information, and how soon can the next movement begin? The research on these questions shows that if this interval is too short (less than 5 s), performance on the next trial will suffer, probably because of insufficient time for evaluation and planning. Overall, though, the post-feedback interval is not particularly powerful in determining learning, and you can focus on more important aspects of the learning environment.

Summary

A learner can receive various kinds of sensory information, but augmented feedback about errors from the instructor is one of the most critical aspects of the learning environment. This kind of information can have several simultaneous roles: It can serve as a motivator; it can influence where the focus of attention is directed; it can provide information about errors and how to correct them; and it can produce a learner dependency, in which case performance suffers when the information is withdrawn. Augmented feedback can take many forms, such as videos and verbal descriptions. Verbal feedback is best when it is simple and refers to only one movement feature at a time, a movement feature that the learner can control.

Augmented feedback can be provided at various time periods relative to the performance—before, during, and after a movement. A number of feedback-related factors have strong influences on learning, such as feedback frequency (including bandwidth and summary procedures) as well as guidance and concurrent-feedback effects. An early principle that anything making feedback more frequent, accurate, and useful will enhance learning has been found to be false and has been replaced by revised viewpoints that focus on the feedback's nature, scheduling, and motivational properties.

HK*PROPEL* ACTIVITIES

HK*Propel* offers these activities to help you build and apply your knowledge of the concepts in this chapter. Additionally, you'll find a key terms flashcard review activity and a key terms quiz, along with audio supplements for selected figures, as indicated by QR codes throughout the chapter.

Interactive Learning

Activity 11.1: Review the types of feedback by matching each to its definition.

Activity 11.2: Given examples of feedback, determine whether each represents knowledge of results or knowledge of performance.

Activity 11.3: Answer a series of questions that will help you understand the effects of concurrent feedback and physical guidance.

Activity 11.4: Tie together concepts discussed throughout the textbook by selecting labels to complete a conceptual model of motor performance.

Activity 11.5: Listen to a discussion that discusses feedback in a vocational setting, then apply what you've learned to a different vocational context.

Principles-to-Application Exercise

Activity 11.6: The principles-to-application exercise for this chapter prompts you to choose an activity and a learner, as well as an aspect of the learner's current performance. You will then create a strategy for providing feedback to that learner in the most beneficial way possible.

Motor Control in Everyday Actions Narratives

The Coach as a Dictionary

The Golfer's Little Helper

Check Your Understanding

1. Define inherent and augmented feedback, highlighting the differences between them. Define knowledge of results and knowledge of performance, highlighting the differences between them. Provide an example of each of these types of feedback that a beginner watercolor artist might experience.
2. Briefly explain how each of the following can affect learning:
   - Frequency of feedback
   - Precision of feedback
   - Feedback schedules
   - Timing of feedback presentation
3. List and briefly discuss four properties of augmented feedback.

Apply Your Knowledge

1. A university wrestling coach is teaching his team some new ways to finish a takedown. One wrestler has been competing for 10 years and is the current national champion, while another is in her first year of university and has much less experience. Discuss some factors that the coach might consider when providing feedback to each of the wrestlers. Explain how the coach might provide feedback that benefits the wrestlers' learning of the new skills and their transfer to a wrestling match.
2. A physical education teacher is beginning a new unit, teaching the game of goalball to her high school class. (In the game of goalball, each player is blindfolded, and the ball used for play emits an auditory signal.) Discuss three types of augmented feedback the teacher can use to provide feedback to the students during the class. Would the amount, precision, and frequency of feedback change from her earlier unit teaching handball? If so, how would it change?

12

Theoretical Perspectives on Motor Learning

Understanding How Learning Occurs

CHAPTER OUTLINE

CHAPTER OBJECTIVES

Chapter 12 discusses various theoretical accounts of the motor learning process. This chapter will help you understand

- the different views on the motor learning process that theories and theoretical constructs provide,
- the strengths and limitations of each theory, and
- a theoretical outlook's important implications for understanding the acquisition of motor skills.

CHAPTER PREVIEW QUIZ

1. What roles do errors play in motor learning?
2. What constraints can be used to promote motor learning?
3. What is the impact of motivation on motor learning?

Scientific theories and theoretical constructs are developed to describe something, often a process, based on experimental evidence. As discussed in chapter 1, theories are formalized constructs that have clear and testable predictions and are sufficiently succinct for research to support or refute their tenets. Other theoretical constructs are less formalized than theories, such as hypotheses or frameworks, but provide useful ways to conceptualize a thing or process. Various theories and theoretical constructs have been proposed about the motor learning process to explain how skills are acquired, retained, and transferred. They rely on considerable experimental evidence, gathered using laboratory and applied skills.

In this chapter, consistent with the main themes and evidence discussed throughout the book, we have focused our attention on theories that are largely based on experimental evidence derived from behavioral motor learning research. In so doing, we do not discuss some important theories that exist at different levels of analysis, such as at the neural level (e.g., the COIN theory by Heald et al., 2021, and the fast/slow learning theory by McDougle et al., 2015). We also do not present theories that were designed to explain general learning phenomena, although frequently tested using motor learning tasks (such as Thorndike's (1927) Law of Effect and Hull's (1943) drive reduction theory).

As you read this chapter, be aware that we have tried to simplify much of the specific background rationale and tenets that underlie the theoretical constructs. Note as well that we have minimized the number of specific terms used by the authors to describe their theoretical constructs. We did this to maintain our writing style, or "voice," in relation to motor learning and performance, to facilitate direct cross-theory comparisons, and to limit the introduction of new jargon. So, consider our descriptions not only as an introduction to these theories and constructs but also as an invitation for you to explore each individual theory in detail by reading the original sources.

This chapter appears at the end of the book for good reasons. As we describe each theory, you should be able to formulate ideas about how they explain the research ideas that were presented in the previous four motor learning chapters. Each construct we present has made important advances to our understanding of the motor learning process. However, each one also has limitations—either in the breadth or scope of the actions they explain or because new research data fail to conform to the theory's predictions. Be aware that although a theoretical construct has limitations, those limitations do not diminish its importance. Remember that theories are not the end, but rather the beginning of the discovery process. By reformulating ideas in novel ways, they have blazed a trail for future research and new theorizing.

Stage Theories

Sometimes it is useful to consider learning as a series of relatively distinct stages (or phases) in the skill acquisition process. These stages should not be confused with the information-processing stages discussed in chapter 2. Rather, they are descriptors of the different levels of skill development. Although several stage theories of motor learning have appeared in the literature (e.g., see Gentile, 1972; Snoddy, 1926), we will discuss two in particular, one by Fitts and another by Bernstein, each developed from a very different perspective (Anson et al., 2005).

The Learning Process: Fitts' Stages

Paul Fitts (1964; Fitts & Posner, 1967) suggested that perceptual-motor learning was largely a cognitive problem that went through three stages of progress. The stages mainly reflect changes in the allocation of attentional resources to the task.

Stage 1: Cognitive

As the name implies, the learner's first problem to overcome is cognitive. The dominant questions concern what to do (and what not to do), when to do it, how to do it, and so on. Figuring out what to attend to in the environment and devising an appropriate movement plan are critical in the **cognitive stage**. Gains in proficiency in this stage are large and occur very rapidly, indicating that better strategies for performance are being discovered, resulting in massive performance improvements. It is not of much concern that performance at this stage is halting, jerky, uncertain, and poorly timed to the external environment; this is merely the starting point for later proficiency gains. Verbal activity (e.g., self-talk) is effective for this initial stage, facilitating a rough approximation of the skill and will diminish later.

Consider the example of learning to play ice hockey. Ice hockey involves two main tasks: skating (whole-body movements on skates that cut into the ice) and stickhandling (using a bladed stick to pass, shoot, and manipulate a rubber disk). The process of maintaining balance is a primary concern, requiring massive amounts of attentional resources just to stay upright. Holding the stick is verbalized, and doing so correctly is important (a right-handed player uses the left hand to hold the stick near the top of the shaft and the right hand to hold it partway down the shaft). Shooting, passing, and manipulating the puck require considerable conscious resources since each of these activities perturbs balance.

Stage 2: Fixation

The performer next enters the **fixation stage** (Fitts also referred to this as the *associative stage*). Most of the cognitive problems dealing with attending to environmental cues and performing the necessary actions have been solved. Several factors change markedly during the fixation stage, associated with more effective movement patterns. As the learner attempts new solutions to movement problems, performance improves steadily, although with some inconsistency from trial to trial. Consistency gradually improves, though movements involving closed skills become more stereotypic and those involving open skills become more adaptable to the changing environment (Gentile, 1972). Enhanced movement efficiency reduces energy costs, and self-talk becomes less important for performance. Learners begin to effectively monitor feedback and anticipate errors. Performers discover environmental regularities that serve as effective cues for timing. Anticipation develops rapidly, making movements smoother and less rushed. This stage generally lasts much longer than the cognitive stage.

In the ice hockey example, rudimentary skill has been achieved by the start of the fixation stage—the learner has acquired the basic motor patterns to skate, shoot, pass, and manipulate the puck, although these require considerable cognitive resources to coordinate simultaneously. The attention allocated to skating and stickhandling has been reduced, allowing the learner to attend to other information, such as locating members of the opposing team and anticipating the actions of teammates.

Stage 3: Autonomous

After considerable practice, the learner gradually enters the **autonomous stage**. This is the stage usually associated with the attainment of expert performance—perceptual anticipation enhances environmental information processing. The decreased attention demanded by both perceptual and motor processes frees the individual to perform simultaneous higher-order cognitive activities, such as making decisions about strategies in sports, expressing emotion and affect in music and dance, and dealing with stress and chaos in emergencies. Self-confidence increases, and the capability to anticipate, detect, and correct errors becomes more finely tuned.

By the time the hockey player reaches the autonomous stage, very little attention is given to the processes involved in skating and stick control or even the simultaneous coordination of these skills. Now the learner's cognitive involvement is invested in higher-order activities of the game—detecting patterns of game flow by both teams, planning strategic plays by going to locations on the ice that could provide an offensive or defensive advantage, or taking advantage of perceived weaknesses of the opponent.

The Learning Process: Bernstein's Stages

In contrast to Fitts' emphasis on attention and the information-processing aspects of skill, Nikolai Bernstein (1967) identified stages of learning from a different level of analysis. Specifically, his concern was the **degrees of freedom problem**—how to effectively control the enormous number of ways in which the body can move.

Stage 1: Reduce Degrees of Freedom

Bernstein suggested that the initial step in solving the degrees of freedom problem was to reduce the conscious regulation of nonessential or redundant body parts—in essence, by "freezing" them or creating coordinated units of action that work together. In some ways, this solution achieved the same goal as Fitts' first stage of learning—by reducing the number of body parts to control, fewer independent motions require attention.

Continuing with the ice hockey example, reducing body motion solves the problem of staying upright and striking the puck in Bernstein's first stage. A steady base is critical; therefore, movements that would destabilize that base, such as taking a long stride or shooting or passing a puck, are reduced in magnitude. The motions of the body during skating are rather rigid, again to avoid destabilizing balance. During this stage, players largely use the stick as a crutch to help maintain balance.

Stage 2: Release Degrees of Freedom

As movement control in stage 1 begins to result in some initial successes, the typical learner attempts to improve performance by releasing some of the degrees of freedom that had initially been frozen. This is particularly useful in tasks that require power or speed, because the degrees of freedom that have been released could allow for faster movement and greater accumulation of forces.

At this stage of learning to play hockey, the learner's skating skills have improved dramatically due to the release of some of the body's degrees of freedom. Rather than appearing to walk on skates, the learner makes a sideward push with one skate and glides forward on the other skate with greater ranges of motion of the body parts. Considerably more trunk rotation is used to move, resulting in much faster and more powerful skating. Control of the puck has also improved through more involvement of the wrist, forearm, and shoulder muscles. The result is greater force production and accuracy in receiving, shooting, and passing the puck, as well as more effective stick-handling control.

Stage 3: Exploiting Passive Dynamics

In Bernstein's final stage, the performer has learned to exploit the passive dynamics of the body—essentially, the energy and motion that come for free with the help of physics (such as gravity and momentum). In Bernstein's final stage, the movement becomes maximally skilled in terms of effectiveness (achieving an end result with maximum assuredness) and efficiency (minimum outlay of energy).

Bernstein's final stage in our hockey example exploits the energy that comes with the fast, dynamic play of the game. Players learn to stop, turn, accelerate, and decelerate with precision and use the passive dynamics not only of their own bodies but also of the energy obtained from on-ice objects, both animate (other players) and inanimate (e.g., the boards that surround the ice rink). Modern skates and sticks are manufactured with materials that are designed to be fully exploited by only the most highly skilled players.

Limitations

One point that is important to keep in mind about both the Fitts and the Bernstein perspectives is that these stages are generic descriptions of performance capabilities and tendencies at any one time in the learning process, understanding that these capabilities change as learning progresses. Neither is an empirically testable theory of learning. Also, neither considers these stages to be nonlinear and unidirectional. Indeed, Fitts considered performance change to be regressive as well as progressive, expecting it to produce tendencies characteristic of a previous stage under conditions of high arousal or after a long layoff from practice (Fitts et al., 1959).

In the photo, this young girl is learning to use chopsticks to pick up her sushi. Note that her parents have tied a rubber band around the tops of the two chopsticks. Describe what effect this would have from (1) Fitts' perspective and (2) Bernstein's perspective.

Task differences also play an important role in the stage views of both Fitts and Bernstein. For instance, automaticity in Fitts' final stage might be achieved for some tasks but never achieved for other tasks. Similarly, the nature of the task might limit the application of Bernstein's stages (Newell & Vaillancourt, 2001). For example, consider learning to do a handstand on the still rings in men's gymnastics. The learner seems to begin learning this task using nearly all the available degrees of freedom (e.g., maintaining balance with hip and trunk movements, using the arms). When the learner is clearly past the initial stage, rather than releasing degrees of freedom, the learner seems to freeze them. The wild hip and arm movements seem to drop out, leaving behind control of balance by the wrists only. This is the opposite order from Bernstein's views, where the learner gains proficiency by freezing, then releasing degrees of freedom. Similarly, Konczak and colleagues (2009) found that, like the still ring's example, expert violinists developed their skill by learning to reduce rather than release motions of their bowing arm.

In sum, the Fitts and Bernstein stage theories provide a good heuristic description of the motor learning process. However, the considerable lack of testable hypotheses and confirming evidence renders them incomplete. In contrast, in the early 1970s, Jack Adams proposed a theory that described motor learning in fine detail based on available empirical evidence and which offered testable hypotheses.

Adams' Closed-Loop Theory

Adams' (1971) learning theory was based on the premise that slow, goal-directed positioning movements result in inherent feedback sensations (called **perceptual traces**) that are stored in memory. Performing a goal-directed movement involves a process that compares current, ongoing inherent feedback (mainly proprioceptive) to these stored perceptual traces using closed-loop processes (see chapter 4). The key ingredient to learning is *strengthening* the correct perceptual trace stored in memory. Adams' theory described the motor learning process as a change in the distribution of perceptual trace strengths as a function of practice.

The Learning Process

The three parts of figure 12.1 illustrate the process of learning, as described by Adams (1971). Early in learning, there is no single, dominant perceptual trace strength, so ongoing movement regulation is made by comparing current inherent feedback to a selected trace in memory, which may or may not be the correct one. Movement regulation will be inaccurate if it is compared to an incorrect perceptual trace. Figure 12.1*a* illustrates this early stage as a nonpeaked normal distribution of the relative frequency of trace strengths. The trace strength for the correct movement is not disproportionally stronger than the nearby incorrect ones in this figure, so frequent errors are likely.

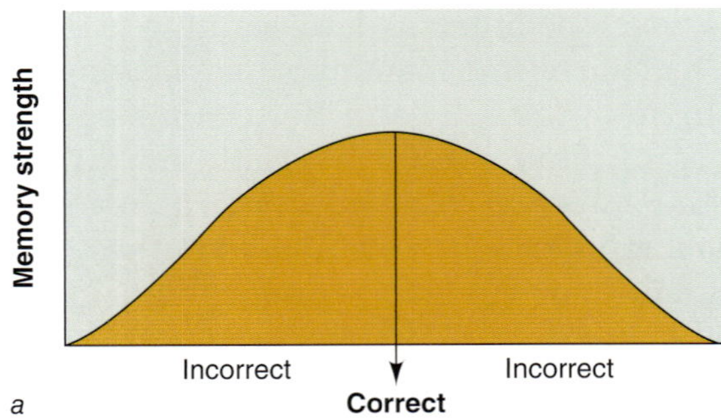

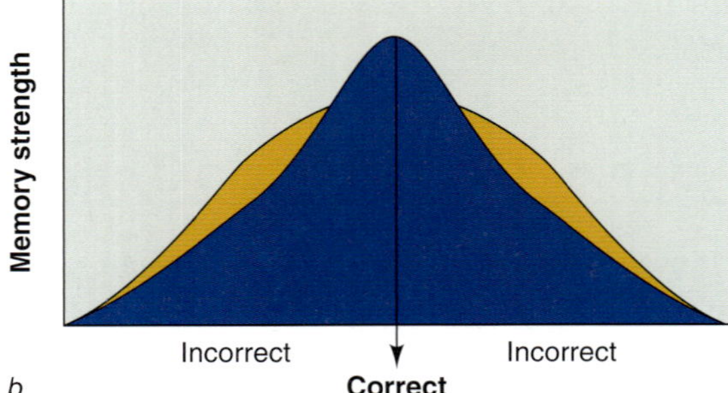

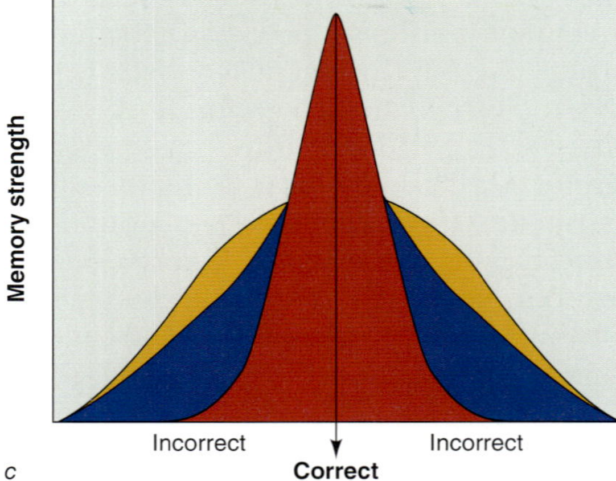

FIGURE 12.1 An illustration of the learning process of Adams' closed-loop theory. Practicing a slow positioning task over many trials results in the accumulation of stored perceptual traces of the resulting inherent feedback. In the graphs, *memory strength* refers to the relative frequency of the perceptual trace strengths for both correct and incorrect movements. The stronger the memory strength, the more likely it will be selected to guide current performance. When augmented feedback accompanies practice, which helps the learner become more accurate, the relative frequency of stored traces for the correct movement increases and, concomitantly, decreases for incorrect movements. Thus, learning shifts the shape of the frequency distribution from *(a)* relatively flat to *(b)* the development of a peak corresponding to the correct perceptual trace to *(c)* a sharply peaked distribution.

With the accumulation of practice attempts, accompanied by augmented feedback, the learner begins to make more and more movements that are correct and relatively fewer and fewer movements that are incorrect. The accumulation of a higher proportion of correct perceptual traces results in a redistribution of these representations in memory (i.e., the shape of the curve becomes leptokurtic). The correct perceptual trace becomes increasingly dominant, illustrated by a distribution with increased peaking that corresponds to the correct movement (see figure 12.1*b* and 12.1*c*).

Limitations

Adams' theory emphasized the roles of both ongoing and previously stored inherent feedback information for guiding slow positioning movements. Augmented feedback is useful to the degree that it helps the learner develop a stronger memory representation for correct inherent feedback through error-detection and correction processes. A key contribution of the theory was the importance given to how memory strength changes as skill improves (the redistribution of perceptual traces). A number of studies found evidence to support the theory, such as the beneficial effect of additional inherent feedback channels (reviewed in Adams, 1987).

A major limitation is that the theory was based on and applicable only to the acquisition of slow, feedback-based movements, which leaves unexplained how very rapid movement skills are learned. The theory also fails to account for findings that errors during practice are good for learning (Lee et al., 2016), as frequently occurs with interleaved practice conditions (see chapter 10). The theory also stands at odds with the physical guidance research (see chapter 11), which shows that forced repetition of only correct movements is poor for retention and transfer. Last, a major limitation was the key role assigned to augmented feedback—essentially, that providing augmented feedback in a way that guides the learner toward experiencing the correct movement (which strengthens the correct perceptual trace) would enhance learning. As we discussed in chapter 11, considerable research has shown that the guiding role of augmented feedback actually diminishes learning. Subsequently, a theory was advanced that accounted for some of the limitations arising from Adams' closed-loop theory.

Schema Theory

Adams' ideas inspired Richard Schmidt to develop a new theory that expanded the application beyond slow, positioning movements and which also accounted for the role of errors in learning. Using the generalized motor program (GMP) concept for performing rapid movements as a basis (see chapter 5), Schmidt (1975) developed the idea of a schema to describe the process of how one learns to select parameters to instantiate a GMP.

Recall from chapter 5 that the skill of throwing, for example, represents a class of movements. In American football, an important aspect of a quarterback's skill is the capability to throw different distances on demand. According to **schema theory**, a GMP for forward passing can be applied to many specific throwing situations by specifying parameters in the movement programming stage, which define how the movement is produced for any one instance. Figure 12.2 depicts a simplified version of the process. The quarterback first assesses the distance to be thrown (a value on the *x*-axis), then, based on the previously learned schema (the blue diagonal line), selects an appropriate force parameter (a value on the *y*-axis). For a relatively short pass (X_1), the schema determines that a relatively low force (Y_1) be applied to the GMP. A relatively longer pass (X_2) would require relatively more force (Y_2).

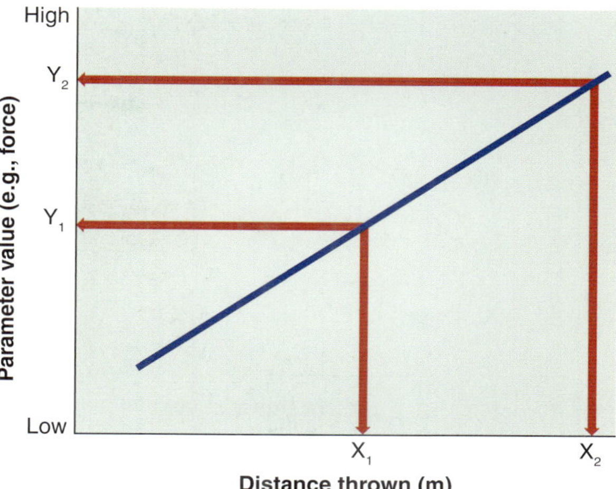

FIGURE 12.2 Schema theory in action. Throwing a football to specific distances (on the *x*-axis) occurs by choosing a force parameter value (on the *y*-axis) that corresponds to the appropriate schema (blue line) for overarm throwing.

The Learning Process

Schema learning occurs according to an abstraction process that relates parameter values (e.g., forces) to outcomes (e.g., distances thrown). Practice (e.g., repeated throws) results in the accumulation of abstracted data points. Early in learning, given relatively few practice attempts, the schema, is a crude and poorly specified relationship between parameters and outcomes. Practice improves the schema, making it a more precise and reliable representation in memory.

In figure 12.2, the thickness of the blue line represents the quarterback's skill level—the thinner the line, the more precise the schema. The thin line in figure 12.2 is presumably for a very skilled quarterback. Figure 12.3 illustrates the process of improving the schema. Instead of a thin blue line, a rather wide region depicts the schema. Early in learning, the developing schema is based on relatively few data points (figure 12.3*a*). The thickness of the area denotes a wide range of variability exists when using the schema. With practice, adding many more data points serves to decrease the area of this schema (see figure 12.3*b*). The reduced variability of the region denotes improved precision with which the schema can generate a movement. Thus, memory strength is represented in the figure as the inherent variability of the schema (the width of the shaded areas in figure 12.3).

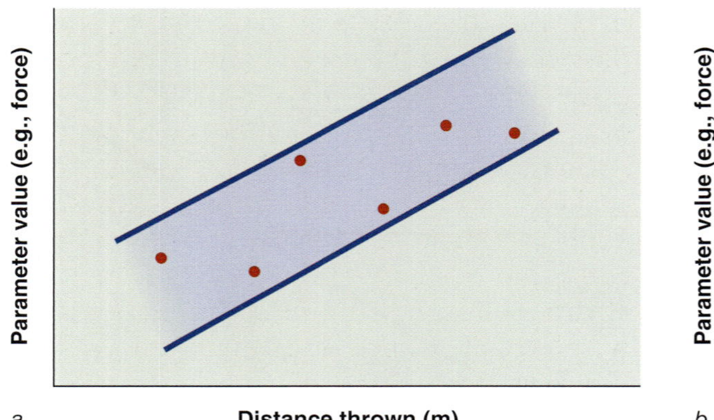

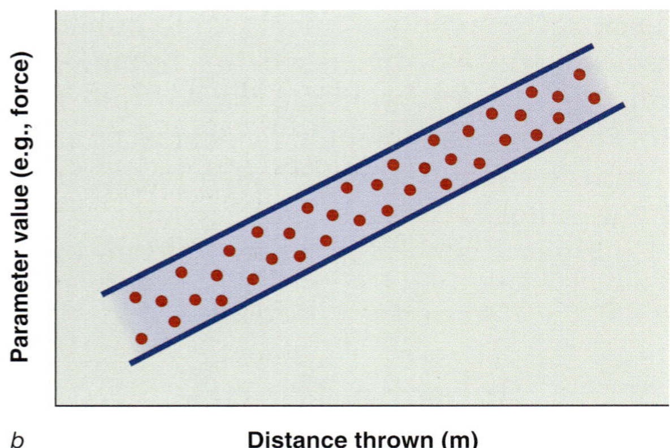

FIGURE 12.3 *(a)* Early in practice, the schema is based on relatively few data points, resulting in a large variability for parameter selection. *(b)* Practice refines the schema with more data points, making the surrounding variability smaller and the process of parameter specification more precise.

Figure 12.4*a* illustrates the imprecision of the schema to accurately specify a force. In this example, a rather large range of forces could be related to one intended distance early in learning. With practice, the schema becomes more precise because the memory representation is based on many more data points, making it less variable (imagine the schema in figure 12.4*b* being based on many thousands of data points). The reduced area of the schema, shown in figure 12.4*b*, reflects the improved capability of the individual to reliably generate the correct parameters to achieve the desired outcome based on the schema.

Schema theory was viewed as a favorable alternative to Adams' **closed-loop theory** for several reasons. First, schema theory could explain the learning of a wider range of actions because the theory was not restricted to slow positioning movements. Second, every movement (correct or incorrect) is a data point that contributes equally well to improving the precision of the schema. Therefore, learning is enhanced as much by errors as by correct movements. And third, the abstractness of the schema explains how one could generate movements that were both previously experienced and completely novel.

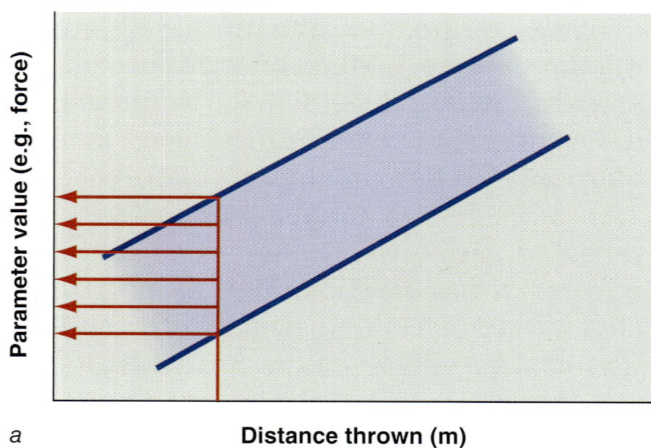

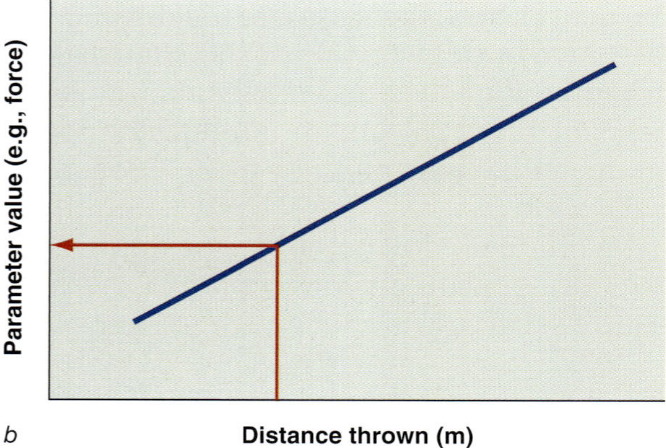

FIGURE 12.4 Practice reduces the imprecision of the chosen force value in parameterizing the generalized motor program as the schema becomes more refined. *(a)* The wide schema associates many potential parameter values (forces) with the desired throwing distance. *(b)* A more finely-tuned schema results in reduced parameter value options available, making the decision more precise.

Limitations

Although the process of schema learning was a strong advance for motor learning theory, a major limitation is the absence of any discussion about how the GMP is learned. Presumably, a prominent feature of a GMP, such as relative timing, would need to be acquired. Would GMP learning be completed separately or in conjunction with schema learning? The theory is silent on the question.

Another limitation, one that applies both to Adams' and Schmidt's theories, is the differential impact of various practice conditions on learning. Both Adams' and Schmidt's theories saw learning as an incremental, somewhat linear progression (increases in trace or schema strength). But, as we saw in chapters 10 and 11, some practice attempts appear to have different value in promoting learning (e.g., the value of a practice trial undertaken in an interleaved order is greater for learning than the value of a practice trial in a blocked schedule). Schema theory predicted that variability of practice would boost learning compared to constant practice. However, schema theory cannot explain why equal amounts of variability result in different learning outcomes when performed in interleaved versus blocked orders.

Passing a football accurately requires the player to throw different distances. In this photo, how can a learner maximize the ability to perform this skill?

In chapter 10, we presented evidence about the contributions to motor learning of cognitive processes, such as those involved in observation, mental practice, and motivation. The absence of a role for purely mental activities in the motor learning process must also be considered a limitation of both Adams' and Schmidt's theories. In the next section, we discuss a theoretical perspective that attempts to account for this limitation.

Challenge Point Framework

One of the issues emerging from chapters 9, 10, and 11 is the important role of cognition in the motor learning process. Several factors that facilitate performance improvements during practice, such as a blocked schedule, immediate feedback, and physical guidance, were found to subvert or degrade learning, as measured in retention and transfer. In contrast, factors that encourage the learner to apply additional resources during practice appear to enhance learning (interleaving, spacing, delayed feedback, etc.). Lee and colleagues (1994) argued that this learning effect was due to enhanced cognitive effort: "the mental work involved in making decisions" during practice (p. 329). When the nature of practice conditions minimizes cognitive effort, the learner will sometimes perform actions on a type of autopilot or by just going through the motions. Conditions of practice that add a degree of difficulty promote additional cognitive effort, which enhances learning. These ideas parallel research on desirable difficulties in human memory (Bjork & Bjork, 2020).

The Learning Process

Guadagnoli and Lee (2004) offer a theoretical idea that expands the role of cognitive effort. According to their **challenge point framework**, the potential for learning depends on the available information to be gained during practice, which the difficulty of the task largely dictates. Performing an easy task, one in which success is highly predictable, does not provide much new information for learning. Conversely, a very difficult task, one that will surely result in failure, provides too much potential information for the learner to assimilate to improve skill. Guadagnoli and Lee termed this the **nominal task difficulty**: the level of difficulty associated with the task itself.

The nominal task difficulty, however, is not the same for everyone or under all conditions. Performing CPR might be relatively easy for a seasoned nurse but relatively difficult for a novice learner. As well, performing CPR in a classroom using a mannequin might be easier than in an emergency (which might include inclement weather, extremely heightened states of anxiety, and so on). Guadagnoli and Lee use the term **functional task difficulty** to describe how the nominal task difficulty changes as a function of the skill level of the learner and the conditions under which it is performed. The same nominal task can be more or less functionally difficult when performed by individuals of different skill levels or under differing conditions of practice.

Many of the factors discussed in chapters 10 and 11 regarding practice conditions and augmented feedback could alter the functional difficulty of a task. The essence of the framework is that the potential learning gain from performance directly relates to functional task difficulty and, theoretically, that there exists an optimal challenge point—a "sweet spot" where the level of task difficulty will result in the optimal amount of information to maximize the learning benefit. For novices, combining tasks and conditions of practice to produce a functionally easy challenge point would be most appropriate for learning. For experts, using tasks and conditions of practice that are much more functionally difficult would best promote learning.

Limitations

The challenge point framework has served as a useful heuristic in several areas of instruction, such as coaching sport skills (Hodges & Lohse, 2022) and teaching health professionals (Nelson & Eliasz, 2023). The framework provides a logical rationale for prescribing methods of practice that increase mental effort workload yet are tailored to the skill levels of the individual.

As a theory of motor learning, however, the framework falls short for several reasons. First, nominal task difficulty is never operationally defined in the challenge point framework. In chapter 6, for example, we discussed Fitts' Law and Schmidt's Law, which precisely defined task difficulty in terms of the properties of the aiming environment and measured outcomes as speed–accuracy trade-off functions. Performance corresponds lawfully to these definitions of nominal task difficulty. The absence of an operational definition of nominal task difficulty in the challenge point framework severely compromises how a level of functional task difficulty could be systematically applied in a real-world setting.

Second, the learning process according to the framework differs greatly from, for example, closed-loop and schema theories, which assign a consequence for learning based on the performance of each movement. The challenge point framework ascribes no learning value for functional task difficulties that result in too much or no information gained and a graded potential for learning for suboptimal challenge points. However, the framework is mute on how much learning depends on the success of the performance. Does performance need to be correct (cf. closed-loop theory), or do all outcomes benefit learning (cf. schema theory)?

Last, the framework fails to consider the affective response of the learner in such a situation (Hodges & Lohse, 2022). In an optimally challenged learning environment, where the functional task difficulty is continuously altered to potentiate the most learning, what is the impact on the learner's motivation level when continually pushing them out of their comfort zone? Does the burden of performing tasks just beyond one's capability affect motivation, and if so, what is the impact on learning? We will come back to this important issue of the role of motivation in learning later in this chapter.

At this point, we shift focus to consider some views of the motor learning process from a different level of analysis. These views de-emphasize the role of information processing. Instead, these views extend the ecological approach to motor control to consider the learning process. Before going further, consider rereading some of the ecological and dynamic systems concepts that were presented in chapter 7.

Dynamic Pattern Theory

The **dynamic pattern theory** considers human movement to be a complex system involving the interaction of moving parts that evolves over time. As we described in chapter 7, some of these parts innately (or spontaneously) work together. For example, when put on a slow-paced moving belt, such as a treadmill, we spontaneously adopt a walking gait—alternating the forward motions of each leg in a rhythmic, phase-locked pattern. If the belt velocity increases, we respond by speeding up our gait. But at some point, as the belt speed increases, the walking pattern becomes inefficient and gait variability increases—the relative phasing of the stride destabilizes (Diedrich & Warren, 1995). One of two possible actions is then likely to occur: (1) We continue with the walking pattern, locomoting inefficiently, expending more and more energy, and risking a fall, or (2) we shift to a running pattern, which reestablishes a stable gait and reduces energy expenditure.

Dynamic pattern theory relies heavily on existing patterns of motor behavior, either innate or learned. These existing patterns are called **attractors**: behavior states that draw the degrees of freedom toward specific patterns of movement and away from other patterns. Walking and running gaits are strong attractors because they coordinate the degrees of freedom involved in locomotion into stable patterns. But attractor strength can change as the system undergoes a transformation due to certain influences. In the gait example, the stability of the walking and running patterns changes as a function of the speed of the treadmill belt.

In chapter 7, we discussed another empirical demonstration of a dynamic pattern—rhythmically coordinating the index fingers of each hand (Kelso, 1984). Even though there are endless possible coordination patterns existing between a 0° and 360° relative phase, only two attractors are innately present at slow speeds for most people: in-phase (0°) and anti-phase (180°). As illustrated in figure 12.5*a*, think of the attractors as magnets that draw the relative timing of the moving fingers toward either a 0° or 180° relative phase. But, as speed increases, only the in-phase attractor remains dominant. The strength of the anti-phase attractor diminishes, causing the pattern to destabilize and increasing the in-phase attractor's dominance (see figure 12.5*b*). These ideas of attractor strength are critically important as we explore how dynamic pattern theory views the learning process (Kelso, 1995).

The Learning Process

The identification of existing attractor states in bimanual timing provided a novel and critically important opportunity for the study of motor learning. All modern theories of learning agree that learning new skills occurs in the background of existing skills. However, the frequent approach to the study of motor learning was to ask the research participant to acquire the skill of performing a completely unique, arbitrary task—one that the researcher could rest assured the participant had never practiced previously. Dynamic pattern theory went beyond those traditional approaches by providing both a theoretical

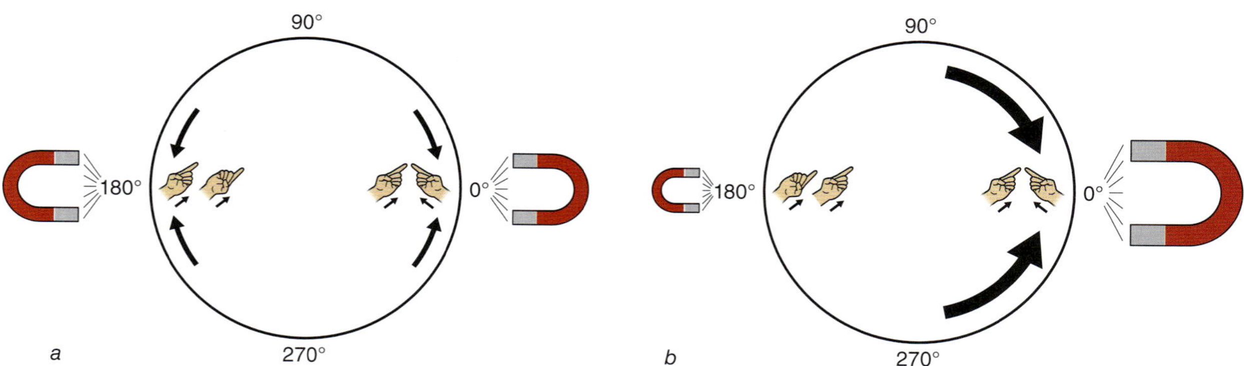

FIGURE 12.5 Illustration of the attractor states in two-finger bimanual timing. The circle represents all possible bimanual relative phase patterns. *(a)* At slow speeds, the system is bistable, having two dominant attractors, in-phase (0°) and anti-phase (180°). *(b)* At faster speeds, the strength of the anti-phase attractor diminishes, and only the in-phase attractor remains dominant.

and experimental avenue for examining how new learning is achieved in the presence of identifiable, existing skills. For example, asking a research participant to practice a 90° relative phasing could be studied in the context of knowing and measuring the strength of innate, stable coordination attractors at 0° (in-phase) and 180° (anti-phase). Changes in the fate of both existing and new coordination patterns as a function of practice were examined within a prescribed theoretical agenda (Schöner et al., 1992).

Many researchers have used the dynamic pattern paradigm to study the acquisition of a novel coordination timing pattern of the fingers or upper limbs, such as a 90° relative phase. Consistent with the theory, most participants begin acquisition of a new coordination pattern in a spontaneous, stable, in-phase or anti-phase pattern, not in a chaotic pattern. Learning is not a matter of acquiring a new pattern from scratch but rather of first breaking away from the attraction of one of the spontaneous patterns, then refining the stability of the new pattern as a stable attractor. In the process of learning the initially bistable dynamic system changes to a tristable system (Kelso, 1995).

Limitations

There are many complexities about the dynamic pattern theory of motor learning that the interested reader should explore but which are beyond the scope of the discussion here (e.g., see Kostrubiec et al., 2012; Schöner et al., 1992). For us, the most important contributions are the exhibited roles of existing patterns in learning new skills. Indeed, in the study by Lee and colleagues (1995), some participants exhibited a specific warm-up decrement (see chapter 2) on a second day of 90° practice by spontaneously reverting to an anti-phase pattern. Such a clear observation of how a system demonstrates the continued influence of previous learning is largely absent in many studies of skill acquisition.

The experimental agenda promoted by dynamic pattern theory has resulted in many empirical investigations. The vast majority of those studies, especially those that have investigated learning, have involved one particular type of motor skill: continuous, cyclical movements in which feedback (inherent and augmented) plays a dominant role. Studies involving the acquisition of new ballistic actions, which require planning and minimize the role of feedback, are largely absent from the dynamic pattern perspective and represent a limitation in the scope of investigation.

Some findings have also failed to support predictions of dynamic pattern theory. For example, since innate patterns differ in stability, a prediction was that the in-phase pattern would create more interference with learning a nearby phase relation than would the anti-phase pattern. In fact, studies have found the reverse—that learning a pattern close to 180° was more difficult than learning a pattern close to 0° (Fontaine et al., 1997; Wenderoth et al., 2002). Also, studies involving the acquisition of a novel bimanual timing skill (Pauwels et al., 2014; Tsutsui et al., 1998) have found contextual-interference effects (see chapter 10). We see no clear theoretical rationale within dynamic pattern theory to explain why interleaved practice would result in stronger learning of a new coordination pattern than blocked practice.

Constraints-Based Framework

A related, ecological approach to learning relies on the concept of **constraints**: certain features that act as boundaries on movement will serve to shape how actions are performed and learned. This theory was developed from two related proposals: (1) Higgins (1977) suggested that movement coordination was determined by the interaction of environmental, biomechanical, and morphological constraints, and (2) Newell (1986) suggested that motor development across the aging process involved an interaction of organismic, environmental, and task constraints. These two views have greatly influenced a field of study now often referred to as the **constraints-based framework** or *constraints-led approach.*

The Learning Process

Button and colleagues (2021) and Gray (2021) have summarized the idea of constraints as a construct that shapes learning, illustrated by the model presented in figure 12.6. In this model, motor learning is a process of *exploration* whereby the interaction of constraints shapes the discovery process. **Organismic constraints** are those factors unique to the individual learner and include body dimensions, cognitive resources, and perceptual-motor abilities. **Environmental constraints** are the physical realities of the world in which we move, including gravity, bases of support (e.g., land, water, space, ice), and perceptual affordances. **Task constraints** are more specific to the engaged activity, such as the dimensions of the tools used in a sport (e.g., size, height, weight, and shape of bats, balls, sticks) and the rules that guide specific motor behavior. The concept of learning as an interaction of these constraints means that it is not one constraint alone that influences learning. Rather, it is the nature of how the three types of constraints interact that determines the progress of learning.

Exploration and discovery learning are critical to the constraints-based framework. This emphasis on discovery stands in stark contrast to what proponents describe as the *traditional approach* to coaching and pedagogy, which relies on prescriptive methods and repetitive drilling of skills. Instead, the constraints-based framework considers the perception and action needs of the individual learner to be the critical determinants of how to organize practice. The role of the coach or instructor is to determine how to alter the task and environmental constraints to meet the needs of each learner. Scenarios are encouraged that pose problems for the learner to solve with situation-specific actions. In this way, practicing a movement solution is encouraged instead of drill-type repetition of specific movements.

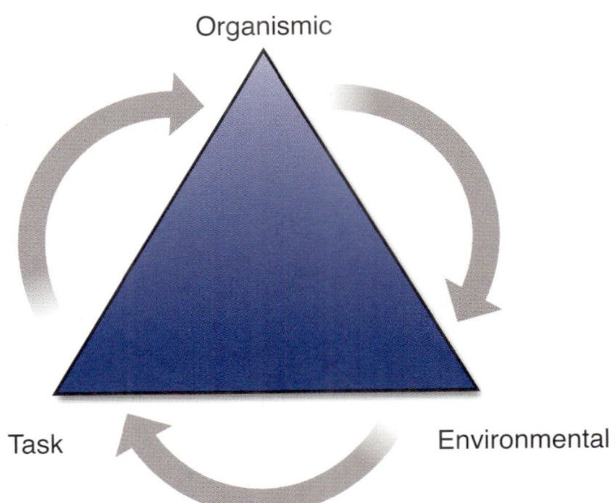

FIGURE 12.6 The constraints-based framework suggests that motor learning is an exploration process of discovery, shaped by the interaction of organismic, environmental, and task constraints.

A study by Gray (2018) provides one example of how a constraints-based framework can boost the discovery learning process. The experiment examined three different approaches to improving a baseball batter's launch angle in a simulated batting task: (1) providing internal focus of attention instructions (such as "Get your hands under the ball"), (2) providing external-focus instructions (such as "Drive the ball over the infield"), or (3) simply telling the learner to try to hit each simulated pitch over a barrier just past the infield with the height adjusted to match the learner's current launch angle.

Figure 12.7 illustrates the discovery learning process, which tracks how the angle of the bat was adjusted over the six weeks of practice under each of the three instruction conditions. The idea here is that more adjustments—representing more explorations and changes in strategy to try to increase launch angles—would increase the batter's variability in bat path angles. As is clear in this figure, internal-focus instructions led to few changes in variability; external-focus instructions led to some changes; but the constraints-based method was the most successful in encouraging the batters to explore ways to increase launch angles. Gray argues that this goal-directed exploration process was responsible for the enhanced performance in various batting statistics seen later in a retention test.

Limitations

There is much to admire about the constraints-based framework. It represents a nuanced approach to learning that considers the needs of the individual in the learning environment. That level of nuance, however, creates a paradox when instructing a group of learners, unless knowledge about individual differences is available. If the instructor considers organismic constraints to be the class average, then the framework loses the basis of its approach—to be attuned to the individual needs.

The constraints-based framework shares similarities with the challenge point framework in that task demands (such as practice order) can be altered to optimize an individual's learning potential. Like the challenge point framework, however, those optimal conditions are rather ill-defined. Indeed, the concept of a constraint itself is so general that it loses much of its explanatory power.

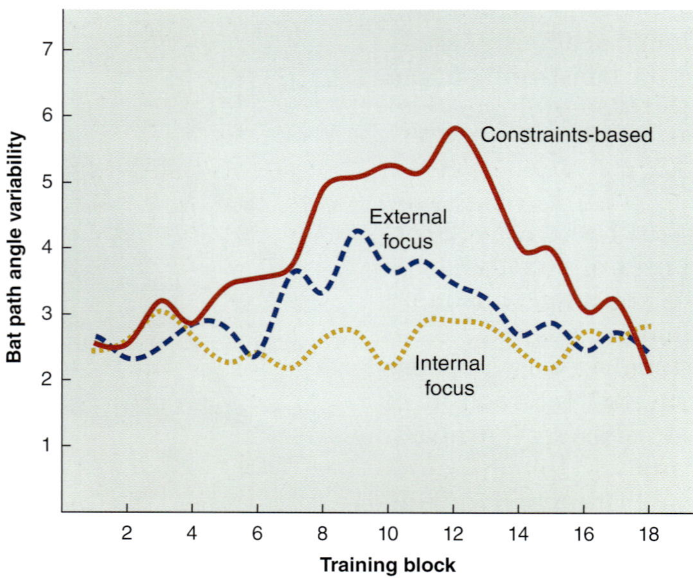

FIGURE 12.7 Variability in bat path angles was largest for the constraints-based framework, indicating increased explorations in self-discovery of methods to increase batting launch angles.

A legitimate question to ask is, What is *not* a constraint on learning? In many ways, the degree of generality with which the framework seeks to explain the learning process, at the same time, reduces its capacity for specific testable predictions with refutable hypotheses.

Last, establishing a set of constraints such as those used in the Gray (2018) study, for example, raises an important issue regarding why learning was enhanced. Although exploration and discovery are certainly valid explanations, one could also argue that constraints serve to enhance the motivational level of the group participants, especially when compared to the control conditions. Perhaps the very incentive to attempt changes in bat angle promoted learning, which was not a motivating factor in the other groups. In the final theory to be discussed, motivation plays a central role in motor learning.

OPTIMAL Theory

The underlying premise of Wulf and Lewthwaite's (2016) **OPTIMAL theory** of motor learning (Optimizing Performance Through Intrinsic Motivation and Attention for Learning) is that a person's attitude toward learning largely determines the effectiveness of practice. OPTIMAL theory suggests that attitude is mainly affected by three factors: expectation to succeed, practice **autonomy**, and focus of attention. For example, the golfer who doubts her ability to hit the ball over a water hazard ends up splashing her next shot in the pond (expectation to succeed). The performer who tells himself that he must make 10 consecutive free throws to improve his foul shooting grudgingly works at doing just that simply because the coach told him to (lack of autonomy in decision-making). The baseball pitcher who is having problems throwing a curve ball for a strike might be focusing on how he grips the ball while throwing (internal focus of attention). The OPTIMAL theory considers how these three factors ultimately determine the effectiveness of practice.

The Learning Process

In chapter 10, we discussed a large body of research showing that motivation plays a significant role in motor learning. Factors such as setting difficult but attainable goals, allowing individuals to self-regulate their practice, and providing positive-normative feedback were all found to enhance motor learning. Yet none of the theories discussed in this chapter considered motivation as part of the motor learning process. This omission about the role of motivation in learning represents the significant contribution of OPTIMAL theory.

A critical role of motivation in skilled performance is the expectation of success. Since expectations are based on experiences, previous successes play a large role in future performance. But, even in the wake of an unsuccessful performance, augmented feedback that bolsters expectations for future performances can enhance motivation. Challenging the learner by setting difficult goals will be motivating if the learner has a reasonable expectation of meeting those challenges.

Wulf and Lewthwaite (2016) also discuss research on the beneficial effects of autonomy support—giving the learner the opportunity to make decisions about the structure of the practice conditions. This autonomy also helps to enhance motivation and the expectation for future good performance. Last, OPTIMAL theory gives an important role to the focus of attention. As discussed in chapters 3 and 9, focusing attention on the intended result of an action (an external focus) facilitates performance in most cases, compared to directing attention to how to produce a movement (an internal focus). A considerable body of research has demonstrated similar findings when learning a motor skill: external-focus instructions result in better performance during practice and, importantly, in retention and transfer too, when compared to internal-focus instructions (Wulf, 2013).

According to OPTIMAL theory, all these positive attitudes—expecting to perform well, having control over one's practice, and focusing on the object or goal of performance—help develop a strong bond between the goal of the action and how the action is performed. Repeated exposures to these positive mindsets serve to strengthen these bonds, which support the learning process.

Limitations

The OPTIMAL theory of motor learning has filled an enormous gap in motor learning theory. No previous theory has provided a fundamental role for the effects of motivation on learning. As well, the theory is replete with testable hypotheses, which is one hallmark of a good theory.

As with the other theories presented in this chapter, however, there are limitations. In general, the theory correlates improved motor performance with improved learning. As we have seen in previous chapters, however, motor learning can be enhanced during practice in which errors in performance are frequent (as in interleaved practice), when errors are physically induced (augmented guidance errors), or when no performance

In this photo, how would the attainment of skill in casting a fly be explained from each of the different theoretical perspectives?

improvement occurs at all (mental practice). OPTIMAL theory would predict that performance with many errors in practice would lead to decreased motivation and, consequently, poorer learning than when errors are infrequent or prevented altogether.

Learning can also be enhanced in the face of lowered expectations. For example, in a study by Simon and Bjork (2001), learners in the blocked-practice group performed worse than members of the random group in a retention test, even though they had expected to perform better (see chapter 10 and figure 10.9). Conversely, random practice had led learners to have a lower expectation of performing well in a retention test. The evidence that expectations did not match the retention test outcomes is opposite to the predictions of OPTIMAL theory.

Summary

The psychologist Kurt Lewin said that "there is nothing as practical as a good theory" (Lewin, 1943). Motor learning theory provides the user with a practical understanding of how skills are improved. For example, when an instructor provides feedback to a learner, she must consider how to give it (verbally, visually, etc.), how much information to give, when to give it, how often to give it, and so on. Delivering feedback in a certain way is based on the understanding that it will work better than any other way. These feedback delivery decisions are based on underlying assumptions about what would best facilitate the learning process, as well as the coach's theories about the learning process.

When a golfer steps onto a driving range to practice his swing, he selects how many balls to hit, which clubs to use, where to hit them, and so on. The golfer decides how to organize the order of practice based on the belief that it will make him a better golfer. The practice decisions are based on the golfer's theory about the learning process.

This chapter has described many good theoretical constructs of motor learning. All of them provided an understanding of the learning process that had practical implications for instruction, coaching, and rehabilitation. None of the theories is correct in every aspect, and we have tried to point out limitations for each. However, each theory offers something unique and practical for the learner of motor skills.

Theories are not built anew—previous research ideas and theoretical constructs contribute greatly to the advancement of new theories. Motor learning theory is no different. For example, William James' writing influenced how Fitts came to view the role of verbalizing behaviors in early motor learning. Adams built upon the strengths and weaknesses of Edward Thorndike's views as the basis for his closed-loop theory of learning. Schmidt drew heavily on the concept of prototypes—rule-based abstracts used in perception. Kelso developed dynamic pattern theory based on knowledge about how physical systems change under differing environmental conditions.

Try not to think of the theories described in this chapter as the culmination or end of a process for conceptualizing motor learning. Rather, think of them as the beginning of the quest for a new, more accurate, and complete account that builds upon the strengths and limitations of what came before. Think of these theories as steps along the way to a more practical theory.

HK*PROPEL* ACTIVITIES

HK*Propel* offers these activities to help you build and apply your knowledge of the concepts in this chapter. Additionally, you'll find a key terms flashcard review activity and a key terms quiz, along with audio supplements for selected figures, as indicated by QR codes throughout the chapter.

Interactive Learning

Activity 12.1: Indicate whether a given understanding of a stage of learning fits with Fitts' or Bernstein's model of skill acquisition.

Activity 12.2: Match specific terms with the theoretical construct.

Activity 12.3: Review your understanding of motor learning theories through a fill-in-the-blank exercise.

Principles-to-Application Exercise

Activity 12.4: The principles-to-application exercise for this chapter prompts you to use the example of archery to describe how the challenge point framework relates the nominal task difficulty to the skill level of the individual.

Check Your Understanding

1. Compare and contrast the role of errors in the learning process of any three theories or theoretical constructs discussed in this chapter.
2. Compare and contrast the role of mental practice in the learning process of any three theories or theoretical constructs discussed in this chapter.
3. Discuss the ecological basis for the dynamic pattern theory and constraints-based approaches to learning. What makes these theories ecological?

Apply Your Knowledge

1. Discuss how each of the theories or theoretical constructs presented in this chapter would affect specific methods used in stroke rehabilitation.
2. Describe how the development of suturing techniques in medical education would progress under Fitts' versus Bernstein's stages of learning.

Glossary

ability—A stable, enduring, innate trait that underlies skilled performance, largely inherited and not modifiable by practice.

absolute constant error (|CE|)—The absolute value of a participant's CE; a measure of amount of bias without respect to its direction.

absolute error (AE)—The average absolute deviation of each of a set of scores from a target value; a measure of overall error.

absolute frequency of feedback—The actual number of feedback presentations given in a series of practice trials.

amplitude—The distance between the two targets in a reciprocal aiming task (*A* in Fitts' Law).

anti-phase—A coordination timing pattern in which two movement components oscillate in 180° relative phase.

arousal—An internal state of alertness or excitement.

attention—A limited capacity to process information.

attractor—Behavior states that draw degrees of freedom toward specific patterns of movement and away from other patterns.

augmented feedback—Information from the measured performance outcome that is fed back to the learner, usually by some artificial means; sometimes called *extrinsic feedback*.

automatic processing—A mode of information processing that is fast, done in parallel, not attention demanding, and often involuntary.

autonomous stage—The third stage of learning proposed by Fitts, in which the attention demands of performing a task have been greatly reduced.

autonomy—Giving the learner the opportunity to make decisions about how their practice conditions will be structured; a feature of OPTIMAL theory.

average feedback—A type of augmented feedback that presents a statistical average of two or more trials rather than results on any one of them.

bandwidth feedback—A procedure for delivering augmented feedback in which error information is provided only if the movement attempt falls outside some range of correctness.

bimanual Fitts' task—The pairing of two Fitts' aiming tasks in which each limb is assigned a target.

blindsight—A medical condition in which the patient can respond to certain visual stimuli while being judged legally blind by other criteria.

blocked practice—A schedule in which many trials on a single task are practiced consecutively; sometimes called *drilled* or *repetitive practice*, or *low contextual interference*.

capability—The internal representation of skill acquired during practice that supports performance on some task.

central pattern generator (CPG)—A centrally located control mechanism that produces mainly genetically defined actions such as walking.

challenge point framework—A framework for establishing optimally challenging practice goals to optimize learning.

choice reaction time—The temporal interval between the presentation of a stimulus and the start of a response; the performer must choose one response from more than one alternative response.

choking—Scenario in which a performer changes a normal routine or fails to adapt to a changing situation, resulting in a failed performance.

closed-loop control system—A type of system control involving feedback, error detection, and error correction that is applicable to maintaining a system goal.

closed-loop theory—A theory of motor learning proposed by Adams (1971), focusing on the learning of slow positioning movements.

closed skill—A skill for which the environment is stable and predictable, allowing organization of movement in advance.

cocktail party effect—A phenomenon of attention in which humans can attend to a single conversation at a noisy gathering, neglecting most (but not all) other inputs.

cognitive stage—The first stage of learning proposed by Fitts, in which the learners' performances are heavily based on cognitive or verbal processes.

comparator—A component of closed-loop control that compares anticipated feedback with actual feedback, resulting in an error signal output.

concurrent feedback—Augmented (usually continuous) feedback that is presented simultaneously with an ongoing action.

constant error (CE)—The signed difference of a score on a given trial from a target value; a measure of bias for that trial.

constant practice—A practice sequence in which only a single task is experienced.

constrained action hypothesis—An explanation of focus of attention effects that attributes an internal focus to conscious movement control and external focus to automated movement control.

constraints—Features that contain or act as limitations to performance.

constraints-based framework—A view of motor learning as a problem-solving process involving the interaction of organismic, task, and environmental constraints.

contextual interference—The interference in performance and learning that arises from performing one task in the context of other tasks; *blocked practice* is defined as low in contextual interference; *interleaved practice* is defined as high in contextual interference.

contingency schedule—A type of interleaved practice schedule in which the decision to repeat the same task or to switch to a different task is based on some measure of performance.

continuous skill—A skill in which the action is performed without any defined beginning or end.

controlled processing—A mode of information processing that is relatively slow, serial, attention demanding, and voluntary.

coordination—The process by which multiple degrees of freedom are combined to produce movement.

coordination dynamics—The study of movement systems as they interact with the environment over time.

correlation coefficient (*r*)—A statistical method that evaluates the strength of a relationship between two variables; it does not imply causality.

criterion task—The ultimate version, condition, or situation in which the skill learned in practice is to be applied; the ultimate goal of practice.

cutaneous receptor—A receptor in the skin that provides inherent information about touch (haptic sensations).

deafferentation—A surgical procedure that involves cutting one or more of an animal's dorsal roots, preventing nerve impulses from the periphery from traveling to the spinal cord.

degrees of freedom—The collection of independent ways in which the body can move.

degrees of freedom problem—The problem of explaining how a movement with many degrees of freedom is controlled or coordinated.

deliberate practice—The type of practice that is effortful and conducted specifically for improving skilled performance.

demonstration—Performance of a skill by an instructor (or a model) to facilitate observational learning.

differential method—A method for understanding behavior by focusing on individual differences and abilities.

discrete skill—A skill that has a recognizable beginning and end; usually brief.

distributed practice—A practice schedule in which the amount of rest between practice trials is relatively long or when practice sessions are spaced apart in time.

dorsal stream—Region of the brain that uses visual information specifically for the control of movement; sent from the eye to the posterior parietal cortex.

double-stimulation paradigm—A method for studying information processing in which a given stimulus (leading to one response) is followed closely by a second stimulus (leading to another response).

dual-task method—A method that uses a secondary (usually continuous) task to assess the attention demands of the criterion task (see *probe-task method*).

dynamic pattern theory—A view of motor control and learning that considers human movement as a complex system involving the interaction of moving parts that evolves over time.

echolocation—Used by animals (and humans) to emit sound waves that bounce off objects; the auditory feedback is used to orient flying or swimming to find food or avoid objects.

ecological approach—A means of studying motor learning and performance by focusing on the dynamic, problem-solving process involving the interaction of movement and the environment.

effective target width (W_e)—The amount of spread, or variability, of movement end points in an aiming task; represents the performer's effective target size; the within-participant standard deviation of the movement distances for a set of trials.

elaboration hypothesis—The idea that frequent switching among tasks (e.g., in interleaved practice) renders the tasks more distinct from each other and more meaningful, resulting in stronger memory representations; one explanation of the contextual-interference effect.

end-state comfort—Planning operations done in advance that assure maximum comfort at movement completion.

environmental constraint—Limitations to performance based on the physical realities of the world in which we move, including gravity, bases of support (e.g., land, water, space, ice), and perceptual affordances.

error amplification—A technique in which a guidance device amplifies the error made during movement production.

error-detection—The learned capability to detect one's own errors through analyzing inherent feedback.

especial skill—A specific representation for one skill (e.g., free throw in basketball) within a broader class of skills (e.g., set shots in basketball).

experimental method—A method of understanding behavior that examines common principles among people through the use of experiments.

expertise—An exceptional level of skill that is attained only after extensive deliberate practice.

external attentional focus—Attention directed outside the body to an object or environmental goal.

exteroception—Sensory information arising primarily from outside the body.

extrinsic feedback—See *augmented feedback*.

faded feedback—The practice of delivering reduced augmented feedback whereby the frequency is decreased systematically across trials.

false-negative normative feedback—An experimental procedure in which learners are misinformed that their performance is less skilled than that of a peer group.

false-positive normative feedback—An experimental procedure in which learners are misinformed that their performance is more skilled than a peer group.

far transfer—Transfer of learning from one task to another in a very different task or setting.

feedback—Information that is "fed back" to the performer either naturally through the senses or artificially, from an external source.

feedback delay interval—The interval of time from the end of the movement until the feedback is presented.

feedforward—Sensory consequences of a movement that are expected to be fed back to the performer.

Fitts' Law—The principle that movement time in aiming tasks is linearly related to the target dimensions; MT = $a + b[\log_2(2A/W)]$, where A = amplitude and W = target width.

fixation stage—The second stage of learning proposed by Fitts in which learners establish motor patterns; also called *associative stage*.

foreperiod—The interval of time between a warning signal and a stimulus to respond in a reaction time task.

forgetting—The loss of an acquired capability for responding; loss of memory.

forgetting hypothesis—The hypothesis that frequent task switching during interleaved practice causes forgetting of movement planning, leading to extensive next-trial planning, resulting in stronger memory representations; a hypothesis to explain the contextual-interference effect.

functional task difficulty—The nominal difficulty of a task when considered in conjunction with the skill level of the performer and the conditions under which the task is being performed.

gait transition—The point at which walking becomes running (and vice versa) in bipedal animals or when gait shifts occur in quadrupeds.

gearshift analogy—A model regarding the learning of motor programs using the analogy of learning to shift gears in a standard-transmission automobile.

generalized motor program (GMP)—A motor program whose output can vary along certain dimensions to produce novelty and generalizability in movement.

general motor ability—A view in which a single general ability was thought to underlie individual differences in motor behavior.

goal setting—A motivational procedure in which the learner is encouraged to set personal performance goals during practice.

Golgi tendon organs—Small stretch receptors located in the tendons that provide precise information about muscle tension.

guidance—A procedure used in practice in which the learner is physically or verbally directed in order to minimize errors during performance.

Hick's Law—The mathematical descriptor showing a linear relationship between choice reaction time and the logarithm of the number of stimulus–response alternatives; RT = $a + b \log2(N)$.

hypervigilance—A heightened state of arousal that leads to ineffective decision making, panic, and often poor performance.

inattentional blindness—A failure to perceive objects in the visual environment when attention is directed to anticipating other objects or events.

index of difficulty (ID)—The theoretical difficulty of a movement in the Fitts tapping task, defined as $\log_2(2A/W)$, where A is target amplitude and W is target width.

individual differences—Stable, enduring differences among people in terms of some measurable characteristic or task performance.

information processing—Approach to the study of behavior that treats the human as a processor of information, focusing on attention, perception, and memory.

inherent feedback—Information provided as a natural consequence of making an action; sometimes called *intrinsic feedback*.

in-phase—A coordination timing pattern in which two movement components oscillate in a 0° relative phase.

instantaneous feedback—Augmented feedback delivered immediately after completion of movement (with no delay).

interleaved practice—A general term that refers to nonrepetitive practice in which the order is systematically or non-systematically varied.

internal attentional focus—Attention directed to body movement, such as motor or sensory information.

invariant feature—A feature of a class of movements that remains constant, or invariant, while surface features change (e.g., relative timing).

inverted-U principle—The principle that increased arousal improves performance only to a point, with degraded performance as arousal increases further.

ironic effects—The tendency to do exactly what you consciously intend *not* to do.

joint receptors—Sensory receptors located in the joint capsule that provide information about joint position.

knowledge of performance (KP)—Augmented feedback about the movement pattern (such as kinetics or kinematics) the learner has just made.

knowledge of results (KR)—Augmented verbal feedback (or at least feedback that can be verbalized) about the success of an action with respect to the environmental goal.

lead-up activities—Special tasks designed to be learned before the practice of a more complicated or dangerous criterion task.

learning curves—A label sometimes applied to a performance curve (a plot of average performance over trials) in the mistaken belief that the changes in performance mirror changes in learning.

long-term memory (LTM)—A virtually limitless memory store for information, facts, concepts, and motor skills.

looked-but-failed-to-see automotive accidents—Traffic accidents in which the driver looked at but failed to notice the presence of a cyclist or pedestrian; believed to be related to inattention blindness.

M1 response—The monosynaptic stretch reflex, with a latency of 30 to 50 ms.

M2 response—The polysynaptic, or functional, stretch reflex, with a latency of 50 to 80 ms.

massed practice—A practice schedule in which the amount of rest between practice trials is relatively short or when practice sessions are concentrated in time.

mental practice—A practice procedure in which the learner imagines successful action without overt physical practice.

mixed reality—Technology that combines virtual reality with physical tasks.

modeling—A practice procedure in which another person demonstrates the skills to be learned.

motor learning—A set of internal processes associated with practice or experience leading to relatively permanent gains in the capability for skilled performance.

motor program—A prestructured set of movement commands that defines the essential details of skilled action with minimal (or no) involvement of sensory feedback.

movement programming—The stage of information processing in which the motor system is readied for the planned action.

movement time (MT)—The interval from the initiation of a movement until its termination.

muscle spindle—Structure in parallel with muscle fibers that provides information about muscle length.

near transfer—Transfer of learning from one task or setting to another that is very similar.

nominal task difficulty—The difficulty of a task without respect to who is performing it or the conditions under which it is performed.

novelty problem—The concern that simple motor programs cannot account for the production of novel, unpracticed movements.

observational learning—The process by which the learner improves a motor skill by observing modeled demonstrations.

open-loop control—A type of system control in which instructions for the effector system are determined in advance and run off without feedback modification.

open skill—A skill for which the environment is unpredictable or unstable, preventing organization of movement in advance.

optical array—The collection of rays of light that are reflected from objects in the visual environment.

optical flow—The change in patterns of light rays from the environment as they flow over the retina during continuous movement of the eye through the environment, allowing perception of motion, position, and timing.

OPTIMAL theory—A theory of motor learning in which a person's expectation to succeed, focus of attention, and autonomy largely determine the effectiveness of practice.

organismic constraint—Limitations on performance due to a learner's body dimensions, cognitive resources, and perceptual-motor abilities.

parameters—Values applied to a generalized motor program that determine a movement's surface features, such as speed, amplitude, or limb used.

part practice—A procedure in which a complex skill is broken down into parts that are practiced separately.

perceptual trace—From closed-loop theory, a representation of sensory feedback that is stored in memory and used for detection and correction of errors.

performance curve—Graphs of average performance for an individual or a group plotted over practice trials; sometimes incorrectly called a *learning curve*.

physical fidelity—The degree to which the surface features of a simulator and the criterion task are identical.

population stereotypes—Habitual stimulus–response relationships that dominate behavior due to specific cultural learning.

post-feedback delay—The interval of time between the presentation of augmented feedback and the start of the next movement.

practice specificity—A finding that learning is very specific—what is learned depends on what is practiced and how practice is conducted.

precision of feedback—The level of precision with which augmented feedback describes the movement or outcome produced.

prediction—The process of using people's abilities to estimate their probable success in various situations.

probe-task method—A method that uses a secondary RT task to assess the attention demands of the criterion task.

proprioception—Sensory information arising from within the body, resulting in the sense of position and movement.

psychological fidelity—The degree to which the behaviors produced in a simulator are identical to the behaviors required by the criterion task.

psychological refractory period (PRP)—The delay in responding to the second of two closely spaced stimuli.

quiet-eye effect—The period of time when a performer fixates the eyes on a target just before movement onset.

random practice—A type of interleaved schedule in which practice trials on two or more different tasks are unsystematically ordered across the practice period; also called *high contextual interference.*

reaction time (RT)—The interval from the presentation of an unanticipated stimulus until the beginning of the response.

reflex-reversal phenomenon—The phenomenon by which a given stimulus can produce two different reflexive responses depending on the function of the limb in a movement.

relative-age effect—Phenomenon in which athletes of an age-normative group who are born early in a given year achieve higher skill levels than those born late in the year.

relative frequency of feedback—The proportion of trials during practice for which feedback is given; absolute frequency divided by the total number of trials.

relative phase—A measure of coordination that describes the motor behavior of two oscillating limbs or objects.

relative timing—The temporal structure or rhythm of action; the durations of various segments of an action divided by the total movement time.

repetition—A type of ineffective practice in which a movement is repeated again and again.

response selection—The stage of information processing in which the system selects a response from a number of alternatives.

response time—The sum of reaction time plus movement time; sometimes called *total time.*

retention test—A performance test provided after a retention interval without practice; sometimes called a *transfer test.*

root-mean-square error (RMSE)—The square root of the average squared deviations of a set of values from a target value; typically used as a measure of overall tracking proficiency.

schema—A learned rule relating movement outcomes to the parameters that were used to produce those outcomes.

schema theory—A theory of learning by Schmidt (1975) based on adding parameters to generalized motor programs.

Schmidt's Law—The principle that effective target width (W_e) in rapid aiming tasks is linearly related to movement velocity; $W_e = a + b(A/MT)$, where A = amplitude and MT = movement time.

self-regulation—Technique used in motor learning studies in which the learners determine how to schedule practice or feedback.

sensory neuropathy—A medical condition in patients who are unable to process their sensory feedback.

serial practice—A type of interleaved schedule in which practice trials on two or more different tasks are systematically rotated across the practice period; also called *high contextual interference.*

serial skill—A skill composed of several discrete skills strung together, often with the order being critical for success.

set—A collection of psychological activities or adjustments underlying performance that can be "lost" after a rest, leading to warm-up decrement.

short-term memory (STM)—A memory store with a limited capacity for holding information; sometimes called *working memory.*

short-term sensory store (STSS)—A functionally limitless memory store for holding literal, sensory information from the various senses very briefly (for only about 1 s).

simple RT—A reaction-time situation in which there is only one possible stimulus and one response.

simulator—A training device that mimics various features of some real-world task.

skill—The capability to bring about a result with maximum certainty, minimum energy, or minimum time; task proficiency that can be modified by practice.

sonification—A process by which features of movement are fed back to the performer as sounds.

spatial anticipation—The anticipation that one of several possible stimuli will occur; sometimes called *event anticipation.*

specificity hypothesis—Henry's hypothesis that individual differences are based on many independent abilities.

speed–accuracy trade-off—The tendency for accuracy to decrease as the movement speed or velocity of a movement increases and vice versa.

split-belt treadmill—A treadmill containing two belts that can cycle at different speeds.

startle RT—A rapid (<100 ms latency) reaction to an unexpected, often very strong, stimulus; used to study the involuntary release of motor programs.

stimulus identification—The stage of information processing in which a stimulus is recognized and identified.

stimulus-onset asynchrony (SOA)—The interval between the onsets of the two stimuli in a double-stimulation paradigm; sometimes called the *interstimulus interval (ISI).*

stimulus–response (S-R) compatibility—The degree of naturalness (or directness) between the stimulus and the response assigned to it.

storage problem—The concern that simple motor programs would require an almost limitless storage capacity for nearly countless different movements.

Stroop effect—Evidence for parallel processing in stimulus identification whereby performance is interfered when naming the font color of words that are semantically related (e.g., the word "red" printed in green font color) compared to words that are semantically unrelated.

summary feedback—Information about the performance on a series of trials that is presented only after the series has been completed.

surface feature—An easily changeable aspect of a movement, such as movement time or amplitude, that does not affect the deep structure (the invariant features).

sustained attention—Maintenance of attention over long periods of work, such as monitoring a radar-based aircraft detection device; sometimes called *vigilance.*

task constraint—Limitations to performance based on the dimensions of the tools used in a sport (e.g., size, height, weight, and shape of bats, balls, and sticks) and rules that guide behavior.

tau (τ)—A variable providing optical information about time-to-contact; the size of the retinal image divided by the rate of change of the image.

temporal anticipation—The anticipation of when a given stimulus will arrive or when a movement is to be made.

tracking—A class of tasks in which a moving object must be followed, typically by movements of a manual control.

transfer of learning—The gain or the loss in proficiency on one task as a result of practice or experience on another task.

transfer test—A performance test in which the task or task conditions have changed; often provided after a retention interval without practice.

trials-delay of feedback—A procedure in which the presentation of feedback for a movement is delayed; during the delay, the learner practices one or more other trials of the same task.

unintended acceleration—Sudden, extreme acceleration of a vehicle accompanied by the perception of a loss of braking effectiveness.

variable error (VE)—The standard deviation of a set of scores about the participant's own average (CE) score; a measure of movement inconsistency.

variable practice—A schedule of practice in which many variations of a class of actions are practiced.

ventral stream—Region of the brain that uses visual information for the identification of an object; sent from the eye to the inferotemporal cortex.

vestibular apparatus—Receptors in the inner ear that are sensitive to the orientation of the head with respect to gravity, rotation of the head, and balance.

virtual reality (VR)—Computer-generated immersive technology that replicates a real-world experience.

warm-up decrement—Temporary worsening of performance brought on by time away from a task and eliminated quickly when the performer begins again.

whole practice—A procedure in which a skill is practiced in its entirety without separation into its parts.

width—The size of a target in aiming tasks (*W* in Fitts' Law).

yoked group—A type of control procedure in which a practice schedule is determined by (and matched to) a learner in a different experimental group or condition.

References

Abbs, J.H., Gracco, V.L., & Cole, K.J. (1984). Control of multimovement coordination: Sensorimotor mechanisms in speech motor programming. *Journal of Motor Behavior, 16*, 195-232.

Abernethy, B. (2001). Attention. In R.N. Singer, H.A. Hausenblas, & C.M. Janelle (Eds.), *Handbook of sport psychology* (2nd ed., pp. 53-85). Wiley.

Abernethy, B., Farrow, D., Gorman, A., & Mann, D. (2012). Anticipatory behavior and expert performance. In N.J. Hodges & A.M. Williams (Eds.), *Skill acquisition in sport: Research, theory and practice* (2nd ed., pp. 287-305). Routledge.

Abernethy, B., & Wood, J.M. (2001). Do generalized visual training programmes for sport really work? An experimental investigation. *Journal of Sports Sciences, 19*, 203-222.

Adams, J.A. (1953). *The prediction of performance at advanced stages of training on a complex psychomotor task.* Res. Bull. 5349. Human Resources Research Center.

Adams, J.A. (1956). *An evaluation of test items measuring motor abilities.* Research Rep. AFPTRCTN5655. Human Resources Research Center.

Adams, J.A. (1961). The second facet of forgetting: A review of warmup decrement. *Psychological Bulletin, 58*, 257-273.

Adams, J.A. (1971). A closed-loop theory of motor learning. *Journal of Motor Behavior, 3*, 111-150.

Adams, J.A. (1987). Historical review and appraisal of research on the learning, retention, and transfer of human motor skills. *Psychological Bulletin, 101*, 41-74.

Adams, J.A., & Dijkstra, S. (1966). Short-term memory for motor responses. *Journal of Experimental Psychology, 71*, 314-318.

Agarwal, P.K., Nunes, L.D. & Blunt, J.R. (2021). Retrieval practice consistently benefits student learning: A systematic review of applied research in schools and classrooms. *Educational Psychology Review, 33*, 1409-1453.

Agethen, M., & Krause, D. (2016). Effects of bandwidth feedback on the automatization of an arm movement sequence. *Human Movement Science, 45*, 71-83.

Ajemian, R., D'Ausilio, A., Moorman, H., & Bizzi, E. (2010). Why professional athletes need a prolonged period of warm-up and other peculiarities of human motor learning. *Journal of Motor Behavior, 42*, 381-388.

Alaker, M., Wynn, G.R., & Arulampalam, T. (2016). Virtual reality in laparoscopic surgery: A systematic review and meta-analysis. *International Journal of Surgery, 29*, 85-94.

Alexander, R.M. (2003). *Principles of animal locomotion.* Princeton University Press.

Allard, F., & Burnett, N. (1985). Skill in sport. *Canadian Journal of Psychology, 39*, 294-312.

Ammons, R.B. (1950). Acquisition of motor skill: III. Effects of initially distributed practice on rotary pursuit performance. *Journal of Experimental Psychology, 40*, 777-787.

Ammons, R.B., Farr, R.G., Block, E., Neumann, E., Dey, M., Marion, R., & Ammons, C.H. (1958). Long-term retention of perceptual motor skills. *Journal of Experimental Psychology, 55*, 318-328.

Ammons, R.B., & Willig, L. (1956). Acquisition of motor skill: IV. Effects of repeated periods of massed practice. *Journal of Experimental Psychology, 51*, 118-126.

Anderson, D.I., Lohse, K.R., Lopes, T.C.V., & Williams, A.M. (2021). Individual differences in motor skill learning: Past, present and future. *Human Movement Science, 78*, 102818. https://doi.org/10.1016/j.humov.2021.102818

Anderson, D.I., Magill, R.A., Sekiya, H., & Ryan, G. (2005). Support for an explanation of the guidance effect in motor skill learning. *Journal of Motor Behavior, 37*, 231-238.

Annett, J. (1959). Learning a pressure under conditions of immediate and delayed knowledge of results. *Quarterly Journal of Experimental Psychology, 11*, 3-15.

Anson, J.G., Elliott, D., & Davids, K. (2005). Information processing and constraints-based views of skill acquisition: Divergent or complementary? *Motor Control, 9*, 217-241.

Arexis, M., & Maquestiaux, F. (2023). Visual illusions influence proceduralized sports performance. *Psychonomic Bulletin & Review, 30*, 174-183.

Armstrong, T.R. (1970). *Training for the production of memorized movement patterns.* Tech. Rep. No. 26. University of Michigan, Department of Psychology.

Arps, G.F. (1920). Work with knowledge of results versus work without knowledge of results. *Psychological Monographs, 28*, 1-41.

Asundi, K., & Odell, D. (2011). Effects of keyboard keyswitch design: A review of the current literature. *Work, 39*, 151-159.

Atkinson, R.C., & Shiffrin, R.M. (1968). Human memory: A proposed system and its control processes. In K.W. Spence, & J.T. Spence (Eds.), *The psychology of learning and motivation: Advances in research and theory* (Vol. 2, pp. 89-195). Academic Press.

Attneave, F. (1959). *Applications of information theory to psychology: A summary of basic concepts, methods, and results.* Holt, Rinehart & Winston.

Baddeley, A.D., & Longman, D.J.A. (1978). The influence of length and frequency of training session on the rate of learning to type. *Ergonomics, 21*, 627-635.

Bahrick, H.P., Fitts, P.M., & Briggs, G.E. (1957). Learning curves—facts or artifacts? *Psychological Bulletin, 54*, 256-268.

Banala, S.K., Kim, S.H., Agrawal, S.K., & Scholz, J.P. (2009). Robot assisted gait training with active leg exoskeleton (ALEX). *IEEE Transactions on Neural Systems and Rehabilitation Engineering, 17*, 2-8.

Barnsley, R.H., Thompson, A.H., & Legault, P. (1992). Family planning: Football style. The relative age effect in football. *International Review for the Sociology of Sport, 27*, 77-87.

Bartlett, F.C. (1932). *Remembering: A study in experimental and social psychology.* Cambridge University Press.

Battig, W.F. (1966). Facilitation and interference. In E.A. Bilodeau (Ed.), *Acquisition of skill* (pp. 215-244). Academic Press.

Battig, W.F. (1979). The flexibility of human memory. In L.S. Cermak & F.I.M. Craik (Eds.), *Levels of processing in human memory* (pp. 23-44). Erlbaum.

Beilock, S.L. (2010). *Choke: What the secrets of the brain reveal about success and failure at work and at play.* Simon & Schuster.

Belen'kii, V.Y., Gurfinkel, V.S., & Pal'tsev, Y.I. (1967). Elements of control of voluntary movements. *Biofizika, 12*, 135-141.

Bender, P.A. (1987). *Extended practice and patterns of bimanual interference.* Unpublished doctoral dissertation, University of Southern California.

Bernier, M., Codron, R., Thienot, E., & Fournier, J.F. (2011). The attentional focus of expert golfers in training and competition: A naturalistic investigation. *Journal of Applied Sport Psychology, 23*, 326-341.

Bernier, M., Trottier, C., Thienot, E., & Fournier, J. (2016). An investigation of attentional foci and their temporal patterns: A naturalistic study in expert figure skaters. *The Sport Psychologist, 30*, 256-266.

Bernstein, N.A. (1967). *The co-ordination and regulation of movements.* Pergamon Press.

Bernstein, N.A. (1996). On dexterity and its development. In M.L. Latash & M.T. Turvey (Eds.), *Dexterity and its development.* Erlbaum.

Bilodeau, I.M. (1966). Information feedback. In E.A. Bilodeau (Ed.), *Acquisition of skill* (pp. 255-296). Academic Press.

Bjork, R.A., & Bjork, E.L. (2019). The myth that blocking one's study or practice by topic or skill enhances learning. In C. Barton (Ed.), *The researchED guide to education myths: An evidence-informed guide for teachers* (pp. 59-72). John Catt Educational.

Bjork, R.A., & Bjork, E.L. (2020). Desirable difficulties in theory and practice. *Journal of Applied Research in Memory and Cognition, 9*, 475-479.

Blouin, J., Gauthier, G.M., Vercher, J.L., & Cole, J. (1996). The relative contribution of retinal and extraretinal signals in determining the accuracy of reaching movements in normal subjects and a deafferented patient. *Experimental Brain Research, 109*, 148-153.

Bourne, L.E., Jr., & Archer, E.J. (1956). Time continuously on target as a function of distribution of practice. *Journal of Experimental Psychology, 51*, 25-33.

Boutcher, S.H., & Crews, D.J. (1987). The effect of a preshot attentional routine on a well-learned skill. *International Journal of Sport Psychology, 18*, 30-39.

Bouwsema, H., van der Sluis, C.K., & Bongers, R.M. (2014). Effect of feedback during virtual training of grip force control with a myoelectric prosthesis. *PLoS ONE*, *9*, e98301. https://doi.org/10.1371/journal.pone.0098301

Boyce, B.A. (1992). Effects of assigned versus participant-set goals on skill acquisition and retention of a selected shooting task. *Journal of Teaching in Physical Education*, *11*, 220-234.

Breslin, G., Hodges, N.J., Steenson, A., & Williams, A.M. (2012). Constant or variable practice: Recreating the especial skill effect. *Acta Psychologica*, *140*, 154-157.

Bridgeman, B., Kirch, M., & Sperling, A. (1981). Segregation of cognitive and motor aspects of visual information using induced motion. *Perception & Psychophysics*, *29*, 336-342.

Broadbent, D.P., Causer, J., Williams, A.M., & Ford, P.R. (2017). The role of error processing in the contextual interference effect during the training of perceptual-cognitive skills. *Journal of Experimental Psychology: Human Perception and Performance*, *43*, 1329-1342.

Brosnan, K.C., Hayes, K., & Harrison, A.J. (2017). Effects of false-start disqualification rules on response-times of elite-standard sprinters. *Journal of Sports Sciences*, *35*, 925-935.

Brown, I.D. (2005). *Review of the "looked but failed to see" accident causation factor.* Road Safety Res. Rep. No. 60. Ivan Brown Associates.

Brown, I.D., Tickner, A.H., & Simmons, D.C.V. (1969). Interference between concurrent tasks of driver and telephoning. *Journal of Applied Psychology*, *53*, 419-424.

Brown, P.C., Roediger, H.L., & McDaniel, M.A. (2014). *Make it stick: The science of successful learning*. Belknap Press.

Bryan, W.L., & Harter, N. (1897). Studies in the physiology and psychology of the telegraphic language. *Psychological Review*, *4*, 27-53.

Bryan, W.L., & Harter, N. (1899). Studies on the telegraphic language: The acquisition of a hierarchy of habits. *Psychological Review*, *6*, 345-375.

Button, C., Seifert, L., Chow, J.Y., Araújo, D., & Davids, K. (2021). *Dynamics of skill acquisition: An ecological dynamics approach* (2nd ed.). Human Kinetics.

Caird, J.K., Simmons, S.M., Wiley, K., & Johnston, K.A. (2018). Does talking on a cell phone, with a passenger, or dialing affect driving performance? An updated systematic review and meta-analysis of experimental studies. *Human Factors*, *60*, 101-133.

Cañal-Bruland, R., Müller, F., Lach, B., & Spence, C. (2018). Auditory contributions to visual anticipations in tennis. *Psychology of Sport & Exercise*, *36*, 100-103.

Carpenter, S.K., Pan, S.C., & Butler, A.C. (2022). The science of effective learning with spacing and retrieval practice. *Nature Neuroscience Psychology*, *1*, 496-511. https://doi.org/10.1038/s44159-022-00089-1

Carron, A.V. (1967). *Performance and learning in a discrete motor task under massed versus distributed conditions.* Unpublished doctoral dissertation, University of California, Berkeley.

Carron, A.V., Loughhead, T.M., & Bray, S.R. (2005). The home advantage in sport competitions: Courneya and Carron's (1992) conceptual framework a decade later. *Journal of Sports Sciences*, *23*, 395-407.

Carter, C. (July 2020). Why the progress you make in the practice room seems to disappear Overnight—Part 2. *The Bulletproof Musician*. https://bulletproofmusician.com/why-the-progress-you-make-in-the-practice-room-seems-to-disappear-overnight-part-2

Catalano, J.F., & Kleiner, B.M. (1984). Distant transfer in coincident timing as a function of practice variability. *Perceptual and Motor Skills*, *58*, 851-856.

Cattell, J.M. (1893). Aufmerksamkeit und reaction. *Philosophische Studien*, *8*, 403-406. English translation in R.S. Woodworth (1947). *Psychological research* (vol. 1, pp. 252-255). Science Press.

Cecilio-Fernandes, D., Cnossen, F., Jaarsma, D.A.C.C., & Tio, R.A. (2018). Avoiding surgical skill decay: A systematic review on the spacing of training sessions. *Journal of Surgical Education*, *75*, 471-480.

Cha, Y.J., Yoo, E.Y., Jung, M.Y, Park, S.H., & Park, J.H. (2012). Effects of functional task training with mental practice in stroke: A meta analysis. *NeuroRehabilitation*, *30*, 239-246.

Chabris, C.F., & Simons, D.J. (2010). *The invisible gorilla: And other ways our intuitions deceive us.* Crown.

Chapanis, A. (1951). Theory and methods for analyzing errors in man-machine systems. *Annals of the New York Academy of Sciences*, *51*, 1179-1203.

Chase, W.G., & Simon, H.A. (1973). Perception in chess. *Cognitive Psychology*, *4*, 55-81.

Chauvel, G., Wulf, G., & Maquestiaux, F. (2015). Visual illusions can facilitate sport skill learning. *Psychonomic Bulletin & Review*, *22*, 717-721.

Cherry, E.C. (1953). Some experiments on the recognition of speech, with one and two ears. *Journal of the Acoustical Society of America, 25*, 975-979.

Chiviacowsky, S. (2021). The motivational role of feedback in motor learning: Evidence, interpretations, and implications. In M. Bertollo, E. Filho, & P.C. Terry (Eds.) *Advancements in mental skills training* (pp. 44-56). Routledge.

Chiviacowsky, S., & Wulf, G. (2007). Feedback after good trials enhances learning. *Research Quarterly for Exercise and Sport, 78*, 40-47.

Choi, Y., Qi, F., Gordon, J., & Schweighofer, N. (2008). Performance-based adaptive schedules enhance motor learning. *Journal of Motor Behavior, 40*, 273-280.

Christina, R.W. (1992). The 1991 C.H. McCloy research lecture: Unraveling the mystery of the response complexity effect in skilled movements. *Research Quarterly for Exercise and Sport, 63*, 218-230.

Chua, L.-K., Jimenez-Diaz, J., Lewthwaite, R., Kim, T., & Wulf, G. (2021). Superiority of external attentional focus for motor performance and learning: Systematic reviews and meta-analyses. *Psychological Bulletin, 147*, 618-645.

Cignetti, F., Schena, F., Zanone, P.G., & Rouard, A. (2009). Dynamics of coordination in cross-country skiing. *Human Movement Science, 28*, 204-217.

Cobley, S., Baker, J., Wattie, N., & McKenna, J. (2009). Annual age-grouping and athlete development: A meta-analytical review of relative age effects in sport. *Sports Medicine, 39*, 235-256.

Cooper, D., Fuller, J., Wiggins, M.W., Wills, J.A., Main, L.C., & Doyle, T. (2024). Negative consequences of pressure on marksmanship may be offset by early training exposure to contextually relevant threat training: A systematic review and meta-analysis. *Human Factors, 66*, 294-311. https://doi.org/10.1177/00187208211065907

Cooper, J.M., & Strayer, D.L. (2008). Effects of simulator practiced and real-world experience on cellphone related driver distraction. *Human Factors, 50*, 893-902.

Coughlan, E.K., Williams, A.M., McRobert, A.P., & Ford, P.R. (2014). How experts practice: A novel test of deliberate practice theory. *Journal of Experimental Psychology: Learning, Memory, and Cognition, 40*, 449-458.

Crossman, E.R.F.W. (1959). A theory of the acquisition of speed skill. *Ergonomics, 2*, 153-166.

Cuddy, L.J., & Jacoby, L.L. (1982). When forgetting helps memory. An analysis of repetition effects. *Journal of Verbal Learning and Verbal Behavior, 21*, 451-467.

Davies, D.R., & Parasuraman, R. (1982). *The psychology of vigilance*. Academic Press.

Davis, R. (1959). The role of "attention" in the psychological refractory period. *Quarterly Journal of Experimental Psychology, 11*, 211-220.

Deci, E.L., & Ryan, R.M. (2000). The "what" and "why" of goal pursuits: Human needs and the self-determination of behavior. *Psychological Inquiry, 11*, 227-268.

de Gelder, B., Tamietto, M., van Boxtel, G., Goebal, R., Sahraie, A., van den Stock, J., Stienen, B.M.C., Weiskrantz, L., & Pegna, A. (2008). Intact navigation skills after bilateral loss of striate cortex. *Current Biology, 18*, R1128-R1129.

deGroot, A.D. (1946/1978). *Thought and choice in chess*. Mouton. (Original work published in 1946).

DeLuca, M., Low, D., Kumari, V., Parton A., Davis, J., & Mohagheghi, A.A. (2022). A systematic review with meta-analysis of the StartReact effect on motor responses in stroke survivors and healthy individuals. *Journal of Neurophysiology, 127*, 938-945.

Dickstein, R., & Deutsch, J.E. (2007). Motor imagery in physical therapist practice. *Physical Therapy, 87*, 942-953.

Diedrich, F.J., & Warren, W.H., Jr. (1995). Why change gaits? Dynamics of the walk-run transition. *Journal of Experimental Psychology: Human Perception and Performance, 21*, 183-202.

Drew, T., Vo, M.L.H., & Wolfe, J.M. (2013). The invisible gorilla strikes again: Sustained inattentional blindness in expert observers. *Psychological Science, 24*, 1848-1853.

Drowatzky, J.N., & Zuccato, F.C. (1967). Interrelationships between selected measures of static and dynamic balance. *Research Quarterly, 38*, 509-510.

Eliasz, K.L. (2016). *The effects of social-comparative feedback during motor skill acquisition in highly motivated learners: Applications to medical education*. PhD thesis, McMaster University. hdl.handle.net/11375/20515

Elliott, D., & Bennett, S.J. (2021). Intermittent vision and goal-directed movement: A review. *Journal of Motor Behavior, 53*, 523-543.

Elliott, D., Hansen, S., & Grierson, L.E.M. (2010). The legacy of R.S. Woodworth: The two-component model revisited. In D. Elliott & M. Khan (Eds.), *Vision and goal-directed movement: Neurobehavioral perspectives* (pp. 5-19). Human Kinetics.

Elliott, D., Helsen, W.F., & Chua, R. (2001). A century later: Woodworth's (1899) two-component model of goal-directed aiming. *Psychological Bulletin, 127*, 342-357.

Elliott, D., & Khan, M. (Eds.). (2010). *Vision and goal-directed movement: Neurobehavioral perspectives.* Human Kinetics.

Elliott, D., & Lee, T.D. (1995). The role of target information on manual aiming bias. *Psychological Research, 58*, 2-9.

Ericsson, K.A., & Pool, R. (2016). *Peak: Secrets from the new science of expertise.* Houghton, Mifflin, Harcourt.

Farrow, D., & Abernethy, B. (2015). Expert anticipation and pattern perception. In J. Baker & D. Farrow (Eds.), *Routledge handbook of sport expertise* (pp. 9-21). Routledge.

Feeley, A.A., Feeley, I.H., Merghani, K., & Sheehan, E. (2022). Use of procedure specific preoperative warm-up during surgical priming improves operative outcomes: A systematic review. *The American Journal of Surgery, 224*, 1126-1134.

Feltz, D.L., & Landers, D.M. (1983). The effects of mental practice on motor skill learning and performance: A meta-analysis. *Journal of Sport Psychology, 5*, 25-57.

Firth, J., Rivers, I., & Boyle, J. (2021). A systematic review of interleaving as a concept learning strategy. *Review of Education, 9*, 642-684.

Fischman, M.G., Christina, R.W., & Anson, J.G. (2008). Memory drum theory's C movement: Revelations from Franklin Henry. *Research Quarterly for Exercise and Sport, 79*, 312-318.

Fitts, P.M. (1954). The information capacity of the human motor system in controlling the amplitude of movement. *Journal of Experimental Psychology, 47*, 381-391.

Fitts, P.M. (1964). Perceptual-motor skills learning. In A.W. Melton (Ed.), *Categories of human learning* (pp. 243-285). Academic Press.

Fitts, P.M., Bahrick, H.P., Noble, M.E., & Briggs, G.E. (1959). *Skilled performance.* Contract No. AF 41 [657]-70. Ohio State University, Wright Air Development Center.

Fitts, P.M., & Peterson, J.R. (1964). Information capacity of discrete motor responses. *Journal of Experimental Psychology, 67*, 103-112.

Fitts, P.M., & Posner, M.I. (1967). *Human performance.* Brooks/Cole.

Fleishman, E.A. (1956). Psychomotor selection tests: Research and application in the United States Air Force. *Personnel Psychology, 9*, 449-467.

Fleishman, E.A., & Parker, J.F. (1962). Factors in the retention and relearning of perceptual motor skill. *Journal of Experimental Psychology, 64*, 215-226.

Fontaine, R.J., Lee, T.D., & Swinnen, S.P. (1997). Learning a new bimanual coordination pattern: Reciprocal influences of intrinsic and to-be-learned patterns. *Canadian Journal of Experimental Psychology, 51*, 1-9.

Forssberg, H., Grillner, S., & Rossignol, S. (1975). Phase dependent reflex reversal during walking in chronic spinal cats. *Brain Research, 85*, 103-107.

Fujii, S., Kudo, K., Ohtsuki, T., & Oda, S. (2010). Intrinsic constraint of asymmetry acting as a control parameter on rapid, rhythmic bimanual coordination: A study of professional drummers and nondrummers. *Journal of Neurophysiology, 104*, 2178-2186.

Garrison, K.A., Winstein, C.J., & Aziz-Zadeh, L. (2010). The mirror neuron system: A neural substrate for methods in stroke rehabilitation. *Neurorehabilitation and Neural Repair, 24*, 404-412.

Gentile, A.M. (1972). A working model of skill acquisition with application to teaching. *Quest, 17*, 3-23.

Gentile, A.M. (2000). Skill acquisition: Action, movement, and neuromotor processes. In J.H. Carr & R.H. Shepherd (Eds.), *Movement science: Foundation for physical therapy in rehabilitation* (2nd ed., pp. 111-180). Aspen.

Gentili, R., Han, C.E., Schweighofer, N., & Papaxanthis, C. (2010). Motor learning without doing: Trial-by-trial improvement in motor performance during mental training. *Journal of Neurophysiology, 104*, 774-783.

Gentner, D.R. (1987). Timing of skilled motor performance: Tests of the proportional duration model. *Psychological Review, 94*, 255-276.

Giboin, L.-S., Gruber, M., Kramer, A. (2018). Three months of slackline training elicit only task specific improvements in balance performance. *PLoS ONE, 13*, e0207542. https://doi.org/10.1371/journal.pone.0207542

Gibson, J.J. (1966). *The senses considered as perceptual systems.* Houghton Mifflin.

Gladwell, M. (2008). *Outliers: The story of success.* Little, Brown.

Gonzalez, C.C., Causer, J., Miall, R.C., Grey, M.J., Humphreys, G., & Williams, A.M. (2017). Identifying the causal mechanisms of the quiet eye. *European Journal of Sport Science, 17*, 74-84.

Gray, R. (2008). Multisensory information in the control of complex motor actions. *Current Directions in Psychological Science, 17*, 244-248.

Gray, R. (2009). How do batters use visual, auditory, and tactile information about the success of a baseball swing? *Research Quarterly for Exercise and Sport, 80*, 491-501.

Gray, R. (2018). Comparing cueing and constraints interventions for increasing launch angle in baseball batting. *Sport, Exercise and Performance Psychology, 7*, 318-332.

Gray, R. (2021). *How we learn to move: A revolution in the way we coach & practice sports skills.* Independently published. ISBN-13: 979-8751331184.

Greenlee, E.T., DeLucia, P.R., & Newton, D.C. (2018). Driver vigilance in automated vehicles: Hazard detection failures are a matter of time. *Human Factors, 60*, 465-476.

Grillner, S. (2021). The execution of movement: A spinal affair. *Journal of Neurophysiology, 125*, 693-698.

Guadagnoli, M.A., Dornier, L.A., & Tandy, R.D. (1996). Optimal length for summary knowledge of results: The influence of task-related experience and complexity. *Research Quarterly for Exercise and Sport, 67*, 239-248.

Guadagnoli, M.A., & Kohl, R.M. (2001). Knowledge of results for motor learning: Relationship between error estimation and knowledge of results frequency. *Journal of Motor Behavior, 33*, 217-224.

Guadagnoli, M.A., & Lee, T.D. (2004). Challenge point: A framework for conceptualizing the effects of various practice conditions in motor learning. *Journal of Motor Behavior, 36*, 212-224.

Güldenpenning, I., Jackson, R.C., & Cañal-Bruland, R. (2023). The science of deceptive human movement. *Human Movement Science, 92*. https://doi.org/10.1016/j.humov.2023.103147

Guthrie, E.R. (1952). *The psychology of learning.* Harper & Row.

Haken, H., Kelso, J.A.S., & Bunz, H. (1985). A theoretical model of phase transitions in human hand movements. *Biological Cybernetics, 51*, 347-356.

Hancock, G.R., Butler, M.S., & Fischman, M.G. (1995). On the problem of two-dimensional error scores: Measures and analyses of accuracy, bias, and consistency. *Journal of Motor Behavior, 27*, 241-250.

Hancock, P.A. (2017). On the nature of vigilance. *Human Factors, 59*, 35-43.

Harris, D.J., Buckingham, G., Wilson, M.R., & Vine, S.J. (2019). Virtually the same? How impaired sensory information in virtual reality may disrupt vision for action. *Experimental Brain Research, 237*, 2761-2766.

Heald, J.B., Lengyel, M., & Wolpert, D.M. (2021). Contextual inference underlies the learning of sensorimotor repertoires. *Nature, 600*, 489-493.

Helm, E.E., & Reisman, D.S. (2015). The split-belt walking paradigm: Exploring motor learning and spatiotemporal asymmetry poststroke. *Physical Medicine and Rehabilitation Clinics in North America, 26*, 703-713.

Helmuth, L.L., & Ivry, R.B. (1996). When two hands are better than one: Reduced timing variability during bimanual movement. *Journal of Experimental Psychology: Human Perception and Performance, 22*, 278-293.

Henry, F.M. (1968). Specificity vs. generality in learning motor skill. In R.C. Brown & G.S. Kenyon (Eds.), *Classical studies on physical activity* (pp. 331-340). Prentice Hall. (Original work published in 1958).

Henry, F.M., & Rogers, D.E. (1960). Increased response latency for complicated movements and a "memory drum" theory of neuromotor reaction. *Research Quarterly, 31*, 448-458.

Herrebrøden, H. (2023). Motor performers need task-relevant information: Proposing an alternative mechanism for the attentional focus effect. *Journal of Motor Behavior, 55*, 125-134.

Heuer, H. (1985). Wiewirktmentale Übung? [How does mental practice operate?] *Psychologische Rundschau, 36*, 191-200.

Heuer, H. (1988). Testing the invariance of relative timing: Comment on Gentner (1987). *Psychological Review, 95*, 552-557.

Heuer, H., & Lüttgen, L. (2016). Robot assistance of motor learning: A neuro-cognitive perspective. *Neuroscience and Biobehavioral Reviews, 56*, 222-240.

Hick, W.E. (1952). On the rate of gain of information. *Quarterly Journal of Experimental Psychology, 4*, 11-26.

Higgins, J.R. (1977). *Human movement: An integrated approach.* Mosby.

Hird, J.S., Landers, D.M., Thomas, J.R., & Horan, J.J. (1991). Physical practice is superior to mental practice in enhancing cognitive and motor task performance. *Journal of Sport and Exercise Psychology, 13*, 281-293.

Hodges, N.J., & Campagnaro, P. (2012). Physical guidance research: Assisting principles and supporting evidence. In N.J. Hodges & A.M. Williams (Eds.), *Skill acquisition in sport: Research, theory and practice* (2nd ed., pp. 150-169). Routledge.

Hodges, N.J., & Lohse, K.R. (2022). An extended challenge-based framework for practice design in sports coaching. *Journal of Sports Sciences*, *40*, 754-768.

Hollerbach, J.M. (1978). *A study of human motor control through analysis and synthesis of handwriting.* Unpublished doctoral dissertation, Massachusetts Institute of Technology.

Howell, M.L. (1956). Use of force-time graphs for performance analysis in facilitating motor learning. *Research Quarterly*, *27*, 12-22.

Hoyt, D.F., & Taylor, C.R. (1981). Gait and the energetics of locomotion in horses. *Nature*, *292*, 239-240.

Huang, S., Layer, J., Smith, D., Bingham, G.P., & Zhu, Q. (2021). Training 90° bimanual coordination at high frequency yields dependence on kinesthetic information and poor performance of dyadic unimanual coordination. *Human Movement Science*, *79*, 102855. https://doi.org/10.1016/j.humov.2021.102855

Hubbard, A.W., & Seng, C.N. (1954). Visual movements of batters. *Research Quarterly*, *25*, 42-57.

Hull, C.L. (1943). *Principles of behavior: An introduction to behavior theory.* Appleton-Century.

Humphrey, N. (1974). Vision in a monkey without striate cortex: A case study. *Perception*, *3*, 241-255.

Hyman, I.E., Jr., Boss, S.M., Wise, B.M., McKenzie, K.E., & Caggiano, J.M. (2010). Did you see the unicycling clown? Inattentional blindness while walking and talking on a cell phone. *Applied Cognitive Psychology*, *24*, 597-607.

Hyman, R. (1953). Stimulus information as a determinant of reaction time. *Journal of Experimental Psychology*, *45*, 188-196.

Ille, A., Selin, I., Do, M.-C., & Thon, B. (2013). Attentional focus effects on sprint start performance as a function of skill level. *Journal of Sports Sciences*, *31*, 1705-1712.

Ishigami, Y., & Klein, R.M. (2009). Is a hands-free phone safer than a handheld phone? *Journal of Safety Research*, *40*, 157-164.

Jackson, R.C., & Cañal-Bruland, R. (2019). Deception in sport. In A.M. Williams, & R.C. Jackson (Eds.), *Anticipation and decision making in sport* (pp. 99-116). Routledge.

Jagacinski, R.J., & Flach, J.M. (2003). *Control theory for humans: Quantitative approaches to modeling performance.* Erlbaum.

James, W. (1890). *The principles of psychology* (Vol. 1). Holt.

James, W. (1891). *The principles of psychology* (Vol. 2). Holt.

Janelle, C.M. (1999). Ironic mental processes in sport: Implications for sport psychologists. *The Sport Psychologist*, *13*, 201-220.

Janelle, C.M., Barba, D.A., Frehlich, S.G., Tennant, L.K., & Cauraugh, J.H. (1997). Maximizing performance feedback effectiveness through videotape replay and a self-controlled learning environment. *Research Quarterly for Exercise and Sport*, *68*, 269-279.

Janssen, L., Crajé, C., Weigelt, M., & Steenbergen, B. (2010). Motor planning in bimanual object manipulation: Two plans for two hands? *Motor Control*, *14*, 240-254.

Kantak, S.S., & Winstein, C.J. (2012). Learning-performance distinction and memory processes for motor skills: A focused review and perspective. *Behavioural Brain Research*, *228*, 219-231.

Keele, S.W. (1968). Movement control in skilled motor performance. *Psychological Bulletin*, *70*, 387-403.

Keele, S.W., & Posner, M.I. (1968). Processing of visual feedback in rapid movements. *Journal of Experimental Psychology*, *77*, 155-158.

Keetch, K.M., Lee, T.D., & Schmidt, R.A. (2008). Especial skills: Specificity embedded within generality. *Journal of Sport and Exercise Psychology*, *30*, 723-736.

Keetch, K.M., Schmidt, R.A., Lee, T.D., & Young, D.E. (2005). Especial skills: Their emergence with massive amounts of practice. *Journal of Experimental Psychology: Human Perception and Performance*, *31*, 970-978.

Kelso, J.A.S. (1984). Phase transitions and critical behavior in human bimanual coordination. *American Journal of Physiology: Regulatory, Integrative and Comparative Physiology*, *246*, R1000-R1004.

Kelso, J.A.S. (1995). *Dynamic patterns: The self-organization of brain and behavior.* MIT Press.

Kelso, J.A.S. (2022). On the coordination dynamics of (animate) moving bodies. *Journal of Physics: Complexity*, *3*. *https://doi.org/10.1088/2632-072X/ac7caf*

Kelso, J.A.S., Putnam, C.A., & Goodman, D. (1983). On the space-time structure of human interlimb co-ordination. *Quarterly Journal of Experimental Psychology*, *35A*, 347-375.

Kelso, J.A.S., Scholz, J.P., & Schöner, G. (1986). Nonequilibrium phase transitions in coordinated biological motion: Critical fluctuations. *Physics Letters A*, *118*, 279-284.

Kelso, J.A.S., Southard, D.L., & Goodman, D. (1979). On the coordination of two-handed movements. *Journal of Experimental Psychology: Human Perception and Performance, 5*, 229-238.

Kelso, J.A.S., Tuller, B., Vatikiotis-Bateson, E., & Fowler, C.A. (1984). Functionally specific articulatory cooperation following jaw perturbations during speech: Evidence for coordinative structures. *Journal of Experimental Psychology: Human Perception and Performance, 10*, 812-832.

Kernodle, M.W., & Carlton, L.G. (1992). Information feedback and the learning of multiple-degree-of-freedom activities. *Journal of Motor Behavior, 24*, 187-196.

Kerr, R., & Booth, B. (1978). Specific and varied practice of motor skill. *Perceptual and Motor Skills, 46*, 395-401.

Kim, O.A., Forrence, A.D., & McDougle, S.D. (2022). Motor learning without movement. *Proceedings of the National Academy of Science, 119*(30), e2204379119. https://doi.org/10.1073/pnas.2204379119

Klapp, S.T. (1996). Reaction time analysis of central motor control. In H.N. Zelaznik (Ed.), *Advances in motor learning and control* (pp. 13-35). Human Kinetics.

Klapp, S.T. (2010). Comments on the classic Henry and Rogers (1960) paper on its 50th anniversary. *Research Quarterly for Exercise and Sport, 81*, 108-112.

Klapp, S.T., Maslovat, D., & Jagacinski, R.J. (2019). The bottleneck of the psychological refractory period involves timing of response initiation rather than response selection. *Psychonomic Bulletin & Review, 26*, 29-47.

Kolarik, A.J., Cirstea, S., Pardham, S., & Moore, B.C.J. (2014). A summary of research investigating echolocation abilities of blind and sighted humans. *Hearing Research, 310*, 60-68.

Konczak, J., vander Velden, H., & Jaeger, L. (2009). Learning to play the violin: Motor control by freezing, not freeing degrees of freedom. *Journal of Motor Behavior, 41*, 243-252.

Kostrubiec, V., Zanone, P.G., Fuchs, A., & Kelso, J.A.S. (2012). Beyond the blank state: Routes to learning new coordination patterns depend on the intrinsic dynamics of the learner—experimental evidence and theoretical model. *Frontiers in Human Neuroscience, 6*. https://doi.org/10.3389/fnhum.2012.00222

Kovacs, A.J., Buchanan, J.J., & Shea, C.H. (2010). Impossible is nothing: 5:3 and 4:3 multi-frequency bimanual coordination. *Experimental Brain Research, 201*, 249-259.

Kozlowski, S.W.J., & DeShon, R.P. (2004). A psychological fidelity approach to simulation-based training: Theory, research, and principles. In E. Salas, L.R. Elliott, S.G. Schflett, & M.D. Coovert (Eds.), *Scaled worlds: Development, validation, and applications* (pp. 75-99). Ashgate.

Krause, D., Agethen, M., & Zobe, C. (2018). Error feedback frequency affects automaticity but not accuracy and consistency after extensive motor skill practice. *Journal of Motor Behavior, 50*, 144-154.

Kunde, W., Skirde, S., & Weigelt, M. (2011). Trust my face: Cognitive factors of head fakes in sports. *Journal of Experimental Psychology: Applied, 17*, 110-127.

Kunde, W., & Weigelt, M. (2005). Goal congruency in bimanual object manipulation. *Journal of Experimental Psychology: Human Perception and Performance, 31*, 145-156.

LaDelfa, N.J., Garcia, D.B.L., Cappelletto, J.A.M., McDonald, A.C., Lyons, J.L., & Lee, T.D. (2013). The gunslinger effect: Why are movements made faster when responding to vs. initiating an action? *Journal of Motor Behavior, 45*, 85-90.

Lage, G.M., Faria, L.O., Ambrósio, N.F.A., Borges, A.M.P., & Apolinário-Souza, T. (2022). What is the level of contextual interference in serial practice? A meta-analytic review. *Journal of Motor Learning and Development, 10*, 224-242.

Lage, G.M., Ugrinowitsch, H., Apolinário-Souza, T., Vieira, M.M., Albuquerque, M.R., & Benda, R.N. (2015). Repetition and variation in motor practice: A review of neural correlates. *Neuroscience and Biobehavioral Reviews, 57*, 132-141.

Landin, D., & Hebert, E.P. (1997). A comparison of three practice schedules along the contextual interference continuum. *Research Quarterly for Exercise and Sport, 68*, 357-361.

Langham, M., Hole, G., Edwards, J., & O'Neil, C. (2002). An analysis of "looked but failed to see" accidents involving parked police vehicles. *Ergonomics, 45*, 167-185.

Lashley, K.S. (1917). The accuracy of movement in the absence of excitation from the moving organ. *American Journal of Physiology, 43*, 169-194.

Lashley, K.S. (1942). The problem of cerebral organization in vision. In J. Cattell (Ed.), *Biological symposia. Vol. VII. Visual mechanisms* (pp. 301-322). Jaques Cattell Press.

Lavery, J.J. (1962). Retention of simple motor skills as a function of type of knowledge of results. *Canadian Journal of Psychology*, *16*, 300-311.

Lavery, J.J., & Suddon, F.H. (1962). Retention of simple motor skills as a function of the number of trials by which KR is delayed. *Perceptual and Motor Skills*, *15*, 231-237.

Leavitt, J.L. (1979). Cognitive demands of skating and stickhandling in ice hockey. *Canadian Journal of Applied Sports Science*, *4*, 46-55.

Lee, D.N., & Aronson, E. (1974). Visual proprioceptive control of standing in human infants. *Perception & Psychophysics*, *15*, 529-532.

Lee, D.N., & Young, D.S. (1985). Visual timing of interceptive action. In D. Ingle, M. Jeannerod, & D.N. Lee (Eds.), *Brain mechanisms and spatial vision* (pp. 1-30). Martinus Nijhoff.

Lee, T.D. (2012). Contextual interference: Generalizability and limitations. In N.J. Hodges & A.M. Williams (Eds.), *Skill acquisition in sport: Research, theory and practice* (2nd ed., pp. 79-93). Routledge.

Lee, T.D., & Carnahan, H. (1990). Bandwidth knowledge of results and motor learning: More than just a relative frequency effect. *Quarterly Journal of Experimental Psychology*, *42A*, 777-789.

Lee, T.D., & Carnahan, H. (2021). Motor learning: Reflections on the past 40 years of research. *Kinesiology Review*, *10*, 274-282.

Lee, T.D., Eliasz, K.L., Gonzalez, D., Alguire, K., Ding, K., & Dhaliwal, C. (2016). On the role of error in motor learning. *Journal of Motor Behavior*, *48*, 99-115.

Lee, T.D., & Genovese, E.D. (1988). Distribution of practice in motor skill acquisition: Learning and performance effects reconsidered. *Research Quarterly for Exercise and Sport*, *59*, 277-287.

Lee, T.D., & Genovese, E.D. (1989). Distribution of practice in motor skill acquisition: Different effects for discrete and continuous tasks. *Research Quarterly for Exercise and Sport*, *60*, 59-65.

Lee, T.D., Ishikura, T., Kegel, S., Gonzalez, D., & Passmore, S. (2008). Do expert golfers really keep their heads still while putting? *Annual Review of Golf Coaching*, *2*, 135-143.

Lee, T.D., & Magill, R.A. (1983). The locus of contextual interference in motor-skill acquisition. *Journal of Experimental Psychology: Learning, Memory, and Cognition*, *9*, 730-746.

Lee, T.D., Magill, R.A., & Weeks, D.J. (1985). Influence of practice schedule on testing schema theory predictions in adults. *Journal of Motor Behavior*, *17*, 283-299.

Lee, T.D., & Schmidt, R.A. (2014). PaR (Plan-act-Review) golf: Motor learning research and improving golf skills. *International Journal of Golf Science*, *3*, 2-25.

Lee, T.D., & Swinnen, S.P. (1993). Three legacies of Bryan and Harter: Automaticity, variability and change in skilled performance. In J.L. Starkes & F. Allard (Eds.), *Cognitive issues in motor expertise* (pp. 295-315). Elsevier.

Lee, T.D., Swinnen, S.P., & Serrien, D.J. (1994). Cognitive effort and motor learning. *Quest*, *46*, 328-344.

Lee, T.D., Swinnen, S.P., & Verschueren, S. (1995). Relative phase alterations during bimanual skill acquisition. *Journal of Motor Behavior*, *27*, 263-274.

Lee, T.D., Wishart, L.R., Cunningham, S., & Carnahan, H. (1997). Modeled timing information during random practice eliminates the contextual interference effect. *Research Quarterly for Exercise and Sport*, *68*, 100-105.

Lee, W.A. (1980). Anticipatory control of postural and task muscles during rapid arm flexion. *Journal of Motor Behavior*, *12*, 185-196.

Lersten, K.C. (1968). Transfer of movement components in a motor learning task. *Research Quarterly*, *39*, 575-581.

Levac, D., Huber, M.E., & Sternad, D. (2019). Learning and transfer of complex motor skills in virtual reality: A perspective review. *Journal of NeuroEngineering and Rehabilitation*, *16*, 121.

Levac, D., Rivard, L., & Missiuna, C. (2012). Defining the active ingredients of interactive computer play interventions for children with neuromotor impairments: A scoping review. *Research in Developmental Disabilities*, *33*, 214-223.

Lewin, K. (1943). Psychology and the process of group living. *Journal of Social Psychology*, *17*, 113-131.

Lewthwaite, R., & Wulf, G. (2010). Social-comparative feedback affects motor skill learning. *Quarterly Journal of Experimental Psychology*, *63*, 738-749.

Lewthwaite, R., & Wulf, G. (2012). Motor learning through a motivational lens. In N.J. Hodges & A.M. Williams (Eds.), *Skill acquisition in sport: Research, theory and practice* (2nd ed., pp. 173-191). Routledge.

Limballe, A., Kulpa, R., & Bennett, S. (2022). Using blur for perceptual investigation and training in sport? A clear picture of the evidence and implications for future research. *Frontiers in Psychology*, *12*, 752582. https://doi.org/10.3389/fpsyg.2021.752582

Lindeburg, F.A. (1949). A study of the degree of transfer between quickening exercises and other coordinated movements. *Research Quarterly, 20*, 180-195.

Liu, J., & Wrisberg, C.A. (1997). The effects of knowledge of results delay and the subjective estimation of movement form on the acquisition and retention of a motor skill. *Research Quarterly for Exercise and Sport, 68*, 145-151.

Locke, E.A., & Latham, G.P. (1985). The application of goal setting to sports. *Sport Psychology Today, 7*, 205-222.

Lordahl, D.S., & Archer, E.J. (1958). Transfer effects on a rotary pursuit task as a function of first-task difficulty. *Journal of Experimental Psychology, 56*, 421-426.

Mackworth, N.H. (1948). The breakdown of vigilance during prolonged visual search. *Quarterly Journal of Experimental Psychology, 1*, 6-21.

MacLeod, C.M. (1991). Half a century of research on the Stroop effect: An integrative review. *Psychological Bulletin, 109*, 163-203.

MacLeod, C.M. (2015). Attention: Beyond Stroop's (1935) colour-word interference phenomenon. In M.W. Eysenck & D. Groome (Eds.), *Cognitive psychology: Revisiting the classic studies* (pp. 60-70). Sage.

Marchal-Crespo, L., Rappo, N., & Riener, R. (2017). The effectiveness of robotic training depends on motor task characteristics. *Experimental Brain Research, 235*, 3799-3816.

Marteniuk, R.G. (1974). Individual differences in motor performance and learning. *Exercise and Sport Sciences Reviews, 2*, 103-130.

Marteniuk, R.G. (1986). Information processes in movement learning: Capacity and structural interference effects. *Journal of Motor Behavior, 18*, 55-75.

Martinez De Quel, O. & Bennett, S.J. (2014). Kinematics of self-initiated and reactive karate punches. *Research Quarterly for Exercise and Sport, 85*, 117-123.

Maslovat, D., & Klapp, S.T. (2024). Trouble doing two differently timed actions at once: What is the problem? *Psychological Review, 13*, 231-246. http://dx.doi.org/10.1037/rev0000383.

Maslovat, D., Klapp, S.T., Jagacinski, R.J., & Franks, I.M. (2014). Control of response timing occurs during the simple reaction time interval but on-line for choice reaction time. *Journal of Experimental Psychology: Human Perception and performance, 40*, 2005-2021.

Maslovat, D., Sadler, C.M., Smith, V., Bui, A., & Carlsen, A.N. (2021). Response triggering by an acoustic stimulus increases with stimulus intensity and is best predicted by startle reflex activation. *Scientific Reports, 11*, 23612. https://doi.org/10.1038/s41598-021-028258

McCracken, H.D., & Stelmach, G.E. (1977). A test of the schema theory of discrete motor learning. *Journal of Motor Behavior, 9*, 193-201.

McDougle, S.D., Bond, K.M., & Taylor, J.A. (2015). Explicit and implicit processes constitute the fast and slow processes of sensorimotor learning. *Journal of Neuroscience, 35*, 9568-9579.

McKay, B., Hussien, J., Vinh, M.-A., Mir-Orefice, A., Brooks, H., & Ste-Marie, D.M. (2022). Meta-analysis of the reduced relative feedback frequency effect on motor learning and performance. *Psychology of Sport & Exercise, 61*, 102165. https://doi.org/10.1016/j.psychsport.2022.102165

McLeod, P. (1980). What can probe RT tell us about the attentional demands of movement? In G.E. Stelmach & J. Requin (Eds.), *Tutorials in motor behavior* (pp. 579-589). Elsevier.

Mechsner, F., Kerzel, D., Knoblich, G., & Prinz, W. (2001). Perceptual basis of bimanual coordination. *Nature, 414*, 69-73.

Mehrholz, J., Platz, T., Kugler, J., & Pohl, M. (2008). Electromechanical and robot-assisted arm training for improving arm function and activities of daily living after stroke. *Cochrane Database of Systematic Reviews, 4*, CD006876. https://doi.org/10.1002/14651858.CD006876.pub2

Merkel, J. (1885). Die zeitlichen Verhaltnisse der Willensthaütigkeit. *Philosophische Studien, 2*, 73-127. Cited in Woodworth, R.S. (1938). *Experimental psychology.* Holt.

Merton, P.A. (1972). How we control the contraction of our muscles. *Scientific American, 226*, 30-37.

Milanese, C., Cavedon, V., Corte, S., & Agostini, T. (2017). The effects of two different correction strategies on the snatch technique in weightlifting. *Journal of Sports Sciences, 35*, 476-483.

Milanese, C., Corte, S., Salvetti, L., Cavedon, V., & Agostini, T. (2016). Correction of a technical error in the golf swing: Error amplification versus direct instruction. *Journal of Motor Behavior, 48*, 365-376.

Monsell, S. (2003). Task switching. *Trends in Cognitive Sciences, 7*, 134-140.

Morgulev, E., Azar, O.H., & Bar-Eli, M. (2020) Searching for momentum in NBA triplets of free throws. *Journal of Sports Sciences, 38*, 390-398.

Nabavinik, M., Abaszadeh, A., Mehranmanesh, M., & Rosenbaum, D.A. (2018). Especial skills in experienced archers. *Journal of Motor Behavior, 50*, 249-253.

Nacson, J., & Schmidt, R.A. (1971). The activity-set hypothesis for warm-up decrement. *Journal of Motor Behavior, 3*, 1-15.

Nashner, L., & Berthoz, A. (1978). Visual contribution to rapid motor responses during postural control. *Brain Research, 150*, 403-407.

National Hockey League Official Rules (2021-2022). National Hockey League.

Néda, Z., Ravasz, E., Brechet, Y., Vicsek, T., & Barabasi, A.L. (2000). The sound of many hands clapping: Tumultuous applause can transform itself into waves of synchronized clapping. *Nature, 403*, 849-850.

Neisser, U., & Becklen, R. (1975). Selective looking, attending to visually specified events. *Cognitive Psychology, 7*, 480-494.

Nelson, A., & Eliasz, K.L. (2023). Desirable difficulty: Theory and application of intentionally challenging learning. *Medical Education, 57*, 123-130.

Neumann, D.L., Walsh, N., Moffitt, R.L., & Hannan, T.E. (2020). Specific internal and external attentional focus instructions have differential effects on rowing performance. *Psychology of Sport & Exercise, 50*, 101722. https://doi.org/10.1016/j.psychsport.2020.101722

Neumann, E., & Ammons, R.B. (1957). Acquisition and long-term retention of a simple serial perceptual-motor skill. *Journal of Experimental Psychology, 53*, 159-161.

Newell, K.M. (1986). Constraints on the development of coordination. In M.G. Wade & H.T.A. Whiting (Eds.), *Motor development in children: Aspects of coordination and control* (pp. 341-360). Nijhoff.

Newell, K.M., Liu, Y.-T., & Mayer-Kress, G. (2001). Time scales in motor learning and development. *Psychological Review, 108*, 57-82.

Newell, K.M., & Vaillancourt, D.E. (2001). Dimensional change in motor learning. *Human Movement Science, 20*, 695-715.

Newell, K.M., & Walter, C.B. (1981). Kinematic and kinetic parameters as information feedback in motor skill acquisition. *Journal of Human Movement Studies, 7*, 235-254.

NHTSA. (n.d.). *Distracted driving.* www.nhtsa.gov/risky-driving/distracted-driving

Nilsen, D.M., Gillen, G., & Gordon, A.M. (2010). Use of mental practice to improve upper-limb recovery after stroke: A systematic review. *American Journal of Occupational Therapy, 64*, 695-708.

Ong, N.T., & Hodges, N.J. (2012). Mixing it up a little: How to schedule observational practice. In N.J. Hodges & A.M. Williams (Eds.), *Skill acquisition in sport: Research, theory and practice* (2nd ed., pp. 22-39). Routledge.

Oppici, L., Dix, A., & Narciss, S. (2021) When is knowledge of performance (KP) superior to knowledge of results (KR) in promoting motor skill learning? A systematic review. *International Review of Sport and Exercise Psychology.* https://doi.org/10.1080/1750984X.2021.1986849

Oullier, O., & Kelso, J.A.S. (2009). Social coordination from the perspective of coordination dynamics. In R.A. Meyers (Ed.), *Encyclopedia of complexity and systems sciences* (pp. 8198-8212). Springer-Verlag.

Park, S.H., Hsu, C.J., Dee, W., Roth, E.J., Rymer, W.Z., & Wu, M. (2021). Enhanced error facilitates motor learning in weight shift and increases use of the paretic leg during walking at chronic stage after stroke. *Experimental Brain Research, 239*, 3327-3341.

Pauwels, L., Swinnen, S.P., & Beets, I.A.M. (2014). Contextual interference in complex bimanual skill learning leads to better skill persistence. *PLOS One, 9*(6). https://doi.org/10.1371/journal.pone.0100906

Peterson, L.R., & Peterson, M.J. (1959). Short-term retention of individual verbal items. *Journal of Experimental Psychology, 58*, 193-198.

Pezzulo, G., Barca, L., Bocconi, A.L., & Borghi, A.M. (2010). When affordances climb into your mind: Advantages of motor simulation in a memory task performed by novice and expert rock climbers. *Brain & Cognition, 73*, 68-73.

Pfordresher, P.Q., & Dalla Bella, S. (2011). Delayed auditory feedback and movement. *Journal of Experimental Psychology: Human Perception and Performance, 37*, 566-579.

Pigott, R.E., & Shapiro, D.C. (1984). Motor schema: The structure of the variability session. *Research Quarterly for Exercise and Sport, 55*, 41-45.

Plamondon, R., & Alimi, A.M. (1997). Speed/accuracy tradeoffs in target-directed movements. *Behavioral and Brain Sciences, 20*, 279-349.

Porter, J.M., & Magill, R.A. (2010). Systematically increasing contextual interference is beneficial for learning sport skills. *Journal of Sports Sciences, 28*, 1277-1285.

Posner, M.I., & Keele, S.W. (1969). Attentional demands of movement. *Proceedings of the 16th Congress of Applied Psychology.* Swets and Zeitlinger.

Poulton, E.C. (1974). *Tracking skill and manual control.* Academic Press.

Proteau, L. (1992). On the specificity of learning and the role of visual information for movement control. In L. Proteau & D. Elliott (Eds.), *Vision and motor control* (pp. 67-103). Elsevier.

Raganathan, R., Cone, S., & Fox, B. (2022). Predicting individual differences in motor learning: A critical review. *Neuroscience and Biobehavioral Reviews, 141,* 104852. https://doi.org/10.1016/j.neubiorev.2022.104852

Raibert, M.H. (1977). *Motor control and learning by the state space model.* Tech. Rep. No. AI-TR-439. MIT Artificial Intelligence Laboratory.

Redelmeier, D.A., & Tibshirani, R.J. (1997). Association between cellular-telephone calls and motor vehicle collisions. *New England Journal of Medicine, 336,* 453-458.

Reznik, D., Henkin, Y., Levy, O., & Mukamel R. (2015). Perceived loudness of self-generated sounds is differentially modified by expected sound intensity. *PLoS One, 10,* e0127651. https://doi.org/10.1371/journal.pone.0127651

Rosenbaum, D.A. (2010). *Human motor control* (2nd ed.). Elsevier.

Rosenbaum, D.A., Chapman, K.M., Coelho, C.J., Gong, L., & Studenka, B.E. (2013). Choosing actions. *Frontiers in Psychology, 4,* 273. https://doi.org/10.3389/fpsyg.2013.00273

Rothstein, A.L., & Arnold, R.K. (1976). Bridging the gap: Application of research on videotape feedback and bowling. *Motor Skills: Theory Into Practice, 1,* 35-62.

Salmoni, A.W., Schmidt, R.A., & Walter, C.B. (1984). Knowledge of results and motor learning: A review and critical reappraisal. *Psychological Bulletin, 95,* 355-386.

Samani, J., & Pan, S.C. (2021). Interleaved practice enhances memory and problem-solving ability in undergraduate physics. *Nature Partner Journal: Science of Learning, 6*(1), 32. https://doi.org/10.1038/s41539-021-00110-x

Sanli, E.A., Patterson, J.T., Bray, S.R., & Lee, T.D. (2013). Understanding self-controlled motor learning protocols through the self-determination theory. *Frontiers in Movement Science and Sport Psychology, 3,* 611. https://doi.org/10.3389/fpsyg.2012.00611

Savir, S., Khan, A.A., Yunus, R.A., Rehman, T.A., Saeed, S., Sohail, M., Sharkey, A., Mitchell, J., & Matyal, R. (2023). Virtual reality: The future of invasive procedure training? *Journal of Cardiothoracic and Vascular Anesthesia, 37,* 2090-2097. https://doi.org/10.1053/j.jvca.2023.06.032

Schaefer, S., & Scornaienchi, D. (2020). Table tennis experts outperform novices in a demanding cognitive-motor dual-task situation. *Journal of Motor Behavior, 52,* 204-213.

Schaffert, N., Braun Janzen, T., Mattes, K., & Thaut, M.H. (2019). A review on the relationship between sound and movement in sports and rehabilitation. *Frontiers in Psychology, 10*(244). https://doi.org/10.3389/fpsyg.2019.00244

Schaffert, N., & Schlüter, S. (2022). The design of interactive real-time audio feedback systems for application in sports. In V. Tzankova & M. Filimowicz (Eds.), *Interactive sports technologies: Performance, participation, safety* (pp. 79-95). Routledge.

Schmidt, R.A. (1969). Movement time as a determiner of timing accuracy. *Journal of Experimental Psychology, 79,* 43-47.

Schmidt, R.A. (1975). A schema theory of discrete motor skill learning. *Psychological Review, 82,* 225-260.

Schmidt, R.A. (1989). Unintended acceleration: A review of human factors contributions. *Human Factors, 31,* 345-364.

Schmidt, R.A., Heuer, H., Ghodsian, D., & Young, D.E. (1998). Generalized motor programs and units of action in bimanual coordination. In M. Latash (Ed.), *Progress in motor control, Vol. 1: Bernstein's traditions in movement studies* (pp. 329-360). Human Kinetics.

Schmidt, R.A., Lange, C., & Young, D.E. (1990). Optimizing summary knowledge of results for skill learning. *Human Movement Science, 9,* 325-348.

Schmidt, R.A., Lee, T.D., Glazebrook, C.M., Studenka, B., & Zelaznik, H.N. (2025). *Motor control and learning: A behavioral emphasis* (7th ed.) [Manuscript in preparation]. Human Kinetics.

Schmidt, R.A., & Sherwood, D.E. (1982). An inverted-U relation between spatial error and force requirements in rapid limb movements: Further evidence for the impulse-variability model. *Journal of Experimental Psychology: Human Perception and Performance, 8,* 158-170.

Schmidt, R.A., Wood, C.T., Young, D.E., & Kelkar, R. (1996). *Evaluation of the BIC J26 child guard lighter.* Tech. Rep. Failure Analysis Associates.

Schmidt, R.A., & Wulf, G. (1997). Continuous concurrent feedback degrades skill learning: Implications for training and simulation. *Human Factors, 39,* 509-525.

Schmidt, R.A., & Young, D.E. (1987). Transfer of movement control in motor learning. In S.M. Cormier & J.D. Hagman (Eds.), *Transfer of learning* (pp. 47-79). Academic Press.

Schmidt, R.A., Young, D.E., Swinnen, S., & Shapiro, D.C. (1989). Summary knowledge of results for skill acquisition: Support for the guidance hypothesis. *Journal of Experimental Psychology: Learning, Memory, and Cognition*, *15*, 352-359.

Schmidt, R.A., Zelaznik, H.N., Hawkins, B., Frank, J.S., & Quinn, J.T., Jr. (1979). Motor-output variability: A theory for the accuracy of rapid motor acts. *Psychological Review*, *86*, 415-451.

Schneider, D.M., & Schmidt, R.A. (1995). Units of action in motor control: Role of response complexity and target speed. *Human Performance*, *8*, 27-49.

Schneider, W., & Shiffrin, R.M. (1977). Controlled and automatic human information processing: I. Detection, search, and attention. *Psychological Review*, *84*, 1-66.

Schöllhorn, W.I. (2016). Invited commentary: Differential learning is different from contextual interference learning. *Human Movement Science*, *47*, 240-245.

Schöner, G., Zanone, P.G., & Kelso, J.A.S. (1992). Learning as a change of coordination dynamics: Theory and experiment. *Journal of Motor Behavior*, *24*, 29-48.

Schutz, R.W., & Roy, E.A. (1973). Absolute error: The devil in disguise. *Journal of Motor Behavior*, *5*, 141-153.

Scripture, C.W. (1905). *The new psychology.* Scott.

Seifert, L., Komar, J., Barbosa, T., Toussaint, H., Millet, G., & Davids, K. (2014). Coordination pattern variability provides functional adaptations to constraints in swimming performance. *Sports Medicine*, *44*, 1333-1345.

Shapiro, D.C., Zernicke, R.F., Gregor, R.J., & Diestel, J.D. (1981). Evidence for generalized motor programs using gait pattern analysis. *Journal of Motor Behavior*, *13*, 33-47.

Shea, J.B., & Morgan, R.L. (1979). Contextual interference effects on the acquisition, retention, and transfer of a motor skill. *Journal of Experimental Psychology: Human Learning and Memory*, *5*, 179-187.

Shea, J.B., & Zimny, S.T. (1983). Context effects in memory and learning movement information. In R.A. Magill (Ed.), *Memory and control of action* (pp. 345-366). Elsevier.

Shergill, S.S., Bays, P.M., Frith, C.D., & Wolpert, D.M. (2003). Two eyes for an eye: The neuroscience of force escalation. *Science*, *301*, 187.

Sherwood, D.E. (1988). Effect of bandwidth knowledge of results on movement consistency. *Perceptual and Motor Skills*, *66*, 535-542.

Sherwood, D.E., Lohse, K.R., & Healy, A.F. (2014). Judging joint angles and movement outcome: Shifting the focus of attention in dart-throwing. *Journal of Experimental Psychology: Human Perception and Performance*, *40*, 1903-1914.

Sherwood, D.E., Schmidt, R.A., & Walter, C.B. (1988). The force/force-variability relationship under controlled temporal conditions. *Journal of Motor Behavior*, *20*, 106-116.

Simmons, S.M., Hicks, A., & Caird, J.K. (2016). Safety-critical event risk associated with cell phone tasks as measured in naturalistic driving studies: A systematic review and meta-analysis. *Accident Analysis and Prevention*, *87*, 161-169.

Simon, D.A., & Bjork, R.A. (2001). Metacognition in motor learning. *Journal of Experimental Psychology: Learning, Memory, and Cognition*, *27*, 907-912.

Simon, D.A., & Bjork, R.A. (2002). Models of performance in learning multisegment movement tasks: Consequences for acquisition, retention, and judgments of learning. *Journal of Experimental Psychology: Applied*, *8*, 222-232.

Simon, D.A., Lee, T.D., & Cullen, J.D. (2008). Win-shift, lose-stay: Contingent switching and contextual interference in motor learning. *Perceptual and Motor Skills*, *107*, 407-418.

Simons, D.J., & Chabris, C.F. (1999). Gorillas in our midst: Sustained inattentional blindness for dynamic events. *Perception*, *28*, 1059-1074.

Simons, D.J., & Levin, D.T. (1998). Failure to detect changes to people in a real-world interaction. *Psychonomic Bulletin & Review*, *5*, 644-649.

Simons, J.P., Wilson, J.M., Wilson, G.J., & Theall, S. (2009). Challenges to cognitive bases for an especial motor skill at the regulation baseball pitching distance. *Research Quarterly for Exercise and Sport*, *80*, 469-479.

Sinnett, S., & Kingstone, A. (2010). A preliminary investigation regarding the effect of tennis grunting: Does white noise during a tennis shot have a negative impact on shot perception? *PLoS One*, *5*, e13148. https://doi.org/10.1371/journal.pone.0013148

Slater-Hammel, A.T. (1960). Reliability, accuracy and refractoriness of a transit reaction. *Research Quarterly*, *31*, 217-228.

Smith, K.L., Weir, P.L., Till, K., Romann, M., & Cobley, S. (2018). Relative age effects across and within female sport contexts: A systematic review and meta-analysis. *Sports Medicine, 48*, 1451-1478.

Snoddy, G.S. (1926). Learning and stability: A psychophysical analysis of a case of motor learning with clinical applications. *Journal of Applied Psychology, 10*, 1-36.

Soderstrom, N.C., & Bjork, R.A. (2015). Learning versus performance: An integrated review. *Perspectives on Psychological Science, 10*, 176-199.

Spruit, E.N., Band, G.P.H., & Hamming, J.F. (2015). Increasing efficiency of surgical training: Effects of spacing practice on skill acquisition and retention in laparoscopic training. *Surgical Endoscopy, 29*, 2235-2243.

Ste-Marie, D.M., & Hancock, D.J. (2015). The use of observation as a method to develop expertise in coaching and officiating. In J. Baker & D. Farrow (Eds.), *Routledge handbook of sport expertise* (pp. 404-413). Routledge.

Ste-Marie, D.M., Law, B., Rymal, A.M., O, J., Hall, C., & McCullagh, P. (2012). Observation interventions for motor skill learning and performance: An applied model for the use of observation. *International Review of Sport and Exercise Psychology, 5*, 145-176.

Stephen, L., Macknik, S.L., King, M., Randi, J., Robbins, A., Teller, J.T., & Martinez-Conde, S. (2008). Attention and awareness in stage magic: Turning tricks into research. *Nature Reviews: Neuroscience, 9*, 871-879.

Strayer, D.L., & Johnston, W.A. (2001). Driven to distraction: Dual-task studies of simulated driving and conversing on a cellular telephone. *Psychological Science, 12*, 462-466.

Stroop, J.R. (1935). Studies of interference in serial verbal reactions. *Journal of Experimental Psychology, 18*, 643-662.

Swinnen, S.P. (1990). Interpolated activities during the knowledge-of-results delay and post-knowledge-of-results interval: Effects on performance and learning. *Journal of Experimental Psychology: Learning, Memory, and Cognition, 16*, 692-705.

Swinnen, S.P., Schmidt, R.A., Nicholson, D.E., & Shapiro, D.C. (1990). Information feedback for skill acquisition: Instantaneous knowledge of results degrades learning. *Journal of Experimental Psychology: Learning, Memory, and Cognition, 16*, 706-716.

Swinnen, S.P., Walter, C.B., Lee, T.D., & Serrien, D.J. (1993). Acquiring bimanual skills: Contrasting forms of information feedback for interlimb decoupling. *Journal of Experimental Psychology: Learning, Memory, and Cognition, 19*, 1328-1344.

Taub, E. (1976). Movement in nonhuman primates deprived of somatosensory feedback. *Exercise and Sport Sciences Reviews, 4*, 335-374.

Taub, E., & Berman, A.J. (1968). Movement and learning in the absence of sensory feedback. In S.J. Freedman (Ed.), *The neuropsychology of spatially oriented behavior* (pp. 173-192). Dorsey.

Thaler, L., & Goodale, M.A. (2016). Echolocation in humans: An overview. *Wiley Interdisciplinary Reviews: Cognitive Science, 7*, 382-393.

Thomas, P.A., & Mathew, K.P. (2023). A broad review on non-intrusive active user authentication in biometrics. *Journal of Ambient Intelligence and Humanized Computing, 14*, 339-360.

Thompson, L.L., Rivara, F.P., Ayyagari, R.C., & Ebel, B.E. (2013). Impact of social and technological distraction on pedestrian crossing behaviour: An observational study. *Injury Prevention, 19*, 232-237.

Thorndike, E.L. (1927). The law of effect. *American Journal of Psychology, 39*, 212-222.

Thorndike, E.L., & Woodworth, R.S. (1901). The influence of improvement in one mental function upon the efficiency of other functions. *Psychological Review, 8*, 247-261.

Tiffin, J., & Rogers, H.B. (1943). The selection and training of inspectors. *Personnel, 22*, 3-20.

Timmermans, A.A.A., Seelen, H.A.M., Willmann, R.D., & Kingma, H. (2009). Technology-assisted training of arm-hand skills in stroke: Concepts on reacquisition of motor control and therapist guidelines for rehabilitation technology design. *Journal of Neuroengineering and Rehabilitation, 6*, 1. https://doi.org/10.1186/1743-0003-6-1

Torres-Oviedo, G., Vasudevan, E., Malone, L., & Bastian, A.J. (2011). Locomotor adaptation. *Progress in Brain Research, 191*, 65-74.

Trowbridge, M.H., & Cason, H. (1932). An experimental study of Thorndike's theory of learning. *Journal of General Psychology, 7*, 245-260.

Tsutsui, S., Lee, T.D., & Hodges, N.J. (1998). Contextual interference in learning new patterns of bimanual coordination. *Journal of Motor Behavior, 30*, 151-157.

Ungerleider, L.G., & Mishkin, M. (1982). Two cortical visual systems. In D.J. Ingle, M.A. Goodale, & R.J.W. Mansfield (Eds.), *Analysis of visual behavior* (pp. 549-586). MIT Press.

Urbin, M.A., Stodden, D., Boros, R., & Shannon, D. (2012). Examining impulse-variability in overarm throwing. *Motor Control*, *16*, 19-30.

van Ulzen, N.R., Lamoth, C.J., Daffertshofer, A., Semin, G.R., & Beek, P.J. (2008). Characteristics of instructed and uninstructed interpersonal coordination while walking side-by-side. *Neuroscience Letters*, *432*, 88-93.

Varlet, M., & Richardson, M.J. (2015). What would be Usain Bolt's 100-meter sprint world record without Tyson Gay? Unintentional interpersonal synchronization between the two sprinters. *Journal of Experimental Psychology: Human Perception and Performance*, *41*, 36-41.

Verbruggen, F., & Logan, G.D. (2008). Response inhibition in the stop-signal paradigm. *Trends in Cognitive Sciences*, *12*, 418-424.

Wadman, W.J., Denier van der Gon, J.J., Geuze, R.H., & Mol, C.R. (1979). Control of fast goal-directed arm movements. *Journal of Human Movement Studies*, *5*, 3-17.

Wakatsuki, T., & Yamada, N. (2020). Difference between intentional and reactive movement in side-steps: Patterns of temporal structure and force exertion. *Frontiers in Psychology*, *11*, 2186. https://doi.org/10.3389/fpsyg.2020.02186

Watson, J.M., & Strayer, D.L. (2010). Supertaskers: Profiles in extraordinary multi-tasking ability. *Psychonomic Bulletin and Review*, *17*, 479-485.

Wegner, D.M. (1994). Ironic processes of mental control. *Psychological Review*, *101*, 34-52.

Weinberg, R.S., & Gould, D. (2024). *Foundations of sport and exercise psychology* (8th ed.). Human Kinetics.

Weiskrantz, L. (2007). Blindsight. *Scholarpedia*, *2* (4), 3047. www.scholarpedia.org/article/Blindsight

Weiskrantz, L., Warrington, E.K., Sanders, M.D., & Marshall, J. (1974). Visual capacity in the hemianopic field following a restricted occipital ablation. *Brain*, *97*, 709-728.

Welchman, A., Stanley, J., Schomers, M., Miall, R., & Bulthoff, H. (2010). The quick and the dead: When reaction beats intention. *Proceedings of the Royal Society of Biological Sciences*, *277*, 1667-1674.

Weller, L., Kunde, W., & Pfister, R. (2018). Disarming the gunslinger effect: Reaction beats intention for cooperative actions. *Psychonomic Bulletin & Review*, *25*, 761-766.

Wenderoth, N., Bock, O., & Krohn, R. (2002). Learning a new bimanual coordination pattern is influenced by existing attractors. *Motor Control*, *6*, 166-182.

Williams, A.M. (2020). Perceptual-cognitive expertise and simulation-based training in sport. In N.J. Hodges & A.M. Williams (Eds.), *Skill acquisition in sport: Research, theory and practice* (3rd ed., pp. 237-254). Routledge.

Williams, A.M., & Hodges, N.J. (2023). Effective practice and instruction: A skill acquisition framework for excellence. *Journal of Sports Sciences*, *41*, 833-849. https://doi.org/10.1080/02640414.2023.2240630

Williams, A.M., & Jackson, R.C. (Eds.). (2019). *Anticipation and decision making in sport*. Routledge.

Wilson, M.R., Causer, J., & Vickers, J.N. (2015). Aiming for excellence: The quiet eye as a characteristic of expertise. In J. Baker & D. Farrow (Eds.), *Routledge handbook of sport expertise* (pp. 22-37). Routledge.

Wing, A.M., & Kristofferson, A.B. (1973). The timing of interresponse intervals. *Perception & Psychophysics*, *13*, 455-460.

Winstein, C.J., & Schmidt, R.A. (1990). Reduced frequency of knowledge of results enhances motor skill learning. *Journal of Experimental Psychology: Learning, Memory, and Cognition*, *16*, 677-691.

Witt, J.K., Linkenauger, S.A., & Proffitt, D.R. (2012). Get me out of this slump! Visual illusions improve sports performance. *Psychological Science*, *23*, 397-399.

Wolfe, J.M., Horowitz, T.S., & Kenner, N.M. (2005). Rare items often missed in visual searches: Errors in spotting key targets soar alarmingly if they appear only infrequently during screening. *Nature*, *435*, 439-440.

Wolfe, J.M., Kosovicheva, A., & Wolfe, B. (2022). Normal blindness: When we look but fail to see. *Trends in Cognitive Sciences*, *26*, 809-819.

Wolpert, D.M., & Flanagan, J.R. (2001). Motor prediction. *Current Biology*, *11*, R729-R732.

Woodworth, R.S. (1899). The accuracy of voluntary movement. *Psychological Review Monographs*, *3*(13).

Woodworth, R.S. (1938). *Experimental psychology*. Holt.

Wright, D.L. (1991). The role of intertask and intratask processing in acquisition and retention of motor skills. *Journal of Motor Behavior*, *23*, 139-145.

Wright, D.L., & Kim, T. (2019). Contextual interference: New findings, insights, and implications for skill acquisition. In N.J. Hodges & A.M. Williams (Eds.), *Skill acquisition in sport: Research, theory and practice* (3rd ed., pp. 99-118). Routledge.

Wright, D.L., Verwey, W., Buchanan, J., Chen, J., Rhee, J., & Immink, M. (2016). Consolidating behavioural and neurophysiologic findings to explain the influence of contextual interference during motor sequence learning. *Psychonomic Bulletin & Review, 23*, 1-21.

Wulf, G. (2007). *Attention and motor skill learning.* Human Kinetics.

Wulf, G. (2013). Attentional focus and motor learning: A review of 15 years. *International Review of Sport and Exercise Psychology, 6*, 77-104.

Wulf, G., & Lewthwaite, R. (2016). Optimizing performance through intrinsic motivation and attention for learning: The OPTIMAL theory of motor learning. *Psychonomic Bulletin & Review, 23*, 1382-1414.

Wulf, G., McConnel, N., Gärtner, M., & Schwarz, A. (2002). Feedback and attentional focus: Enhancing the learning of sport skills through external-focus feedback. *Journal of Motor Behavior, 34*, 171-182.

Wulf, G., McNevin, N.H., & Shea, C.H. (2001). The automaticity of complex motor skill learning as a function of attentional focus. *Quarterly Journal of Experimental Psychology, 54A*, 1143-1154.

Wulf, G., & Toole, T. (1999). Physical assistance devices in complex motor skill learning: Benefits of a self-controlled practice schedule. *Research Quarterly for Exercise and Sport, 70*, 265-272.

Wunderlich, F., Heuer, H., Furley, P., & Memmert, D. (2020). A serial-position curve in high-performance darts: The effect of visuomotor calibration on throwing accuracy. *Psychological Research, 84*, 2057-2064.

Yao, W., Fischman, M.G., & Wang, Y.T. (1994). Motor skill acquisition and retention as a function of average feedback, summary feedback, and performance variability. *Journal of Motor Behavior, 26*, 273-282.

Yerkes, R.M., & Dodson, J.D. (1908). The relation of strength of stimulus to rapidity of habit-formation. *Journal of Comparative Neurology and Psychology, 18*, 459-482.

Young, D.E., & Schmidt, R.A. (1990). Units of motor behavior: Modifications with practice and feedback. In M. Jeannerod (Ed.), *Attention and performance XIII* (pp. 763-795). Erlbaum.

Young, D.E., & Schmidt, R.A. (1992). Augmented kinematic feedback for motor learning. *Journal of Motor Behavior, 24*, 261-273.

Zehr, E.P. (2005). Neural control of rhythmic human movement: The common core hypothesis. *Exercise and Sport Sciences Reviews, 33*, 54-60.

Index

Note: The italicized *f* and *t* following page numbers refer to figures and tables, respectively.

About the Authors

Timothy D. Lee, PhD, is a professor emeritus in the department of kinesiology at McMaster University in Hamilton, Ontario. He has published extensively in motor behavior and psychology journals since 1980, has served as an editor for the *Journal of Motor Behavior* and *Research Quarterly for Exercise and Sport*, and has been an editorial board member for *Psychological Review*. Before his retirement, his research was supported primarily by grants from the Natural Sciences and Engineering Research Council of Canada.

Lee has been a member, secretary-treasurer, and president of the Canadian Society for Psychomotor Learning and Sport Psychology (SCAPPS) and a member of the North American Society for the Psychology of Sport and Physical Activity (NASPSPA), the Psychonomic Society, and the Human Factors and Ergonomics Society. In 1980, he received the inaugural Young Scientist Award from SCAPPS, and in 2011 he was named a fellow of the society—its highest honor. He was named an international fellow by the National Academy of Kinesiology in 1999 and awarded the Distinguished Scholar Award by NASPSPA in 2017. His leisure-time passions include golf and music.

Richard A. Schmidt, PhD (1941-2015) was a professor emeritus in the department of psychology at UCLA. At the time of his death, Schmidt ran his own business, Human Performance Research, conducting research and consulting in the area of human factors and human performance. Widely acknowledged as one of the leaders in research on motor behavior, he had more than 40 years of experience in motor learning and performance.

The originator of both schema theory and impulse-variability theory (also called Schmidt's Law), he founded the *Journal of Motor Behavior* in 1969 and was editor for 11 years. He authored the first and second editions of *Motor Control and Learning* in 1982 and 1988 and the first edition of this book, *Motor Learning and Performance*, in 1991.

Schmidt was highly recognized for his contribution of a lifetime of research and writing. He received honorary doctorates from the Catholic University of Leuven in Belgium in 1992 and the Université Joseph Fourier in France in 1998. He was a longtime member of the North American Society for the Psychology of Sport and Physical Activity (NASPSPA), where he served as president in 1982 and received the organization's two highest honors: the Distinguished Scholar Award (for lifetime contributions to research in motor control and learning) in 1992 and the President's Award (for significant contributions to the development and growth of NASPSPA) in 2013. He was also a member of the Human Factors and Ergonomics Society and the Psychonomic Society and received the C.H. McCloy Research Lectureship from the American Alliance for Health, Physical Education, Recreation and Dance. His leisure-time passions included sailboat and Porsche racing.

Books

Ebooks

Continuing Education

Journals ...and more!

US.HumanKinetics.com
Canada.HumanKinetics.com

Sign up for our newsletters!

Get the latest insights with regular newsletters, plus periodic product information and special insider offers from Human Kinetics.